# THE STRING QUARTETS OF BEETHOVEN

Cavatina
adagio molto espressivo
aus dem Quartett op. 130
sotto voce
1

# THE *String Quartets* OF *Beethoven*

EDITED BY

William Kinderman

UNIVERSITY OF ILLINOIS PRESS
Urbana, Chicago, and Springfield

Publication of this volume was assisted by grants from the Society for Music Theory, the American Musicological Society, and the Research Board of the University of Illinois at Urbana-Champaign.

*Frontispiece:* Beethoven's autograph score for the beginning of the Cavatina movement of the Quartet in B♭ Major, op. 130. Artaria 208, p. 1, Staatsbibliothek zu Berlin—Preussischer Kulturbesitz, Berlin, Musikabteilung. Printed with permission.

First Illinois paperback, 2020

∞ This book is printed on acid-free paper.
1 2 3 4 5 C P 5 4 3 2 1

The Library of Congress cataloged the cloth edition as follows:
The string quartets of Beethoven / edited by William Kinderman.
p. cm.
Includes bibliographical references (p. ) and index.
ISBN 0-252-03036-2 (cloth : alk. paper)
1. Beethoven, Ludwig van, 1770–1827. Quartets, strings.
2. String quartet—Analysis, appreciation. I. Kinderman, William.
MT145.B425S75 2006
785'.7194'092—dc22 2005002730

PAPERBACK ISBN 978-0-252-08515-4

# CONTENTS

Introduction *1*
WILLIAM KINDERMAN

1. Transformational Processes in Beethoven's Op. 18 Quartets *13*
WILLIAM KINDERMAN

2. Metrical Dissonance and Metrical Revision in Beethoven's String Quartets *31*
HARALD KREBS

3. Peak Experience: High Register and Structure in the "Razumovsky" Quartets, Op. 59 *60*
MALCOLM MILLER

4. Beethoven's "Harp" Quartet: The Sketches in Context *89*
LEWIS LOCKWOOD

5. "Haydns Geist aus Beethovens Händen"? Fantasy and Farewell in the Quartet in E♭, Op. 74 *109*
NICHOLAS MARSTON

6. Aspects of the Genesis of Beethoven's String Quartet in F Minor, Op. 95 *132*
SEOW-CHIN ONG

7. "So träumte mir, ich reiste . . . nach Indien": Temporality and Mythology in Op. 127/I *168*
BIRGIT LODES

8. Plenitude as Fulfillment: The Third Movement of Beethoven's String Quartet in B♭, Op. 130 *214*
ROBERT HATTEN

9. The Genesis of the Countersubjects for the *Grosse Fuge* *234*
WILLIAM E. CAPLIN

10. Opus 131 and the Uncanny *262*
JOSEPH KERMAN

11. Beethoven's Last Quartets: Threshold to a Fourth Creative Period? *279*
WILLIAM KINDERMAN

APPENDIX
Chronology and Sources of the String Quartets *323*

Selected Bibliography *331*

Index *345*

# THE STRING QUARTETS OF BEETHOVEN

# INTRODUCTION

## *William Kinderman*

No group of compositions occupies a more central position in chamber music than Beethoven's string quartets, yet the meaning of these works continues to stimulate debate. The achievements of Haydn in his op. 33 collection and Mozart in his famous "Haydn" set had already brought the string quartet to peaks of stylistic development by the 1780s. The refined cultural position of the genre was reflected in the old adage, echoed by Goethe in 1829, that in a quartet "one hears four reasonable people conversing with one another."[1] Building on the conversational aura and integrated textures of these models, Beethoven used the quartet as the medium for some of his boldest and most advanced ideas. These works convey wit and humor, pathos and drama, and the last quartets in particular seem to push beyond established traditions to discover whole new seas of thought and feeling.

The distribution of the quartets across Beethoven's career neatly displays the three recognized "periods" of his creativity. A "classical" phase in the op. 18 set from 1800 is followed by a "heroic" phase, as embodied in the three "Razumovsky" Quartets, op. 59, and—many years later—by the introspective and exploratory final cluster of quartets: opp. 127, 132, 130, 131, and 135.[2] In 1809–10, furthermore, toward the end of the "heroic" period, yet long before the emergence of his late style, Beethoven wrote a contrasting pair of quartets, the so-called "Harp" Quartet in E♭ Major, op. 74, and the *Quartetto serioso* in F Minor, op. 95. This tally of sixteen quartets is augmented by his arrangement in 1802 of the Piano Sonata in E Major, op. 14 no. 1, as a string quartet in F major, and by the formidable double image of his great B♭ Quartet, op. 130, with its two radically different finales: the titanic "Great Fugue," op. 133, and the more congenial Rondo he wrote as a substitute finale in 1826. Thus the total number of Beethoven's quartets may be regarded as seventeen or even eighteen.

The present collection of essays explores these works from a variety of perspectives. In some instances, fresh critical approaches or new methods of musical analysis help us to come to terms with the expression and originality of the music. The study of unfamiliar sources, such as Beethoven's musical sketches, can shed light on features of the works that would otherwise remain obscure. Nonetheless, any scholarly study of the Beethoven quartets belongs in a historical context, as a contribution to the ongoing discourse that began about these pieces two centuries ago. For that reason, it may be useful to briefly review here some aspects of this ever-changing context of critical reception.

Since they first appeared, Beethoven's quartets have sparked enthusiasm and provoked some resistance. An announcement in the *Allgemeine musikalische Zeitung* from August 26, 1801, referred to the op. 18 set as "very difficult to play and by no means popular." Although some details are shadowed in obscurity, these quartets clearly were first heard in private performances, in the same social milieu that supported the quartets of Haydn and Mozart. Some of Beethoven's closest friends were string players, including Karl Amenda and Wenzel Krumpholz (violinists) and Nikolaus Zmeskall von Domanovecz (a cellist who also composed string quartets). Prince Franz Joseph Lobkowitz, who commissioned the six quartets of op. 18, maintained an orchestra as well as an excellent quartet, and he himself played the violin. This was an amateur environment par excellence, and it offered a small but discerning audience for new compositions.

Of special importance for Beethoven was the "Knabenquartett" ("boy quartet"), a paid quartet ensemble established soon after his arrival in Vienna through the sponsorship of his generous patron Prince Karl Lichnowsky.[3] This initiative enabled the twenty-three-year-old Beethoven to work closely with a group of excellent young string players, including the sixteen-year-old violinist Ignaz Schuppanzigh, as well as second-violinist Louis Sina and violist Franz Weiß, then lads of fifteen. (The cellists were older, more experienced players: Nikolaus Kraft, Beethoven's friend Zmeskall, and later Joseph Linke.) These musicians met on Thursday mornings at Count Razumovsky's, and on Friday mornings at Lichnowsky's, to play quartets of Haydn and Mozart, along with music by other composers, especially Beethoven. The group had remarkable longevity, continuing as the "Schuppanzigh Quartet" in later years, with sponsorship from Razumovsky following Beethoven's break with Lichnowsky in October 1806. This was the ensemble that first played many of the Beethoven quartets before the general public beginning in 1804, and it maintained a prominent role in Viennese musical life until Schuppanzigh's sudden death in 1830.[4] During the late 1790s, Beethoven's work with this emerging ensemble offered him a laboratory for his biggest compositional project of the first Vienna decade.

The number of quartets in op. 18—six—emulates the practice of Haydn and Mozart in their famous sets, and typically for Beethoven, his engagement with his distinguished predecessors is direct and confrontational. Certain organizational parallels stand out. In the opening Allegro of the F-Major Quartet, op. 18 no. 1, Beethoven's single-minded concentration on the initial six-note turn figure recalls Haydn's monothematic concentration, although Beethoven carried this device even further than would Haydn; the "reasonable conversation" is taken to the brink of obsessiveness. (Op. 18 no. 1 was not the first composed, but Beethoven must have regarded it as the appropriate opening salvo for this magnum opus of his early Vienna years.) The witty and gracious Quartet in G Major, op. 18 no. 2, invites comparison with Haydn's quartet in this key from his op. 33. The A-Major Quartet, op. 18 no. 5, on the other hand, is modeled, especially in its slow-movement variations, on Mozart's quartet in the same key from his "Haydn" set, K. 464. The position of this Mozartian homage as the fifth piece within the opus even parallels the placement of Mozart's K. 464 as no. 5 of his op. 10.[5] Some commentators have recognized the most direct influence of Haydn and Mozart in the D-Major Quartet, op. 18 no. 3, and Joseph de Marliave found in it "the most perfect achievement within Beethoven's capacity in the old quartet style."[6]

Each of the op. 18 quartets displays a strongly differentiated character, and the C Minor Quartet, op. 18 no. 4, must count as one of Beethoven's most controversial compositions. Earlier critics responded positively to this work, and Theodor Helm, writing in 1885, considered the C-Minor Quartet as a worthy counterpart to Beethoven's popular *Sonate pathétique* for piano, in the same key. Regarding the beginning of the quartet, he wrote: "Now I ask the reader just to cast a glance at the music example and earnestly ask himself whether a quartet movement by Haydn or Mozart can display such a broad and unified, forward-driving melody? You will definitely have to answer 'no.'"[7] Yet, influential later commentators wrote disparagingly about the piece, bolstering their arguments with suspicions about an earlier origin of the work—speculations that remain unconfirmed.[8] Hugo Riemann, in his *Meisterführer* handbook of 1910, concluded, "It is very probable that the C minor Quartet is a rapidly executed remake of a substantially older composition (which was perhaps not a quartet)."[9] Riemann based his theory on the absence of surviving sketches for the quartet and on its apparent motivic similarities with another work, the Duet for Viola and Cello in E♭ Major "with two eyeglasses obbligato." In his classic study *The Beethoven Quartets,* Joseph Kerman builds upon Riemann's observations in a sweeping negative assessment. He considers the C-minor first movement to be "more crudely written than anything in the other Op. 18 Quartets" and regards the entire C-Minor Quartet as "the exceptional work in the Op. 18 series; exceptional, by its weakness, in the entire corpus of the Beethoven quartets."[10]

A more appreciative assessment of the C-Minor Quartet in relation to its companion works has been offered by Robert Simpson, who stresses the distinctive moods of these pieces and the presence of ironic humor:

> These six works [of Op. 18], sometimes to the point of recklessness, express a wider range of colour and feeling than any group of six by Haydn or Mozart. Opposite the bluntness of the C minor lies the almost genteel elegance of the A major, informed by an amused restraint with a trace of irony in it—"So you think me crude?" The C minor goes in for crunching homophony, the A major for suave polyphony; the young composer whose rude manners could shock was also at this time very careful about his dress. But neither work courts superfluity, and the disconcertingly slender first movement of the A major is in its way as ironically

> elliptic as that of the C minor, which bluffly shoulders its way past . . . Neither the C minor nor the A major aims at profundity—only the F major does that—and, so far as the C minor Quartet is concerned, much harm has been done by the expectations aroused by Beethoven's famous 'C minor mood', as if there were such a thing in a generalized sense. C minor often incites Beethoven to blunt energy, but never to the same mood twice . . . We seem to digress, but the point is that most criticisms of Op. 18, No. 4, miss its sardonic humour by expecting a C minor Titan.[11]

## A New Exploration of Musical Potential

If Beethoven laid claim to equality with Haydn and Mozart in his op. 18 set, he was clearly disinclined to continue cultivating the genre in a similar way during the early years of the new century. Just a few years separate the completion of op. 18 in 1800 from the composition of the "Razumovsky" Quartets, op. 59, in 1806, yet how profound are the differences in technique and sensibility! These works embody a new concept of music as *process,* whereby the potential for development of basic musical elements is probed on a broad scale. As part of this new exploration of musical potential, Beethoven could begin with what seem to be mere fragments and enact a process of creative development within the work itself. The beginning of the F-Major Quartet, op. 59 no. 1, with the main theme in the cello heard under the accompaniment, is one such example. The meaning of this theme seems inextricably bound up with its rising contour and overall registral ascent—an idea with important ramifications at later points in the form. The stepwise ascent of the first four notes is intensified through a fourfold rhythmic augmentation to whole notes as the theme reaches its culmination in mm. 16–19, imparting enormous forward thrust to the music. That forward-driving quality Helm admired in op. 18 no. 4 is here taken to another level.

A divergent view of this passage is offered by James Webster, who describes Beethoven's "systematic use of register as a compositional resource, as in the expansion from the middle to extremes of high and low in the first nineteen bars of op. 59, no. 1," as "not entirely original," citing Haydn's Quartet in C Major, op. 20 no. 2, from 1772, as an antecedent.[12] Yet the beginning of Haydn's quartet is rather different: its theme does not emerge under the accompaniment, and its successive thematic entries are not coordinated with a gradual ascent in register, as in op. 59 no. 1. Webster underestimates the originality of Beethoven's creative development in maintaining that "neither his heroic style nor his ensuing lyric phase around 1810 fundamentally altered" the style he shared with Haydn and Mozart.[13] This view fails to give enough recognition to the new artistic dimensions of the "Razumovsky" Quartets, such as the registral strategies that are evident from the outset of the F-Major Quartet. Such relationships are not confined to individual themes or even whole movements. Nevertheless, many of Beethoven's evolving artistic resources do remain indebted to the legacy of Haydn and Mozart, whose works also provided precedents for the cyclic unification of multimovement compositions. In op. 59 no. 1, for instance, the initial rising series of notes prefigures the finale of the quartet, where the cello takes up in the same register the Thème russe—a theme that Beethoven employed in response to a request from his Russian patron, Count Andreas Razumovsky. This tune was drawn from an anthology of Russian melodies published at Saint Petersburg in 1790.[14] The initial motivic kernel from the outset of op. 59 no. 1 is bound up with the cyclic integration of the whole work, yet ultimately it is drawn from the preexisting Russian tune.

Another development of a primal motive comes in the second movement of op. 59 no. 1, the Allegretto vivace e sempre scherzando. This unpredictable movement begins in deceptive simplicity: a rhythm on a single note is softly tapped out by the cellist. The composite theme in its fullness is not the starting point, as in earlier practice, but arises instead as a consequence of the musical development itself. Such procedures are bound to bewilder listeners who do not grasp the music as a larger, unfolding process. Beethoven has embodied in these pieces a shift to a fundamentally new aesthetic perspective. Isaiah Berlin's comments about the transition from Enlightenment to Romantic attitudes applies here: "There is no copying, there is no adaptation, there is no learning of the rules, there is no external check, there is no structure which you must understand and adapt yourself to before you can proceed. The heart of the entire process is invention, creation, making, out of literally nothing, or out of any materials that may be to hand."[15]

The "Razumovsky" Quartets jolted conservative musicians out of their complacency. Beethoven's biographer Alexander Wheelock Thayer commented about op. 59 that "Perhaps no work of Beethoven's met a more discouraging reception from musicians than these now famous Quartets."[16] Stories about the first "Razumovsky" quartet being dismissed as "crazy music" and of its Allegretto vivace being trampled underfoot in anger by one of the best cellists of the day remind us of the changing reception context of such challenging works of art.[17] With hindsight, it is not surprising that the C-Major Quartet, op. 59 no. 3, proved at first to be the most accessible of the quartet trilogy. A reviewer of all three quartets in 1807 described the works as "not generally comprehensible, with the exception of the third in C major, which must win over every friend of music through its individuality, melody, and harmonic strength."[18] Yet with the passage of time, the two less "comprehensible" quartets of op. 59, in F major and E minor, ultimately surpassed no. 3 in popularity. The C-Major Quartet displays a mixture of retrospective and futuristic qualities, with certain bold features, such as the chromatic slow introduction, showing an affinity to earlier models—in this case, especially to Mozart's "Dissonant" Quartet, K. 465, in the same key. Another break with the past in this last "Razumovsky" quartet is its perpetuum mobile finale, whose muscular virtuosity and blending of fugal procedure with dramatic sonata rhetoric leave behind all traces of graceful conversation. The genre seems transformed here from music for the private salon to music for the concert hall. The opening fugal theme outlines stepwise falling fourths, inverting and compressing the melodic contour from the beginning of op. 59 no. 1. In the spacious unfolding of its motivic textures, the finale of op. 59 no. 3 seems almost orchestral, calling to mind the finales of two symphonies in this key: Mozart's "Jupiter" Symphony[19] and Beethoven's own Fifth Symphony. In this C-major quartet, as in its companion works, Beethoven strove toward a new artistic vision and transcended the boundaries of genre.

Beethoven's ability to transform "any materials that may be to hand" into artistic coinage is illustrated in a colorful story from his student Carl Czerny. Czerny reported that around 1809 the composer Ignaz Pleyel came to Vienna with his latest string quartet, which was performed at the home of Prince Lobkowitz, the sponsor of Beethoven's op. 18. Beethoven was in attendance and was then urged to perform at the piano. He was hesitant to play and became irritated, and then suddenly grabbed one of the parts from Pleyel's quartet—the second violin part—and began to improvise. "Never had one heard something so ingenious, so captivating, so brilliant from him; but in the middle of his fantasy one could still hear plainly a banal run drawn from the violin part . . . He had built his entire beautiful improvisation upon this figure."[20] Hartmut Krones has identified the "banal run" in the Rondeau finale of Pleyel's G-Major Quartet, op. 8 no. 2, and discovered its transformation in the trio of Beethoven's Quartet in E♭ major, op. 74, from 1809.[21] Tellingly, this quartet received its first private performance at Lobkowitz's home, and it was published with a dedication to the prince. Yet, as Nicholas Marston points out in his chapter in the present volume, a much more important dimension of this quartet is its extensive engagement with the last of Haydn's op. 76 quartets. Op. 74 was evidently the first large-scale work that Beethoven took up after Haydn's death on May 31, 1809. Study of the sketches offers new perspectives on this quartet, as is shown in the essay by Lewis Lockwood. Both Marston and Lockwood draw attention to the relevance of improvisatory and cadenza-like passages in their discussions of this piece, which until now has been somewhat neglected in the scholarly literature.

The contrasting companion work to op. 74, the Quartet in F Minor, was dedicated to Beethoven's friend Zmeskall. It was composed in 1810 but waited until 1816 to be published, when it appeared with the deceptively high opus number 95. If the "Razumovsky" Quartets are explorers in expansive ways, the F-Minor Quartet breaks new ground with its terse, elliptical concentration and its handling of sharp contrasts. The pithy density of this *Quartetto serioso,* as it was dubbed by Beethoven, poses special challenges, and he was clearly aware that this music would not be so readily understood by audiences. The uncompromising character of the piece is encapsulated in his provocative comment that it "is written for a small circle of connoisseurs and is never to be performed in public."[22] Another fascinating dimension of the F-Minor Quartet resides in its deep affinity with a contemporary work—the *Egmont* music—as is explored by Seow-Chin Ong in his contribution to the present volume.

## Beethoven as a "Deaf Seer"

The remarkable op. 95 in F Minor is a harbinger of Beethoven's last quartets, which have long been regarded as some of the most complex and demanding works of his entire oeuvre. Undoubtedly it is these final quartets, composed during 1824–26, that have posed the strongest challenges to listeners and players. A sharp division of opinion about these ambitious compositions surfaced immediately. An early reviewer of the E♭-Major Quartet, op. 127, observed, "Judgements about the last works of this master are very divergent, indeed not seldom completely contradictory. One person says that one can find nothing more beautiful and marvelous than this very quartet, which represents the highest that music can offer; another person says on the other hand: 'No, everything is unclear here, all is confused; there is no clear idea that is developed, since in every measure there are sins against accepted rules; the already deaf composer must indeed have been unbalanced to bring this piece into being.'"[23]

This review, from about the time of Beethoven's death in 1827, raised a matter that surfaced in many early discussions of the music: the impact of the composer's deafness upon his works. The last quartets were composed when Beethoven was almost completely deaf. Were their unaccustomed features a product of this debility of the composer, and did they mark a decline in his artistic powers?

In this regard, K. M. Knittel has singled out Richard Wagner's centennial "Beethoven" essay of 1870 as a major turning point in the positive reception of the late style, on the grounds that Beethoven's deafness, which was previously regarded as the handicap that explained the eccentricities of these works, was seen by Wagner as an enabling factor that had shielded Beethoven from the turmoil of the outer world and enhanced his ability to dwell in the inner world of the imagination.[24] For Wagner, Beethoven was a deaf "seer" who led the way to new artistic perspectives.[25]

Although Wagner's essay was undoubtedly influential, Knittel underestimates the extent to which Beethoven's later works had already found acceptance before 1870. As Wilhelm von Lenz put it in his 1855 book *Beethoven: Eine Kunststudie,* "In the year 1827 one would have been regarded as a musical black sheep if one had wished to hear something from Beethoven's third-period style. These treasures are now common property."[26] Of course, the works first needed to be heard in order to be appreciated. Yet the four brothers Müller, a quartet from Brunswick, had premiered Beethoven's op. 131 already in the first year of their ensemble's existence, in 1828, and they went on tour performing the Beethoven quartets beginning in the 1830s.[27] A subsequent quartet that emphasized Beethoven's later quartets in performance was the ensemble founded by the Austrian violinist Joseph Hellmesberger in 1849. The report on performances of the Hellmesberger Quartet in Vienna that appeared in the *Neue Zeitschrift für Musik* in 1859 is revealing:

> I begin with Hellmesberger's Quartet, whose first cycle is now underway . . . The masterworks of [Beethoven's] last period: the C-sharp minor (Op. 131) and E-

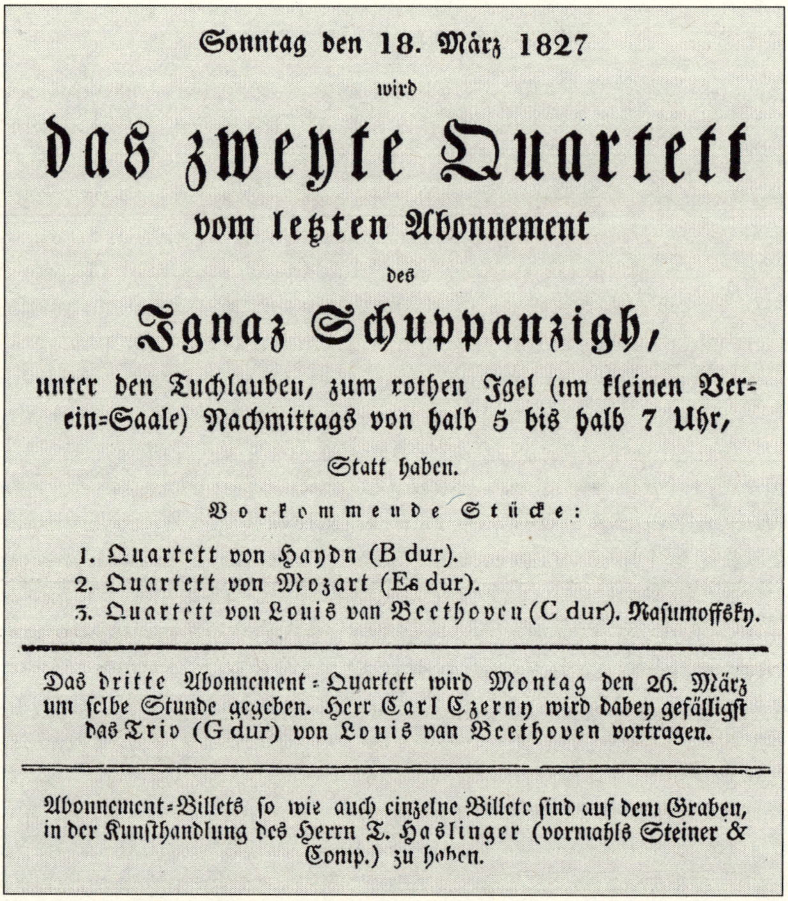

Sonntag den 18. März 1827
wird
das zweyte Quartett
vom letzten Abonnement
des
Ignaz Schuppanzigh,
unter den Tuchlauben, zum rothen Igel (im kleinen Ver-ein=Saale) Nachmittags von halb 5 bis halb 7 Uhr,
Statt haben.

Vorkommende Stücke:

1. Quartett von Haydn (B dur).
2. Quartett von Mozart (Es dur).
3. Quartett von Louis van Beethoven (C dur). Rasumoffsky.

Das dritte Abonnement=Quartett wird Montag den 26. März um selbe Stunde gegeben. Herr Carl Czerny wird dabey gefälligst das Trio (G dur) von Louis van Beethoven vortragen.

Abonnement=Billets so wie auch einzelne Billete sind auf dem Graben, in der Kunsthandlung des Herrn T. Haslinger (vormahls Steiner & Comp.) zu haben.

Announcements of concerts of the Schuppanzigh Quartet during Beethoven's final illness. The concert time of 4:30 P.M. on March 26, 1827, with Carl Czerny in a performance of the G-Major Trio of op. 1, became Beethoven's last hour.

flat major (Op. 127) quartets, as well as the first public performance here of the *Grosse Fuge* (Op. 133) [were featured]. It is Hellmesberger's great service to have made this prophetic and progressive artist so popular among us . . . The crowning contribution of this quartet [is] that even a many-faceted structure, Beethoven's quartet fugue, was listened to so attentively by the entire audience and after its completion greeted so warmly and with so much applause. For even a very practiced score reader will require many repetitions to grasp this musical pyramid . . . Finally, the sounding of both fugue themes, the one simple and the other in double counterpoint, was crowned with resounding bravos. That says a great deal.[28]

Thoughtful writings on Beethoven's later music also began to appear by mid-century, such as Hermann Hirschbach's 1839 essay "Über Beethovens letzte Streichquartette," with its praise of the "novelistic" character of the late quartets,[29] Ernst von Elterlein's book *Beethoven's Clavier-Sonaten,* which appeared in 1856,[30] and Adolph Bernhard Marx's two-volume study of Beethoven's life and works, published in 1859.[31] By the 1850s, the progressive features of Beethoven's later musical language were seen as urgently relevant to new developments in composition, as is illustrated by Wagner's own enthusiasm at this time for the C♯-Minor Quartet, op. 131. At Zurich in 1854, he organized and coached a performance of this work, and he also contributed analytical notes on the piece.[32] The importance of late Beethoven to the midcentury musical avant-garde is reflected as well in Felix Draeseke's 1861 essay "The So-Called Music of the Future and Its Opponents," in which he wrote that "it is not surprising that Beethoven's third period seemed destined to shake the absolutist regime of the main tonality for the first time, and that another thirty years had to pass, before this system was actually put aside."[33]

Serious engagement with Beethoven's later music had gained considerable momentum by the 1850s, and this development was fueled not by changing views about Beethoven's deafness but by the novelty and power of the works themselves. The originality of these compositions, which so often provoked initial resistance, was itself a major factor in their success. Beethoven's own awareness of this tensional relation in the reception of his music is implied in his comment that the F-Minor Quartet was "never to be played in public" and in his description of the "Hammerklavier" Sonata, op. 106, as "a sonata that will give pianists something to do" and that would "be played 50 years hence"—a fairly accurate prediction because, apart from Liszt, von Bülow, and Clara Schumann, few pianists tackled the immense challenges of this great sonata before the last decades of the nineteenth century.

That the later string quartets have also given scholars "something to do" can be readily demonstrated through the writings on any one of these works. Consider for instance the quartet that most preoccupied Wagner, op. 131 in C♯ Minor. Wagner's own enthusiastic discussion of the quartet in his centennial "Beethoven" essay is a curiously unsatisfactory tribute.[34] A more detailed discussion is contained in Theodor Helm's aforementioned 1885 monograph *Beethovens Streichquartette,* which later became familiar in English-speaking countries through the translation of much of its content in Joseph de Marliave's *Beethoven's Quartets* in 1928.[35] The view of op. 131 as a pinnacle of Beethoven's achievement was fully developed by Helm. He wrote that "the novelty, freedom and spirituality of the nevertheless lucid and strictly logical form, the speaking soulfulness of the content into every note, every measure, finds its purest embodiment in the C♯ minor Quartet," wherein "as in few string quartets the unfolding of a definite psychological idea is undeniable."[36]

Donald Francis Tovey, in his own Beethoven centennial essay of 1927,[37] approached the music along somewhat different lines, seeking to show how the immense "freedom" of the C♯-Minor Quartet, with its seven numbered movements within a single gigantic continuity, was nevertheless guided by a principle of "normality" or controlling logic. Joseph Kerman's 1966 book *The Beethoven Quartets* took Tovey's essay as a point of departure in exploring the large-scale integration of op. 131.[38] In the present collection of essays, Kerman has returned to the C♯-Minor Quartet thirty-eight years later to probe deeper insights, this time into the "uncanny" dimension of this impressive work. Another attempt to plumb the depths of op. 131 is Robert Winter's investigation of Beethoven's creative process based on the sketches and drafts, sources so voluminous that much remains to be done, even on op. 131.[39]

"We do not understand music—it understands us."[40] This aphorism by Theodor Adorno well expresses the quandary and fascination many listeners have experienced in approaching Beethoven's late quartets. This music resists full elucidation yet invites engagement from many perspectives, and it is not surprising that the emphasis in this book falls on these seemingly inexhaustible works, Beethoven's last essays in the genre. The richness of this music calls forth a variety of approaches, ranging from Robert Hatten's discernment of expressive "plentitude" in the exquisite Andante con moto ma non troppo of op. 130 to Birgit Lodes's analysis of mythic timelessness lodged in the binary oppositions of the opening movement of the first of these astonishing works, op. 127 in E♭ Major.

Many of the chapters in the present volume originally were read as papers at the conference "Beethoven's String Quartets: A Classical or Modernistic Legacy?" held at the University of Victoria, British Columbia, in March 2000, in conjunction with the Beethoven quartet cycle of the Lafayette Quartet; the study by Lockwood was presented at the symposium "Beethoven and the Creative Process," held at the University of Illinois at Urbana-Champaign in May 2003. Since these conferences, the essays included here have been revised for print, with new material added in the Appendix to provide the reader with an overview of sources related to the quartets. The Selected Bibliography offers a guide to further reading and research. All translations are those of the authors unless otherwise noted.

Grateful acknowledgment is made to several individuals and institutions for their support of this project, including Robin Kearton Boynton, Andrew Granade, and especially Bradley Decker, who produced many of the music examples. Erik Horak-Hult provided valuable assistance in preparing the final typescript for publication. Thanks are due as well to the staff of the University of Illinois Press, and particularly its director, Willis Regier. The publication of this book was generously supported by the Research Board of the University of Illinois at Urbana-Champaign, the Society for Music Theory, and the Manfred Bukofzer Publication Endowment Fund of the American Musicological Society.

## Notes

1. Goethe's often-cited comment, which appeared in a letter to Carl Friedrich Zelter of November 9, 1829, echoes the notion of a "quartet conversation" (Quartett-"Gespräch"), an eighteenth-century idea that had assumed wide currency by 1800. See in this regard Ludwig Finscher, *Studien zur Geschichte des Streichquartetts* (Kassel: Bärenreiter, 1974), 285–88.

2. The opus numbers of the late quartets are not aligned with their chronology.

3. For a discussion of Lichnowsky's Knabenquartett, see Oldřich Pulkert, "Das Knabenquartett des Fürsten Lichnowsky," in *Ludwig van Beethoven im Herzen Europas,* ed. Oldřich Pulkert and Hans-Werner Küthen (Prague: České lupkové závody A. G., 2000), 452–58.

4. There was an interruption in the activities of the quartet from 1816 to 1823 because of Schuppanzigh's absence from Vienna during these years.

5. On this point see Jeremy Yudkin, "Beethoven's 'Mozart' Quartet," *Journal of the American Musicological Society* 45 (1992), 70.

6. Joseph de Marliave, *Beethoven's Quartets,* trans. Hilda Andrews (London: Oxford University Press, 1928), 17.

7. Theodor Helm, *Beethovens Streichquartette* (Leipzig: Fritzsch, 1885), 21.

8. Sketches for the C-Minor Quartet are lacking, but it is possible that Beethoven composed the quartet from autumn 1799 to early 1800 in a lost sketchbook that might also have contained work on pieces including the Horn Sonata, op. 17; the Septet, op. 20; the First Symphony, op. 21; and the Third Piano Concerto, op. 37.

9. *Beethoven's Streichquartette* (Berlin: Schlesinger'sche Buch- und Musikhandlung, [1910]), 8.

10. *The Beethoven Quartets* (New York: Norton, 1966), 68, 71.

11. "The Chamber Music for Strings," in *The Beethoven Reader* (New York: Norton, 1971), 246–47.

12. "Traditional Elements in Beethoven's Middle-Period String Quartets," in *Beethoven, Performers, and Critics: The International Beethoven Congress, Detroit, 1977,* ed. Robert Winter and Bruce Carr (Detroit, Mich.: Wayne State University Press, 1980), 99–100.

13. "The Concept of Beethoven's 'Early' Period in the Context of Periodization in General," *Beethoven Forum* 3 (1994), 25.

14. Lwow/Pratsch, *Sobranije narodnich russkich pesen s ich golosami* (Saint Petersburg, 1790; new edition Moscow, 1955).

15. Isaiah Berlin, *The Roots of Romanticism,* ed. Henry Hardy (Princeton, N.J.: Princeton University Press, 1999), 119.

16. *Thayer's Life of Beethoven,* ed. Elliot Forbes (Princeton, N.J.: Princeton University Press, 1964), 409.

17. Ibid.

18. This review, from the *Allgemeine musikalische Zeitung* (1807), col. 400, is cited in *Ludwig van Beethoven: Die Werke im Spiegel seiner Zeit; Gesammelte Konzertberichte und Rezensionen bis 1830,* ed. Stefan Kunze (Laaber: Laaber, 1987), 72.

19. See in this regard Peter Gülke, ". . . *immer das Ganze vor Augen": Studien zu Beethoven* (Stuttgart: Metzler, 2000), 237–38. Ludwig Finscher also stresses the use of orchestrated textures in op. 59 (article "Streichquartett" in *Die Musik in Geschichte und Gegenwart,* vol. 12 (Kassel: Bärenreiter, 1965), column 1576. Helm reports that the finale of op. 59 no. 3 was often excerpted and arranged for string orchestra (*Beethovens Streichquartette,* 117).

20. *Erinnerungen aus meinem Leben,* ed. Walter Kolneder (Strassburg: Heitz, 1968), 45. A very similar report of Beethoven improvising on a motive from the cello part of a quintet by Daniel Steibelt in 1798 stems from Beethoven's student Ferdinand Ries; see *Thayer's Life of Beethoven,* 257.

21. "Streichquartett Es-Dur 'Harfenquartett' op. 74," in *Beethoven: Interpretationen seiner Werke,* vol. 1, ed. Albrecht Riethmüller, Carl Dahlhaus, and Alexander Ringer (Laaber: Laaber Verlag, 1994), 587.

22. *The Letters of Beethoven,* vol. 2, ed. Emily Anderson (London: Macmillan, 1961), 606; *Ludwig van Beethoven: Briefwechsel Gesamtausgabe,* vol. 3, ed. Sieghard Brandenburg (Munich: Henle, 1996), 306. See also Kurt von Fischer, "'Never to be performed in public': Zu Beethovens Streichquartett op. 95," *Beethoven-Jahrbuch* 9 (1973/77), 87–96. This letter by Beethoven was written to Sir George Smart in London in October 1816.

23. *Allgemeine Musikzeitung zur Beförderung der theoretischen und praktischen Tonkunst* 1 (1827/28); cited in *Ludwig van Beethoven: Die Werke im Spiegel seiner Zeit,* ed. Stefan Kunze, 557.

24. See K. M. Knittel, "Wagner, Deafness, and the Reception of Beethoven's Late Style," *Journal of the American Musicological Society* 51 (1998), 49–82. Wagner's "Beethoven" is contained in his *Prose Works,* vol. 5, trans. William Ashton Ellis (London, 1896).

25. In his "Beethoven" essay, Wagner wrote, "A musician sans ears!—Can one conceive an eyeless painter? / But the blinded *Seer* we know" (*Actors and Singers: Richard Wagner,* trans. W. Ashton Ellis [Lincoln: University of Nebraska Press, 1995], 91–92).

26. *Beethoven: Eine Kunststudie,* by Wilhelm von Lenz, reprint with notes by Alfred Kalischer (Berlin: Schuster & Loeffler, 1921), 174. The original text is as follows: "Im Jahre 1827 hätte man auch noch für einen musikalischen Schwarzkünstler gegolten, wenn man etwas von der dritten Stylart Beethovens hören lassen sollten. Diese Schätze sind jetzt Gemeingut." In the translation, the term *black sheep,* is less than adequate in rendering von Lenz's term *Schwarzkünstler,* with its overtones of black magic and outcast status.

27. On the quartet of the Müller brothers, see Tully Potter, "From Chamber to Concert Hall," in *The Cambridge Companion to the String Quartet,* ed. Robin Stowell (Cambridge: Cambridge University Press, 2003), 45; and Helmut Wirth, "Kammermusik," in *Die Musik in Geschichte und Gegenwart,* vol. 7 (Kassel: Bärenreiter, 1958), column 479.

28. Quoted and translated by Robert Winter in "Performing the Beethoven Quartets in Their First Century," in *The Beethoven Quartet Companion,* ed. Robert Winter and Robert Martin (Berkeley: University of California Press, 1994), 28–57.

29. See John Daverio, "Manner, tone, and tendency in Beethoven's chamber music for strings," in *The Cambridge Companion to Beethoven,* ed. Glenn Stanley (Cambridge: Cambridge University Press, 2000), 152. Hirschbach's essay was issued in four installments in the *Neue Zeitschrift für Musik* during 1839.

30. Ernst von Elterlein, *Beethovens Clavier-Sonaten* (Leipzig: Heinrich Matthes, 1856). Elterlein's book contains discussions of each of the last five sonatas in pp. 96–118.

31. Adolph Bernhard Marx, *Ludwig van Beethoven: Leben und Schaffen,* 2 vols. (Berlin: 1859; reprinted Hildesheim and New York: Georg Olms, 1979).

32. See in this regard Ernest Newman, *The Life of Richard Wagner,* vol. 2 (New York: Knopf, 1937), 447.

33. This essay was delivered as a lecture at Weimar on August 8, 1861, printed in the *Neue Zeitschrift für Musik* 55 (1861), and reprinted in *Felix Draeseke Schriften 1855–1861,* ed. Martella Gutierrez-Denhoff and Helmut Loos (Bonn: Gudrun Schröder Verlag, 1987), 315–36; quotation on p. 327. The reference here to a shaking of "the absolutist regime of the main tonality" presumably refers to the striking tonal ambiguity of the slow fugal movement that begins the quartet.

34. Kerman has pointed out on the basis of Cosima Wagner's diary entries how ambivalent Wagner felt about the fugue of op. 131. See Kerman, "Beethoven Quartet Audiences: Actual, Potential, Ideal," in *The Beethoven Quartet Companion,* 18, 21.

35. As Kerman has pointed out (*The Beethoven Quartets,* 384), the note describing this situation was omitted from the 1961 reprint of Marliave's book.

36. Helm, *Beethovens Streichquartette,* 223.

37. "Some Aspects of Beethoven's Art Forms," in *Music and Letters* 3 (1927), republished in *Essays and Lectures on Music* (London, 1949).

38. *The Beethoven Quartets* (New York: Norton, 1966, republished in paperback, 1979). The discussion of the C♯-Minor Quartet is found in pp. 325–49.

39. *Compositional Origins of Beethoven's Opus 131* (Ann Arbor, Mich.: UMI Research Press, 1982).

40. Theodor W. Adorno, *Beethoven: The Philosophy of Music; Fragments and Texts,* ed. Rolf Tiedemann, trans. Edmund Jephcott (Cambridge: Polity Press, 1998), xi. This note by Adorno is found in the earliest of his notebooks containing fragmentary writings on Beethoven.

CHAPTER ONE

# Transformational Processes in Beethoven's Op. 18 Quartets

*William Kinderman*

The six quartets of op. 18 are the magnum opus of Beethoven's first decade at Vienna, and they stand somewhat apart from his later contributions to the quartet genre. Although less admired in writings about the composer than the "Razumovsky" Quartets or the late quartets, the op. 18 quartets are probably the most frequently performed, and they occupy a key historical position at the threshold to the nineteenth century. The very number of six pieces reminds us of the important legacy of Haydn and Mozart, and particularly of Haydn's "Russian" Quartets, op. 33, and Mozart's "Haydn" Quartets. Beethoven knew these works intimately, and reminiscences of both of his distinguished predecessors can be detected in his op. 18.

Beethoven produced the op. 18 quartets in two phases of three quartets each, as is confirmed by the recent discovery of receipts held in the Lobkowitz Archive in the Czech Republic.[1] In order of composition, he first wrote the Quartet in D Major, op. 18 no. 3, followed by the F-Major and G-Major quartets, op. 18 nos. 1 and 2. The latter two pieces were originally completed in 1799, and on June 25 Beethoven presented his friend Karl Amenda with a set of parts for the work in F major that became op. 18 no. 1. In this copy, the piece is described as "Quartetto No. II," implying that at this point the D-major quartet still stood at the head of the series. More than a year later, after Beethoven had composed the following quartets in C minor, A major, and B♭ major, he felt an urgent need to revise the quartets in F major and G major. The main work of revision took place during the summer of 1800.[2] Writing to Amenda a year later, on July 1, 1801, Beethoven cautioned his friend not to circulate the earlier version of op. 18 no. 1, because he had "only now learned how to write quartets properly."[3]

This chapter concerns the relation between integration and contrast in the quartets placed by Beethoven at the head of this pivotal opus, op. 18 no. 1 in F Major and no. 2 in G Major, as well as in the final quartet of the series, op. 18 no. 6. There is abundant evidence that he strove toward a tight unity of organization in crafting these pieces, at the same time pursuing heightened dramatic oppositions within and between individual movements. The surviving musical sketches and other sources cast a revealing and suggestive light on his compositional struggles and aesthetic goals. My particular concern will be how Beethoven devised transformational passages in certain movements of the quartets, wherein the strongest contrasts coexist with a high degree of integration.

## Quartet in F Major, Op. 18 No. 1

The opening Allegro con brio of the F-Major Quartet is the very touchstone of motivic integration in the High Classic style. The opening pair of statements of the six-note turn figure in the four instruments, neatly profiled by rests, embodies a lucid declaration of a working principle, whereby the fundamental motivic material heard at the outset serves as a consistent foundation for the texture of an entire movement. Such structural concentration can impose limiting and almost deterministic conditions. In this Allegro con brio, one is never distant from this primary motive, which also punctuates transitions and episodes in the formal design. It is as if the unfolding music continually remembers this basic topic, resulting in the tight sense of unity.

Yet Beethoven's aim often seems to go beyond the pursuit of unity for its own sake. In the present case, one indication of this ambition may be the fact that in revising the Amenda version of the quartet, he considerably reduced the number of appearances of the main motive. In the first version of the quartet, this motive appears 130 times, whereas in the revised piece, the turn figure occurs just 109 times. This revision, made once Beethoven had "learned to write quartets properly," implies that he had come to regard his earlier reliance on the turn figure as excessive.

The existence of the Amenda version has attracted considerable commentary, including an entire book devoted to a comparison of the two versions of the first movement.[4] Janet Levy, the book's author, perceives various problems in the first version of the development and sees the last bars of the development in this version as "among the most miscalculated in the entire movement."[5] As Levy and, before her, Carl Waack and Hans Josef Wedig have observed,[6] Beethoven's revamped development section generates far more momentum and intensity in its drive to the recapitulation than did the passage in the original Amenda version. In this regard, it is somewhat surprising that Levy does not reassess the recapitulatory arrival in light of its enhanced preparation. In comparing the two versions, she writes that "In each version the first eight measures of the recapitulation are the same as those of the exposition."[7] She concludes that "decisive points in the form . . . are not fundamentally revised. Nor are the other moments that most basically delineate the large structure—the very beginnings of the development, recapitulation, and coda."[8] Actually, the outset of the recapitulation is not the same as in the Amenda version. Although the notes themselves are unchanged, there is a significant intensification in dynamics at the point of recapitulation, from *forte* to *fortissimo* (Examples 1.1a and b).

This change in dynamics is not an isolated nuance; one of Beethoven's striking alterations, in the thoroughly rewritten passage preceding the recapitulation, con-

*Example 1.1a.* Quartet in F Major, op. 18 no. 1, I, mm. 175–95, in original, "Amenda" version.

*Example 1.1b.* Quartet in F Major, op. 18 no. 1, I, mm. 165–87 in final version.

sists of a rethinking of the dynamic balance of the approach to the big tonic cadence. Previously, the eight preceding measures had been *fortissimo,* and the actual recapitulation only *forte.* This stronger dynamic level of the Amenda version, in conjunction with the vivid animation of the part writing, including sixteen-note scales and syncopated chords, produces a massive sound that does not connect effectively to the beginning of the recapitulation. In his revision, Beethoven reversed the dynamic levels here, and he connected one section to the next through *crescendo* markings on the three lower parts two bars before the arrival, and on the first violin one bar before. These *crescendo* indications prescribe that the vigorous energy of the rewritten development should connect to the emphatic moment of recapitulation.

Joseph Kerman describes the effect of this recapitulation as "blatant, and no less so for being thoroughly typical of the man."[9] He claims, "The present recapitulation has points of ingenuity, but it provides no true outcome for the frenetic, rather silly preparation."[10] Yet this critique applies more to the Amenda version than to the final version of the quartet. It seems true enough that an effect of blatancy or disjointedness can easily arise through inadequate performance, but this outcome may be precisely what Beethoven attempted to guard against in his revision. In the final version, the *fp* markings imply that the basic dynamic level throughout is soft, with the *sf* accents arising out of this restrained level of sound. Increasing intensity is generated through rhythmic activity and registral expansion, among other means; but a major challenge in performance is precisely to avoid any premature *crescendi* before these are specified in the last two bars before the return.

In its final version, the passage indeed displays "points of ingenuity," whereby the main motive is drawn into processes of variation and transformation. For instance, as Beethoven built up the rhythmic energy and textural density of the music, he replaced the rather neutral, familiar presentation of the turn motive with a more decisive, emphatic version. This is heard in the cello twelve bars before the big cadential arrival. Beethoven shaped a kind of rhythmic abstract of the motivic pattern, while eliminating the turn figure altogether. Instead, the lowest pitches are placed on the downbeats of each measure, whereas the first note of each group of three repeated upbeat pitches is given an accent in mm. 167–69. In comparison to the original motive, these accents are placed where the neighbor note, G, had stood. A dynamic accent thus compensates for the energy otherwise achieved through use of the neighbor note and helps preserve an audible relation to the original turn figure. Through such means, Beethoven retained a close relation to his original motive even as he pulled out the stops in this powerful drive to the recapitulation.

There is another sense in which this rewritten passage in op. 18 no. 1 represents significant rethinking of a "decisive point in the form." Such a recapitulation in the Classical Style presents an opportunity to revisit the opening idea that had stood alone, without preparation, at the outset of the piece. The two soft unison statements of the motive are striking but restrained, as befits a germinal idea at the beginning of an extended discourse. In addition, the exposition contains a counterstatement of the turn figure in its double presentation in mm. 9–12, and on this occasion the dynamic level is shifted to *forte*. Here is yet another reason why the recapitulation should go beyond the dynamic level of *forte* to *fortissimo*. The forceful preparation for this presentation, together with its broader spacing, motivates the most emphatic rendering of the motto figure. Beethoven's treatment of the development and recapitulation shows how much is latent in his basic material. Surprising power emerges from what had appeared to be elegant conversational rhetoric. In other words, a certain disproportion or imbalance in the weighting of the formal divisions may be an outcome of Beethoven's basic aesthetic approach. There is, to be sure, a fairly tight motivic foundation for the driving momentum at the end of the development. The pervasive sixteenth-note figuration, for example, is ultimately linked to the pair of sixteenth notes in the seminal turn figure itself. This derivation can be most clearly heard at the end of the exposition, where a series of repetitions of the turn motive in the first violin leads into a series of rapid descending scales, before a variant of the turn, two octaves lower, grounds this intensity into the four repeated quarter notes that close the exposition.

In the coda of the movement, new variants of the turn figure help to bring about the final cadential resolution. Twenty bars from the end, the motive is reshaped so that its closing interval ascends by step instead of dropping a fourth. This reshaping allows the chain of such motives in the first violin to outline the rising line F–G–A–B♭–C–D—a pattern that had been foreshadowed in the *fortissimo* unison phrase heard about twenty bars earlier (Examples 1.2a and b). Now a whispered statement of the turn figure on the dominant already announces a cadence. But it takes a subtle rhythmic realignment of the turn motto to finally do the trick: in the last measures Beethoven compressed the head of the motive and lengthened the tail, as the drop of the fourth to C rebounds into a witty cadential resolution (Example 1.2c). Here again, the accents (which were not yet present in the Amenda version) are purposeful and much to the point. They help to signal the process of thematic completion, marking and emphasizing the rhetorical extension of the familiar version of the motivic cell. The omnipresent turn motive lacks the ability to achieve closure without this added twist.

*Example 1.2a.* Quartet in F Major, op. 18 no. 1, I, coda, mm. 273–83.

*Example 1.2b.* Quartet in F Major, op. 18 no. 1, I, coda, mm. 292–301.

*Example 1.2c.* Quartet in F Major, op. 18 no. 1, I, coda, mm. 308–end.

## Quartet in G Major, Op. 18 No. 2

Soon after tackling the revision of the F-Major Quartet, Beethoven decided to revamp the G-Major Quartet, as well, and he undertook that task by the summer of 1800. The movement that was most substantially changed was the second movement, the Adagio cantabile. Originally this movement was marked Largo, and its similarities to the work as we know it were surprisingly limited. In the revision, the original meter was altered from 4/4 to 3/4, and the thematic material was significantly reworked. Furthermore, there is no sign, in the original sketches for the movement contained in the Grasnick 2 sketchbook,[11] of the striking middle section of the movement in Allegro tempo. Yet this passage is particularly arresting. Kerman finds that "Precedent for so whimsical an insertion of a fast dance into an *Adagio* is hard to find," and he relates this compositional decision to the use of dance "parodies," such as turn up repeatedly in the late quartets.[12]

Fresh light has been cast on this episode by the recent publication of a sketchleaf known as the "Scala leaf"; this manuscript contains one of Beethoven's drafts for the new middle section, which originally belonged together with related entries in the Autograph 19e sketchbook.[13] As this source shows, he was especially preoccupied with the handling of the transition from the end of the opening section in slow tempo to the rapid, dance-like middle section. The transition as written on the top of the recto side of the Scala leaf is shown in Example 1.3a, in Richard Kramer's transcription; the finished version is shown in Example 1.3b. There are two alternative versions on the Scala leaf, depending whether the word *oder* ("or") is taken to signal a continuation to the beginning of staff 2. The sixteenth-note figure at the end of staff 1 presumably marks the beginning of the Allegro and hence continues into the episode in 2/4 meter. Both of these alternative versions are longer than the finished work, because Beethoven placed the "all[egro]" notation in the draft after the change of key to F major, at the outset of the continuous motion in sixteenth notes. In the work as we know it, the change to the fast tempo occurs already in the opening phrases in employing sixteenth notes in F major, with these phrases already written in 2/4 time.

*Example 1.3a.* Scala leaf, recto, staves 1–2.

*Example 1.3b.* Quartet op. 18 no. 2, II, mm. 20–38.

A version of the transition closer to the finished work actually occurs on the facing page of the reconstructed sketchbook, a leaf now housed in Stockholm at the Stiftelsen Musikkulturens framjande.[14] Yet even if the transition on the Stockholm leaf resembles the finished work more closely, the version of the following Allegro is rather different.[15] The motivic texture of the Allegro episode on the Stockholm leaf is less consistently based on the motive of four sixteenths outlining a stepwise pattern outlining a third. In the end, Beethoven remained extremely close throughout the episode to the motivic pattern that is highlighted at the transition from the end of the slow section to the beginning of the Allegro.

This join between the two sections rewards close attention. Kramer refers to this moment as a "juncture where the new Allegro interrupts the Adagio cantabile,"[16] whereas Kerman finds Beethoven indulging here in "a more or less irresponsible juncture of disparate styles—a gesture of weariness or desperation, it almost seems, with a type of slow thematic material that no longer satisfied the composer."[17] It seems unnecessary to postulate that the Allegro was born out of the composer's supposed frustration with the noble Adagio cantabile. There is no evidence that he was weary with this material, even if he did take efforts to thoroughly revise the first version of the movement. Indeed, this kind of contemplative, lyric Adagio is characteristic of early Beethoven, and movements of this general type are found in some of the most ambitious early piano sonatas, such as in the impressive slow movement in this key, marked "con gran espressione," of the Sonata in E♭ Major, op. 7.

Is Beethoven "irresponsible" in venturing this surprising thematic juxtaposition as the basis for the ternary form? The entire opening section is shown in Example 1.4, which continues in Example 1.3b. Clearly, he was exploring here a new type of heightened contrast, at once structural and expressive in nature. For one, the Allegro does not actually "interrupt" the Adagio cantabile. The Adagio unfolds with great breadth and achieves its lyric peak in a shift through an augmented-sixth chord to a widely spaced C-major chord in 6/4 position, five bars from the close of the section in slow tempo. This is the climax; the several measures that follow are a quiet postlude. The closing *pianissimo* phrases round off the structure while recalling the contour of the head of the theme, in its original register.

The reference to the beginning of the theme is sensitively handled. The first five-note *pianissimo* phrase of the postlude is a variant of the opening upbeat of the original theme, the rising fourth G–C. Beethoven then drew the Adagio section to a serene close by augmenting the falling triadic pattern of the first notes of the theme: the G is sustained throughout the next five-note gesture in the first violin, and the two last pitches fall through the third to the root of the C-major triad. This same motivic pattern—G–C–G–E–C—forms the head of the Adagio theme, and it also appears in the passage leading to the melodic climax in mm. 19–20. In these bars, the measured fall through the notes of the C-major triad is heard twice in the high register before the stepwise push to the mediant leads to the peak of the entire opening period. In the transition from the Adagio to the Allegro, Beethoven accelerated

*Example 1.4.* Op. 18 no. 2, II, mm. 1–19.

the five-note phrase that is itself a decorated version of the opening upbeat of the movement. After two tentative introductory bars in the first violin in the faster tempo, the dance parody unfolds in earnest, with its own binary form of two repeated halves. The effect of contrast is indeed startling. The Allegro does not maintain the measured decorum of the serious outer sections of the movement. This "whimsical insertion," in Kerman's formulation, seems to mock the serious aria in which it is embedded.

Yet this passage, too, embodies a transformational process, for it is audibly linked to the opening motto theme of the Adagio cantabile. As we have seen, the first motives of the Allegro are derived from the rising fourth of the opening upbeat of the theme. The next notes of that subject include the falling triadic degrees from fifth to third to tonic, followed by a semitone drop to the leading tone and then an upward rise to the second degree of the scale. The intervallic outline is thus 5–3–1–7–1–3–2. It is remarkable how closely the main motive of the Allegro mimics this intervallic pattern. The faster tempo and use of figural diminution disguise the relation, yet the structural skeleton is extremely similar. Beethoven began in m. 28 on C, the fifth degree of F major, then placed A and F on the strong beats of the following measure, touched the leading tone E in m. 29, and continued with a rise through F♯ to G, the second degree, in m. 30. The underlying structural outline is thus practically identical to that heard in bars 1–2 of the Adagio cantabile (see Figure 1.1).

Further evidence of the derivational process lies in the falling stepwise sixteenth notes, a texture that is so characteristic of the dance-like Allegro. Instead of the almost ponderous falling motion through the triad in the Adagio, the Allegro deftly fills in these gaps, generating a lively perpetual motion that is sustained through sequential patterns. Remarkably, the basic texture of the three stepwise sixteenths actually appears before the Allegro even begins, in the tranquil postlude of the opening Adagio. A developing process of thematic derivation connects the Adagio cantabile with the Allegro.

Attentive hearing thus reveals that this pairing is not so wild and capricious as first appears. The relation of the Adagio and Allegro is not arbitrary. Still, an effect of astonishing contrast is undoubtedly part of the aesthetic meaning of the work. Beethoven has succeeded here in a seemingly paradoxical endeavor: to maximize differences between the two sections while retaining a tangible structural link. A point of this music is to show how the imagination can negotiate between seemingly incompatible realms, linking strange worlds together in a tensional balance. There is a sense in which Beethoven may have been "irresponsible" to the reflective character of the Adagio when he wedded it to the frenetic Allegro. But his vision of artistic freedom encouraged him to move beyond a unitary perspective to explore opposing and complementary ideas. The somewhat static character of the Adagio cantabile, with its heavy cadences and portentous pauses, invites juxtaposition with its antipode, the swift and nimble interlude supplied by the Allegro. In this sense, each of the two sections of the movement can be regarded as a complement or critique of the other. The quest for a paradoxical unity of opposites seems all the more fitting here in view of the humorous spirit of the quartet as a whole.[18]

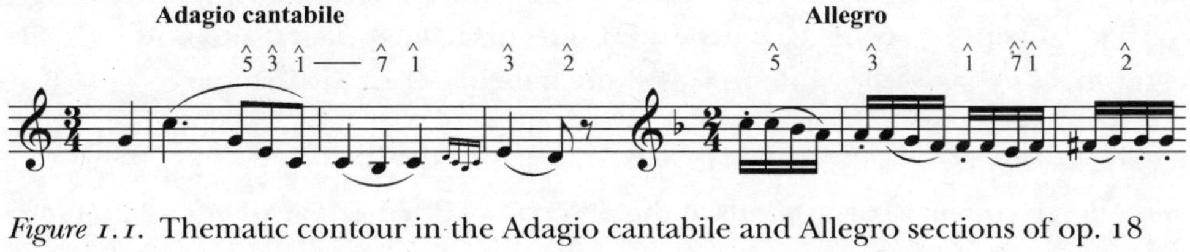


*Figure 1.1.* Thematic contour in the Adagio cantabile and Allegro sections of op. 18 no. 2, II.

## Quartet in B♭ Major, Op. 18 No. 6

It seems scarcely accidental that Beethoven rewrote the slow movement of op. 18 no. 2 at around the same time he conceived the final work of the series, the Quartet in B♭ Major, op. 18 no. 6.[19] For the finale of op. 18 no. 6 offers the most striking wedding of opposites in the entire opus: an Adagio labeled "La Malinconia" ("Melancholy"), which leads into a swinging, dance-like rondo finale in 3/8 time, marked "Allegretto quasi Allegro." Judging from the evidence of the sketches, these two movements seem to have been connected in their genesis. After having freshly composed op. 18 no. 6, with its unusual dualistic finale, Beethoven soon turned to the revision of the Adagio of the G-Major Quartet and then resolved to embed in that piece a contrast of comparable force.

In the G-Major Quartet, the dance-like perpetuum mobile occupies the center of the ternary form, whereas in the finale of op. 18 no. 6, the dance-like Allegretto becomes the main thematic material, though prefaced by and balanced against the mysterious Adagio marked "Melancholy." Despite basic differences, there are some conspicuous similarities in the way the dance-like music is handled. In both works, the faster music follows an Adagio of serious, weighty character and responds to this profundity with lively animation, as is expressed in a busy, continuous musical texture. The ternary design of op. 18 no. 2 allows for only a single change in character, whereas in op. 18 no. 6 there is a more extensive alternation of material in the two contrasting tempi.

In his study of the genesis of op. 18 no. 6, Richard Kramer has traced the evolution of La Malinconia, beginning from early sketches that show no evidence of including the initial Adagio.[20] As he observes about the sketching of the finale, "The areas most heavily sketched are the points of liaison between the Malinconia and the Allegretto. The final integration of the two tempos toward the end of the movement, beginning just before m. 195, occupied Beethoven's thoughts evidently to the exclusion of the main body of the Allegretto."[21]

A duality of character states had appeared in some of Beethoven's earlier works, such as his piano piece "Lustig-traurig" ("Funny-Sad"), WoO 54, in C major/minor. A familiar example that is more comparable to op. 18 no. 6 is the first movement of the *Sonate pathétique*, op. 13, which was completed shortly before the quartet project. This movement juxtaposes a solemn, brooding Grave with a brilliant, turbulent Allegro con brio. Although the initial material in the slow tempo functions as an extended introduction to the Allegro, it also returns at the outset of the development and in the coda. In op. 18 no. 6, "Melancholy" also recurs at later stages, and only with difficulty does the 3/8 Allegretto shake off the memory of La Malinconia.

It is instructive to consider the psychology of such character polarities in Beethoven's music. In the case of the *Sonate pathétique*, the relation between the Grave and Allegro con brio corresponds to the percepts of Friedrich Schiller's aesthetics.[22]

If the gloomy slow introduction suggests a subjective awareness of human suffering, the main Allegro section seems to posit resistance to such suffering and a refusal to accept that condition as permanent and irremediable. Under such circumstances, a relapse into or alternation of contrasting soul states is convincing, since a psychological transition does not obliterate an awareness or memory of the preceding condition. Carl Dahlhaus has addressed some related dramatic aspects of Beethoven's instrumental music: "Although a drama is a goal-directed process, its dialectic remains essentially unresolved. In other words, the structure of a drama is at once and inseparably both teleological and paradoxical: the action presses on towards an end, but leaves behind it the intuition of an undetermined state of ideas, characters, and points of view that reciprocally 'relativize' each other. This undetermined state continues to be realized throughout the dramatic process; and, vice versa, the meaning of the action is not revealed by its ending but by the totality of the stages through which it passes, with all the contradictions that are expressed on the way."[23]

Beethoven's use of the term *melancholy* conjures up associations with two slow movements from this phase of his career: the Largo e mesto of the Sonata in D Major, op. 10 no. 3, and the Adagio affettuoso ed appassionato in the first of the op. 18 quartets. Both movements are in the key of D minor and share certain stylistic features. In their somber tone evocative of tragic resignation and their sensitive use of musical rhetoric, both pieces invite close attention. In each case, there is a striking rapport of sound with silence—a cessation that carries the implication of death. Amenda reported that Beethoven associated the Adagio of op. 18 no. 1 with the tomb scene in Shakespeare's *Romeo and Juliet*. This association is confirmed by several entries in the Grasnick 2 sketchbook. The most fascinating single sketch, found at the top of page 9, carries the inscription "les derniers soupirs" ("the last sighs").[24] Yet the musical content of this sketch relates even more closely to the Largo e mesto of op. 10 no. 3 than to the quartet (Examples 1.5a and b).

The correspondence is particularly strong to the end of the development of the sonata movement, where the falling sigh figure in the upper voice is set off by rests, leading before the cadence to D minor to a strongly emphasized interval of the diminished seventh, B♭–C♯. To be sure, the quartet movement also shows a highly arresting treatment of sonorities and silences at this point, and the dynamic contrasts preceding the recapitulation were even more drastic in the original 1799 version of the quartet, with a *fortissimo* diminished-seventh chord leading to a triple pianissimo dominant-seventh just three bars later.

Each of these movements has a more unified character than the finale of op. 18 no. 6, in which the dramatic process is conditioned by the strong polarity of La Malinconia and its German dance sequel in 3/8 meter. There is something Haydnesque about such a slow introduction acting as preface while lending expressive weight to a swift main movement, and it is typical of Haydn in such circumstances to foreshadow the faster section in the slow introduction.[25] Herein lies an important ques-

*Example 1.5a.* Grasnick 2 sketchbook, p. 9, staves 1–2.

*Example 1.5b.* Sonata in D Major, op. 10 no. 3, II, mm. 40–41.

tion relating to Beethoven's penchant for transformational processes: Is the dance-like Allegretto merely juxtaposed to "Melancholy" as a study in contrasts, or does it grow out of the Adagio by reshaping the substance of the preceding music?

Commentators have remained silent about the precise musical relationship between La Malinconia and the main body of the finale. Hugo Riemann writes about the thematic duality: "Whether he [Beethoven] depicts a struggle or wishes to display two personalities set against one another (he was early on already an accomplished character painter) is for a grasp of the music completely unimportant; for this purpose one need not know the actual underlying idea, and we have no means to explore it."[26] Kerman regards the Adagio as "an emotional sphinx, dealing with pathos entirely from the outside, revealing an almost heartless preoccupation with its own harmonic meditations over those of the poor melancholic," but he also finds that "the aggregation of *Adagio* and *Allegretto* sections . . . is a case of the whole being larger than the sum of the parts."[27]

Close attention to the melodic relations between the *Adagio* and the *Allegretto* suggests how a sense of the "larger whole" is conveyed (Example 1.6a and b). The soft, delicately mysterious opening phrase of "Melancholy" starts in the first violin on the third degree, D. After three repetitions of this pitch, the phrase continues with a drop of a third to the tonic, B♭, followed by a stepwise linear ascent leading from the tonic to the dominant. The four-bar phrase then concludes with a turn figure emphasizing the fifth degree, F. In its motivic makeup, the opening phrase thus consists of three main parts: the opening repeated notes on the third degree with their char-

*Example 1.6a.* Quartet in B♭ Major, op. 18 no. 6, IV, beginning of "La Malinconia."

*Example 1.6b.* Quartet in B♭ Major, op. 18 no. 6, IV, beginning of Allegretto quasi Allegro.

acteristic rhythm; the rising line from tonic to dominant; and the slow turn figure articulated on the highest note of the phrase.

At the outset of the Allegretto quasi Allegro, the first-violin line picks up each of these three motivic elements, absorbing them into the continuous texture in sixteenth notes. The descending-third D–B♭ is contained here in the upbeat figuration to m. 1, with the interval of the falling third spelled out through conjunct motion. Immediately following is a stepwise line rising through four ascending steps to outline a diminished fifth, from A to E♭. What about the turn figure, which is so prominent in La Malinconia? This motivic element, too, is present at the beginning of each of the opening measures. The turn is rendered as B♭–A–B♭ in bar 1 and as C–B–C in m. 2. It is probably not coincidental, moreover, that Beethoven placed a dynamic inflection in the form of an accent at the end of each turn, with this articulation reinforced in the other instruments. This treatment recalls the treatment of some four-note turns in La Malinconia, in which the final outcome note is emphasized by a *forte* marking.

It is thus possible to hear the beginning of the German dance as a lively rhythmic transformation of those same motivic elements that were so mysteriously suspended in La Malinconia. This interpretation sheds light on the "underlying idea" of Beethoven's unusual wedding of contrasts, which is richer and more concrete in its psychological meaning than has often been recognized. The return of the thematic juxtaposition of "Melancholy" and Allegretto near the end of this rondo finale is noteworthy in this connection. Here is a one possible source of inspiration for Schubert's famous setting of Goethe's *Gretchen am Spinnrade.* Schubert's song shows remarkable insight into the distraught psychological state of Gretchen, who, increasingly obsessed by her thoughts of Faust and ultimately by his kiss, breaks off her repetitive activity of spinning and only with difficulty is able to resume it. Similarly, the implied protagonist in Beethoven's narrative design in the quartet again becomes haunted by La Malinconia at this point and is made temporarily unable to sustain the dance-like vivacity. After starting up in A minor, beginning in m. 160, the Allegretto almost immediately loses itself and breaks off into silence in the middle of the fourth bar. Only a renewed preoccupation with the driving sequential patterns of the dance points the way to a return of the theme in the tonic B♭ major, and later to the arrival of the brilliant coda, marked Prestissimo. The threshold to this final stage is a slowed-down, poco adagio presentation of those basic phrases from the dance, which invites us once more to hear a transformational relationship between the Malinconia phrases and the contour of the German dance.

A sensitive performance can convey the dialectic tension between these themes—particularly the way the Allegretto reshapes the musical structure of "Melancholy" while transforming it. Every note counts in this process, as can be shown by reviewing the opening phrase of the dance. The opening F connects to the last notes of the Adagio while grounding the phrase to come; the detached articulation of the D and C and slur on the B♭ allow us to hear the return of the falling third D–B♭ from the Adagio as now filled in with vivacious new energy. As previously noted, the turn figure on B♭ is here worked directly into the rhythmic continuity, and the motivic idea of a rising linear series through a fifth supplies the remaining notes of the basic thematic configuration of the Allegretto. Fittingly, the sequential pattern of the music allows the highest note D in the upbeat figure to be surpassed by E♭ in bar 1, and then by F in bar 4. Above all, the Allegretto represents music of energetic continuity, whose faithful reliance on the pattern heard at the outset ensures an ongoing audible connection to the Adagio.

This kind of transformational process did not remain an isolated experiment for Beethoven. The most impressive later work that develops this approach is another finale composed more than twenty years later, that of the Piano Sonata in A♭ Major, op. 110, with its duality of Arioso dolente and fugue. This finale is divided between appearances of the lamenting song and aspiring fugue, and its most crucial moment of transformation occurs when the inverted fugue subject appears *una corda* in the exact registral position previously occupied by the most despairing version of the Arioso dolente. Hence we can feel in satisfactory performance how one soul state is transformed into another, and Beethoven even wrote above the ensuing passage, "gradually coming anew to life."[28] There can be no doubt that this psychological content belongs to the fundamental meaning of the music, and every adequate engagement with these works needs to go beyond the mere surface of notes to perceive the organic interrelationships that can bring those notes to life.

## Notes

1. For a discussion of these and other documents relating to the genesis of the quartets, see Sieghard Brandenburg, "Beethovens Streichquartette op. 18," in *Beethoven und Böhmen: Beiträge zu Biographie und Wirkungsgeschichte Beethovens,* ed. Sieghard Brandenburg and Martella Gutierrez-Denhoff (Bonn: Beethoven-Haus, 1988), 259–302. Receipts bearing Beethoven's signature show that he received 200 gulden from Prince Lobkowitz for the first three quartets on October 14, 1799, and 200 gulden for the remaining three quartets on October 18, 1800. These documents are reproduced in Jaroslav Macek, "Die Musik bei den Lobkowicz," in *Ludwig van Beethoven im Herzen Europas,* ed. Oldřich Pulkert and Hans-Werner Küthen (Prague: České lupkové závody A.G., 2000), 181, 183.

2. The sketches for the revision of these quartets are contained in the sketchbook Autograph 19e, which has been published in reconstructed form in facsimile and transcription, with commentary, edited by Richard Kramer, as *Ludwig van Beethoven, A Sketchbook from the Summer of 1800: Sketches for the String Quartets Op. 18, Nos. 1, 2, and 6, the Piano Sonata Op. 22, and for Various Other Works* (Bonn: Beethoven-Haus, 1996). The sketchbooks preceding and following Autograph 19e also contain work on the op. 18 quartets. These have been published as *Beethoven: Ein Skizzenbuch zu Streichquartetten aus Op. 18,* 2 vols., ed. Wilhelm Virneisel (Bonn: Beethoven-Haus, 1974), and *Ein Notierungsbuch von Beethoven aus dem Besitze der Preussischen Staatsbibliothek zu Berlin,* ed. Karl Lothar Mikulicz (Leipzig: Breitkopf & Härtel, 1927; reprinted Hildesheim and New York: Georg Olms, 1972). The autograph scores of the op. 18 quartets have not survived. The original Amenda version of op. 18 no. 1 is printed in *Beethoven Werke: Abteilung VI Band 3 Streichquartette 1,* ed. Paul Mies (Munich: Henle, 1962), 124–50.

3. *Beethoven Briefe,* vol. 1, ed. Sieghard Brandenburg (Munich: Henle, 1996), L. 67. The original German text is as follows: "—dein Quartett gieb ja nicht weiter, weil ich es sehr umgeändert habe, indem ich erst jezt recht *quartetten* zu schreiben weiss, was du schon sehen wirst, wenn du sie erhalten wirst" (p. 86).

4. Janet Levy, *Beethoven's Compositional Choices: The Two Versions of Opus 18, No. 1, First Movement* (Philadelphia: University of Pennsylvania Press, 1982).

5. Ibid., 73.

6. Carl Waack, "Beethovens F-dur Streichquartett Op. 18 No. 1 in seiner ursprünglichen Fassung," *Die Musik* 12 (1904): 418–20; Hans Josef Wedig, *Beethovens Streichquartett op. 18 nr. 1 und seine erste Fassung* (Bonn: Beethoven-Haus, 1922).

7. Levy, *Beethoven's Compositional Choices,* 75.

8. Ibid., 95.

9. Joseph Kerman, *The Beethoven Quartets* (New York: Norton, 1966), 35.

10. Ibid.

11. These sketches are found in *Beethoven: Ein Skizzenbuch zu Streichquartetten aus Op. 18,* ed. Wilhelm Virneisel (see note 2).

12. Kerman, *The Beethoven Quartets,* 51–52.

13. This source has been published in facsimile and transcription as *Ein neuentdecktes Skizzenblatt vom Sommer 1800 zu Beethovens Streichquartett op. 18 Nr. 2,* ed. Richard Kramer (Bonn: Beethoven-Haus, 1999); the leaf belongs in the reconstructed Autograph 19e sketchbook, between fols. 21 and 22.

14. This leaf is transcribed in Kramer's transcription volume of Autograph 19e, p. 66. It is catalogued as str qt MMS 271 in the Nydahl Collection at the Stiftelsen Musikkulturens framjande, as recorded in Bonnie and Erling Lomnas, *Catalogue of Music Manuscripts* (Stockholm: Musikaliska akademiens bibliotek, 1995), 28.

15. In fact, this draft lacks the notation "Allegro," but a shift to a faster tempo is clearly implied by the context of the surrounding sketches, including the notation "all[egro]" on the Scala leaf.

16. *Ludwig van Beethoven: Ein neuentdecktes Skizzenblatt vom Sommer 1800,* 7.

17. Kerman, *The Beethoven Quartets,* 52.

18. For a discussion of humor and paradox in early Beethoven, see my article "Beethoven's High Comic Style in Piano Sonatas of the 1790s, or 'Beethoven, Uncle Toby, and the Muckcart-driver,'" *Beethoven Forum* 5 (1996): 119–38.

19. Richard Kramer observes sketches for an unused piece, which probably once had been intended for the finale of op. 18 no. 2, in close proximity to entries for La Malinconia. See Kramer, "Ambiguities in *La Malinconia,*" *Beethoven Studies* 3, ed. Alan Tyson (Cambridge: Cambridge University Press, 1982), 36, note 5. Also, some sketches for music that found its way into the finale of the Piano Sonata in B♭ Major, op. 22, may have been conceived in relationship to the finale of what became op. 18 no. 6. See Kramer, *A Sketchbook from the Summer of 1800,* transcription vol., 19.

20. Kramer, "Ambiguities in *La Malinconia,*" 35; these sketches are found in the edition of *A Sketchbook from the Summer of 1800,* transcription vol., 46–47.

21. *A Sketchbook from the Summer of 1800,* transcription vol., 21.

22. For a discussion of aesthetic affinities between Schiller and Beethoven, as well as the relevance of Schiller's aesthetics to the *Sonate pathétique,* see my study *Beethoven* (Oxford: Clarendon, 1995), esp. 4–14, 45–50.

23. Carl Dahlhaus, *Ludwig van Beethoven: Approaches to His Music,* trans. Mary Whittall (Oxford: Clarendon, 1991), 127–28.

24. *Beethoven: Ein Skizzenbuch zu Streichquartetten aus Op. 18,* ed. Wilhelm Virneisel, transcription vol., 47.

25. Haydn, of course, typically employed such introductions at the outset of first movements of his symphonies.

26. *Ludwig van Beethovens Leben von Alexander Wheelock Thayer, nach dem Original-Manuskript deutsch bearbeitet von Hermann Deiters,* ed. and expanded by Hugo Riemann, vol. 2 (Leipzig: Breitkopf & Härtel, 1922), 196.

27. Kerman, *The Beethoven Quartets,* 82.

28. For a detailed study of op. 110 from this perspective, see my essay "Integration and Narrative Design in Beethoven's Piano Sonata in A♭ Major, Opus 110," *Beethoven Forum* 1 (1992): 111–45.

CHAPTER TWO

# Metrical Dissonance and Metrical Revision in Beethoven's String Quartets

*Harald Krebs*

Many writers have remarked on the prevalence of metrical conflict in Beethoven's music. Michael Broyles has stated, for example, "Of all Classical composers, Beethoven especially exploited meter to generate tension and conflict."[1] Barry Cooper observes that a particular kind of metrical conflict—the "violent off-beat sforzando"—is more common in Beethoven's music than in that of any other composer.[2] Numerous specific examples of metrical conflict have been identified in Beethoven's music. Broyles mentions relevant passages from a number of Beethoven's orchestral works, including the third movement of the *Eroica* Symphony, the Fourth Symphony (which, he feels, "represents Beethoven's most intense use of syncopation as a structural device"), the *Egmont* overture, and the *Coriolan* Overture.[3] The first movement of the *Eroica* Symphony is probably the most frequently cited work in this connection; Edward T. Cone, Carl Dahlhaus, Barry Cooper, David Epstein, and William Kinderman, for example, have commented on its cross-rhythms, offbeat sforzandi, and syncopations.[4] Striking metrical conflicts have also been noted in Beethoven's piano sonatas (for instance, in the opening movements of op. 14 no. 2, op. 31 no. 1, and op. 101),[5] in his songs,[6] in his string quartets,[7] and in other genres.[8]

A few authors, including William Rothstein, Roger Kamien, and Richard Cohn, have identified particular conflicts (mostly on a hypermetrical level) in Beethoven's music and also have traced Beethoven's treatment of those conflicts through a work or movement.[9] The examination of the operation of metrical conflict within large contexts has been the focal point of my own work, as well (although in my case, the emphasis has been on the metrical rather than the hypermetrical level).[10] This chapter involves an investigation of metrical conflicts (or "metrical dissonances") in Beethoven's string quartets, employing an approach that makes it possible to label particular dissonances, and then to track them through a composition. My approach posits two basic types of metrical dissonance. Grouping dissonance involves the superposition on the notated meter of a grouping of pulses that is incongruent with the metrical grouping. (Hemiola is a specific type of grouping dissonance.) Displacement dissonance (syncopation) consists of the superposition on the notated meter of a congruent but nonaligned pulse grouping.[11] Both types are amply illustrated in Beethoven's string quartets, as is demonstrated by Examples 2.1 and 2.2. Example 2.1 shows a small selection of displacement dissonances in Beethoven's quartets. Each example is festooned with numbers; these are not intended to encourage the counting of pulses while listening to the music, nor to suggest that listening to the music requires such counting, but are simply a convenient means of making visible the layers of pulses that combine to form given metrical dissonances. The position of the numbers in the score indicates the regular pulses of metrical layers and of conflicting, "antimetrical" layers; metrical layers are indicated below the score, antimetrical layers above. The numbers themselves indicate the quantity of unit pulses encompassed by the pulses of those layers. Parenthesized numbers indicate pulses that are not articulated in the music but are implied by the context. I refer to the number associated with a given layer as the "cardinality" of that layer, and to the given layer as a "2–layer," or "3–layer," and so forth, depending upon its cardinality. The value of the unit pulse, obvious in each example, is chosen so as to avoid fractional cardinalities. I have assigned to each metrical dissonance in Example 2.1 a label beginning with "D" (for *displacement*), followed by the cardinality that is shared by the metrical and antimetrical layers, a plus sign (denoting displacement), and finally a number designating the quantity of pulses by which the pulses of the layers are separated.

There is space here to discuss only a few of the passages shown in Example 2.1. The selection includes many displacement dissonances whose antimetrical layers arise from dynamic accents in all instrumental parts (see Examples 2.1a and 2.1b); this is the most common method of creating displacement dissonance in Beethoven's music. Not all of his displacement dissonances, however, are so obvious. In Example 2.1c, there are no dynamic accents; instead, durational accents (long durations following short ones), then also density accents (sudden increases of density) suggest an antimetrical 3–layer beginning on the notated second beats, and harmony and melodic grouping reinforce the metrical 3–layer.[12] The resulting dissonance is D3+1 (because the antimetrical 3–layer is displaced by one quarter-note pulse in relation to the metrical 3–layer). Example 2.1d similarly begins with a displacement dissonance that does not arise from dynamic accentuation. The metrical 2–layer is suggested by the melodic rhythm, whose strongest durational accents coincide with

*Example 2.1.* Displacement dissonances in Beethoven's string quartets.

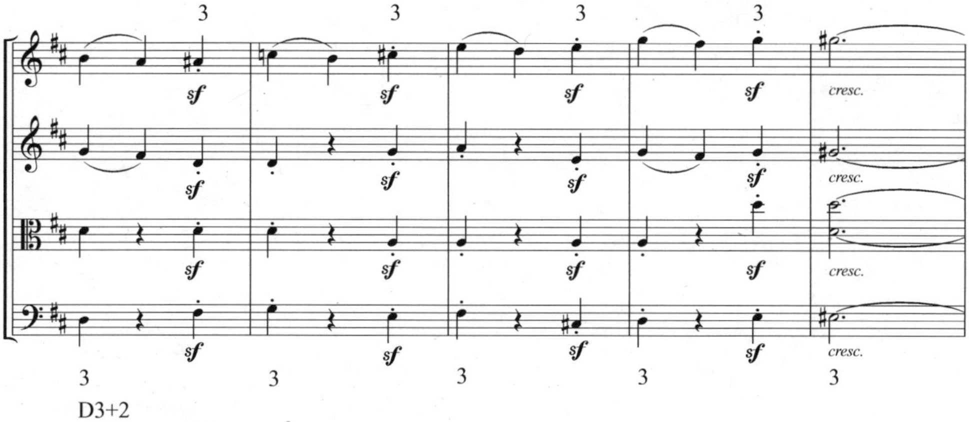


*a.* Op. 18 no. 3, III, mm. 16–20.

*b.* Op. 18 no. 5, II, beginning of Trio.

*c.* Op. 95, III, mm. 1–7.

*Example 2.1, continued. d.* Op. 74, IV, mm. 1–8.

*e.* Op. 135, II, mm. 1–8.

*f.* Op. 132, II, mm. 1–8.

downbeats. The harmonic rhythm, however, results in the strong articulation of an antimetrical duple layer. The conflicting 2–layers form the displacement dissonance D2+1—a dissonance that plays an important role in the remainder of the theme and of the movement. In Example 2.1e, displacement dissonance results from the placement of durational accents on metrically weak beats. I include this example primarily in order to demonstrate compound displacement dissonance; while the cello and viola present a metrically aligned triple layer, the two violins play different displaced layers. Such multiple displacement is not difficult to render by a string quartet, which is why Beethoven used it quite frequently in this medium.

One of Beethoven's most subtle displacement dissonances is shown in Example 2.1f. This theme could be heard as reinforcing the metrical triple layer; the initial notes in the bars would then be appoggiaturas or retardations. Performers, guided by Beethoven's notation, usually play the theme in accordance with this analysis. I believe, however, that a second potential metrical interpretation will emerge even from a performance influenced by the notation—the interpretation shown by the 3s on second beats. The main harmonic tones of the theme consistently lie on second beats; the harmonies can be heard as changing on beat 2 in each bar, and these regular harmonic changes result in an antimetrical 3–layer. Beginning in m. 5, durational accents on the downbeats (the half notes in mm. 5 and 7) strongly reinforce the metrical triple layer and almost drive the antimetrical 3–layer into hiding. This almost imperceptible displacement dissonance foreshadows more audible dissonances of this class in the Trio section.[13] (The 2s in Example 2.1f will be discussed later.)

Whereas grouping dissonances are somewhat less common in Beethoven's music than are displacements, their frequency is nevertheless astonishing. Example 2.2 is a sampling of grouping dissonances from the quartets. Numbers are used here much as in Example 2.1. The labels attached to each example, however, now consist of a "G" (for *grouping*) followed by two numbers separated by a slash; the numbers represent the different cardinalities of the layers involved in the given grouping dissonance.

Some of Beethoven's grouping dissonances arise from the sustention of individual pitches for durations that conflict with the overall meter, often with a mysterious effect of temporarily stepping outside the world established by the context (see Examples 2.2a and 2.2b). Example 2.2b follows an opening theme saturated with displacement dissonance (see Example 2.1e). The repeated B♭s announced by all instruments after the double bar create a duple layer that conflicts with the metrical and antimetrical triple layers announced earlier; the resulting grouping dissonance enhances the strangeness that the foreign pitches already bring to the passage. This grouping dissonance soon yields to displacement dissonance (as shown in the last two measures of Example 2.2b), which effectively prepares the return of the displacement-ridden opening theme. Beethoven ends the movement with a grouping dissonance similar to that shown in Example 2.2b; the final *forte* chord, to be sure, is on a down-

*Example* 2.2. Grouping dissonances in Beethoven's string quartets.

*a.* Op. 59 no. 2, I, mm. 99–107.

*b.* Op. 135, II, mm. 16–22.

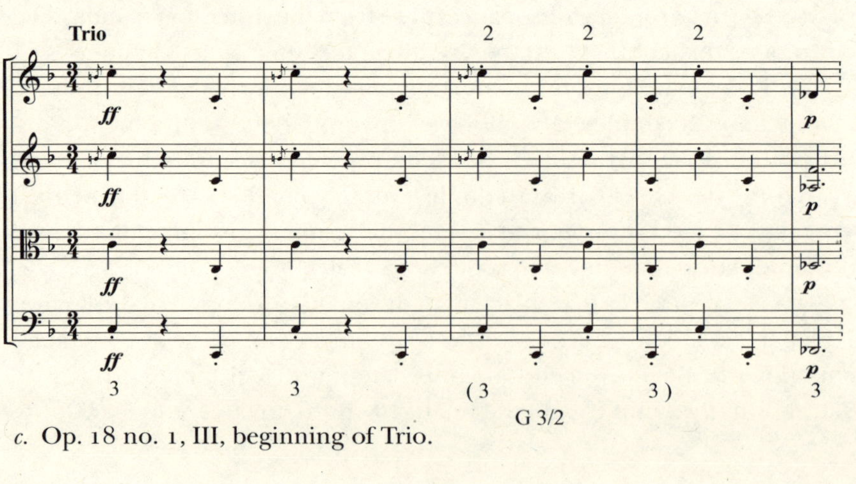


*c.* Op. 18 no. 1, III, beginning of Trio.

*d.* Op. 59 no. 1, II, mm. 404–8.

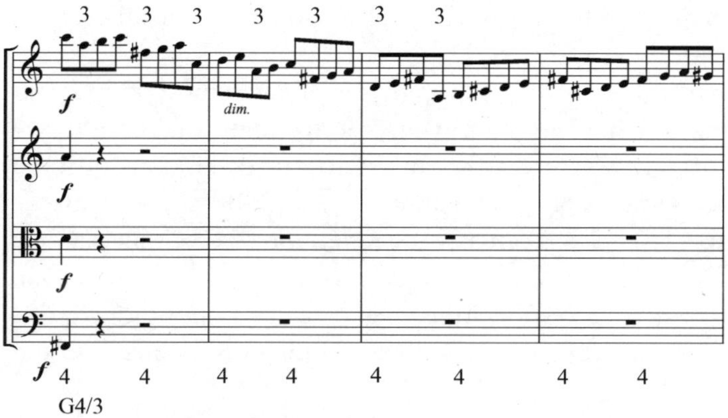


*e.* Op. 59 no. 3, IV, mm. 60–63.

*f.* Op. 132, IV, mm. 1–5.

*Example* 2.2, *continued. g.* Op. 132, II, mm. 41–45.

beat and thus suggests an attempt to restore metrical consonance, but this state of consonance is quite precarious.

The antimetrical layers of Beethoven's grouping dissonances most often result from the repetition of a pattern that falls short of an expected metrical duration (see Examples 2.2c to 2.2e). At times, features other than pattern repetition contribute to the formation of the antimetrical layer; in Example 2.2d, for instance, harmonic change reinforces the duple layer also created by the repetition of a contour pattern.

Joseph Kerman states that the opening measures of the Alla marcia from op. 132 (Example 2.2f) "cannot be quite as innocent as they pretend"—and indeed, this apparently simple surface is perturbed by a complex grouping dissonance.[14] In the first four measures, the metrical 4–layer is rather difficult to hear (although significant harmonic changes weakly corroborate it, especially in mm. 2 and 4). Much more clearly audible in these opening measures, however, is an antimetrical 3–layer. In m. 1, this layer is initiated by the dynamic, durational, registral, and density accents on the notated second beat, and it is continued by the harmonic change three beats later. The pause in m. 2 is too long for an accurate continuation of the triple layer, but listeners could easily impute this inaccuracy to a fermata, or to the notorious laxity of performers in counting silences. The situation in mm. 3–4 is similar; thereafter, the 3–layer is abandoned and the grouping dissonance resolved.

To conclude this brief overview of grouping dissonance in Beethoven's string quartets, I return briefly to the Allegro non tanto from op. 132 (Example 2.1f). I have already indicated the possibility of hearing a displacement dissonance in this theme, but there is also a hint of grouping dissonance. Harmonic changes, necessarily ambiguous in an octave texture, can be heard not only in accordance with the two layers of 3s in the example, but also with the 2s shown at the top. The initial note of each two-bar phrase segment would, in this hearing, link with the second note, in the manner of an appoggiatura embellishing the subsequent harmonic tone. The following repeated notes form an obvious pair, continuing the harmony just announced. The subsequent two notes a third apart can then be heard as together establishing a new harmony. The result is a duple layer, which conflicts with the two triple layers. Later in the movement, an overt hemiola brings this conflict to the surface (see Example 2.2g).[15]

Metrical dissonances serve two main functions in Beethoven's string quartets (and in his works in general). Many of them occur at points of climax or just before cadences; they thus create an effect of tension, even disorientation, which is then resolved as (or just after) the climax is reached, or as the cadence takes place. But Beethoven just as frequently inscribed metrical dissonance into his opening themes, such that metrical dissonance became part of the *Grundgestalt* of the given movement. Climactic or cadential usage of metrical dissonance was fairly common before Beethoven (although Beethoven's usages of this type are generally much more dramatic and obvious than those of his predecessors); thematic metrical dissonance, however, is a Beethovenian innovation (a few movements by J. S. Bach and Haydn excepted).[16]

I turn now to a more detailed discussion of two movements from Beethoven's early quartets. I have selected two particular movements for investigation, partly because they are in themselves very interesting from a metrical perspective, but also because sketch materials and early versions were accessible to me, making possible the investigation of Beethoven's revisions of metrical structure.

The Scherzo section of the third movement of op. 18 no. 6 is unusual among the early quartets because it employs metrical dissonance pervasively rather than intermittently. The conflicts in the Scherzo section are indicated in Example 2.3 by uncircled numbers (the circled numbers are bar numbers). The metrical 6– and 2–layers are shown below each brace of the score. Antimetrical layers are shown at higher points of the score.

The metrical six-eighth-note layer is quite clearly presented within the opening measures of the Scherzo. It is remarkable, however, how little corroboration these measures provide for the metrical 2–layer (the quarter-note layer); notice how many of the 2s below the braces are parenthesized, indicating duple pulses that are not clearly articulated. The only hints at the metrical 2–layer in the initial eight measures occur in mm. 1–3, where the placement of tonic harmony on first and third quarter-note beats suggests metrically aligned two-eighth-note durations. After the double bar, the metrical 2–layer becomes slightly more prominent; it is implied by harmonic changes on the third beats of mm. 8 and 10, by harmonic changes in m. 14, and by harmonic changes and second-beat *sforzandi* in mm. 15–18. In mm. 19–22, the clear articulation of the metrical 2–layer by the second violin, viola, and cello results in a definite sense of three-four meter. When the opening theme returns at m. 22, this 2–layer is again obscured. Another process of clarification begins, however, with mm. 30–31, where the cello's second-beat *sforzandi* restore some sense of quarter beats. In m. 33, the 2–layer is enunciated by three of the four instruments, then hinted at by second-beat *sforzandi* in mm. 34–35. In the remainder of the Scherzo section, the

*Example 2.3.* Metrical analysis of op. 18 no. 6, III, mm. 1–48.

cresc.

metrical 2–layer is again difficult to perceive. At the very end of the section, octave leaps in the first violin (mm. 47–48) briefly suggest this layer. Clarification of the metrical 2–layer coincides with significant points within the harmonic framework and formal structure of the Scherzo—the retransitional prolongation of the dominant at mm. 15–22, and the subsequent return of the opening theme in the tonic; the important cadence to the tonic at mm. 33–34; and the ending of the Scherzo.

Even on the rare occasions where one or more of the instruments articulates the metrical 2–layer, contradictory layers are presented by the other instruments. Such layers are all the more in evidence where the metrical 2–layer is in abeyance. The result is a great variety of metrical dissonance. Most of the dissonances of the movement are announced within the opening measures. At the very beginning, dynamic accents occur on the sixth eighth-note pulses of several measures; the displaced six-eighth-note layer (shown by the 6s above the first-violin part) interacts with the metrically aligned layer of the same cardinality, which is clearly expressed by durational accents in cello and viola and by the points of harmonic resolution, to create the displacement dissonance D6+5. This dissonance returns at the restatement of the opening theme in mm. 23–27 and 34–37. The opening theme also contains the displacement dissonance D2+1; it is formed by the interaction of the metrical 2–layer and a displaced 2–layer created by the rhythm of pitch change within the melody (shown by the 2s between the violin staves). This displacement dissonance is present throughout most of the Scherzo. A particularly blatant example occurs at mm. 19–21, where the metrical and antimetrical 2–layers are simultaneously announced with great clarity.

The opening theme also contains grouping dissonance. The notation implies a grouping of eighth notes into threes. This grouping is, however, more than a notational matter; it is also suggested by the harmonic changes (alternations of V and I). The superposition of the resulting 3–layer on the metrical and antimetrical 2–layers results in the grouping dissonance G3/2, a dissonance just as pervasive in the movement as the displacement dissonance D2+1. It is particularly pronounced at mm. 15–18, where numerous pulses of both the 2– and the 3–layers are emphasized by dynamic accents.

Not all of the metrical dissonances of the movement are present within the opening theme; Beethoven saved a few metrical tricks for later passages. In mm. 15–18, he stated some new displacement dissonances along with G3/2; dynamic accents create displaced six-eighth-note layers and, in interaction with the metrically aligned 6–layer, the dissonances D6+2 and D6+3. The former dissonance returns in mm. 34–35, the latter in mm. 37–38 and in the retransition after the Trio (not shown in Example 2.3). D6+3 could, of course, also be interpreted as a grouping dissonance, for it implies the division of six-eighth-note groups into two groups of three, which could be heard as forming G3/2.

Another dissonance not present within the opening measures appears in mm. 12–13. At this point the 3–layer prevalent in mm. 1–11 disappears; the eighth notes in the first violin part are instead grouped into fours by a repeated melodic pattern.

The pattern could be heard as starting at various points (I have shown only one possibility), but no matter where one hears the initiations, the pattern repetitions interact with the metrical 6–layer to create G6/4, the augmentation of the initial G3/2. This dissonance returns at 39–41, where melodic pattern repetition again creates a 4–layer. G6/4 is in mm. 39–41 allied with D2+1 (as it was in mm. 12–14); in mm. 42–48, G6/4 disappears while D2+1 continues. The effect is one of diminishment of the degree of metrical dissonance—an appropriate gesture for the approach to the end of the movement.

In Beethoven's sketches for the movement, we can trace the genesis of some of the metrically intricate passages.[17] What seems to be the first sketch of the passage in mm. 12–14 (in which D2+1 is associated with G6/4) appears within a single-voice continuity draft of the Scherzo section (see Example 2.4a). The sketch of mm. 12–14 contains the seeds of the final form in terms of pitch; it is based on motion by descending thirds (although in the final version, those thirds are embellished by lower neighbors). In terms of meter, too, there is some similarity to the final version: the displaced 2–layer, and thus the dissonance D2+1, is already present in the sketch. The 4–layer of the final version, however, and the dissonance G6/4, are not yet in evidence. There is a displaced 6–layer (formed at the double bar by durational accents, and from m. 12 onward by registral accents and beginnings of patterns); in interaction with the implicit metrical 6–layer, it results in D6+3—a dissonance not used within mm. 12–14 in the final version, but employed immediately thereafter (in mm. 15–18). The path to the final version, then, involved the disentangling of the first sketch's compound dissonance D6+3/D2+1, as well as the addition of the new dissonance G6/4 to the retained D2+1.

We can follow a portion of this path in another sketch of mm. 12–14, a few pages after the sketch shown in Example 2.4a (see Example 2.4b). Here, Beethoven preserved the descending-third structure and the displacement D2+1 but inserted the incomplete lower neighbors that characterize the passage in the final version. This addition resulted in the disappearance of the displaced 6–layer and the emergence of a 4–layer, each segment of the 4–layer consisting of two eighth notes that are chord tones, and two that are neighbors. The final version's combination of D2+1 and G6/4 was now in place. The specific positioning of the 4–layer within the measure is different from in the final version; the final alignment, however, appears as a revision just above the original version (see the upper staff of Example 2.4b). This revision, subsequently incorporated into two rewrites on the verso of the same folio (Kramer, p. 41, lines 3–4, and p. 42, line 2), is almost identical to the published work.

Recall that mm. 12–14 of the final version are similar to mm. 39–41 (both passages bring together D2+1 and G6/4). Beethoven seems to have intended a close relationship between these two points even at early stages of the compositional process. The earliest sketch for mm. 12–14 (Example 2.4a) is very similar to an early sketch for the later passage (Example 2.5a) in terms of pitch (falling thirds) and meter (D2+1 plus D6+3). Comparing the metrical structure of Example 2.5a with that of the final

*Example 2.4.* Sketches of op. 18 no. 6, III, mm. 12–14.

*a.* Sketch with D2+1 and D6+3 (Kramer, p. 37, lines 4–5).

*b.* Sketch with D2+1 and G6/4 (Kramer, p. 40, line 3).

version of the ending, we find that this early sketch already contains the D2+1 that characterizes the ending of the final version; durational accents and pitch changes determine a displaced two-eighth-note layer. In addition to D2+1, the sketch contains D6+3 (in the first three measures), the antimetrical 6–layer resulting, as in Example 2.4a, from registral accents within the melody; this dissonance is not present in the final version of the ending. Although one of the dissonances in the sketch passage is different from the one ultimately selected, Beethoven's metrical strategy was already that of the final version: by eliminating D6+3 after three measures while retaining D2+1—by moving from a combination of dissonances to a single dissonance—Beethoven gradually reduced the degree of dissonance as he approached the final cadence of the section.

A few pages later, Beethoven sketched the ending of the Scherzo again (Kramer, p. 38, line 1—Example 2.5b). In terms of pitches, this sketch differs more from the final version than the one shown in Example 2.5a. Metrically, however, it more closely approaches the final version; the overall strategy is that of the final version, as are the precise dissonances. D2+1 and G6/4 are first presented together (the new 4–layers are shown in Example 2.5b), whereupon G6/4 is eliminated to leave only D2+1, which remains in effect until the end.[18] The remaining sketches for the ending remain metrically similar to Example 2.5b, although the pitches are adjusted (see Kramer, p. 40, lines 5, 7, 8, and 10—counting only complete lines—and p. 41, line 9).

*Example* 2.5. Sketches for op. 18 no. 6, III, mm. 39–41.

*a.* Sketch with D2+1 and D6+3 (Kramer, p. 34, line 5).

*b.* Sketch with D2+1 and G6/4 (Kramer, p. 38, line 1).

The first movement of op. 18 no. 1 is less pervasively metrically dissonant, but metrical dissonance plays no less significant a role than in the Scherzo of op. 18 no. 6. Beethoven's strategy here was to begin in a metrically consonant fashion and introduce dissonance only gradually. The first theme is fully consonant. Near the end of the transition, there is a hint at G3/2; the reiterated eighth–eighth–eighth–quarter motive in the second violin and viola, in conjunction with durational accents on downbeats, suggests a grouping of the measures' six-eighth notes into threes (Example 2.6a). In the lead-in to the second theme, displacement dissonance appears for the first time (Example 2.6b); D2+1 forms a foil for the first portion of the second theme, which is primarily consonant (although the antimetrical slurring and beaming of that theme constitute a vestigial remnant of the preceding displacement dissonance).

In the final portion of the exposition, metrical dissonance proliferates, resulting in a growing sense of excitement and tension. The most significant cadence in the exposition (the expanded cadential progression in the key of V at the end of the second theme) is highlighted by the grouping dissonance G6/4; its 4–layer arises from pattern repetition within a passage of sixteenth-note figuration (Example 2.6c).[19] The immediately following reinforcements of the cadence to the dominant involve the same dissonance in a different guise (Example 2.6d); the eighth notes in this passage group into fours on the basis of a repeated contour pattern. This passage also hints at the displacement dissonance D6+2 (notice the *fp* on the second beat of m. 84). More G6/4 in the sixteenth-note version occurs at the end of the exposition (Example 2.6e).

The development section expands upon pitch motives from the exposition, along with most of the exposition's metrical dissonances. The section begins with G6/4 in sixteenth notes (shown in Example 2.6e). At the climaxes of the subsequent fugato section, the D6+2 hinted at in mm. 84 and 92 is developed (see Example 2.6f); the antimetrical layer is formed by insistent dynamic accents in conjunction with

*Example* 2.6. Metrical dissonances in op. 18 no. 1, I (second version); 1 = eighth note.

*a.* mm. 49–53 (exposition—end of transition).

*b.* mm. 55–58 (exposition—beginning of second theme).

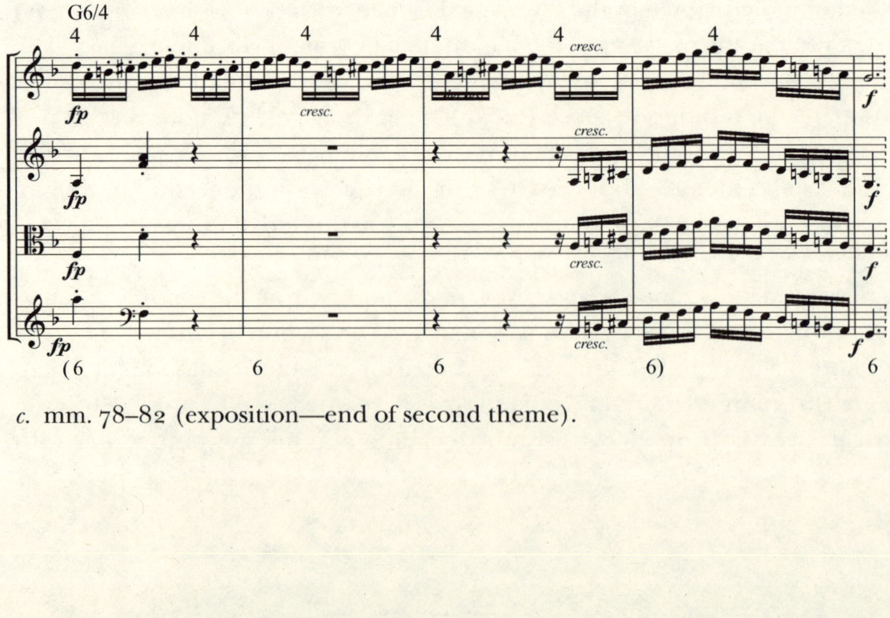


*c.* mm. 78–82 (exposition—end of second theme).

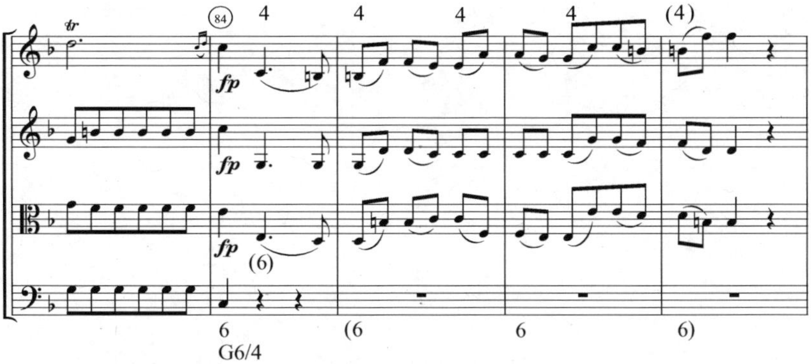


*d.* mm. 83–87 (exposition—beginning of closing theme).

*e.* mm. 109–18 (end of exposition and beginning of development section).

*Example 2.6, continued. f.* mm. 145–50 (climax within fugato passage in the development section).

*g.* mm. 164–76 (retransition).

*h.* mm. 310–13 (end of movement).

durational accents on second beats. The resolution of this dissonance during the section immediately following contributes immensely to that section's sense of stability and relative calm.[20]

In the following retransition (Example 2.6g), an intense and complex state of metrical dissonance provides a renewed sense of activity and tension. The retransition brings a number of the dissonances of the movement together, namely D6+2 (note the *sforzandi* on second beats); G6/4 (in its sixteenth-note guise—mm. 169–70 and 173–75); and the diminution of G6/4, G3/2 (mm. 167–70), which is now stated much more powerfully than in the transition, the 3–layer being emphasized by *sforzandi*.[21] A new displacement dissonance also appears: D6+4, created by the first violin's *sforzandi* in mm. 167–68. Because the retransition is so intensely dissonant—its metrical state is by far the most complex in the movement—the recapitulatory restatement of the metrically consonant opening theme provides a profound sensation of harmonic—as well as metrical—resolution. Furthermore, the statement of G6/4 at its beginning and end lends the development section a pleasing symmetry.

Most of the remainder of the movement replicates the metrical states of the exposition. It is worth mentioning, however, that the return of D6+4, the retransition's new dissonance, adds a special verve to the concluding measures (Example 2.6h).

The sketches reveal a great deal about the evolution of these metrical dissonances.[22] As is typical of Beethoven, the sketches contain no *sforzandi* at all, so that the dissonances just described are less overt. Furthermore, most of the sketches (again, as is typical) are one-line sketches, so that superpositions of multiple layers of motion are not as clearly evident as in the full score. Nevertheless, the sketches yield much information about Beethoven's original metrical ideas for the movement, which are sometimes quite different from those that underlie the final version. The sketches relate primarily to the first version of op. 18 no. 1. Where differences exist between the two versions, these will be mentioned.

The displacement dissonance D2+1 leading into the second theme was not part of Beethoven's earliest plans; what is apparently the first sketch of the passage shows unsyncopated repeated eighth notes (first two bars of Example 2.7a). It was only in the second sketch of the exposition, a page later, that Beethoven added the syncopation and, hence, D2+1 (p. 40, line 8). Furthermore, the vestigial dissonance in the second theme was not present in the first sketch; the durational accents produced by the dotted eighth notes emphasize the metrical 2–layer to a much greater extent than do the undotted eighths of both completed versions of the movement. The slurs (I am assuming that Beethoven meant each corresponding group of the sketched theme to be slurred, although he wrote out only one of the slurs) cannot seriously disturb the metrical layer so clearly announced by the durational accents.

The grouping dissonance G6/4 is already prominent in the sketches. The eighth-note version of G6/4 (as shown in Example 6d) is present in the first sketches of the passage. The first appearance of G6/4 in the guise of sixteenth-note figuration (in mm. 78–82, refer to Example 2.6c) was not part of Beethoven's very first notations but was added as an insertion at an early stage (see the "vi-de" in Example 2.7b). The similar G6/4 that ends the exposition was sketched on the lines just after this insertion (see the end of line 11 and beginning of line 12 in Example 2.7b); it appears that the first passage immediately suggested the second one.

The sixteenth-note version of G6/4 was not part of Beethoven's first idea for the beginning of the development section; his original plan was to employ the metrically consonant opening theme (as is evident from the end of line 12 in Example 2.7b). The idea of using G6/4 to open the development section seems to have occurred to Beethoven during a second sketch of the section (Example 2.7c). He began this sketch page with the transposed first-theme material sketched earlier, but later, on line 2, he wrote several bars of sixteenth-note material incorporating a 4–layer, closely approaching the pitches of the completed development opening.[23] The final pitch content (with preservation of the metrical dissonance G6/4) was worked out in two sketches, the more extensive of which is shown in Example 2.7d. It appears from these sketches that the metrical idea for the beginning of the development anteceded the definitive pitch structure.

D6+2 as a climactic metrical dissonance for the development section is already hinted at in the sketches; although there are no *sforzandi*, durational accents on second beats result in a weak version of the dissonance. Beethoven added *sforzandi* to the second beats in both completed versions of the movement.[24]

The sketches for two passages of the movement are particularly revealing from a metrical standpoint, namely those for the conclusion and those for the retransition. Two early sketches for the ending incorporate D6+2 (one is shown in Example 2.8a); in both, the antimetrical layer is created by durational accents on second beats.[25] Higher on the same page, Beethoven tried out an ending using G6/4, the 4–layer being created by repeated contracted statements of the opening motive (Example 2.8b). A third sketch for the ending on this page (Example 2.8c) contains virtually

*Example* 2.7. Sketches of selected metrically dissonant passages of op. 18 no. 1, I (exposition and development).

*a.* Sketch of the beginning of the second theme (Virneisel, p. 39, line 6).

*b.* Sketches of the end of the second theme and the end of the exposition (Virneisel, p. 39, lines 8 and 10–12).

*Example* 2.7, *continued.* *c.* Sketches of the beginning of the development section (Virneisel, p. 41, lines 1–2).

*d.* Later sketch of the beginning of the development section (Virneisel, p. 44, line 5).

no metrical dissonance (except for the hint at D6+2 created by the last interval—a density accent on the second beat—a vestige of D6+2 that is retained in the completed versions). It is this sketch that Beethoven ultimately selected as the concluding idea; it corresponds to the first violin part at the end of the first completed version (which, in turn, is like the final version of the ending except that it lacks the antimetrical *sforzando* stabs). In the first version, however, metrical dissonance is added by the lower strings; these instruments, after resting on beat 2, burst into activity on the third beats (imagine Example 2.6h without the *sforzandi*). The result is weak D6+4. In the final version, the dynamic accents, added to the existing density accents, intensify this dissonance.

In sum, analysis of the sketches of the ending and of the ending of the two completed versions reveals Beethoven's basic plan of incorporating into the final measures one of the significant metrical dissonances of the movement. He considered the incorporation into the final measures of D6+2 and of G6/4, but he finally selected D6+4 (and intensified it in the second completed version).

The metrical history of the retransition is even more complex. As was mentioned, the purpose of the retransition from a metrical standpoint is to pile up dissonances

*Example 2.8.* Sketches of the ending of op. 18 no. 1, I.

Note: [*unl*] designates illegible notations in the manuscript.

*a.* Sketch with D6+2 (Virneisel, p. 45, lines 15–16).

*b.* Sketch with G6/4 (Virneisel, p. 45, line 6).

*c.* Sketch with no apparent metrical dissonance (Virneisel, p. 45, line 3).

so that the sense of resolution inherent in the impending metrically consonant recapitulation becomes all the more pronounced. Much of Beethoven's work on the retransition was concerned with the adjustment of its mix of metrical dissonances of both types.

The earliest sketches for the retransition contain only displacement dissonance. One of the first sketches that can with near certainty be linked with the retransition is shown in Example 2.9a.[26] Durational accents on second beats in the lower voice of this two-voice sketch create a weak form of D6+2; the retransition of the second version of the movement contains this dissonance, although it is there intensified by the

*Example* 2.9. Sketches of the retransition of op. 18 no. 1, I.

*a.* Sketch with D6+2 and D6+4 (Virneisel, p. 41, lines 4–5).

*b.* Sketch with G6/4 (Virneisel, p. 41, lines 13–14).

*c.* Sketch with G6/4 and D6+4 (Virneisel, p. 44, lines 9–10).

Note: [*unl*] designates illegible notations in the manuscript.

*d.* Sketch with multiple metrical dissonances (Virneisel, p. 49, lines 1–8).

use of dynamic accents in the violins and viola (see Example 2.6g, mm. 167–73). Durational accents on the third beats in the upper voice of Example 2.9a result in weak D6+4, a dissonance retained in both of the completed versions.

Another metrical building-block for the retransition appears in a sketch on two lower lines of the same page (Example 2.9b). The metrical hallmark of this sketch is G6/4, the 4–layer being generated by imitated and repeated groups of eight sixteenth notes. This sketch is similar to mm. 177–80 of the first completed version.

Further sketches for the retransition are shown in Example 2.9c. On the upper line of this excerpt, Beethoven wrote repeated hemiolic scalar figures similar to those that characterize mm. 169–70 and 173–74 of the second version. Line 10 (apparently continuous with line 9; the clef change from treble to bass indicates a change of instrument) is very similar to the second version's cello part in mm. 171–72; here the 4–layer disappears and is replaced with a displaced 6–layer, created by durational accents on third beats. The sketch contains six such accents, as opposed to four in the second completed version. Here, then, the grouping dissonance G6/4 and the displacement dissonance D6+4 are juxtaposed, as they are in both completed versions.

A sketch of the retransition in quartet score is shown in Example 2.9d. Here, Beethoven brought together the various metrical elements found in previous sketches, though the mixture was not yet the final one. It is apparent that he originally considered beginning the retransition with a 4–layer and hence with G6/4, the 4–layer being created by the repetition of scalar segments in the first violin part. He then crossed out the repetition of the figure, thereby eliminating G6/4; by placing long note values (durational accents) on the third beats of the first two measures of the sketch, he hinted at a displaced 6–layer and thus at D6+4. G6/4, extracted from the beginning of the sketch, does appear in its third measure, where repeated scale segments form a 4–layer. D6+4 briefly returns, the displaced layer again formed by durational accents on third beats (now in the cello). Imitated descending-scale figures in cello and viola then form a 4–layer and hence G6/4. At the opening of this sketch, Beethoven added the bouncing eighth–eighth–eighth–quarter motive in the cello part, thus hinting at G3/2—an ingredient not present in any earlier sketches of the retransition. As comparison with Example 2.6g will reveal, this sketch quite closely approaches the final version of the retransition.

Later stages of the compositional process, however, continued the search for the best balance between grouping and displacement dissonance. Figure 2.1 summarizes the metrical differences among the sketch shown in Example 2.9d, the first completed version, and the final version. The measure numbers are those of the final version; there is a one-to-one correspondence between the measures of the three versions. Different types of lines show the measures in which particular metrical dissonances are in effect in the various versions. The graph makes clear that D6+4 and, more dramatically, G6/4 lose ground during the final revisionary stages. G6/4, which is almost continuous in the first completed version, is confined to just two two-measure spurts in the final version. D6+2, on the other hand, assumes much more prominence

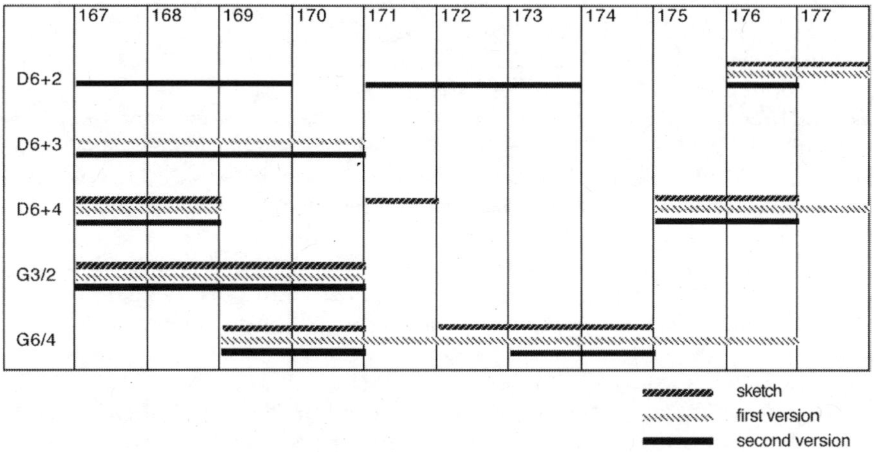


*Figure 2.1.* Comparison of metrical structure in three versions of the retransition of op. 18 no. 1, I.

in the final version than in the earlier ones. D6+3, with which Beethoven experimented at the opening of the retransition in the first completed version, is deintensified in the final version.[27] It appears that the motivation for these metrical revisions was to simplify the metrical state of the retransition yet retain its sense of a pileup of dissonances as a foil for the coming recapitulation.

The sketches show Beethoven's meticulous working-out of particular metrical dissonances or combinations of dissonances, at times in a number of different pitch incarnations; definitive ideas for metrical structure are sometimes in place before ideas in the pitch domain. The sketches show Beethoven devising particular metrical strategies and attempting to realize them with a variety of specific metrical dissonances. They reveal his efforts to find an optimal combination of different metrical layers by pruning a layer here, or adding a new layer there. Such discoveries clearly demonstrate that Beethoven regarded metrical dissonance as an important element of his music, and they encourage us to continue to investigate this element in both his completed works and in his sketches.

## Notes

1. Michael Broyles, *Beethoven: The Emergence and Evolution of Beethoven's Heroic Style* (New York: Excelsior, 1987), 146.

2. Barry Cooper, *Beethoven and the Creative Process* (Oxford: Clarendon, 1990), 47. Offbeat *sforzandi* may actually be even more common in the music of Robert Schumann than in that of Beethoven.

3. Broyles's discussion of metrical conflict in the four works is found, respectively, on pp. 251, 174–77, 165–67, and 145–48.

4. Edward T. Cone, *Musical Form and Musical Performance* (New York: Norton, 1968), 73; Carl Dahlhaus, *Ludwig van Beethoven: Approaches to His Music,* trans. Mary Whittall (Oxford: Clarendon, 1991), 137; Barry Cooper, *Beethoven and the Creative Process,* 47; David Epstein, *Beyond*

*Orpheus: Studies in Musical Structure* (Cambridge, Mass.: MIT Press, 1979), 131–32; William Kinderman, *Beethoven* (Oxford: Oxford University Press, 1995), 91. I discuss the metrical conflicts in this movement in *Fantasy Pieces: Metrical Dissonance in the Music of Robert Schumann* (New York and Oxford: Oxford University Press, 1999), 74–77.

5. For analyses of metrical conflict in the opening theme of the first movement of op. 14 no. 2, see Joel Lester, *The Rhythms of Tonal Music* (Carbondale: Southern Illinois University Press, 1986), p. 64, and Dahlhaus, *Beethoven,* 162; Lester briefly analyzes metrical conflict in op. 31 no. 1 and op. 101, respectively, in *Rhythms,* 26–28. I refer to additional examples of metrical conflict in the piano sonatas in *Fantasy Pieces,* 73.

6. William Rothstein draws attention to a "shadow meter," out of phase with the notated meter, in the sixth song of *An die ferne Geliebte,* in "Beethoven with and without 'Kunstgepräng': Metrical Ambiguity Reconsidered," in *Beethoven Forum* 4, ed. Christopher Reynolds, Lewis Lockwood, and James Webster (Lincoln: Nebraska University Press, 1995), 166–69.

7. Sylvia Imeson, for example, mentions intriguing instances of "rhythmic play" in the second movement of op. 132, particularly the varying placement of the eighth–eighth–quarter motive within the measure, in *"The time gives it proofe": Paradox in the Late Music of Beethoven,* American University Studies, Series XX (Fine Arts), vol. 29 (New York: Peter Lang, 1996), 133–36. Janet M. Levy discusses metrical conflicts in the two versions of the first movement of op. 18 no. 1 in *Beethoven's Compositional Choices: The Two Versions of the Opus 18, No. 1, First Movement* (Philadelphia: University of Pennsylvania Press, 1982), 28–30, 36–38, 50, 71–72, 74, etc.

8. See, for example, my analysis of metrical conflict in the first movement of the Piano Trio, op. 70 no. 1, in "Rhythmische Konsonanz und Dissonanz," *Musiktheorie* 9/1 (1994): 29–32.

9. William Rothstein, "Beethoven with and without 'Kunstgepräng'"; Roger Kamien, "Conflicting Metrical Patterns in Accompaniment and Melody in Works by Mozart and Beethoven: A Preliminary Study," *Journal of Music Theory* 37/2 (1993): 311–48; Richard Cohn, "The Dramatization of Hypermetric Conflicts in the Scherzo of Beethoven's Ninth Symphony," *19th-Century Music* 15/3 (1992): 188–206.

10. I introduced my analytical approach in "Some Extensions of the Concepts of Metrical Consonance and Dissonance," *Journal of Music Theory* 31/1 (1987): 99–120, and I elaborated on it in *Fantasy Pieces,* 22–61. The consonance-dissonance metaphor was first applied to rhythm by Hector Berlioz; see "Berlioz on the Future of Rhythm," in Barzun, *Berlioz and the Romantic Century* 2, 338. I traced the history of the employment of the metaphor in *Fantasy Pieces,* 3–18.

11. I developed the idea of two categories of metrical dissonance in "Some Extensions," where I called them "type A" and "type B." The terms *grouping dissonance* and *displacement dissonance* were first assigned to my categories by Peter Kaminsky in "Aspects of Harmony, Rhythm and Form in Schumann's *Papillons, Carnaval,* and *Davidsbündlertänze,*" Ph.D. dissertation, University of Rochester, 1989, 27.

12. The terminology for types of accent is based on Joel Lester, *The Rhythms of Tonal Music,* 18–40.

13. See, for example, the displacement dissonance at mm. 141–46 (D3+2). This is one of the passages analyzed by Sylvia Imeson; see note 7.

14. Joseph Kerman, *The Beethoven Quartets* (New York: Alfred A. Knopf, 1967), 262.

15. I am not suggesting that performers should attempt to bring out the antimetrical layers shown in my analysis of the opening of this movement. I do believe, however, that they should avoid overemphasizing the notated downbeats, so as to allow listeners to construct alternative metrical interpretations (which they might then be able to associate with later passages of the movement).

16. An example by Bach of metrical dissonance within an opening theme is the "Tempo di Minuetta" from the fifth Partita (G3/2). Haydn's string quartets contain a number of such examples. The third and fourth movements of op. 76 no. 6 open with displacement dissonance

(density accents on second beats). At the opening of the third movement of op. 77 no. 1, displacement dissonance results from dynamic and durational accents on second beats. The opening theme of the second movement of op. 77 no. 2 contains grouping dissonance; an antimetrical 2–layer is created by the repetition of a falling-fifth motive and later by the repetition of an eighth–eighth–quarter figure.

17. My source for sketches of Beethoven's op. 18 no. 6 is Richard Kramer, ed., *Ludwig van Beethoven: A Sketchbook from the Summer of 1800,* facsimile and transcription (Bonn: Beethoven-Haus, 1996).

18. Note that there are many possible ways to parse the sketch melody in 4s; depending upon which parsing one selects, there are six or seven pulses of the 4–layer, as opposed to four in the final version.

19. The term *expanded cadential progression* is William Caplin's; see his "The 'Expanded Cadential Progression': A Category for the Analysis of Classical Form," *Journal of Musicological Research* 7 (1987): 215–57, and *Classical Form: A Theory of Formal Functions for the Instrumental Music of Haydn, Mozart, and Beethoven* (New York and Oxford: Oxford University Press, 1998), 61, 67, 77, etc.

20. The relatively placid mood of this new section impelled Janet Levy to call it a "plateau"; see Janet M. Levy, *Beethoven's Compositional Choices,* 62.

21. The dynamic accents that form the grouping dissonance G3/2 could also be interpreted as hinting at another displacement dissonance, namely D6+3.

22. My source for sketches of op. 18 no. 1 is Wilhelm Virneisel, ed., *Ein Skizzenbuch zu Streichquartetten aus op. 18,* 2 vols., facsimile and transcription (Bonn: Beethoven-Haus, 1972), p. 74. Editorial clefs and key signatures have been added to the transcriptions provided by Virneisel.

23. It is not absolutely clear that Beethoven intended this material, upon its first conception, for the beginning of the development; there is a gap between the rejected first-theme-based development sketch and the sixteenth-note material.

24. Transcriptions of the relevant sketches for the climaxes of the *fugato* passage are shown in Virneisel p. 41, line 8 and p. 43, lines 11–12. As Janet Levy points out (*Beethoven's Compositional Choices,* 50), there are important metrical differences at this point in the two completed versions. In the first version, Beethoven emphasized the downbeats as well as the second beats with *sforzandi;* in fact, in the measures equivalent to the final mm. 133–34 and 145–46, only the first violin plays antimetrical accents, while the other three instruments emphasize the downbeats with *sforzandi.* Levy makes the point that the strong accentuation of the downbeats in the first version minimizes forward motion in the passage. Another effect of the downbeat *sforzandi,* however, is to weaken the dissonance D6+2; their elimination in the revised version results in the greater relative prominence of the antimetrical layer and hence in a clearer statement of D6+2.

25. The other sketch for the ending containing D6+2 is just above the one shown in Example 2.8a (Virneisel p. 45, lines 13–14). This sketch is reminiscent of the usages of D6+2 in the developmental fugato passages; see Example 2.6f.

26. This sketch appears in close proximity to the sixteenth-note material shown in Example 2.7c, which I hypothetically labeled as a sketch for the opening of the development section. It is, then, possible that Beethoven originally intended it for an earlier portion of the development section. The insistent prolongation of the dominant in Example 2.9a, however, strongly suggests a retransitional function.

27. In the first completed version, this dissonance arises from an imitation of the cello's eighth–eighth–eighth–quarter motive, which is removed in the second version. Janet Levy discusses this revision in *Beethoven's Compositional Choices,* 69–71. In the second version, D6+3 exists only weakly, as a possible hearing—not, in my opinion, the most likely one.

CHAPTER THREE

# Peak Experience

## High Register and Structure in the "Razumovsky" Quartets, Op. 59

*Malcolm Miller*

If the C major Quartet seems ready to go off the cliff at any minute, in this it only exaggerates a quality discernible in the others. None of them is a work at rest; all of them are explorers, and Beethoven may have been as amazed as anyone else to see where they were going.

—Joseph Kerman, *The Beethoven Quartets*

One of the most astonishing exploratory aspects of the "Razumovsky" Quartets, op. 59, is their innovative treatment of register as a structural and expressive resource. Beethoven deployed different registers not only for sonorous or coloristic effect but also to create coherent large-scale structures by means of long-range linear patterns. Particularly in the linear progressions of the highest registers, the op. 59 quartets exhibit exciting narrative processes, which correlate with tonal and formal design. Although the significance of registral peaks at certain points has received some attention, there has been little detailed study of register as a structural parameter in these works. The comprehensive study of such large-scale registral connections enables us to reassess some of Beethoven's compositional strategies and their narrative implications. Detailed analysis, moreover, demonstrates how registral structure reinforces Beethoven's individual use of sonata principle, both within and between movements, and how it serves to unify each work while promoting cyclic coherence within the op. 59 set as a whole.

A fruitful starting point for the interpretation of long-range linear progressions in the highest register is provided in Lewis Lockwood's seminal essay on Beethoven's "Razumovsky" Quartet in F Major, op. 59 no. 1.[1] Lockwood finds that Beethoven's strategic use of the upper register has important formal implications that "break decisively with the classical quartet tradition and establish a new point of departure for the later development of the genre."[2] In his discussion of the first movement, he considers the successive returns of the opening subject as a means of generating an innovative form in which the registral expansion of the opening phrase acts as "a paradigm for the movement as a whole."[3] The peak $C^4$ prior to the start of the recapitulation (m. 242), "dramatically left hanging at this great height,"[4] represents a significant structural landmark en route to the climactic $C^4$ in the coda (m. 386).[5] Lockwood's analysis thus highlights the large-scale structural significance of registral connections and their impact on the work's unconventional design: a sonata form, without exposition repeat, that reaches its goal in the coda.[6]

The most extensive account of registral treatment in these pieces to date is contained in Bruce Campbell's unpublished dissertation on the "Razumovsky" Quartets, in which he notes that "variations in texture act as articulating devices as do also density and register."[7] Campbell frequently pinpoints registral peaks and interprets these within the context of Schenkerian tonal and motivic theory, as middleground or foreground octave displacements of the "obligatory register." Thus Campbell is more concerned with the structural role of particular peak pitches than with linear connections between widely separated events, and he does not explicitly address Beethoven's large-scale formal strategies.

Schenker's own analytic approach to register extended beyond the obligatory register to the strategic use of extremes, an aspect explored early on by the Schenkerian theorist Ernst Oster in an article that draws on examples from Bach to Brahms.[8] Oster's starting point is Schenker's commentary to Beethoven's Sonata in E, op. 109, in which the connection is drawn between two registral peaks of G♯$^3$ (m. 23) and $B^3$ (m. 42), "two tones which viewed superficially have nothing to do with each other enter into a relationship merely through the register in which they appear."[9] Oster develops the perception to show how register is useful as a means of "clarifying certain contrapuntal, structural or thematic motivic connections and relations" and also serves as "one of the main elements of composition . . . on an equal footing with harmony, counterpoint and thematic development."[10] Oster's analyses of works by Beethoven and Schubert demonstrate how registral connections may circumvent the main higher-level linear structures and thus create an autonomous layer. In Beethoven's Bagatelle in G Minor, op. 119 no. 1, the replication of the descent from registral peaks $C^3$ to B♭$^2$ in mm. 19–20 in the coda is considered as a fulfillment of an earlier unsatisfied process. Oster notes that although the events are not "structurally connected," the registral connection creates its own sense of narrative. Register, whether high or low, he observes, is "the chief element which makes two points . . . stand out and thus be related and connected."[11] More than merely clarifying other structures, register can create its own connections that bypass otherwise important events. Oster adds that when such a connection "occurs, it constitutes one of the most remarkable features of the particular composition."[12] The significance of Oster's remarks consists in the way that the Schenkerian vision of the organic whole is refracted and refined to incorporate a notion of large-scale linear direction, patterning, and closure.

In that sense, both Schenker and Oster offer a theoretical springboard for the more radical approach of Robert Fink, whose theory of high registral connections is accompanied by a revisionist understanding of hierarchic reductive analysis.[13] In place of Schenkerian structural levels, Fink locates the coherence of a work in the narrativity embodied in the immediate surface of the music, a particularly useful approach to explicate postmodern music without reference to tonal hierarchy. Yet his discussion of Beethoven mediates between the analysis of the surface and deep-level coherence. His main example, the Credo of the *Missa solemnis,* highlights the strategic use of the octave above $G^3$. Fink asks, "Why not . . . simply link up all the high notes and see what kind of structure they outline?"[14] and justifies this approach by describing the high tessitura above $G^2$ as a "danger zone" characterized by vocal strain.[15] The idea of "strain" could similarly be extended to instrumental music, reflected by finger stretches on string instruments and general difficulties inherent in the wide leaps and control of dynamics and articulation in extreme registers. Tessituras that expand the envelope of playability, Fink contends, contain "widely separated events which share a distinctive sound energy—an audible sense of 'high-wire' risk."[16] It is reasonable to extend Fink's explanation of salience in the upper register to include parameters such as texture (including melodic peaks), instrumentation, articulation, and dynamics. Although the highest register tends to be used rather sparingly, it is often highlighted when it appears, through sharply characterized musical gestures.

According to Fink's view, the listener, remembering the salient moments where the linear progression comes to the fore, "leapfrogs between them," tracing linear dramas or "mechanisms of desire" that ignore the intervening music. Thus connections are established through "our perceptual tendency to link up the high points of musical experience . . . untransformed sounds on the musical surface."[17] Fink's metaphorical use of words such as *striving, desire, denial,* and *arrival* to describe the patterns draws on an awareness of melodic and harmonic teleology, implication, and realization.[18]

Focusing solely on the highest register, Fink recognizes the connections between widely separated peak pitches that produce long-range patterns equivalent to Schenker's *Stufen,* which determine the "notes in between," giving rise to the foreground. The prolongation of these rising *Stufen* "in our listening minds" is, according to Fink, analogous to Schenker's notion of hierarchical "long-range hearing." As an example, Fink analyses the Credo of the *Missa solemnis,* pinpointing a "Mixolydian ascent" where $G^2$ moves to $B\flat^2$ via $A\flat^2$, the flattened seventh degree (see Figure 3.1).[19]

The ascent appears in the musical surface of the Credo at mm. 17–20 and mm. 430–33, yet also, more importantly, in a large-scale progression linking registral peaks between those widely separated moments, creating a coherent linear "plot."[20] Though Fink describes the registral extremes as "untransformed sounds," the full structural

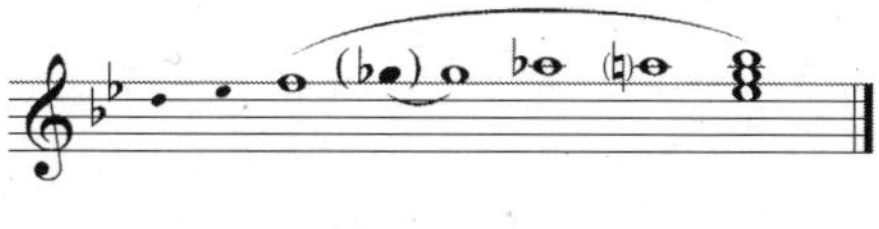

*Figure 3.1.* The "mixolydian ascent."

meaning of the resultant linear patterns, Fink's "plot," is a function of their harmonic and tonal context. The significance of such context is highlighted in William Kinderman's rewarding reading of the Credo, where registral peaks are interpreted as structural signposts and elements in long-range patterns, and also as extramusical symbols that add depth to an appreciation of Beethoven's text setting.[21] His discussion focuses on the slow Incarnatus section, an "interpolation within the larger framework of the whole Credo," introduced by the B♭ cadence at "descendit de coelis," which reaches a registral peak on the word *coelis*.[22] When repeated by the orchestra, the peak $A^3$ at m. 117 does not resolve upward to $B\flat^3$ but is transformed into the dominant in D, the key of the Incarnatus, where the plunge to the lower register, Kinderman suggests, offers an analogy for the descent from heaven to earth.[23] The return to $A^3$ at m. 200 as part of an F-major chord is interpreted as a continuation of the line from the earlier $A^3$ at m. 117, leading through to the recapitulation.[24] Thus the high register connects two events widely separated in time, imbuing two sections of a sonata movement, exposition and recapitulation, with dramatic meaning, the opposition of heaven and earth embodied in the word *coelis*.[25] Kinderman's analysis indicates how the peak pitches are affected by their deep structural context.[26] His reading concurs with Fink's notion that structural levels may buttress the registral prolongations[27] and shows how Beethoven's strategic deployment of peaks contributes to the impact of tonal structures and their musical symbolism.

The combination of linear and narrative elements in these approaches is systematically expressed in Leonard Meyer's theory of implication, realization, and so-called "gap-fill," with its concomitant notions of expectation, denial, and fulfillment.[28] Briefly summarized, the theory focuses on the implication for a rising or descending linear progression to continue toward logical completion—in tonal music, usually on the tonic. At the same time, any leap creates a gap that demands to be filled by stepwise motion. The "gap-fill" process is especially useful in describing the effect of a stylistic gesture distinctive to Beethoven: a powerful leap in the opposite direction that sets up an ascent to a registral peak. Such a gesture is exemplified in the interruption of the Credo mentioned earlier, and also in the numerous wide leaps and extreme registral contrasts encountered frequently in the instrumental works, particularly the string quartets. In addition to their rhetorical effect, such leaps serve several other functions, such as the subversion of a linear rise to the high register, the creation of a large gap that requires filling, and the restoration of a registral balance by moving farther in the opposite direction. All these functions can have the effect of intensifying drama and creating tension and forward motion. Beethoven's "bungee jumps," as one might fancifully describe them, display all the boldness and risk of sport, relying on the performer's skill to ensure safety at all times.

My analytical discussion of the "Razumovsky" Quartets, op. 59, aims to mediate Fink's focus on the musical surface with the Schenkerian hierarchic approaches of Campbell and Oster. My graphic notation, based on Meyer's linear analysis, focuses on the uppermost octave, in order to highlight connections between peak pitches, which my commentary interprets within the broader structural context of the work as a whole.[29]

## Analysis of the Three "Razumovsky" Quartets, Op. 59

### *Quartet in F Major, Op. 59 No. 1*

*Overview* The linear patterns in the highest register outline a rise to the peak $C^4$, yet they are articulated in various ways, as illustrated in Figure 3.2. (The notated pitches are to be read one octave higher, as indicated.) In the first movement, $C^4$ is attained at the climax of the development, and it is established as a stable goal at the climax, within the coda. In the second movement, $C^4$ is a dissonant neighbor note to the main structural goal, $B\flat^3$, whereas in the third movement, $C^4$ functions as dominant of the tonic minor. In the coda of the finale, $C^4$, after several appearances as

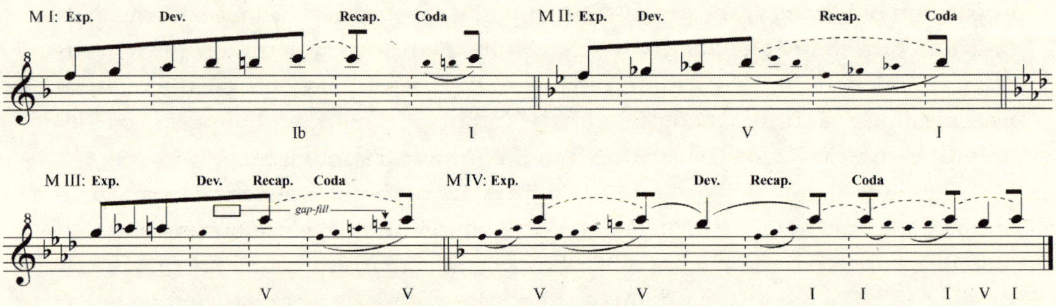


*Figure 3.2.* High-register linear progressions in all four movements of op. 59 no. 1.

Explanation of graphic notation:

The graphic notation employed here aims to highlight the main high-register linear progressions, indicated by beamed notes. A few important secondary linear progressions are indicated in smaller note heads. Arrows are used to highlight connections between widely separated progressions. Identical registral peaks are connected with dotted lines. An open box indicates an important unresolved gap; its resolution is shown by dotted lines and arrows leading to the missing pitch. In the analyses of individual movements, measure numbers are given for all peak pitches and progressions are aligned with formal divisions such as sonata exposition, development, recapitulation, and coda, as well as subdivisions of first and second theme groups, transitions, and rondo episodes. Where a peak occurs in several places in the same section measure numbers are linked by "/," e.g. 14/36.

root of the secondary tonic C, appears over a long-awaited root-position tonic, which restores tonal stability and brings the work to its climactic goal. What is striking in the use of $C^4$ across the work and the means used to attain it, is the evidence of a deliberate, strategic use of the highest register to maintain tension and enable resolution over the largest scale. Moreover, the first, third, and final movements each present a gap-fill motion from $A^3$ to $C^4$ that highlights the missing $B\flat^3$, resolved with the emphasis of $B\flat^3$ at various salient points. The strategy of denial and fulfillment of linear expectation and control of tonal tensions infuses the work with complex drama. That strategy is pervasively deployed in similar ways throughout op. 59 and, as the following analyses demonstrate, operates as a structural parameter hand in hand with the formal and tonal design of each movement and each work as a whole.

*I Allegro* Each division of the sonata structure fulfills a clear and significant role within the linear drama that sustains tension over the whole movement, as illustrated in Figure 3.3.

The main rising linear progression is initiated by the peak $F^3$ attained in the first group (m. 19) and continues to $G^3$ in the transition (mm. 41–42), reinforced by its reiteration in the second group (m. 48; mm. 71–74; mm. 87–89). The progression rises to $B\flat^3$ at the outset of the development (m. 111), as root of the temporary tonic. A varied ascent to $B\flat^3$ (via $E\flat^3$–$F^3$–$G\flat^3$–$A\flat^3$) halfway through (m. 175) reinterprets the peak as a dissonant ninth to the dominant of the temporary tonic D♭. $B\flat^3$ reappears finally in the dominant preparation (m. 240), as a seventh striving forcefully up to $C^4$ (m. 242) via $B^3$. As a dominant, $C^4$ is unstable and, following the subsequent three-octave plunge, the $C^4$–$F^3$ gap (m. 250) is left unfilled. Resolution occurs in the recapitulation, where $C^4$ is regained at m. 318. However, there is still a salient gap from $A^3$ to $C^4$ here, reiterated later at mm. 331–32, where $C^4$ is again emphasized by means of a plunge of almost three octaves (to the viola's F♯). The missing B♭ is supplied in the final appearance of the first theme in the coda, for the first time stated over a stable root-position pedal point (see Example 3.1).

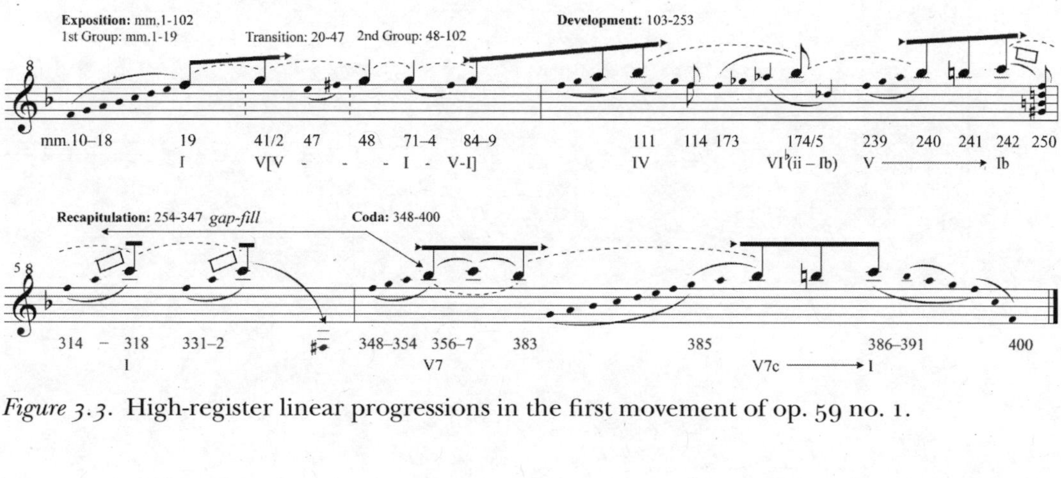


*Figure 3.3.* High-register linear progressions in the first movement of op. 59 no. 1.

*Example 3.1.* Op. 59 no. 1, I, mm. 330–400.

362
371
377
383
390
cresc.
più f
dim.
ten.

Here the theme rises via $F^3$–$G^3$–$A^3$, initially reaching $C^4$ as a neighbor note to $B\flat^3$ (mm. 356–57), which fills the earlier gap and simultaneously creates further expectation for the emphasis of $C^4$ and its concomitant structural closure. That climactic event occurs at mm. 385–86, where, reinforced by the two violins' octave doublings, the line rises through $B\flat^3$ to $B^3$ and on to $C^4$, echoing the gesture heard near the end of the development (mm. 240–42). There the move had culminated on a first-inversion tonic (m. 242), but here the high $C^4$ is sustained for five measures over a bass moving from V7 to I, harmonizing $C^4$ as a strong root-position tonic for the very first time. The use of *sforzando* accents on the dominant chord acts as a subtle means of enhancing the tonic resolution by reducing its expected emphasis and contributes thereby to the impressive serenity and exquisite sonority of this passage. The role of the lofty, prolonged $C^4$ is further highlighted by the subsequent linear descent through three octaves to middle C (m. 394) before the music retrieves $F^3$ and the obligatory register F (m. 400). This decisive closing gesture confirms high-level closure and supports the interconnection of similar structural moments across the span of the four-movement design.

*II Allegretto vivace e sempre scherzando* In the second movement, described by Kerman as "a thoroughly novel formal synthesis,"[30] $C^4$ is again the peak, but its very different context and function as neighbor note to the tonic, $B\flat^3$, renders it a climax rather than goal. As shown in Figure 3.4, there is an overall ascending progression from $F^3$ in the exposition to the dissonant $C^4$ in the development and, after a dramatic descending leap in the recapitulation, a new ascent is made to $B\flat^3$ in the coda.

The exposition does not go above $F^3$ and $G^3$, yet curiously, the second group descends to $E\flat^3$, which contrasts with the generally higher register of the second group in the first movement (and also, significantly, in the first movements of op. 59 nos. 2 and 3). This relaxation reflects the atypical use of the dominant minor as a secondary key.

In the development, $A\flat^3$ and $A^3$ are attained in transpositions of the first theme, first group (m. 157 and m. 213, respectively). There is a brief sequential ascent to $C^4$ in m. 229, followed by a stepwise descent. As mentioned, in contrast to $C^4$ in the first movement, $C^4$ is here harmonized as a powerful dissonance, the major ninth of V9♭ within the temporary tonic E♭ major, whereas $B\flat^3$ receives emphasis as the dominant.

The recapitulation begins with the first group in reverse sequence, with the first theme again reaching $F^3$ and $G^3$ (m. 342). With the transposition of the second group,

*Figure 3.4.* High-register linear progressions in the second movement of op. 59 no. 1.

the range extends up to G♭$^3$–A♭$^3$ at the two high-register appearances of the theme (m. 373 and m. 386). The implication to continue up to B♭$^3$ is fulfilled in the coda. According to some editors, B♭$^3$ is briefly attained in a development of the first theme in m. 434, where it is unstable, as V of the temporary tonic E♭.[31] A more conclusive appearance of B♭$^3$ occurs near the end of the coda. A prominent repeated F$^3$ in mm. 462–64 is intensified as a high trill in mm. 465–67. This trill signals an upward arpeggiation of the tonic triad in each instrument in turn, sounding across all of the pitch registers and reaching B♭$^3$ as the peak in m. 468. As in the first movement, the attainment of the high registral goal near the conclusion is given much temporal and textural prominence here. The following plunge of more than two octaves is softly articulated as a pizzicato chord, and in the emphatic closing gesture Beethoven recaptured the upper-register D$^3$ in the penultimate chord.

*III Adagio molto e mesto* The third movement, in the tonic minor, outlines a linear ascent from G$^3$ to C$^4$, each stage of which corresponds to the concise sonata design, as illustrated in Figure 3.5. The exposition presents the eloquent first subject in a low register, with the peak G$^3$ introduced in the transition as a dominant (m. 21). G$^3$ is regained in the second subject (m. 28) and extended through A♭$^3$ to A$^3$ (m. 36), a pitch emphasized by its dramatic diminished-seventh harmony and by the sudden drop of more than two octaves at the climactic cadence.

The line regains G$^3$ and F$^3$ in the development, and also in the transposition up one octave of the first subject in the recapitulation (mm. 86–90). Yet it is in the second subject that the goal C$^4$ is attained, the rising triad of the theme transposed up a fifth to the tonic key. Nevertheless, the rising line is incomplete because of the leap from A♭$^3$ to C$^4$ (m. 101), which is recalled at A♭$^3$ of the climactic cadence (m. 108). The linear implication is fulfilled in the coda, where C$^4$ is reached by step in a cadenza-like passage,[32] yet with a gap from C$^4$ to A♭$^3$ in the descent (m. 130). Closure is not yet complete, however, as this C$^4$ is poised over a dominant pedal within a transitional passage, and the B♭$^3$ gap is still operative. The process set up in the third movement is completed only in the finale, when C$^4$ is articulated over a root-position tonic chord, which also contributes to high-level closure for the entire work.

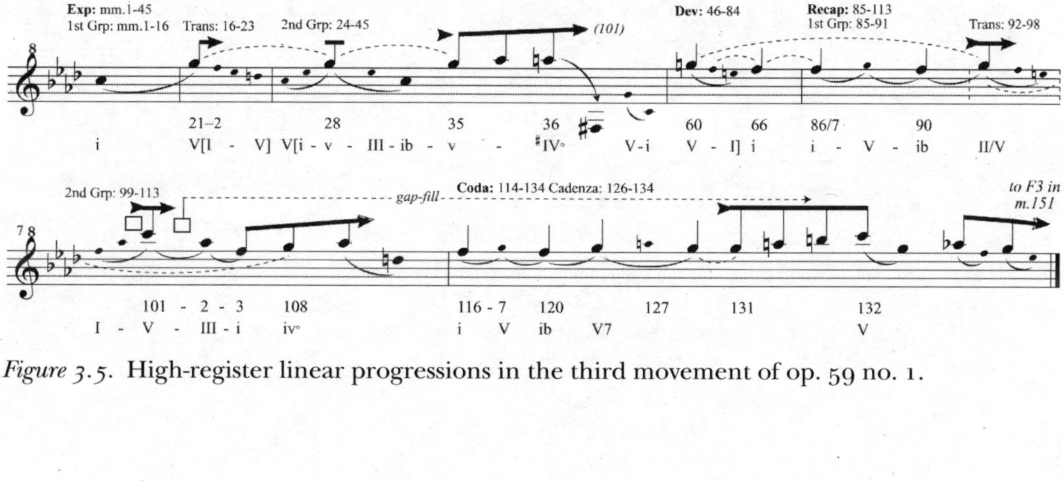


*Figure 3.5.* High-register linear progressions in the third movement of op. 59 no. 1.

*IV Thème russe. Allegro* In contrast to the steady ascent to the $C^4$ in earlier movements, the linear patterns in the finale unfold in the highest register from processes of implication and realization. As shown in Figure 3.6, the peak $C^4$ appears virtually at the outset of this sonata movement, within the first subject, the Thème russe, each time supported by dominant harmony. It is approached by a leap from $A^3$, a move that draws attention to the missing $B\flat^3$, which is immediately supplied in the descent $C^4$–$B\flat^3$–$A^3$ (mm. 18–20). The step motion and leap are reversed in the closing theme of the second group, where there are two identical ascents to $C^4$ via $B^3$ (m. 68 and mm. 91–92) followed by leaps down to $A^3$ (m. 69 and m. 92). $C^4$ here is harmonized as root of the new tonic, C. The ascending and descending gaps highlight the missing $B\flat^3$, which is strongly emphasized in both the development section and in the coda.

In the development, $B\flat^3$ first appears at m. 145 as part of the Neapolitan chord (E♭) within the temporary tonic D minor (VI of the main tonic), approached by step from $A^3$. $B\flat^3$ reappears in the *fortissimo* passage at m. 157, where it is followed by a falling progression, though the rising implication of $A^3$–$B\flat^3$ is fulfilled by the reappearance of $C^4$ near the beginning of the recapitulation featuring the Thème russe at mm. 190–91, another *fortissimo* passage. Beethoven reinforced the linear connection between these passages through the dynamics and the rhythmic texture, with the second passage recapturing and even surpassing the energy of the first climax.

Because the $A^3$–$C^4$ leaps resume in the recapitulation, it is the function of the coda to provide the missing $B\flat^3$ and effect closure (Example 3.2). This use of $B\flat^3$ first occurs in the descent $C^4$–$B\flat^3$–$A^3$ (mm. 250–52–55) near the start of the coda, where $C^4$ is supported for the first time by tonic harmony in root position; however, the closure is short-lived and followed by a further leap away from $C^4$ (mm. 259–61).

Beethoven's remarkable rhetorical interruptions here, and the reiteration of B♭ in different octaves with pauses (mm. 264–66), emphasizes the registral issue and the gap, which is filled only with the $B\flat^3$ prior to the final Adagio restatement of the Thème russe (mm. 306–9). This restatement in turn sets up an implication for continuation to the final C4, which duly arrives in the theme itself (mm. 312–13). However, al-

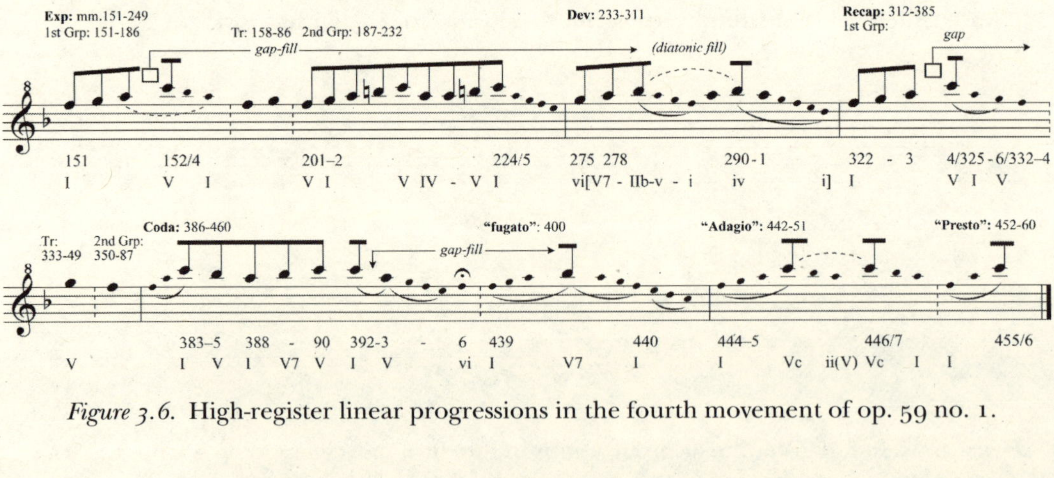


*Figure 3.6.* High-register linear progressions in the fourth movement of op. 59 no. 1.

*Example 3.2.* Op. 59 no. 1, IV, mm. 248–327.

Example 3.2, continued.

though both gap and linear progression are complete, not until the final, robust emphasis in the Presto, played *fortissimo* (mm. 323–24), is closure effected, with the long-awaited articulation of $C^4$, grounded by root-position tonic harmony. This final $C^4$ restores the stability that was attained in the serene passage at the close of the first movement but avoided in the two central movements. The $C^4$ thus represents a registral climax and structural goal of the whole work.

## *Quartet in E Minor, Op. 59 No. 2*

*Overview* As in the first and third op. 59 quartets, in this work $C^4$ acts as a salient registral peak. Yet unlike its role in those works, due to the key, E minor, $C^4$ (and, momentarily, $C\sharp^4$) functions as a structural dissonance to the consonant $B^3$, which is clearly emphasized as a structural goal. The $C^4$–$B^3$ motive highlights the crucial "Neapolitan" clash between the keys of F and E minor, a feature commented on by Kerman, Campbell, and others. This motive is "deconstructed" with the climactic appearance of $C^4$ in the finale and its high-level resolution to $B^3$ (Figure 3.7).

*I Allegro* Significantly, the main peak $B^3$ is not present in the first movement, but an expectation for $B^3$ is set up by an incomplete rise from the consonant $G^3$ to $A^3$, shown in Figure 3.8. In the exposition, $G^3$ appears in the second subject group (m. 39) and rises to $A^3$ as V of the secondary-tonic G major (m. 43), the implication to rise balanced by a return to $G^3$ (m. 55). In the recapitulation, the equivalent progression occurs within the tonic major, moving from $E^3$ to $F\sharp^3$ and back (mm. 179, 184, 194–95). The rising implication of $E^3$ to $F\sharp^3$ reinforces the progression $G^3$–$A^3$ in the coda (m. 250), where $A^3$ is retrieved as the dissonant seventh of V7 in the main tonic E minor. $A^3$ is left hanging saliently, the high register reinforced by the sudden plunge of an octave and a half, to $D\sharp^2$. Thus there is an unresolved tension, a combination of the implications to rise to $B^3$ and descend to G, on account of the V7 harmony. (When $A^3$ reappears next, it happens briefly in the slow movement at m. 57, as part of a I6 chord in the temporary tonic D.)

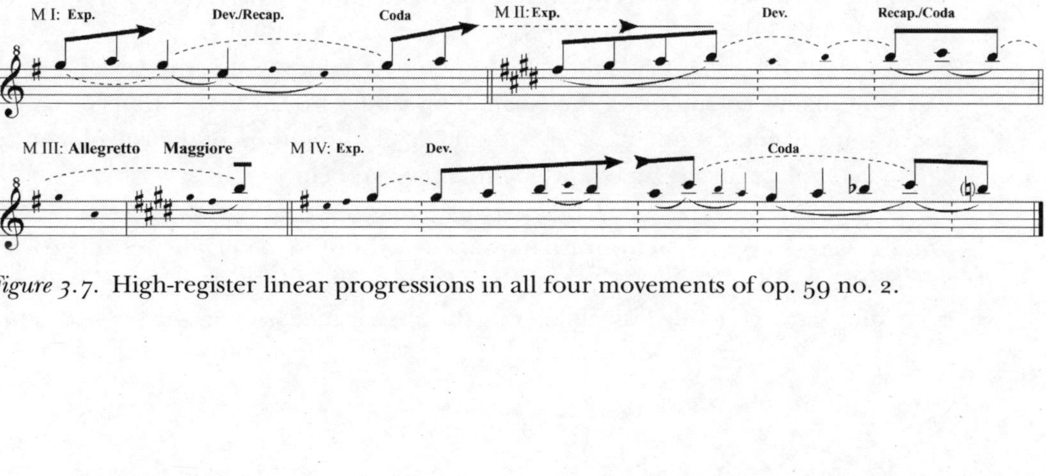


*Figure 3.7.* High-register linear progressions in all four movements of op. 59 no. 2.

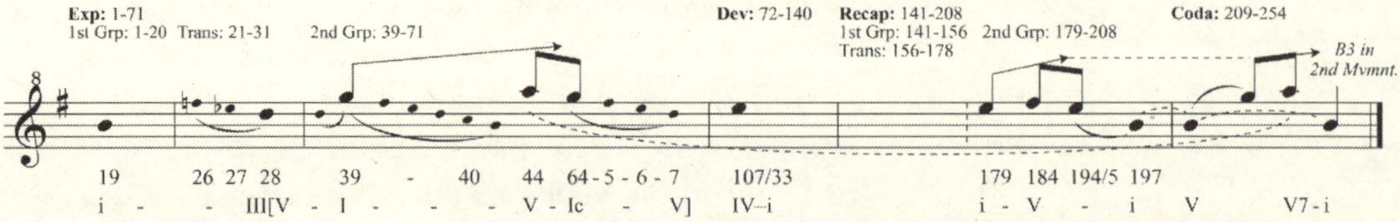


*Figure 3.8.* High-register linear progressions in the first movement of op. 59 no. 2.

*Figure 3.9.* High-register linear progressions in the second movement of op. 59 no. 2.

*II Molto Adagio* The sonata design of the poignant slow movement is straightforward and reinforced by registral structure. According to Carl Czerny, Beethoven conceived this music while "contemplating the starry heavens"; and Daniel Gregory Mason has written in this regard about "the spread of the notes not horizontally across wide tracts, but vertically from lowest bass to highest treble."[33] As in the first movement, the first subject group and transition remain in low registers during the exposition and recapitulation, but the second subject groups and development are distinguished by different contexts for the peak $B^3$. As shown in Figure 3.9, $B^3$ first occurs in the secondary key B major (m. 28), then at m. 43 in the cadenza-like closing section of the exposition, each time supported by a tonic second-inversion chord. In the development, $B^3$ appears as a dissonance in the diminished-seventh chord of a cadence in F♯ minor (m. 68). There are gaps in the ascent to and descent from $B^3$, in contrast to the smooth, stepwise motion of both exposition and recapitulation, with a subsequent deep descent from $F\sharp^3$ to G (m. 70). In the recapitulation, $B^3$ appears at m. 106, as at m. 28, in the second subject, but here it is the fifth of the tonic chord of E major. When this pitch reappears in the closing theme (m. 124), it is surpassed and capped by $C\sharp^4$, a local neighbor note, which resolves immediately. This is the highest note of the work and of the op. 59 set as a whole (Example 3.3).

Though far less emphatic than the $C^4$ in the final movement, the peak $C\sharp^4$ hints at an alternative resolution of the Neapolitan clash C–B through a transformation to the tonic major. Eventually, a more dramatic neutralization of the Neapolitan relation takes place, in the final movement, discussed below.

*III Allegretto—Maggiore* In the third movement, as illustrated in Figure 3.10, the peak $B^3$ (m. 114) occurs in the Trio, "Maggiore," approached by leap from $G\sharp^3$, with the ascending gap being filled much later by the appearance of $A^3$ in the finale. $B^3$ thus

*Example 3.3.* Op. 59 no. 2, II, mm. 106–128.

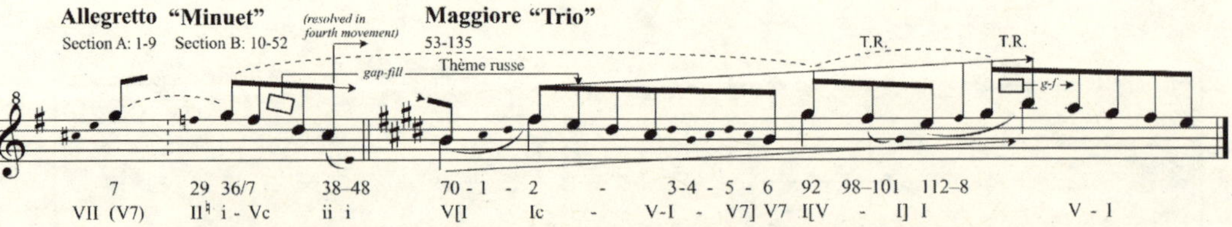


*Figure 3.10.* High-register linear progressions in the third movement of op. 59 no. 2.

reinforces the peak already emphasized in the second movement, and the missing $A^3$ highlights the unresolved problem of the first movement, which was temporarily resolved in the second.

The straightforward Minuet-Trio form is underscored by the registral progression. The first part, the "minuet," outlines an arpeggiated rise to $G^3$, functioning as seventh of $V^7$ of VII (m. 7) in the first section, and in the second section rising through a tonicized $F^3$ (m. 29, the Neapolitan relation) to $G^3$ as part of the tonic E minor (mm. 36–37). A gap in the descent back to $E^3$ remains unfilled at the end of the Scherzo, to be filled by the $E^3$, supported by tonic harmony (m. 93) following a descending pattern from $G\sharp^3$ through $F\sharp^3$ (m. 92), and also by the subsequent emphatic $E^3$s of the Thème russe (mm. 112–18) with which the Maggiore concludes. Similarly, the reiterated $C^2$s at the end of the first part (mm. 38–48) are not resolved to $B^2$, resulting in a lack of closure in the *da capo* repetition.

The Maggiore provides resolution of these implications, strengthening the connection between the two parts.[34] Here the Thème russe is presented contrapuntally, first by viola, then by second violin, followed by cello, and finally by first violin in mm. 70. The first violin touches $F\sharp^3$ on a weak beat (m. 72), then later $G\sharp^3$ (m. 92) in counterpoint with the Thème russe in the bass. Yet the main registral climax is clearly reserved for the first violin's final tonic statement of the Thème russe (mm. 112–18) reinforced by *fortissimo* dynamics and *sforzando* accents in the two lower parts. At this point, the $A^3$ gap appears in the ascent to $B^3$, though it is filled in the subsequent descent.

*IV Finale—Presto* Register and sonata design are, again, inextricably interrelated in the Presto finale. The form is sonata-rondo, where the return of the rondo theme/first subject after the development is withheld, resulting in a "reverse-recapitulation," with the second subject beginning in the tonic (m. 216). An extended developmental coda after the recapitulatory rondo theme (m. 275) leads to one further appearance of the rondo theme and codetta. As illustrated in Figure 3.11, the rondo theme remains in the same register on each appearance, articulating a rising progression to $E^3$ and subsequent descent to $G^2$, but the peak $C^4$ occurs, significantly, in both the development and coda, as well as in the recapitulated second group.

The first occurrence is as a dissonant neighbor note (m. 210) to the main struc-

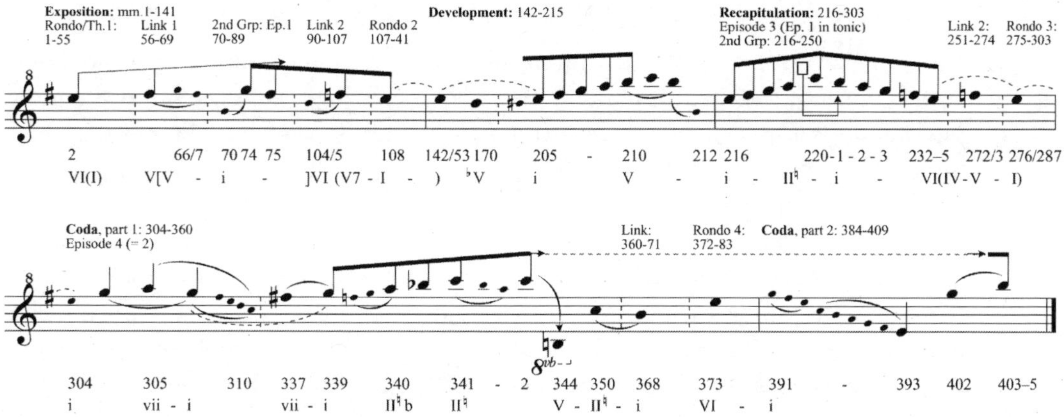


*Figure 3.11.* High-register linear progressions in the fourth movement of op. 59 no. 2.

tural $B^3$ in the dominant preparation, prior to the recapitulation. This climactic moment corresponds with the transition from first to second subjects (mm. 66–68), where the peak $E^3$ of the rondo theme/first subject is raised toward $B^3$ via $F\sharp^3$ and $G\sharp^3$. However, at m. 210 *sf* accents stress the harmony note $B^3$ over the higher $C^4$.[35] Immediately following, at m. 220, $C^4$ reappears as the peak of the second subject, yet it is underscored on this occasion in a consonant harmonization, as the fifth of F major, Neapolitan of E minor. This cadence is too short-lived to become a full resolution, which occurs only when $C^4$ returns, ascending via $B\flat^3$, at the climax of the coda (mm. 304–60, sometimes described as a "second development"), in a rhetorically powerful moment (mm. 340–42). Here it is underlined by *f* and *ff* dynamics, heavily emphasized on two successive downbeats, the second of which is reinforced with an F-major triad in implied root position. The peak $C^4$ set into relief here by a plunging descent to low B in the ensuing phrase, which regains the same C emphasis an octave lower, $C^3$ (m. 350), reiterating the gesture and again focusing attention on register through contrast.

Campbell observes that in mm. 339–41, "The last third $F^3$–$G^3$–$A^3$ introduces the Neapolitan chord as lower auxiliary . . . The $C^4$ enters *fortissimo* in the next measure: *this tone will go unresolved linearly until the very end of the coda*" [italics mine].[36] The resolution to which he refers is the reiteration of $B^3$ (mm. 403–5) in the final measures of the Più Presto, supported by a root-tonic triad and unassailed by any dissonant Cs. This affirmation of $B^3$ purges the semitone motive C–B that pervades the entire work and also neutralizes its Neapolitan clash. These emphatic shifts from $B^2$ to $C^3$, heard when the main Rondo theme appears in C major (mm. 23, 36, 129), seem to be resolved here, as well. The delay of the resolution of $C^4$ to $B^3$ thus serves more than a localized rhetorical function: it is a strategy of vital structural significance that effects closure of large-scale motivic and tonal processes of the entire work.

## *Quartet in C Major, Op. 59 No. 3*

*Overview* $C^4$ is introduced early on in the work but is established as tonic goal only at the climax of the first movement; as shown in Figure 3.12, in the two subsequent movements it appears as part of secondary tonalities. In the second movement in A minor, $C^4$ is attained at a cadence in C major in m. 50; much later, in m. 125, there is a descent by step via $B\flat^3$ and $A\flat^3$, within a remarkable chromatic shift to E♭. In the Trio of the third movement, $C^4$ is regained by a leap from $A^3$. Thus the finale is required to fulfill two functions: to retrace the chromatic modulation of the second movement, by rising through $A\flat^3$ and $B\flat^3$, and to fill the gap left in the third movement in the final diatonic progression $G^3$–$C^4$. $C^4$ appears only in the coda, at the climax, effecting closure for the movement and the work as a whole.

*I Introduction Andante con moto: Allegro vivace* The movement as a whole outlines a rising linear progression, one of Fink's "arrows of desire," from $G^3$, a main focus of both first- and second-theme groups of the exposition and of the development section, to the peak pitch $C^4$. This progression occurs incomplete three times, twice with a gap between $A^3$ and $C^4$, illustrated in Figure 3.13. The missing $B^3$ is supplied only at the climax of the recapitulation (m. 250), thereby providing structural closure in the highest register. Apart from its stepwise approach, the final appearance of $C^4$ differs in several ways from the earlier peaks. In the first group second theme (in the exposition at m. 56 and recapitulation at m. 205) it is metrically weak, placed on the fourth beat of the measure, yet it is salient due to its gestural emphasis, the approach by a rising arpeggio leap, an implied root-tonic harmonization, and its solo texture. A sudden contrast of the violin's lowest note G in the next measure, echoing the similar gesture that concludes the introduction, heightens the impact of $C^4$ retrospectively. As Campbell states, m. 56 "contains . . . the highest note of the movement, followed by the violin's lowest. Such a gesture is quite typical of a concerto . . . as commentators have been quick to point out."[37] The parallel passage in the recapitulation comes in mm. 204–5. Later in the recapitulation, $C^4$ is approached through $G^3$ and $A^3$; three successive linear ascents peak on $A^3$. The first ascent reaches $A^3$ in m. 221; the second ascent at m. 238 falls by step to $G^3$ and $F^3$; the third ascent at m. 243 drops a fifth to $D^3$.

It is the fourth ascent that supplies the missing $B^3$ and reaches $C^4$ at the climactic tonic cadence in m. 250. This $C^4$ differs from the earlier $C^4$ peaks, and it effects closure due to its downbeat emphasis and its role as tonic in root position. In addition, the five-octave interval from $C^4$ to the cello's bass C creates the widest registral

*Figure 3.12.* High-register linear progressions in all four movements of op. 59 no. 3.

spacing of the piece. This arrival point also marks the closure of the *Urlinie* (the resolution via D to C at the close of the second subject) and thus represents a fascinating correlation between hierarchical and high-registral structures.

Yet, remarkably, even this strong conclusion is left open to a certain degree. A codetta (mm. 260ff.) featuring a rising chromatic progression to $C^3$ serves retrospectively to highlight the movement's use of linear patterns and recalls the unresolved implications of the slow introduction. The introduction, involving a slow-motion ascent from $D^2$ to $D^3$ (see Figure 3.13), concludes with a strong sense of unresolved expectation. $D^3$, at first harmonized by a diminished seventh, is left dangling dramatically after a "bungee jump" of almost two octaves to F, the plummeting pitch returning to a dominant-seventh harmony at the pause. The $D^3$ is only resolved with the appearance of $C^3$ (m. 36) in the first theme of the first subject group, described by Kerman as a "rhapsody" for solo violin, and more emphatically with $C^3$ as tonic (m. 43) in the second theme. In the codetta, the rising chromatic progression to $C^3$ calls to mind the introduction's final $D^3$ and resolves it. Thus this analysis of high-register patterns sheds light on hitherto overlooked connections between the slow introduction and main movement.[38]

*II Andante con moto quasi Allegretto* In the evocative A-minor slow movement, $C^4$ is again the registral peak (m. 50), yet its role is distinct from that in the first movement, on account of its harmonic function as tonic of the secondary-tonality C major at the cadence to the second group. As shown in Figure 3.14, the peak $C^4$ is immediately followed by a descent to $F^3$ and $A\flat^3$ (m. 50), emphasizing the flat sixth relation of the first subject ($F^1$–$E^1$, m. 2) while also creating a gap due to the missing B♭. Although the development section reaches a peak of only $E\flat^3$, the recapitulation (m. 101ff.)

*Figure 3.13.* High-register linear progressions in the first movement of op. 59 no. 3.

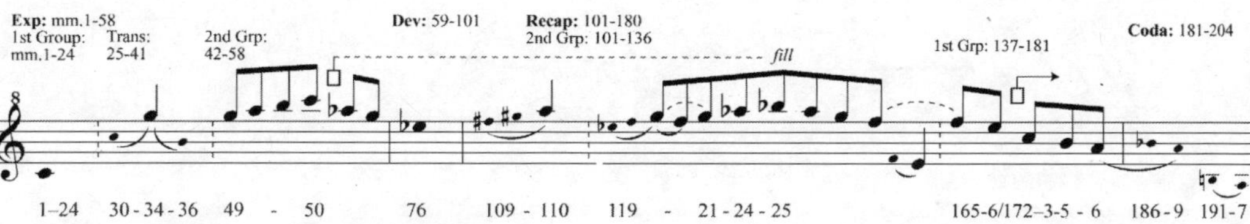


*Figure 3.14.* High-register linear progressions in the second movement of op. 59 no. 3.

regains $A^3$, but the gap from the missing B♭ is not filled until m. 125, the climax of the remarkable recapitulation of the second subject.[39] Kerman colorfully observes that here "the second subject moves as though freed into an unexpectedly ethereal register."[40] Campbell hints at a larger significance, observing that "the flight of fancy or aspiration that is represented by the obbligato of mm. 123–26 *symbolically occupies the highest register* and recalls passages with similar texture in the slow movement of 59/2" [italics mine].[41] Certainly the overall high-registral descent from $C^4$ to $B\flat^3$–$A\flat^3$–$G^3$ highlights the importance of the second subject's modulation to E♭, remarkable in view of its tritonal relation to A minor. It represents a high-level resolution of the earlier gap through $B\flat^3$ and initiates closure of the progression in the highest octave. From $G^3$ the progression descends to the tonic $A^2$ in the recapitulation of the first subject.

*III Menuetto Grazioso—Trio* In this movement, the peak $C^4$ is delayed, significantly, until the second section of the Trio (mm. 71–73), where it is the fifth of the subdominant key, F. The movement's simpler design is reflected in the single rising progression to $C^4$ from $F^3$, with a leap from $A^3$ creating a gap to be filled in the finale. As shown in Figure 3.15, the first section of the Minuet's closed, rounded binary form maintains a low register, but the repeat of the first theme in the second section rises to $C^3$ and thence to $F^3$ (mm. 28, 31, 36).

The third statement of $F^3$ falls via $E^3$ to $D^3$ (m. 36). The $D^3$ is left unresolved, whereas at the cadence $D^2$ resolves to $C^2$ (m. 38). Consequently, the appearance of the expected $C^3$ early in the Trio (m. 40) creates a connection between Minuet and Trio analogous to the $D^3$–$C^3$ connection between the slow introduction and exposition in the first movement. Similarly, the $G^3$ in the Trio's first section (mm. 47, 51–53) extends the Minuet's rising progression $C^3$–$F^3$, further reinforcing the relationship. Highlighting the salience of the peak register, both $G^3$ and $C^4$ are emphasized through threefold repetition (mm. 51–53 and 71–73) and a subsequent leap down more than three octaves to the violin's lowest note.

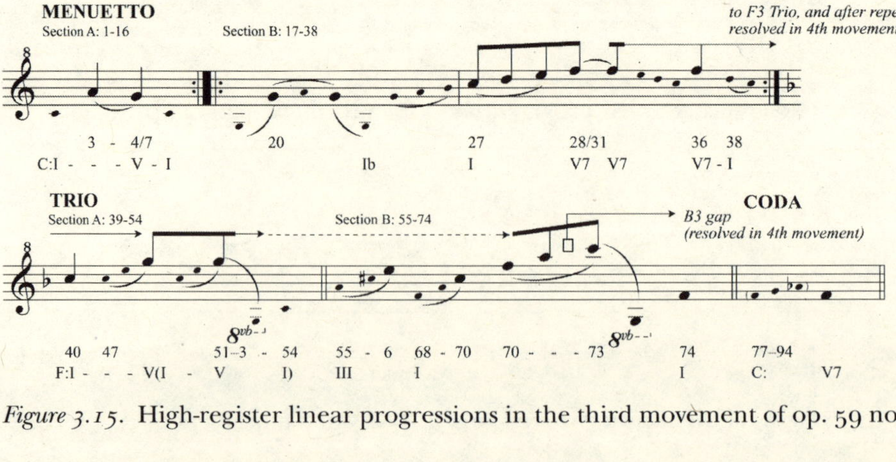


*Figure 3.15.* High-register linear progressions in the third movement of op. 59 no. 3.

*Allegro molto* In the coda to the finale, the culmination of high-level registral processes of the entire work takes place, with the arrival and emphasis of C⁴ (m. 423) contributing to what Kerman has described as Beethoven's "display of might."[42] As illustrated in Figure 3.16, C⁴ forms the goal of an extended linear progression from G³ that begins diatonically as G³–A³, then veers chromatically to the flattened-mediant E♭ with G³–A♭³–B♭³ (echoing the second movement), eventually resuming the diatonic ascent. At a larger level, C⁴ also completes the progression from the first movement following the reinterpretation of C⁴ within secondary tonalities in the second and third movements.

A fugal exposition takes the place of the usual first subject group of this movement, best described as a hybrid of sonata principle and fugue. The last instrument to enter with the subject is the first violin, which twice reaches G³ and its upper neighbor note A³ (mm. 41, 45). The second subject group, after a low start, rises from D³ (m. 65) through E³ (mm. 78, 80) to G³ (m. 81), with a gap to be filled by F³ at the close of the exposition. The line continues up purposefully to B♭³ via A♭³ (mm. 89–90), a peak reinforced by the strident interruption of the violin's three-octave plunge (mm. 90–91). As Campbell notes, "The B♭³ of m. 91 still stands by this point as the highest tone heard in the movement . . . while this is characteristic of the dynamic

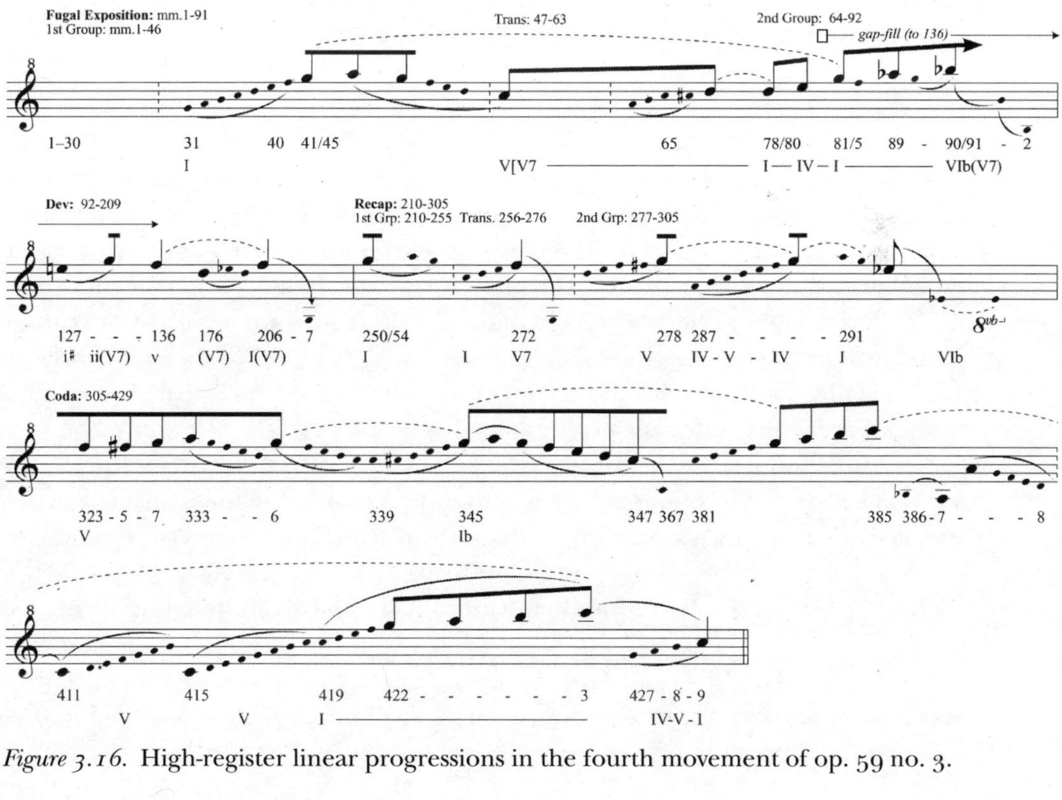


*Figure 3.16.* High-register linear progressions in the fourth movement of op. 59 no. 3.

climaxes of the movement, it is only in the second group that *register is exploited as a textural end in itself*" [italics mine].[43]

The progression to B♭$^3$ has a strong rising implication, which is not realized until C$^4$ in the coda. In between, the development reaches only G$^3$, with F$^3$ prior to the recapitulation (mm. 207–9) filling the gap of the E$^3$–G$^3$ progression (mm. 132–35), and the fugal exposition in the recapitulation (with the addition of a quarter-note countersubject) again reaches G$^3$ and A$^3$ (mm. 250, 254).

In the coda scale beginning at m. 381, the implications of both the G$^3$–A$^3$ and A$^3$–B♭$^3$ progressions are realized for the first time with a rise through B$^3$ to C$^4$ (mm. 381–85). The bold reiteration of registral peaks in these final measures has attracted much comment, such as Campbell's description of "the rapid sweeping over the registers confined not just to first violin but given to all."[44] There has been little mention, however, of the larger linear progression and of the reason for the return to C$^4$ after the dramatic three-octave descent (mm. 385–86). This startling plunge to B♭ (an echo of the similar gestures at mm. 91–92 and mm. 304–5) creates a new gap that is filled only with the renewed ascent to C$^4$, the registral peak and goal of the movement and the whole piece.[45] As mentioned earlier, in both second and third movements, C$^4$ appears within secondary tonal/harmonic contexts, whereas here in the finale, C$^4$ is at last reached over a tonic chord. The first arrival at C$^4$ (m. 385) is short-lived and brusquely interrupted, but a second appearance (m. 423) is sustained and powerfully emphatic, and is quitted by a more gradual descent, rather than a sudden plunge, to the obligatory register to close (Example 3.4).

## Cyclic Unity in Op. 59

Analysis of progressions in the highest register offers an illuminating perspective on the notion of cyclic unity, expressed as an overarching linear coherence. As illustrated in Figure 3.17, the three quartets outline a progression in which B$^3$ acts as a lower neighbor note, between C$^4$ as dominant, in op. 59 no. 1, and C$^4$ as tonic, in op. 59 no. 3. This neighbor-note pattern is a higher-level manifestation of the C$^4$–B$^3$ motif found within the works themselves, especially op. 59/2, and thus further expresses the cyclic unity of the set. Yet there is a sense in which C$^4$ acts as a peak throughout, its different facets generating a coherent narrative process.

In op. 59 no. 1, C$^4$ represents the peak of a linear structure that reinterprets it as a dissonance in the second movement, requiring resolution in the finale. C$^4$ is a dissonance in op. 59 no. 2, a peak rather than a goal, which underlines the Neapolitan conflict at the heart of the tonal and motivic argument of the work. As used in op. 59 no. 3, C$^4$ is transformed from dominant to tonic and again functions to resolve tension created by the linear pattern moving to B♭ in the second movement, transforming it to the diatonic pattern in C major. Thus there is both symmetry and process across the three works, with the enigmatic C♯$^4$ of op. 59 no. 2 remaining unresolved at the set's midpoint. Yet there is a sense in which the C♯$^4$–C$^4$ transformation

*Example 3.4.* Op. 59 no. 3, IV, mm. 381–429.

*Example 3.4, continued.*

*Figure 3.17.* Cyclic coherence in op. 59.

emanates from the Neapolitan tension central to the E-Minor Quartet, resolved via $C^4$ to $B^3$ in the last movement. And it is that Neapolitan relationship, as expressed in the C-major implication of the Thème russe finale of op. 59 no. 2, which has led Kerman and other commentators to suggest connection between the second and third quartets.

## Conclusion

The recognition of the highest register as a distinctive sonorous domain harboring its own possibilities of connectedness has far-reaching structural implications. As analysis demonstrates, the linking up of "high events" in the op. 59 quartets reveals significant linear patterns. Most often these are rising lines, which Robert Fink dubs "arrows of desire," quite distinct from the descending linear structures of the hierarchical Schenkerian approach, yet at some points the patterns correlate. The Meyerian approach has enabled us to highlight the large-scale coherence of the upper register both within and between the movements. All three quartets may be seen to project large-scale linear patterns that maintain tension within each movement and across the four-movement span, with some implications for cyclic coherence. In each work, strategic deployment of the upper register articulates and reinforces Beethoven's individual exploration and expansion of the Classic-Romantic sonata principle, adding its own layer of narrative coherence. For instance, in each first movement, the second subject groups generally extend the first group and transition, moving from a lower to a higher register. My analyses further suggest that investigation of high register structures in other instrumental and vocal works by Beethoven would bear fruit in interpretation of style and expression.

In the "Razumovsky" Quartets, the expansion of structure characteristic of Beethoven's heroic period extends into the domain of extreme registers. The deployment of high registral patterns here is far more complex than in the more classical op. 18 set and anticipates the more radical use of high register in the late quartets, for example the strategic emphasis on $C\sharp^4$ in the coda of the finale of op. 131. Kerman has described the "Razumovsky" Quartets as "explorers, experimenters,"[46] and Maynard Solomon has drawn attention to "the startling use of pizzicato for expressive purposes in the slow movements of no. 1 & 3, the brilliant string writing and voicing, which refashions the characteristic Classic style, the rich harmonic patterns and the extraordinary rhythmic drive; and the creation of flowing and continuous melodies."[47] To this list we may add Beethoven's innovative structural deployment of the highest register, which distinguishes these masterpieces as peaks of heroic musical inspiration.

## Notes

1. Lewis Lockwood, "Process versus Limits: A View of the Quartet in F Major, Opus 59 No. 1," in *Beethoven: Studies in the Creative Process* (Cambridge, Mass.: Harvard University Press, 1992), 198–208; see particularly 200–205.

2. Ibid., 198.

3. Ibid., 200.

4. "[T]he violin I soars into its highest register and reaches the pitch c in the stratosphere. It is then dramatically left hanging at this great height while the exposition figure from mm. 20–29 returns as the first item in the recapitulation." Ibid., 203.

5. "[A]t mm. 373–87 it resumes the opening c–f tetrachord and expands it, reaching a high point in the first violin in a way that is reminiscent of the development . . . at last the theme appears in its upper register in the first violin and fortissimo." Ibid.

6. "[T]he dynamic tension created by the thematic, harmonic and registral strategy for the entire movement, achieved by postponing a root-supported tonic statement of the first theme until the coda." Ibid., 208. Lockwood's analysis of the autograph manuscript argues that the cancellation of the repeat of the development and recapitulation was motivated by structural decisions relating to proportions and the desire to delay the final statement of the main theme until the very last moment.

7. Bruce Campbell, "Beethoven's Quartets Opus 59: An Investigation into Compositional Process," Ph.D. dissertation, Yale University, 1982.

8. Ernst Oster, "Register and the Large-Scale Connection," in *Readings in Schenker Analysis and Other Approaches,* ed. Maury Yeston (New Haven, Conn.: Yale University Press, 1977), 54–71. The article was originally published in the *Journal of Music Theory* 5/1 (1961).

9. Heinrich Schenker, *Das Meisterwerk in der Musik,* vol. 2 (Munich: Drei Masken Verlag, 1926), cited ibid., 54–55.

10. Oster, "Register and the Large-Scale Connection," 55.

11. Ibid., 60.

12. Ibid.

13. Robert Fink, "Going Flat: Post-Hierarchical Music Theory and the Musical Surface," in *Rethinking Musicology,* ed. Nicholas Cook and Mark Everist (London: Faber, 1996), 102–37. Fink's article is based on his doctoral dissertation, "'Arrows of Desire': Linear Structure and the Transformation of Musical Energy," University of California, Berkeley, 1994.

14. Ibid., 109.

15. Ibid. Regarding the Missa, Fink observes that the "choral tessitura leads us to associate pitches according to a surface variable only intermittently respected by reductive analysis: the strain inherent in choral high notes."

16. Ibid.

17. Ibid., 107, 112.

18. Ibid., 112.

19. Ibid., 109.

20. Ibid., 112. Fink's interpretation of the large-scale progression is as follows: "A coherent linear 'plot' emerges: a full Mixolydian ascent at bar 17; a dramatic cadence a2–b2 at bars 117–18 without the Mixolydian inflection—a cadence which on repetition stalls on a2; the retaking of a2 after 75 bars of Adagio at bars 196–201; the retaking of B♭$^2$ after almost 100 *more* bars at bars 290–4, and a final ecstatic Mixolydian ascent through A♭$^2$ and A$^2$ to B♭$^2$ at bars 430–3."

21. William Kinderman, *Beethoven* (Oxford: Oxford University Press, 1995), 238–83.

22. Ibid., 240.

23. Ibid., 241. "Here the full orchestral forces drop out, with a precipitous plunge in regis-

ter for the *Incarnatus* . . . the descent from heaven is thereby reflected in a sudden transformation of the musical texture."

24. Ibid., 242. The peak pitch A at mm. 199–200 is "a point of reference back to the suspended unresolved sonority at the end of 'descendit de coelis,' . . . the beginning of an extended thematic unit . . . later repeated . . . leading up to the recapitulation."

25. Ibid. Kinderman observes that "the F major sonority used for the word 'heaven' is thus a cornerstone in the formal architecture of the *Credo,* linking its first and third sections and initiating the development, while at the same time creating a symbolic role for the music that transcends any details of tone painting."

26. See Chapter 10 in Kinderman's *Beethoven.* He later highlights a similar structural significance in the E♭- chord initially stated at the outset of the Credo, which becomes a "referential sonority." He points out that it always appears with $G^2$ as highest pitch, later echoed in the high G2 used by the solo violin in the Benedictus, there interpreted as tonic of G major, not mediant of E♭.

27. Fink observes, "There is certainly no reason for a Schenkerian reduction of the *Credo* to fail: or any a priori reason why the structural levels of such an analysis might not actually buttress some of the deliberately loose 'prolongations' outlined." Fink, "Going Flat," 114.

28. Leonard B. Meyer, *Explaining Music: Essays and Explorations* (Chicago: University of Chicago Press, 1973). For a theoretical extension of Meyer's theories, see Eugene Narmour, *The Analysis and Cognition of Basic Melodic Structures: The Impact-Realization Model* (Chicago: Chicago University Press, 1977).

29. The graphic notation is an original approach that I have also used in my article "Beethoven's Early Piano Quartets WoO 36 and the Seeds of Genius," in *Arietta: Journal of the Beethoven Piano Society of Europe* 4 (Spring 2004).

30. Kerman, *The Beethoven Quartets,* 106.

31. Wilhelm Altmann, in his introduction to the Eulenberg Score of op. 59 no. 1 (London and Mainz), iii, observes that although Beethoven's autograph score shows the first violin as $F^3$–$G^3$–$D^3$ at m. 434, which is followed by various editions (including the Henle Urtext edition), other editions adopt $F^3$–B♭$^3$–$D^3$, assuming an error on Beethoven's part and reproducing the melodic outlines used eight measures earlier by the cello.

32. Ibid., 112. Kerman describes the passage as "perfectly gauged in psychological justness and in its larger rhythm."

33. See *Thayer's Life of Beethoven,* ed. Elliot Forbes (Princeton, N.J.: Princeton University Press, 1964), 408–9, and Gregory Mason, *The Quartets of Beethoven* (New York: Oxford University Press, 1947), 111.

34. Campbell does not comment about the use of register here, except to make an initial general remark about the Trio's "airy texture" and enhanced use of the "upper registers." See Campbell, "Beethoven's Quartets Opus 59," 184.

35. Ibid., 230. Campbell observes that the significance of the first peak $C^4$ is motivic, noting, "The highest register is used over the dominant pedal, characteristically highlighting $B^3$–$C^4$, the basic motivic half-step. The high register is maintained as the recapitulation begins, removing one parameter of emphasis." As this statement indicates, the lack of contrasting registers in this case is also significant.

36. Ibid., 234.

37. Ibid., 250.

38. Campbell and other commentators, who note a lack of connection between the slow introduction and main movement, have hitherto ignored these connections. See Robert Simpson, "Chamber Music for Strings," in *The Beethoven Companion,* ed. Dennis Arnold and Nigel Fortune (London: Faber, 1967), 241–78.

39. Ibid. Due to the recapitulation of the second group first, Robert Simpson has described

the movement as a "reversed sonata form." Campbell underlines the "unusual hybrid of ternary form (song form) and sonata procedure," in which the "complexity and control of Sonata Form enlarges the central section to equal the outer sections." Campbell, "Beethoven Quartets Opus 59," 278.

40. Kerman, *The Beethoven Quartets,* 148–49.

41. Campbell, "Beethoven's Quartets Opus 59," 265.

42. Kerman, *The Beethoven Quartets,* 144.

43. Campbell, "Beethoven's Quartets Opus 59," 310.

44. Ibid., 315.

45. The motive at mm. 387–88 also transforms the fugal motive with its supertonic harmony, whereas the implication of the low D continuing down to the tonic C is left unresolved until C reappears, rising again to $C^4$.

46. Kerman, *The Beethoven Quartets,* 153.

47. Maynard Solomon, *Beethoven* (New York: Schirmer, 1977), 201.

CHAPTER FOUR

# Beethoven's "Harp" Quartet

## The Sketches in Context

*Lewis Lockwood*

DEDICATED TO THE MEMORY OF
JOHN DAVERIO

Eighteen hundred nine was a hard year in Vienna. In April the beleaguered Austrian regime declared war on France for the third time in seventeen years and then suffered predictable humiliation as Napoleon's armies swept over them and marched on the city. A few weeks later, the royal family fled the city to safety in Hungary, while the ordinary citizens left behind (including Beethoven) endured siege, fierce bombardment, and a French military occupation that lasted until November. On July 26, Beethoven wrote to Breitkopf & Härtel, "[W]e have been experiencing misery in a highly concentrated form . . . [and] since May 4th [the day of the archduke's departure] I have produced very little coherent work, at most a fragment here or there. The whole course of events has affected both my body and soul."[1] And in November he wrote, "[W]e are enjoying a little peace after violent destruction, after suffering every hardship that one could conceivably endure."

Yet this year for Beethoven was one of great productivity. It began auspiciously in January when he skillfully improved his financial status by threatening to accept an invitation from Jérôme Bonaparte to become court music master at Kassel in Westphalia. This move at once precipitated an attractive counteroffer from Beethoven's three main Viennese patrons: the young Archduke Rudolph and Princes Lobkowitz and Kinsky. The result was a legal contract signed on March 1, by which this trio of benefactors accepted Beethoven's conditions for remaining in Vienna and gave him greater security than ever before. They guaranteed him an annual salary of 4,000 florins, payable for life, and promised a yearly concert of his works in a major local theater. The agreement even hinted that he might eventually become Imperial Kapellmeister. Besides this vote of financial confidence—the only substantial one he ever received—his publishing career continued to develop. Despite these times of misery and war, in April and May Breitkopf & Härtel published the first editions of the Cello Sonata op. 69 and the Fifth and Sixth symphonies, thus further consolidating Beethoven's position as the musical leviathan of his time.

His output of new works was, in fact, remarkable. From January onward he worked intensively on the Fifth Piano Concerto and finished it by the end of March, as shown by a massive outpouring of finale sketches in the first thirty-nine pages of the sketchbook Landsberg 5, which he used from March to October. That the Fifth Piano Concerto followed the Choral Fantasy, which he had hurriedly prepared for the famous concert of December 22, 1808, hints at Beethoven's awareness of ordering his major projects and regaining his full powers of composition. Coming after the oddly hybrid Choral Fantasy—part cantata, part fantasy for piano and orchestra—the "Emperor" Concerto not only returns to the heroic style but does so with a vision that is far more redolent of strength and exaltation than of tragedy and commemoration, as in the Third Symphony. Thereafter, Beethoven tackled the "Lebewohl" Piano Sonata, op. 81a, his emotional and programmatic reflection on the departure and return of Archduke Rudolph (begun in May, probably finished in the summer); then the single string quartet op. 74, for which sketches appear near the end of Landsberg 5. He evidently composed the quartet between May and September, but if we can believe his dismal letter of late July, he probably wrote most of it in August and September. The last important sketches in Landsberg 5, as reconstructed and edited by Clemens Brenneis, are for two more piano works—the Variations op. 76 and the Fantasy op. 77.[2] Before the year was out, he had also finished the F♯ Major Piano Sonata, op. 78, and its complement, the little Sonata in G Major, op. 79. It is interesting to see the experimental quartet op. 74 composed amid a fierce concentration on piano works, including a concerto, sonatas, variations, and a fantasy.

Throughout much of 1809, Beethoven was also preparing to take Archduke Rudolph as composition pupil, a job he expected to start when the royal family returned. Accordingly, he gave time to reading and compiling extracts from treatises by Fux, C. P. E. Bach, Kirnberger, Albrechtsberger, and Türk, besides sketching exercise-like passages. In his then-current sketchbook he jotted down an idea for a D-major quintet that he thought of as a potential "monument to Johann Sebastian Bach," and just at this time he asked Breitkopf to send him scores of choral works by Mozart, Haydn, and J. S. Bach.

Accordingly, in the first nine months of 1809 Beethoven returned to several basic genres—the piano concerto, the piano sonata, and the string quartet—in three large and experimental works. The first is his grandest concerto; the second, his first fully programmatic piano sonata; the third, op. 74, marks his return to the quartet genre after the massive innovations of the op. 59 trilogy. That all three big works are in the same key, E♭ major, might be a coincidence. Yet there is no other time in his entire career when Beethoven composed three successive major works in the same key. Further, both the Fifth Concerto and the "Lebewohl" Sonata were dedicated to the archduke (the sonata in a highly personal way), and the recipient of op. 74 was Lobkowitz. Although the dedications might merely seem to confirm the their prominence as patrons, we should also remember that these two benefactors had just guaranteed Beethoven a lifetime income. The archduke then remained for many years the most important supporting figure of Beethoven's entire career, as a generous and accessible member of the royal family, and as the only high aristocrat who became Beethoven's pupil, as pianist and composer.

I apologize for taking so long to get to the point, but these are some of the necessary contextual conditions for thinking about the sketches for op. 74. We can reckon this quartet among the most remarkable products of the years from 1808 to 1812, the romantic twilight of Beethoven's second maturity. And yet it is a work that has drawn puzzled responses from Beethoven commentators past and present.

We have to begin with the quartet's basic movement-plan and aesthetic profile. The four-movement structure is typical for Beethoven's quartets up to this time, but his choices of tempo, key, character, and formal plan establish a new paradigm. The tempo of the slow introduction, "Poco Adagio" is rare for him. He had first used this marking in the *Prometheus* ballet of 1800–1, in the scene in which the two clay creatures slowly come to life. Then it appeared in two songs—one of the Gellert songs (op. 48) of 1803, and the 1805 setting of *An die Hoffnung*. It turned up twice in 1809—in this quartet's slow introduction and as the opening tempo of the Piano Fantasy op. 77. Thereafter, he never used it again.

Beethoven's choice of keys, with the subdominant A♭ major for the Adagio ma non troppo and the submediant C minor for the Scherzo, produce a cycle with the tonic only for the first and last movements. He had tried this unusual scheme fairly recently, in the idiosyncratic Piano Trio in E♭, opus 70 no. 2, of 1808, in which the first and last movements frame a jocular 2/4 Allegretto in C major and a romantic intermezzo in A♭ major. In op. 74 the variations finale, in Allegretto 2/4, links by association to a handful of earlier works that close not with a dynamic finale in Allegro or Presto, but with a quiet and commodious Allegretto that gives breathing space for subtle effects. Witness such antecedents as the rondo finales of the piano sonatas op. 22 and op. 31 no. 1, and the A-major variations movement that closes the violin sonata op. 30 no 1. After those examples, the Allegretto finale of op. 74 is the next one of the kind, and it was soon followed by the comparable variations finale of the violin sonata op. 96.

The primary sources for the compositional history of op. 74 are the sketches, all in the sketchbook Landsberg 5, and the autograph manuscript, now in Kraków. The sketches cover all four movements, but at different stages of development. Those for the first movement are already fairly advanced, whereas the sketches for the other movements range from embryonic ideas to mature drafts and revisions. As to the slow introduction, we have no sketches for it at all, suggesting it was written late and worked out elsewhere. Beethoven was still revising it in the autograph, which also has alterations of significant details for all four movements (none of them yet discussed in the literature).

The sketchbook Landsberg 5, as noted earlier, was Beethoven's primary compositional diary from March to October, and we are fortunate to have the recent and authoritative edition of the whole book as reconstructed, transcribed, and edited by Clemens Brenneis. Published in two volumes, one a full facsimile and the other a complete transcription, it sheds light on all the major works of these eight months and discloses many interesting jottings and occasional entries for works that never got beyond the sketch stage. One unfortunate editorial decision governs the format of the transcription. Brenneis's excellent transcriptions are not presented in "diplomatic" form—that is, they are not published in a format that closely resembles the original layout of each page. Instead, the transcriptions are simply distributed on the printed pages in a format of convenience. The result is that the visual appearance of the original pages can only be discovered by consulting the corresponding facsimile. And because the published facsimile is of merely adequate clarity and sharpness, it is not easy to get a sense of how Beethoven actually worked on any given sketch page or pages, let alone the true relationship of entries that connect to each other across several staves or pages. These and related issues are discussed in a thorough and perceptive review of the edition by Nicholas Marston in *Beethoven Forum* 6.[3]

From the beginning of op. 74 we are in a new world of Beethoven quartet writing, and as the work progresses it reveals an increasingly complex aesthetic profile. From movement to movement, the work displays unusual extremes of character. This juxtaposition of contrasts is evident in the larger relationship of the four movements, and also in the thematic organization of the first movement.

The slow introduction establishes the tonic, E♭ major, yet it immediately destabilizes that tonic by means of an immediate pull toward the subdominant by way of the flat seventh, D♭. As Schoenberg noted, the opening motif with its descending sixth and rising fourth to D♭, then followed in the motif's second statement by a chromatic rise to D♮, provides a basic intervallic shape, a gestalt, that finds its way with ease into the primary thematic material of the Allegro.[4] The pitch D♭ is strongly reinforced later in the slow introduction, at mm. 12–13, where it breaks out on a sudden *forte* eruption as the upper pitch of the dominant seventh of A♭, and again at m. 17, where an intensified version of the same eruption brings it in upper register (this D♭ at 17 is the highest pitch in the entire introduction). And this same D♭ remains a key element throughout the introduction, as the first violin threads its way slowly up a chromatic scale from low D♮ at m. 18 to the high D♭–D♮, at mm. 23–24, which finally produces—for the first time in the work—a root-position V–I cadence onto the tonic E♭ major. The whole thrust of the introduction has been to deflect the tonic toward the subdominant and to explore that region by means of mysterious harmonic progressions that never return to the tonic until the arrival of the Allegro.

The Allegro shows Beethoven's craft at its rarest, beginning with an exposition that, in a short span of 53 measures, presents a startling variety of differentiated musical ideas. I construe the exposition to have as many as nine distinct figures. Compare the exposition of the first movement of his *Eroica* Symphony, which has perhaps six such clearly differentiated figures in a span of 153 measures, almost three times longer than this one.

Let me go through the exposition and take note of the basic sequence of figures and elements.

1. The first segment reaffirms the tonic with an emphatic three-note rising tonic triad (mm. 25–26), with bass moving from tonic in root position to V/6 (compare the opening of op. 59 II!).[5]
2. At once there follows what we take to be the "first theme," which is actually a composite of the first-violin theme and the flowing countertheme in the second violin. The first-violin theme, with its legato shape at the beginning that gives way to the dotted figures of mm. 29–30, provides motivic material in both halves that will serve as substance for later elaboration. The consequent of the first-violin theme is the "answer" in the viola at mm. 31–32, which repeats the opening figure but brings it to a firm cadence on the tonic at m. 35. The complexity of the thematic elements is stabilized by the clear harmonic support of the tonic pedal and subsequent cadence (mm. 32–35), and by the middle voices.
3. Now comes the first pizzicato segment, mm. 35–42. This is the most famous moment in the entire quartet, and it appears five times in the movement. Its first role is as an early transition segment that sets up the first harmonic shift from structural tonic to structural dominant. Later, the same rising pizzicato figures reappear in modified form at the end of the development section (mm. 125–34), where they build the dominant preparation for the recapitulation. Then the exposition version returns in newly expanded form in the recapitulation at mm. 153–68. Finally, the pizzicato makes two appearances in the coda: first, again modified, in the lower strings under the first-violin cadenza (mm. 221–39, etc.), and then at the very end of the movement for the final tonic affirmation (mm. 251–54).

It's safe to say that this extended use of pizzicato as a structural feature is unprecedented in the quartet literature. An informal search shows that the role of plucked string passages in classical chamber music had been extremely limited. As a special closing effect, Haydn and Mozart in their quartets employed pizzicato for such moments as the final V–I cadences of slow movements, especially in soft dynamics, and Beethoven in op. 18 had done the same. He had expanded its role in op. 59, above all in the slow movements of nos. 1 and 3, but always primarily in the cello as a special way of articulating an elaborate melodic bass line. In op. 74 he was seeking much more than a percussive, coloristic effect. The phrase at mm. 35–42 consists of two overlapping five-bar subphrases that exchange textures. The first subphrase features pulsating triadic eighth notes arco in the upper strings, while the lower strings in dialogue pluck arpeggiated quarter-note pairs (reminiscent of the rising quarter-note triad that had begun the Allegro). In the second subphrase, all is reversed in role and register, with the plucked figures in the upper strings (see Example 4.1c). This contrast of registers and roles sets the stage for the pizzicato passages in the development and coda, and also for the expanded tonic repetition in the recapitulation. Indeed, the immediate juxtaposition of high and low registers in a quartet exposition reminds us at once of the famous contrasting high and low half-note chords in the first movement of op. 59/I, which also have an antecedent in the finale of op. 18/VI, "La Malinconia" (see Examples 4.1a and 1b).[6] This is just one of the ways in which op. 74 capitalizes on discoveries Beethoven had made in earlier quartets.

From here on in the exposition, now in the dominant, more varied subthemes appear. These are, in order, the rhythmically energetic passage from 42 to 47, followed by the lively eighth-note figures of mm. 48–52. At 52 appears the likeliest candidate for a "principal" second theme, though there really isn't one in this exposition. Now flowing sixteenth notes in contrary motion enter the scheme, reaching up to a high point—B♭[3] at mm. 56–57. This passage in turn gives way to a poignant new

*Example 4.1.* Registral alternation in earlier quartets.

*a.* Op. 18 no. 6, finale, mm. 1–17.

*b.* Op. 59 no. 1, I, mm. 83–96; op. 59 no. 1, I, development, mm. 142–156.

*Example 4.1, continued. c.* Op. 74, I, exposition, mm. 31–48.

theme at 58–59 with running sixteenths below it, then to a highly articulated cadence (68–69), and at last to two sets of closing figures. The first of these, at 70–72, brings syncopated accents into the discourse for the first time. The second and final closing figure (mm. 74–77) quietly confirms B♭ major in quarter- and whole-note patterns that close the whole *prima parte* (as Beethoven would have called it).

I will not undertake a similar parsing of the development and recapitulation here, though these sections have many remarkable moments. But we can hardly fail to note the strong emphasis on C major in the second half of the development, where the texture is reduced to the dotted figures derived from the second half of the main theme, while the inner strings buzz in divided eighth-note patterns. Nor can we overlook the dramatic way in which the dynamic in the development at first builds to a powerful *ff* climax at m. 92, where the implied registral span is, briefly, an enormous five octaves, with the cello low C at the bottom. Beethoven sustained the dynamic at *forte* for many measures (94–111), then gradually reduced it to *pp* at 123, precisely as the dominant preparation begins with its pizzicato arpeggios, then shifted to arco as the rhythmic diminutions build to full climax at 138.

Nor can we pass over the amazing coda, in which the first violin suddenly tears loose at m. 221 with a long virtuosic cadenza for twenty-five measures, while the lower strings at first articulate the pizzicato rising quarter-note arpeggios, then turn to the most characteristic figure of the main theme in an attempt to integrate this startling new element into the material of the movement. Thereafter, all is clear as the material makes its final use of arpeggiated triads in complementary directions, sustaining the tonic to the end.

With this picture of the first movement before us, what pertinent questions can we ask regarding the sketches? First, we want to know how the larger idea of the movement grew—that is, which of these distinctive segments were essential to the design from early on, and which were added at later phases. Second, we can look into the specific shaping of motives, rhythms, themes, and even whole sections, to see how the formation of the movement took place and which elements may have been elaborated later, perhaps in the autograph stage.

Here are some provisional answers. First, it is clear, as Nottebohm observed, that much work on the first movement must have taken place elsewhere, before or during Beethoven's sketches in Landsberg 5.[7] The sketches in Landsberg 5 for the first movement mainly concern the development, recapitulation, and coda. Further, the Landsberg 5 material for the later movements is in a much earlier stage of compositional development, and this fact shows that the primary invariant for the work was the first movement, against which the other movements were added. Yet even the basic early ideas for the slow movement and Scherzo, however primitive, show the familiar profiles of both movements in formation, whereas Beethoven's ideas for the finale underwent much more drastic changes.

Thus the slow movement, from the very outset, was to be in A♭ major and in 3/8; furthermore, Beethoven's initial idea for the opening theme, in middle register in the second violin, was to begin as a turning theme around the pitch 1, leading in four measures to a half-cadence on the dominant (Example 4.2a). The third movement, from the outset, was to be in C minor with a strong initial gesture using repeated notes on tonic and then dominant, followed by running-scale passages in the cello (Example 4.3a).

As things developed, the first of these basic ideas, using repeated notes to form the Scherzo theme, was fleshed out and elaborated, and the running-scale-figure idea in the cello moved to the Trio. As for the variations finale, its main theme began life in a form very different from what it evolved into. The first idea for it, on page 70 of the sketchbook, shows an opening interval strikingly similar to the opening intervallic shape of the slow introduction, the pitch 5 (B♭) descending by leap to 7 (D), then moving stepwise to 1 (E♭). The larger shape of the theme, with its energetic flow of eighth-note and quarter-note motion, has other affinities to the first-movement material; these resemblances were then buried as the theme evolved into its final form, with its carefully calibrated sequential dotted figures, which gradually emerged in the sketches and become the basic material of the finale main theme (see Examples 4.4a, b, c).

To draw some of these loose threads together, let us turn back to the first-movement sketches in Landsberg 5. Most of the entries for the first movement are for passages in need of sharpening and improvement, and some are for highly strategic places within the movement. One that catches our eye is on page 70, st. 14–15, a try-out for a way of ending the development section and arriving at the tonic for the recapitulation (Example 4.5b). From this sketch we see that at an early stage there was no hint of using pizzicato for this passage, but that a figure of four eighth notes was designed to build in intensity through rising sequences, then give way to strongly punctuated quarter notes on downbeats, with rests between, that would lead through a cadence to the tonic—with a characteristic D♭–C motion in the bass to complicate the cadence. The letters "d.c." at the end of the sketch imply that we are at the point of recapitulation, as is clear from not only the E♭ downbeat but from the rising tonic triad shown by the last two notes of the last measure.

*Example 4.2a.* Op. 74, initial sketch for Adagio (Landsberg 5, p. 70).

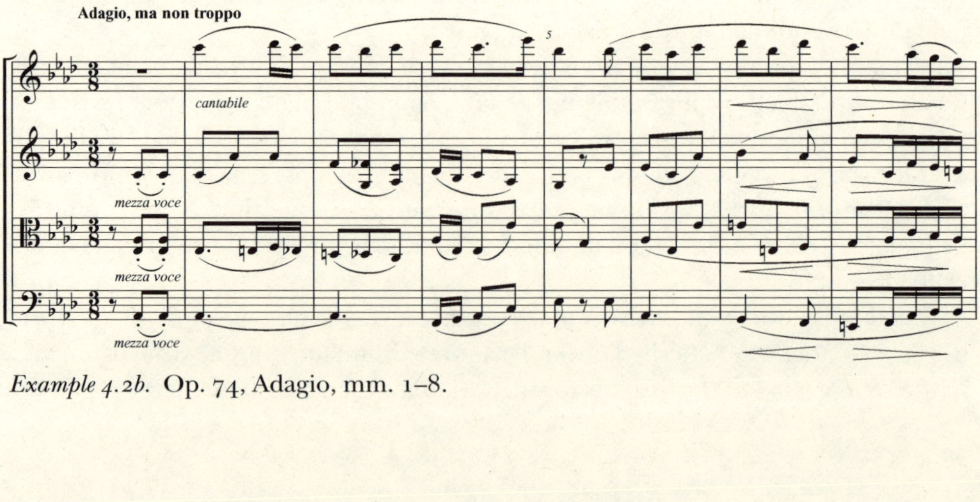


*Example 4.2b.* Op. 74, Adagio, mm. 1–8.

*Example 4.3a.* Op. 74, initial sketch for third movement (Landsberg 5, p. 70).

*Example 4.3b.* Op. 74, III, mm. 1–6; op. 74, Trio, beginning.

*Example 4.4a.* Op. 74, initial sketch for main theme of finale (Landsberg 5, p. 71).

*Example 4.4b.* Op. 74, sketch for finale variation.

*Example 4.4c.* Op. 74, finale, beginning.

When Beethoven returned to work on this passage, eight pages later in the sketchbook (page 78), he had completely changed his mind about how to end the development (Example 4.6).

Brenneis has extracted several layers of readings from the palimpsest on this page, and from his work we find the following basic new elements:

1. The previous sequential four eighth-note figures are now gone, replaced by a succession of pedal-point double stops on various members of the dominant-seventh harmony (as we see in the final version, in the first-violin, from mm. 101 to 113).
2. Against the sustained-dominant harmony, Beethoven now wanted rising quarter-note arpeggiated figures, but, as he wrote in a verbal note, he wanted to delay the introduction of the dominant-seventh pitch, A♭, until the end of the passage. He wrote,

*Example 4.5a.* Early sketch for end of development and lead-in to recapitulation (Landsberg 5, p. 71/14–16).

*Example 4.5b.* Landsberg 5, p. 70/14–15.

"immer B bis zum letztenmal as" ("always B♭ until, at the last time, A♭"). The sequence of arpeggios in the sketch grows in intensity by diminution of note values: from quarter notes in 4/4 to quarter-note triplets, to groups of four eighth notes; to eighth-note triplets, clustering more thickly as they approach the resolution to the tonic. Beethoven even considered a further momentary diminution to four sixteenths in the first violin a half-measure before the tonic resolution, but he then thought better of it. There is no clear sign in the sketch to show pizzicato, which he used to tremendous effect in the final version, but all the sketch versions offer the possibility of pizzicato for the rising quarter-note pairs. In the final score he maintained the pizzicato as long as he could expect it to be playable, only changing to arco at m. 134 at the shift to eighth-triplets. Of course he would have to shift to arco at some point in the sequence, in order to gain the force and momentum needed for this decisive arrival at the tonic. The autograph manuscript shows the final stage, without massive changes.

One other place in the first movement calls for brief comment. That is the first-violin "cadenza" or arpeggiated free fantasia in the coda, accompanied by the lower strings (mm. 221–46). This passage, like no other in the quartet literature up to this time, may have been a Beethovenian gesture toward the French "quatuor brillant," a type of string quartet then in vogue in French circles, in which the first-violin part called for high technical virtuosity and the lower parts were its vassals. Examples by Baillot, Kreutzer, and Rode, the three leading French violinists of the period, form the backbone of this literature, in which the first violin is by far the leading voice, so

*Example 4.6.* Later sketch for end of development and lead-in to recapitulation (Landsberg 5, p. 78).

[?] d
F
[2./3. Fassung]
[Ms.: as]
[3]
[Recap]
Violne [?]
[?]
Vi=[-> Z.16]
[4. Fassung]
Vi=[-> Z.16]
Vl[cl]lo[?]
[3. Fassung]
[1. Fassung]
[2. Fassung]
[4. Fassung]
8va [------------ ]
[Notierung weiter gestr.]
[erst:]
[--> Z.14]
[--> S.79, Z. 16]

much so that when Baillot played as quartet leader in chamber music concerts, he played standing up while the three others remained seated.[8] Beethoven met all three violinists at various times and wrote violin sonatas for two of them, Kreutzer and Rode. The sharp contrast between this type of quartet and the long-familiar four-part-dialogue textures of the Haydn-Mozart-Beethoven tradition may well find expression in this remarkable passage.

In the final version of op. 74, seventeen measures into the coda, just as the material seems to be moving through a crescendo toward a final cadence, the first violinist suddenly breaks into a series of diminished-seventh sixteenth-note passaggi that lasts for four measures and then expands into more wide-ranging string-crossing arpeggios, eventually sustaining its intensity in *forte* and culminating in a powerful cadence to the tonic in *ff* at mm. 245–46. Against this outburst, the other instruments respond first by renewing the upward pizzicato quarter-note figures for twelve measures, and then they resume the basic arco motif from the beginning of the exposition. Eventually, all three lower voices join in arco to build the cadence to the tonic. As I have stated elsewhere, it is as if the lower voices are trying to persuade the high-flying solo violin I to come back into the quartet texture.[9] When they succeed, the movement is ready for its final affirmation of the tonic, once more in rising quarter-note triads that are first plucked, then shift to arco for the needed full sound of the quartet, as they have always done before.

Did Beethoven project this virtuosic cadenza at the sketch stage? And if so, what was the idea for it? In Landsberg 5 we find, indeed, a modest evolution of ideas that yields some insight. The later sketch pages for the first movement show three drafts for the coda, in quick succession. In the first (p. 79, st. 4–6) we find the end of the recapitulation followed simply by the rising quarter-note tonic figures for the ending, and in the first version there is apparently no idea of a true coda at all (Example 4.7).

This idea is quickly revised in favor of a version in which the opening motif of the first theme makes an appearance (p. 80, st. 8–10), but without any sixteenth-note passages (Example 4.8). And then, at the top of page 81, staves 1–2, occurs for the first and only time the idea of the flamboyant arpeggios in the first-violin part, with the rising quarter-note figures below; this idea wends its way through the sketch page on several disjointed staves, then leads to the big tonic cadence that is to end the whole cadenza and moves eventually to the final cadence and the double bar (p. 80, st. 10). The whole idea has some affinities with an abortive cadenza-like sketch for a piano concerto in A minor, which he tried out briefly a few pages earlier while sketching various items. (See Example 4.9).[10]

We should also remember that 1809 seems to be the year in which Beethoven composed a whole series of cadenzas for his first four piano concertos, intending them for his virtuoso student and patron Archduke Rudolph.[11] But in the coda of the first movement of op. 74, we can pretty well infer from the sketch evidence that the idea of the first-violin cadenza passage was an old-fashioned "sudden inspiration" that arose as he was working out the shape and style of the coda and making basic decisions as

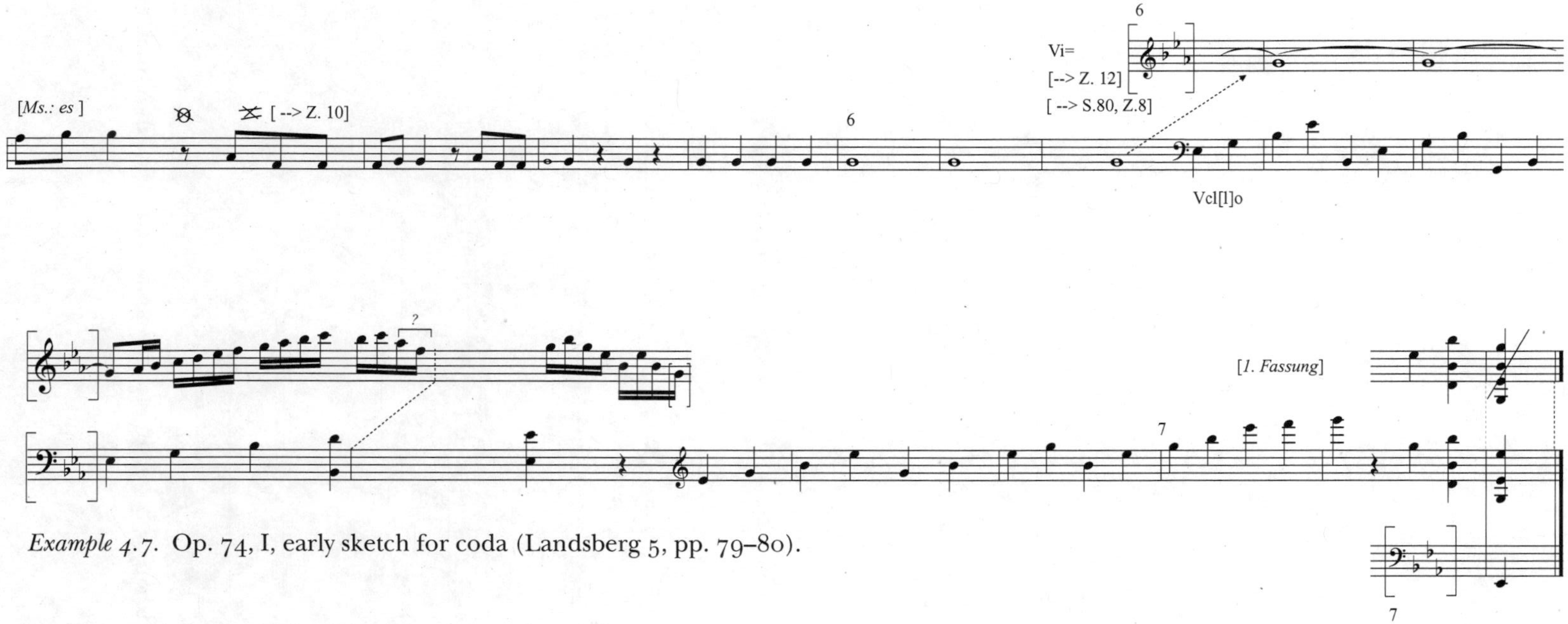


*Example 4.7.* Op. 74, I, early sketch for coda (Landsberg 5, pp. 79–80).

*Example 4.8.* Later sketch for coda (Landsberg 5, pp. 80–81).

*Example 4.9.* Landsberg 5, p. 73: an idea for a piano concerto in A minor.

to how it should be integrated with the earlier portions of the movement. One result of this enormous extension of an originally short coda is that, in the final version, the coda is comparable in length to the earlier principal sections.

The coda cadenza feels at first like an extraneous intrusion upon the reasoned logic of the quartet medium, a passage displaced from the concerto into the domesticated world of the quartet. But if we consider that this movement has from the very beginning been engaged in a process of integrating dissimilarities, of welding into a coherent whole the most disparate elements of any exposition he had written in chamber music, then we see that the cadenza plays a crucial role. It becomes the crowning point of the extremes of texture and style that Beethoven brought together within a single movement and which he then proceeded to integrate in larger terms by uniting the four heterogeneous movements of this remarkable work. Questions and issues like these are just some of the unexpected consequences of perusing the sketches, which can point the way to thoughts that might not have occurred to us in studying the finished composition alone.

## Notes

1. *Beethoven: Briefe,* ed. Sieghard Brandenburg, vol. 2 (Munich: Henle, 1996), no. 392.

2. *Ludwig van Beethoven. Ein Skizzenbuch aus dem Jahre 1809* (Landsberg 5), vol. 1: facsimile (Bonn: Beethoven-Haus, 1992); vol. 2: Übertragung, Einleitung, und Kommentar von Clemens Brenneis (Bonn: Beethoven-Haus, 1993).

3. Nicholas Marston, "Landsberg 5 and Future Prospects for the *Skizzenausgabe,*" *Beethoven Forum* 6 (1998): 207–34.

4. See Schoenberg's posthumously published treatise *Der musikalische Gedanke* (in the original German) and in English translation as *The Musical Idea,* edited and translated by Patricia Carpenter and Severine Neff (New York: Columbia University Press, 1995), 187–89. I have commented on these examples in my paper "On Schoenberg's View of the Beethoven Quartets," in *Music of My Future: The Schoenberg Quartets and Trio,* ed. Reinhold Brinkmann and Christoph Wolff (Harvard University Department of Music, 2000), 43–36. The papers in this volume were all delivered in a conference, in honor of my late and admired colleague David Lewin, that took place at Harvard in February 1999.

5. A number of other Beethoven works in E♭ major have prominent rising tonic triad figures at or near their openings, a point that I have made and discussed in relation to Mozart's *The Magic Flute* and its Masonic content, in my *Beethoven: The Music and the Life* (New York: Norton, 2003), 100 and passim.

6. See op. 18 no. 6, finale, which opens with three four-measure phrases contrasting in register (mm. 1–12) and then moves immediately into one-measure contrasts (mm. 12–13, 14–15, 16–17). In op. 59 no. 1, first movement, the well-known half-note registral contrasts are found at mm. 85–90, 144–51, and 332–37.

7. Gustav Nottebohm, *Zweite Beethoveniana* (Leipzig: C. F. Peters, 1887), 91.

8. Jean Mongredien, *French Music from the Enlightenment to Romanticism, 1789–1830,* English trans. (Portland, Ore.: Hal Leonard, 1996), 289–99.

9. See my *Beethoven: The Music and the Life,* 327.

10. I am indebted here to a paper by Dr. Alexander Fisher that was prepared for a graduate seminar on the Beethoven quartets some years ago.

11. See Max Unger, *Eine Schweizer Beethovensammlung: Katalog* (Zurich: Verlag der Corona, 1939), 24–29; and W. Hess, ed., *Ludwig van Beethoven: Sämtliche Kadenzen* [facsimile of autographs of the cadenzas] (Zurich: Edition Eulenburg, 1979). Leon Plantinga, in *Beethoven's Concertos* (New York: Norton, 1999), 294, also accepts 1809 as the probable date for the cadenzas.

CHAPTER FIVE

# "Haydns Geist aus Beethovens Händen"?

## Fantasy and Farewell in the Quartet in E♭, Op. 74

*Nicholas Marston*

IN MEMORIAM
PHILIP RADCLIFFE
(1905–86)

## I

To chart the critical reception of Beethoven's String Quartet in E♭, op. 74, from its publication in 1810—some twelve months after its composition—to the present is, very broadly speaking, to observe a twofold mutation in its perception: firstly, from a "modernistic" work into one that stands as a monument to Beethoven's classical heritage; and secondly, from a serious, even dark, work of deep personal feeling into one that is open, conventional, and unchallenging.[1] Although the author of a review of the first edition published in the Leipzig *Allgemeine musikalische Zeitung* in May 1811 did not yet know it as the "Harp" Quartet, he was nonetheless struck by the comic (*launig*) effect of the pizzicato passages from which the soubriquet later arose. For him, these passages jarred with the fundamental seriousness of the movement and were but one example of the striking diversity and plenitude of ideas that characterized it—or rather, that made it all but impossible to characterize in any definitive way. Its sparse melodic continuity and humorous to-ing and fro-ing from one idea to another gave the impression of a free fantasia more than of an ordered whole. The following slow movement was a dark nocturne breathing more than a dark melancholy, and seeming increasingly to strain against the limits of *die schöne Kunst,* particularly in the ominous confusion of its second half, where it lost its way. The harmonic complexities of this movement might provide a useful object of study for younger composers, the author decided, but it should not be taken as a model for imitation. The Scherzo was likened to the war dance of some uncivilized nation, and even the closing theme and variations offered something more profound and original than was customary in a finale, with the result that the entire composition became imbued with these qualities. In short, op. 74 allied itself much more to Beethoven's previous three quartets (op. 59) than to his first six (op. 18): the op. 18 quartets exemplified, in their individual movements, qualities of melodiousness, unity, and fixed character that raised them to the status of masterworks and enabled them to be placed alongside the works of Haydn and Mozart, whereas op. 59 breathed the air of a very different planet. Easy intelligibility had given way here to a profundity and learnedness that courted the incomprehensible. Lacking knowledge and experience of Beethoven's later music (including the Quartet in F Minor, op. 95, which had been composed by late 1810 but would not be published until 1816), this reviewer read op. 59 and op. 74 as "modern" music, compared to the "classical" ideal represented by op. 18.[2]

In 1852, in his *Beethoven et ses trois styles,* Wilhelm von Lenz was in a position to take a longer perspective. Yet for him op. 74, although it was "a capital work," remained "severe and grandiose," and he quoted with implicit approbation the *AMZ* assessment of it as "more serious than cheerful, more profound and rich in artistry than agreeable and pleasant."[3] It was, moreover, a middle-period work, or rather one written in what von Lenz called Beethoven's "second style."[4]

The subsequent view of Adolph Bernhard Marx, who in 1863 could place op. 74 as the first of Beethoven's "last quartets," contrasted starkly with earlier assessments. Marx's chapter on these works began by emphasizing the unique power of music to conjure dreamlike states in which nothing is fixed or definite—a twilight zone of fluidity and uncertainty. In Beethoven's last works, Marx wrote, the string quartet became the primary medium for the expression of this "dreamlife"; and in op. 74 the first signs could be perceived of that self-abandonment to the most intimate and dissolving (*auflösend*) feelings that would come to dominate the later music, even if the counterbalance of a vigorous, manly strength was still clearly evident.[5]

Marx was insistent on the pervasiveness of this fundamental dualism throughout the quartet. The basic mood of the first movement was one of deep, intimate feeling and melancholy, albeit occasionally relieved (for example, by the pizzicato "Harp" passages). That same mood underlay the slow movement from beginning to end; for Marx it was as though every note were dipped in a tear, as a heart overflowing with feelings lamented its anxious suffering in the secrecy of the night (recall the *AMZ* reviewer's description of this movement as a dark nocturne). Only the third movement proved capable of providing a counterweight to this prevailing mood and of reasserting "the complete Beethoven in all his virility"; the unexpected and unassuming simplicity of the finale's variation theme (Marx was quick to contrast this and the corresponding movement of the Fifth Symphony, with its unmistakable sense of culminatory triumph over former struggles) might offer a sense of relief, self-content, or renunciation, but the darker basic mood was still not overcome: for example, the cadence on V/VI at the midpoint of the theme signified for Marx a "continuing grief" that connected to the introduction and the fundamental melancholy of the first movement.

Marx's dualistic reading of op. 74 reappeared in Theodor Helm's 1885 account, in a book avowedly indebted to the earlier author's work but intended also as a corrective to what Helm took to be Marx's underrepresentation of some of the Beethoven quartets. The *AMZ* reviewer had been content to ally op. 74 with the "Razumovsky" Quartets in opposition to op. 18, but Helm concurred with Marx's view of op. 74 as fundamentally "late," in the sense that it and the succeeding quartets were linked by an underlying expression of "subjectivity," as opposed to the "objectivity" of op. 59. Op. 59 had expressed the sorrows and joys of the whole world, rather than Beethoven's own personal emotions: "a psychological distinction that appears clearly enough by comparison with the quartets from op. 127, and even predominantly already from op. 74 onward."[6]

Consider now a range of (largely Anglo-American) twentieth-century assessments of the "Harp" Quartet. Walter Riezler's 1936 study dispensed with it in a single brief paragraph and characterized it, aside from the "impetuous" Scherzo, as "light and easy-going music, free of all tension." In 1965, Philip Radcliffe suggested that, in contrast to op. 59, both op. 74 and op. 95 "move gradually in the direction of the sparer texture and more withdrawn manner of the last works." Viewed as a whole, however, "it presents in some ways a less vividly marked personality than the 'Rasumovsky' Quartets." Two years later, Joseph Kerman also linked it with op. 95; the quartet in his view evinced "a poise and control that mark a decided advance over the earlier period (or sub-period)." But there were telling differences, too: "[T]he E♭ Quartet is an open, unproblematic, lucid work of consolidation . . . The F-minor Quartet is an involved, impassioned, highly idiosyncratic piece, problematic . . . , advanced in a hundred ways. *One work looks backward, perhaps, the other forward.* Or to put it better, one work looks outward, the other inward" [italics mine]. One sees well here how the tendency to group these two works together in Beethoven's quartet output risks "normalizing" op. 74 in order to underscore the peculiarities of op. 95: Kerman's description of the later quartet—impassioned, forward-looking, inward-looking—could well be Marx's of op. 74. As Paul Griffiths has put it, Beethoven's own description of op. 95 as "serioso" "has had the unfortunate effect of suggesting that its immediate predecessor . . . does not have to be taken so seriously." Maynard Solomon, doubtless with Kerman's account in mind, speaks of "a lyrical, contemplative, and expressive work which . . . retreats from the innovative thrust of the *Rasumovsky* Quartets and returns to the central vocabulary of the Viennese high-Classic style . . . one senses that Beethoven was attempting to reestablish contact with styles from which he had largely held aloof after 1802." Robert Winter and Robert Martin, in contrast, describe it as "genial and inviting of access." Kerman's "unproblematic" assessment was repeated in *The New Grove* (1980) and has since reappeared, unchanged, in Scott Burnham's revision of that text for the new millennium.[7] The twofold mutation, from the personal to the impersonal and from the "modernistic" to the "classic," seems complete—and difficult to dislodge.

## II

The conception of op. 74 as a backward-looking piece—though this is not at all to be taken as indicating what he terms "dependency" or "compositional insufficiency"—has been explored in considerable detail by James Webster, in a study of traditional elements in Beethoven's middle-period string quartets.[8] Webster cites its relatively modest scale, the placement of the slow movement in the subdominant, and the conjuration of Fuxian second-species counterpoint in the third-movement trio in support of his thesis, and he suggests specific allusions to works by Mozart and Haydn. Of these, the most pronounced are the similarities between the variation theme of Beethoven's finale (and Webster notes that the presence of a variation finale is "the most obvious traditional feature in Op. 74") and the variation theme of the first movement of Haydn's Quartet, op. 76 no. 6 (see Examples 5.1a–b): "Both themes consist of continual repetitions of a motive; in each case this motive outlines a third, and its initial appearance connects the pitches $G^1$ and $B\flat^1$; each first half ends with a half cadence approached by contrary motion to an octave in the outer parts; both use dotted eighths and sixteenths . . . ; in both, the motivic statements are detached from each other . . . ; and in both, the harmonic structure of the first half is curiously nonfunctional, with various subdominants and tonics alternating in odd ways, and various chords placed unexpectedly in inversion rather than root position."[9]

Acknowledging Webster's work, Elaine Sisman has further developed the case for a compositional relationship between these two E♭-major quartets, arguing that Haydn's quartet is "'about' the idea of repetition," whereas Beethoven's "reflects a preoccupation with the idea of alternation." Sisman concludes that the finale of op. 74 "contributes another example of confronting the Classical models and, while overtly alluding to them, inventing its own decorum."[10] Again, there is no suggestion of slavish imitation or modeling here, but rather an essentially creative engagement with an earlier tradition. Perhaps the most obvious *dis*similarity between Haydn's theme and Beethoven's, beyond their differing formal designs, concerns the metrical play in op. 74, where at the outset the consistent denial of the downbeat in the lower three instruments and its light articulation in the first violin causes the perceived meter to shift by a half-measure. Sisman is unaware of any earlier variation theme that so "consistently obscures its downbeat" by these means;[11] yet Haydn's op. 76 no. 6 again offers a precedent, not in its variation theme but in the theme of its own sonata-form finale (see Example 5.2a). Here the three-eighth-note upbeat is again open to at least two other conflicting interpretations (Example 5.2b), though the second of these is perhaps less likely than the first. Nor is this the only respect in which

Haydn's finale theme seems to inform Beethoven's. As Example 5.2c illustrates, the I–ii–V7–I progression in Haydn's measures 1–4 supports a middleground upper-voice descent $B\flat^1$–$A\flat^1$–$G^1$, just as in Beethoven's measures 1–6; the surface melodic activity of both openings is also strikingly similar, as already noted by Webster.

It is to this opening portion of their themes that both composers return at the conclusion of their respective finales, in each case transferring the top voice up from the one-line to the two-line octave (Examples 5.3a–b). Although Beethoven set this concluding thematic reference in octaves, Haydn employed a tonic pedal, above which there is a momentary inflection to the subdominant in measures 160–61 (moreover, the *sforzandi* in these and the subsequent measure momentarily place the theme in yet another ambiguous metrical setting). The tendency to slip toward the subdominant is one that colors the first movement of op. 74 very strongly, from the very first bar of the slow introduction onward; thus it is striking to find that Haydn made a similar move in his opening variation theme: in measures 21–22, which correspond to measures 5–6 of the A section of the theme, what there had been a straightforward unfolding of the tonic triad through voice exchange in the outer instruments is now inflected heavily toward the subdominant, particularly through the prominent E♭–D♭ movement in the cello part; Examples 5.3c–d illustrate the similarity to the opening of op. 74, where E♭–D♭ is heard in both outer voices of the texture.

In fact, the role in op. 74 of an intrusive D♭ extends well beyond the first movement to comprehend the entire quartet.[12] One of its most bizarre appearances occurs in the slow movement, which is itself in the subdominant key and moves to its own subdominant—D♭ major—for the central episode (mm. 87–102). The transition passage leading from this episode back to the tonic key and to the second "variation" of the main theme (mm. 115ff.) is marked by a sudden breakdown in melodic and rhythmic flow: the music hesitates over a parallel succession of 6/3 harmonies with the ($E\flat^2$)–$D\flat^2$–$C^2$ in the upper voice before all four instruments take up the latter two pitches in *fortissimo* octaves. It is a disturbing moment, as brief as it is powerful, and unlike anything else in the movement: if there is a parallel at all, it is to be found in the first movement, at measures 88–89, where D♭–C "sets off a celebration of sorts," as Richard Kramer has put it in a discussion of op. 74 that, in contrast to the views cited above, stresses the forward-looking tendency of the work. Kramer finds that "from the skewed harmonic rhythm of its opening measures, its narrative unfolds in a language beyond convention—or rather, the signs of convention are consumed in a new poetics."[13] And yet a more distant precursor, not directly of the octaves but of the 6/3 harmonies from which they spring, is to be found once again in the opening theme of Haydn's quartet, at measures 9–10, where D♭ occurs for the first time (Examples 5.4a–b).

If the allusion to Haydn's quartet is persuasive in this instance, then Beethoven's endeavor seemingly involves a grotesque distortion or inflation of its innocuous source material.[14] And something of the grotesque, in the dictionary sense of "figures or designs characterized by comic distortion or exaggeration,"[15] may also be said to in-

*Example 5.1a.* Haydn, op. 76 no. 6, I, theme.

*Example 5.1b.* Beethoven, op. 74, IV, theme.

*Example 5.2a.* Haydn, op. 76 no. 6, IV.

*Example 5.2b.* cf. Ex. 5.2a.

*Example 5.2c.* Haydn, op. 76 no. 6, IV; Beethoven, op. 74, IV.

*Example 5.3a.* Haydn, op. 76 no. 6, IV, mm. 154–end.

*Example 5.3b.* Beethoven, op. 74, IV, mm. 185–88.

*Example 5.3c.* Haydn, op. 76 no. 6, I, mm. 9–27.

*Example 5.3d.* Beethoven, op. 74, I, mm. 1–9.

*Example 5.4a.* Haydn, op. 76 no. 6, I, mm. 9–18.

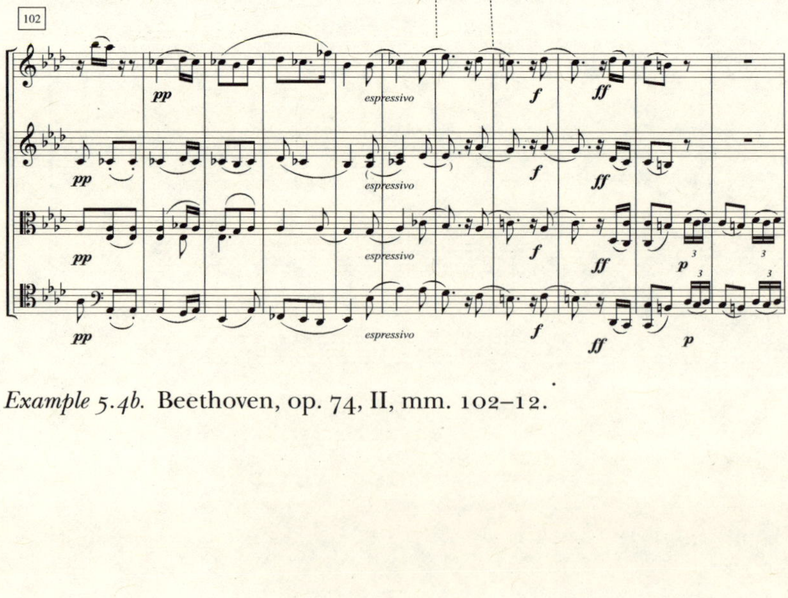


*Example 5.4b.* Beethoven, op. 74, II, mm. 102–12.

here in the third-movement trio of op. 74, for which Haydn's op. 76 no. 6 again provides a provocative context. In the Trio (called "Alternativo"), Haydn almost trumped Beethoven himself in finding his base material in a fundamental element of the tonal language, namely the descending and ascending scale that is treated as a cantus firmus, passing "logically and inexorably" through the quartet from bottom to top and top to bottom.[16] An analysis of Beethoven's trio theme combining voice-leading and metrical reduction helps to reveal the extent to which it behaves as a "comic distortion or exaggeration" of Haydn's more sedate model (Example 5.5).

## III

To the extent that the various intertextual references noted above seem convincing, they impose a duty to consider the nature or quality of the relationship of Beethoven's to Haydn's work. Why might Beethoven have chosen to make such references, and in what spirit was he doing so? By 1809 he certainly needed no compositional prop such as Mozart's K. 464 might have offered in the composition of his op. 18 no. 5, or the development section of the "Jupiter" in the composition of his own First Symphony, op. 21;[17] and in any case, large-scale apprentice-like "modeling" is an inappropriate way in which to conceptualize the piecemeal, fragmentary pickings that Beethoven found in Haydn's music on this occasion. Furthermore, to posit op. 74 as a straightforward act of homage also seems wide of the mark, given the seeming travesty obtaining in the case of the third-movement trio, and perhaps the outburst in the slow movement, also. How are we to read Beethoven's appropriation of Haydn here?

Let us return for a moment to the trio. Its contrapuntal texture has often been associated with the voluminous copying of examples of species counterpoint undertaken by Beethoven in 1809;[18] in the same connection, Webster suggests that the counterpoint may have been "Beethoven's reaction to the drudgery of beating musical sense into the noble head of the Archduke Rudolph."[19] But Hartmut Krones brings to bear an anecdote, related by Carl Czerny, that tells of Beethoven improvising upon

*Example* 5.5. Beethoven, op. 74, III, trio; Haydn, op. 76 no. 6, III, "Alternativo."

an inconsequential scale passage in a violin part from a Pleyel quartet he had heard performed at the home of Prince Lobkowitz (the dedicatee of op. 74) in 1808 or 1809.[20] For present purposes, the literal veracity of the anecdote is less important than its function as a reminder of Beethoven's ability, acknowledged elsewhere by Czerny, to build elaborate and extensive improvisations on the most unpromising material, often just "a few insignificant notes."[21] With this in mind, the quality of Beethoven's use of Haydn's op. 76 no. 6 in his own op. 74 might best be described as improvisatory: the exploding of Haydn's "Alternativo" cantus firmus, as of the dyad D♭–C; the reworking of the motivic substance of the variation theme; the exaggeration of metrical ambivalence at the beginning of the finale; one can imagine all these forming under Beethoven's fingers at the keyboard during one of those reluctant, spontaneous improvisations of the kind recalled by Czerny.

"Improvisation," whether conducted physically (in sketching on paper, as well as on an instrument) or purely mentally, is an inevitable early stage in the process of composition; it is "the initial free search for ideas, in the course of which a main idea is generated, and is subsequently elaborated into a composition."[22] And although the finished composition will typically suppress every trace of the process by which it comes to be what it is, one musical genre of Beethoven's day was distinguished precisely by its foregrounding of the appearance of having been spontaneously improvised, or of "narrating" its own composition, even if that appearance was the result of considerable compositional artifice: the free fantasia.[23] As already noted, the 1811 *AMZ* review of op. 74 had already likened the first movement to a free fantasia. Such a view was not uncommon, being symptomatic of what Peter Schleuning has described as the disappearance around the beginning of the nineteenth century of a "distinction between the main corpus of the standard genres and the 'breakaway' genre of the free fantasia";[24] even the first movement of the *Eroica* had been described in the *AMZ* as "in reality a daring and wild fantasia designed on a very large scale."[25] Such descriptions were not always approbative; rather, the degree of compositional license permitted in the free fantasia was seen as a potential threat to order and decorum if allowed to spread to other genres. Thus Amadeus Wendt, writing in the *AMZ* in 1815, could claim that "many works of Beethoven, for example, various symphonies and sonatas of his, can only be understood and evaluated as *musical fantasies*"; and, Wendt claimed, in contributing to a trend "*to make musical fantasy dominant in the domain of the world of notes,*" Beethoven "has caused great damage, and his powerful spirit has manifested a very detrimental influence upon the art" [italics mine].[26]

The "damage" might be said to have begun with Beethoven's two piano sonatas op. 27, published in 1802 with the title "Sonata quasi una fantasia."[27] The fantasia-like elements are well known and include, in each work, the use of unconventional movement sequences, including the avoidance of a sonata-form first movement; the use of unconventional formal types; the use (particularly in op. 27 no. 1) of frequent tempo changes; and the attenuation of the independence of constituent movements through the use of *attacca* directions. This last element addresses one of the most obvious conflicts between the sonata and fantasia genres, namely the typical multimovement design of the former and the single-movement design of the latter. On the other hand, within its single-movement design the fantasia could tolerate extreme sectional contrast, but such contrast in the sonata was normally achieved between rather than within movements. *Contrast* here refers to more parameters than just tonality, though tonality is a key element. As Robert Winter has noted of the tonal design of the seven-movement String Quartet in C♯ Minor, op. 131, "[A] single movement moving from its tonic of C♯ minor through D . . . A . . . E . . . G♯ . . . and finally back to the tonic would scarcely have raised an eyebrow among Beethoven's musical forebears. Similarly, a multi-movement work restricted to the tonic and subdominant was commonplace."[28] In op. 131 Beethoven reversed "these two sets of relationships," creating thereby "a work which is neither, strictly speaking, one long movement nor a succession of independent movements."[29]

A little-remarked aspect of the op. 27 sonatas is that they exemplify the extremes of tonal contrast or continuity adumbrated here by Winter. The three movements of op. 27 no. 2 share C♯ as their tonic: tonal contrast is supplanted by modal contrast, with the central movement cast in the parallel major (notated as D♭). This scheme is by no means uncommon for Beethoven: indeed, all his multimovement works in E (op. 14 no. 1, op. 59 no. 2, op. 90, and op. 109) adhere to it, as do many others (for example, op. 9 nos. 2 and 3, op. 10 no. 3, op. 12 no. 2, op. 18 no. 4, op. 23, op. 26, op. 28, op. 102 no. 2, and op. 111). The example of op. 27 no. 1 is more unusual. Throughout his career, Beethoven remained observant of the convention that, in the case of four-movement works, only one movement—usually the slow movement—would be in a key other than the tonic.[30] But in op. 27 no. 1 he opted for the maximum degree of tonal contrast available to him, by placing both inner movements in nontonic keys to give the overall scheme E♭–c/C–A♭–E♭. The *attacca* directions function to promote the sense of a series of tonally contrasted sections within a single, continuous movement in E♭.

Although the tendency toward maximal tonal contrast between movements finds its culmination in the late quartets, and specifically in op. 131, it is exceedingly rare prior to that stage. Indeed, op. 27 no. 1 appears to have only two four-movement, three-tonic successors, each in the same key, E♭ major. The earlier of them, the Piano Trio op. 70 no. 2, adopts the same key scheme as the sonata (whereas its companion piece, the "Ghost" Trio, op. 70 no. 1, parallels the single-tonic scheme of op. 27 no. 2); moreover, in opening with a slow introduction that returns unexpectedly before the close of the first movement, as well as in eschewing a genuine slow movement, it exhibits two other characteristics of the "quasi una fantasia" experiment of op. 27. And the second successor to op. 27 no. 1 is none other than op. 74. Beethoven again adopted the same complex of keys as in the sonata and the trio, though in op. 74 the two nontonics are reversed: the slow movement in A♭ is succeeded by the Scherzo and trio in C minor-major. The movement sequence is more conventional than that in the sonata or the trio, but the work again begins with slow music (the slow introduction is obviously indebted to the fantasia), and the third and fourth movements are linked by an *attacca,* made more dramatic by the tonally open ending of the third movement. Some listeners may even be disposed to hear in the final three repeated chords of the slow movement a preparation in augmentation for the anacrusis of the Scherzo: all the more so, perhaps, in view of the fact that at one stage in sketching op. 74 Beethoven pondered an *attacca* between these two movements also.[31]

The foregoing is meant to suggest that the comparison made between the first movement of op. 74 and the free fantasia in the 1811 *AMZ* may be grounded in the quartet's belonging to a small group of "private" works in E♭ in which Beethoven revisited the op. 27 project. And to those works already mentioned may be added another: the Piano Sonata in E♭, op. 31 no. 3. Although not exhibiting the three-key scheme of op. 27 no. 1, op. 70 no. 2, and op. 74, this four-movement sonata shares with the piano trio the characteristic of having no real slow movement (see Tables 5.1 and 5.2). Moreover (and notwithstanding its Allegro marking), the first movement is heavily characterized by a ruminative, brooding quality, born of the opening bars, that is suggestive of fantasia.[32] This first movement, like those of op. 27 no. 1 and op. 70 no. 2, is thus relatively muted compared to the hard-hitting finale, cast either as a sonata rondo (op. 27 no. 1) or as a substantial sonata form (op. 31 no. 3, op. 70 no. 2). Herein lies a significant distinction between these three works and op. 74, whose relatively lightweight variation finale—recall Marx's sense of surprise—

*Table 5.1.*

| *Op. 27 no. 1* | *Op. 31 no. 3* | *Op. 70 no. 2* | *Op. 74* |
|---|---|---|---|
| Andante—Allegro —Andante | Allegro | Poco sostenuto— Allegro ma non troppo | Poco Adagio—Allegro |
| Allegro molto e vivace | Scherzo: Allegretto vivace | Allegretto | Adagio ma non troppo |
| Adagio con espressione | Menuetto: Moderato e grazioso | Allegretto ma non troppo | Presto—Più presto quasi prestissimo—Presto |
| Allegro vivace | Presto con fuoco | Allegro | Allegretto—un poco più vivace—Allegro |

*Table 5.2.*

| *Op. 27 no. 1* | *Op. 31 no. 3* | *Op. 70 no. 2* | *Op. 74* |
|---|---|---|---|
| E♭–C–E♭ | E♭ | E♭ | E♭ |
| c–C | A♭ | C–c | A♭ |
| A♭ | E♭ | A♭ | c–C–c |
| E♭ | E♭ | E♭ | E♭ |

seems almost incongruous following the massive and violent five-part movement of which it functions as the outcome. But incongruity and the juxtaposition of radical contrasts—no less between the serene *cantabile* of the slow movement and the Scherzo, as between Scherzo and finale—is rather the point if, as was more apparent in the nineteenth century than in the twentieth, we hear op. 74 as a "quartetto quasi una fantasia."

## IV

The year 1809, in which op. 74 was composed, seems in any case to bear witness to what Elaine Sisman calls "Beethoven's renewed preoccupation with the idea of *fantasia*." By *fantasia* she is careful to understand not simply a musical genre but "a complex of related principles," also. In particular, she links *fantasia* with the "characteristic," through which she reads the three piano sonatas of 1809: op. 78 in F♯, op. 79 in G, and op. 81a in E♭ ("Das Lebewohl").[33] Two other works of this year openly proclaim their generic allegiance: around April 1809 Beethoven completed the Choral Fantasia, op. 80, by composing its solo piano introduction, which he had improvised at the premiere given during the marathon benefit concert of December 22, 1808. Elements of another fantasia improvised on that notorious occasion may have been incorporated into the Fantasia, op. 77, on which Beethoven worked in the autumn of 1809, probably while finalizing op. 74.[34] Like the quartet, the fantasia ends with a theme and variations; and in scrutinizing Beethoven's remarks on improvisation found in the sketchbook of 1807–8, Sisman reads in them the suggestion "that feelings were the compositional origin of a fantasy, variations the end point."[35] Similarly, Annette Richards has interpreted op. 77 as "enact[ing] the process of *Fantasieren* as the term was used by Haydn, not simply as an evocation of wandering and extra licence but as the performance of the process of invention, the pre-compositional search for ideas upon which the musical discourse will eventually elaborate."[36]

String quartet, the most elevated instrumental medium of late-eighteenth-century music and thus the pinnacle of compositional artifice, and fantasia, representing the spontaneous outpouring of intimate feeling unmediated by ratiocination, would seem to be the most antithetical of musical genres.[37] Yet the slow movement of Haydn's op. 76 no. 6 is a fantasia beginning and ending in B major (the key of Beethoven's op. 77 variations), its genre title supplied in the score by the composer.[38] There is thus a certain irony in the fact that this seems to be the only movement in op. 76 no. 6 from which Beethoven appears not to have drawn in op. 74. Yet there *is* a sense in which Haydn's fantasia is conjured in Beethoven's music, albeit a hardly obvious one. Sisman reminds us that *fantasia* connotes "a complex of related principles as well as a musical genre."[39] In making this point, she draws particularly on Quintilian's codification of rhetoric, in which *fantasia* connotes a figure whereby "things absent are presented to our imagination with such extreme vividness that they seem actually to be before our very eyes."[40] The slow movement of op. 76 no. 6 does something very similar, in that it vividly brings before our ears another slow movement from the same set of quartets: the second movement—in E♭ major!—of the "Sunrise" Quartet, op. 76 no. 4 (see Examples 5.6a–b).[41] If anything, the allusion of the one movement to the other is even more audible at their conclusions (Examples 5.6c–d). Whereas op. 76 no. 6 ends poised over the tonic pedal reached at m. 106, the corresponding pedal E♭ in op. 76 no. 4 is embellished by its lower neighbor, D, and D is itself so embellished, resulting in a momentary impression of "V7/G♭" on the second beat of measures 70 and 72.

This movement from E♭ to "D♭" and back through the mediating D may be compared with the last appearances of the troublesome D♭ in the finale of op. 74. There, in the coda, D♭ twice functions as the bass of a chromatic neighboring harmony to the tonic, in a gesture that strongly recalls Haydn's op. 76 no. 4 (Examples 5.7a–b). Prior to this, in Variation 6, Haydn's ending is again recalled when the tonic pedal underlying the first half lurches down to a D♭ pedal after the double bar; the tonic is regained equally peremptorily by the return to E♭ via D, supporting chord V6/5, in measure 138 (Example 5.7c). Finally, Example 7d reveals how the activity of the cello around E♭–D♭–D–E♭ in Variation 6 relates to that of the first violin in the slow introduction to the first movement, where the "maverick" D♭, as I have called it, originates.[42]

The distinct aptness of Haydn's title for the slow movement of op. 76 no. 6 will now be evident. But if the "absent thing" evoked by that movement is the corresponding movement from op. 76 no. 4, Beethoven reverses the order of fantasy, making the op. 76 no. 4 movement the "fantasia" through which the slow movement of op. 76 no. 6 is conjured in his own op. 74. Finally, the idea may be extended to both quartets as wholes: Beethoven's is a "quartetto quasi una fantasia" in the further sense that it evokes the earlier master's opus.

## V

To return to the fantasia as a musical genre or style: the most straightforwardly fantasia-like music in op. 74 is surely that of the chromatic and fragmented slow introduction. In discussing the corresponding part of the "Lebewohl" sonata, Sisman is able to stress the richly signifying gestures—horn fifths, the characteristic "lamento" descending bass, the rising dotted figure—by means of which absence, loss, and memory are "figured."[43] The op. 74 introduction seems largely to eschew any such means, although for Marx its tendency to slip toward the subdominant was an important element in creating and preserving the melancholic *Stimmung* that he heard as basic to the movement. That tendency is of course basic to the initial four-note motive E♭$^2$–G$^1$–A♭$^1$–D♭$^2$, which in Marx's reading functions effectively as a vital *fantasia* conjuring precisely the image of an absence: for him, this motif was an expression of the most intimate feeling, its interrogatory form and subdominant orientation signifying a melancholy-laden reminiscence. Indeed, he even went so far as to suggest an imaginary distant lover's "Denkest du mein?" as a kind of suppressed accompanying text, similar to the "Le-be-wohl" that Beethoven himself supplied at the beginning of op. 81a.[44]

We know, of course, the identity of the departing person to whom Beethoven's "Lebewohl" was addressed: the autograph manuscript identifies Archduke Rudolph, and even the date of his departure (May 4, 1809) from Vienna.[45] Such is not the case with op. 74, and neither is there any prima facie reason to accept Marx's hermeneutic reading as binding: we might simply dismiss it as a romantic fantasy of the most trivial kind. But the archduke's was not the only departure from Vienna in May 1809. On the 31st, some four weeks after Rudolph's temporary flight from the capital, Haydn died, leaving Vienna and Beethoven forever. If Beethoven's op. 74 is a "fantasia" on Haydn's op. 76 no. 6, the "absent thing" that it evokes is not merely the older composer's E♭ quartet, but Haydn himself—even, perhaps, the entire musical tradition that he had come to embody. Thus may we map Quintilian's understanding of *fantasia* onto another aspect of the generic tradition, namely the association of the fantasia with images of grief and sorrow: with the topic of lament. The tradition of the fantasia as lament or tombeau has been discussed by Schleuning, who cites especially C. P. E. Bach's Fantasia in B♭, Wq. 61 (1787), in which a polonaise by the composer's deceased brother Wilhelm Friedemann is twice quoted. This makes of C. P. E. Bach's work what Schleuning calls a "clear case of an intimate fantasia-tombeau [continuing] the tradition of veiled secrecy in the fantasia."[46]

It is extraordinary—though perhaps not insignificant—that we have no verbal record of Beethoven's reaction to Haydn's death. Richard Kramer, pondering Beethoven's (re)turn to strict counterpoint in 1809, reasons that the death, like that of Albrechtsberger previously, on March 7, "cannot have failed to have touched Beethoven deeply. One may imagine that a sense of loss and of impending isolation . . . might have been tempered by a balancing sense of liberation, for here were the two eminent witnesses who could testify to Beethoven's halting struggle to ascend the Fuxian ladder."[47] Kramer notes, too, Beethoven's request, in a letter to Breitkopf & Härtel dated July 26, 1809, for scores by Haydn, Mozart, J. S. Bach, C. P. E. Bach, and others, and relates this request to the thesis that Beethoven was considering his position in the apostolic succession. In the end, op. 74 is for Kramer, as for Philip Radcliffe, a work that, "in its quiet way . . . signals ahead to later narratives."[48] But it is also a work that engages profoundly with its heritage, invoking and confronting the mature Haydn head-on, in the substance of the final work of that composer's last completed quartet opus: an opus published, moreover, in 1799, when Beethoven was hard at work on his own first set of quartets.

What ultimately remains elusive is the exact nature of that confrontation. Kramer's formulation inevitably calls to mind the Bloomian "anxiety of influence," and with it the associated figure of the "strong poet" who "achieve[s] strength by confronting the anxiety of influence, by wrestling with [his] great precursors." Bloom's observation that "freedom [of meaning in a poem] is wholly illusory unless it is achieved against a prior plenitude of meaning, which is tradition, and so also against

*Example 5.6a.* Haydn, op. 76 no. 6, II, mm. 1–14.

*Example 5.6b.* Haydn, op. 76 no. 4, II, mm. 1–14.

*Example 5.6c.* Haydn, op. 76 no. 6, II, mm. 106–end.

*Example 5.6d.* Haydn, op. 76 no. 4, II, mm. 69–end.

*Example 5.7a.* Beethoven, op. 74, IV, mm. 161–66.

*Example 5.7b.* Haydn, op. 76 no. 4, II: mm. 71–74.

*Example 5.7c.* Beethoven, op. 74, IV: mm. 121–44.

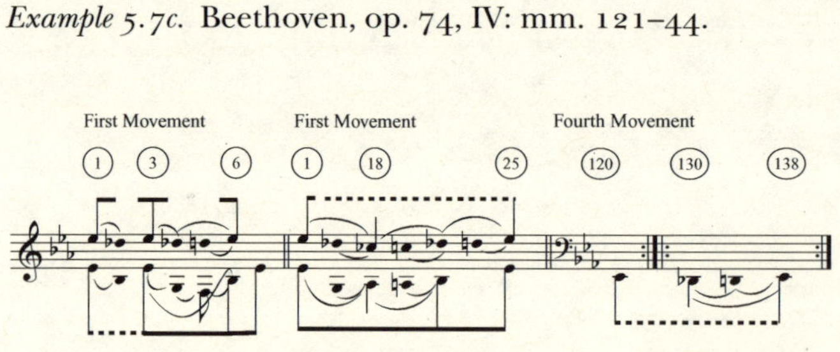


*Example 5.7d.* Beethoven, op. 74, I and IV.

language," is also pertinent.[49] *Ave atque vale:* Was Beethoven come to bury Haydn, not to praise him?[50] "Quartetto quasi una fantasia," certainly; but we may also come to hear op. 74 as Beethoven's "Lebewohl" Quartet, telling of farewell and absence—but in this case, of no earthly return.

## Notes

1. The chapter title refers to Count Waldstein's famous prediction that on going to Vienna in 1792 Beethoven would receive "Mozarts Geist aus Haydns Händen"; for a facsimile, see *Ludwig van Beethovens Stammbuch,* ed. Hans Gerstinger (Bielefeld: Velhagen and Klasing, 1927), fol. 12, and p. 16 in the accompanying text volume.

2. *AMZ* 13 (1811), cols 349–51; repr. in *Ludwig van Beethoven: Die Werke im Spiegel seiner Zeit,* ed. Stefan Kunze (Laaber: Laaber Verlag, 1987), 207–9.

3. Wilhelm von Lenz, *Beethoven et ses trois styles* (St Petersburg: Bernard, 1852), 86, 152–53.

4. Ibid., 86. In his slightly later *Beethoven: Eine Kunststudie* (Kassel, 1855–60), von Lenz seems curiously to have mistaken the date of composition of op. 74, believing that it lay between op. 18 and op. 59 and thus marked a transition between the impersonal style of the first and the more personal style of the second period. On the question of Beethoven's style periods, see James Webster, "The Concept of Beethoven's 'Early' Period in the Context of Periodizations in General," *Beethoven Forum* 3 (1994): 1–27.

5. Adolf Bernhard Marx, *Ludwig van Beethoven: Leben und Schaffen,* vol. 2 (Berlin: Otto Janke, 1863), 310–17, from which the paraphrases in the following paragraph are also taken.

6. Theodor Helm, *Beethoven's Streichquartette. Versuch einer technischen Analyse dieser Werke im Zusammenhange mit ihrem geistigen Gehalt* (Leipzig: E. W. Fritzsch, 1885); see the foreword, esp. pp. v–vi. Margaret Notley has discussed Helm's account of the slow movement of op. 74 in "Late Nineteenth-Century Chamber Music and the Cult of the Classical Adagio," *19th-Century Music* 23 (1999): 40–41.

7. Walter Riezler, *Beethoven,* trans. G. D. H. Pidcock (London: Forrester, 1938; orig. Berlin: Atlantis, 1936), 173; Philip Radcliffe, *Beethoven's String Quartets* (London: Hutchinson, 1965), 82, 89; Joseph Kerman, *The Beethoven Quartets* (London: Oxford University Press, 1967), 156; Paul Griffiths, *The String Quartet* (London: Thames and Hudson, 1983), 92; Maynard Solomon, *Beethoven* (London: Cassell, 1977), 210; Robert Winter and Robert Martin, eds., *The Beethoven Quartet Companion* (Berkeley: University of California Press, 1994), 197; Joseph Kerman and Alan Tyson, "Beethoven, Ludwig van," in *The New Grove Dictionary of Music and Musicians,* ed. Stanley Sadie, 20 vols. (London: Macmillan, 1980), ii, 384, rev. Scott G. Burnham in *The New Grove Dictionary of Music and Musicians,* second edition (London: Macmillan, 2001), iii, 102. A more Marx-influenced interpretation may be found, however, in Joseph de Marliave, *Beethoven's Quartets,* trans. Hilda Andrews (Oxford: Oxford University Press, 1928), where op. 74 is identified as "the key to the soul of Beethoven" (p. 152).

8. James Webster, "Traditional Elements in Beethoven's Middle-Period String Quartets," in *Beethoven, Performers, and Critics: The International Beethoven Congress, Detroit, 1977,* ed. Robert Winter and Bruce Carr (Detroit: Wayne State University Press, 1980), 94–133.

9. Ibid., 122–23.

10. Elaine R. Sisman, *Haydn and the Classical Variation* (Cambridge, Mass.: Harvard University Press, 1993), 246.

11. Ibid., 242.

12. See Nicholas Marston, "Analysing Variations: The Finale of Beethoven's String Quartet Op. 74," *Music Analysis* 8 (1989): 318–20.

13. Richard Kramer, "*Gradus ad Parnassum:* Beethoven, Schubert, and the Romance of Counterpoint," *19th Century Music* 11 (1987): 113.

14. William Kinderman has noted Beethoven's recourse to travesty in some of the Diabelli Variations: see his *Beethoven's Diabelli Variations* (Oxford: Clarendon Press, 1987), 68–75, and especially 70.

15. See *The Oxford English Dictionary,* 2nd edition, ed. J. A. Simpson and E. S. C. Weiner (Oxford: Clarendon Press, 1989), vi, 874, A. 1. b.

16. Sisman, *Haydn,* 184.

17. Jeremy Yudkin, "Beethoven's 'Mozart' Quartet," *Journal of the American Musicological Society* 45 (1992): 30–74; Carl Schachter, "Mozart's Last and Beethoven's First: Echoes of K. 551 in the First Movement of Opus 21," in *Mozart Studies,* ed. Cliff Eisen (Oxford: Clarendon Press, 1991), 227–51.

18. See, for example, Kerman, *The Beethoven Quartets,* 165–66. On the counterpoint transcriptions, see Gustav Nottebohm, "Generalbass und Compositionslehre betreffende Handschriften Beethoven's und J. R. v. Seyfried's Buch 'Ludwig van Beethoven's Studien im Generalbasse, Contrapuncte' u. s. w.," in *Beethoveniana: Aufsätze und Mittheilungen* (Leipzig: Peters, 1872), 154–203. Landsberg 5, the sketchbook containing all the known sketches for op. 74, also contains numerous copyings from theoretical sources, including Fux, Kirnberger, and Albrechtsberger: see *Ludwig van Beethoven: Ein Skizzenbuch aus dem Jahre 1809 (Landsberg 5),* ed. Clemens Brenneis, 2 vols. (Bonn: Beethoven-Haus, 1993).

19. Webster, "Traditional elements," 122.

20. Hartmut Krones, "Streichquartett Es-Dur, 'Harfenquartett' Op. 74," in *Beethoven: Interpretationen seiner Werke,* ed. Albrecht Riethmüller, Carl Dahlhaus, and Alexander L. Ringer, 2 vols. (Laaber: Laaber Verlag, 1994), i, 586–87, where the finale of Ignaz Pleyel's Quartet in G, op. 8 no. 2, is suggested as likely to be the work in question. For the original source, see Carl Czerny, *Erinnerungen aus meinem Leben,* ed. Walter Kolneder (Strasbourg: P. H. Heitz, 1968), 45–46.

21. Carl Czerny, *On the Proper Performance of All Beethoven's Works for the Piano,* ed. Paul Badura-Skoda (Vienna: Universal Edition, 1970), 15.

22. Annette Richards, *The Free Fantasia and the Musical Picturesque* (Cambridge: Cambridge University Press, 2001), 85, where may also be found a translation of Haydn's remarks on the role of *phantasieren* in his own compositional process.

23. Ibid. Richards discusses the "tension between apparent chaos and underlying order" in the fantasias of C. P. E. Bach: see pp. 34–72 (the quotation is from p. 48).

24. Peter Schleuning, *The Fantasia II: 18th to 20th Centuries,* trans. A. C. Howie (Cologne: Arno Volk Verlag, 1971), 15.

25. *AMZ* 7 (1804), col. 321, translated in Schleuning, *The Fantasia,* 15.

26. Amadeus Wendt, "Thoughts about Recent Musical Art, and van Beethoven's Music, Specifically His *Fidelio,*" trans. in Wayne M. Senner, Robin Wallace, and William Meredith, *The Critical Reception of Beethoven's Compositions by His German Contemporaries,* vol. 2 (Lincoln: University of Nebraska Press, 2001), 199, 200. Richardson, *The Free Fantasia,* 199, cites a similar assessment made by Gerber in 1817.

27. See Timothy Jones, *Beethoven: The "Moonlight" and Other Sonatas, Op. 27 and Op. 31* (Cambridge: Cambridge University Press, 1999).

28. Robert Winter, "Plans for the Structure of the String Quartet in C Sharp Minor, Op. 131," in *Beethoven Studies 2,* ed. Alan Tyson (London: Oxford University Press, 1977), 135.

29. Ibid., 134.

30. The Seventh Symphony provides a double exception, in that the slow movement is in the tonic *minor* and the Scherzo in the flat submediant.

31. I have dealt with the aspect of movement-to-movement continuity in the op. 74 sketches in Landsberg 5 in my "Landsberg 5 and Future Prospects for the *Skizzenausgabe,*" *Beethoven Forum* 6 (1998): 207–33, esp. 218–20.

32. The relevance of the fantasia topic to the corresponding movement of op. 31 no. 2 is self-evident.

33. Elaine Sisman, "After the Heroic Style: *Fantasia* and the 'Characteristic' Sonatas of 1809," *Beethoven Forum* 6 (1998): 67, 68.

34. Sketches for all these works are contained in Landsberg 5. In "Landsberg 5 and Future Prospects," I have suggested that a projected C-minor sonata, which itself draws heavily on fantasia style, may have been connected with the genesis of op. 74: see 214–17.

35. Sisman, "After the Heroic Style," 75–76. For a photograph of the sketchleaf (Bonn, *Mh* 75) discussed there and in Sisman's n19, see Alan Tyson, "The Home-Made Sketchbook of 1807–08," *Beethoven-Jahrbuch, Jahrgang 1978/1981,* ed. Martin Staehelin (Bonn: Beethoven-Haus, 1983), 199.

36. Richards, *The Free Fantasia,* 198.

37. On the status of the quartet, see Heinrich Christoph Koch, *Musikalisches Lexikon* (Frankfurt am Main: August Hermann der Jüngere, 1802), cols. 1209–10; also Leonard G. Ratner, *Classic Music: Expression, Form, and Style* (New York: Schirmer, 1980), 125–28, including a translation of Koch's article.

38. For a discussion of this movement see Sisman, *Haydn,* 181–83.

39. Sisman, "After the Heroic Style," 68.

40. Quintilian, *Institutio oratoria,* trans. H. E. Butler (Cambridge, Mass.: Harvard University Press, 1920), VI. ii. 29; translation quoted from Sisman, "Pathos and the Pathétique: Rhetorical Stance in Beethoven's C-minor Sonata, Op. 13," *Beethoven Forum* 3 (1994): 84.

41. Although the slow movement of op. 76 no. 4 is not given the title "fantasia," it shares with that of op. 76 no. 6 the characteristic of frequent repetition, in various keys, of its opening idea. Sisman (*Haydn,* 183) has identified such repetitions as "one important strand of the capriccio-fantasia tradition in the later eighteenth century." Other fantasia-like elements in the op. 76 no. 4 slow movement are self-evident.

42. Marston, "Analysing Variations," 318; see also p. 320, Ex. 11 for the source of Ex. 5.7d above.

43. Sisman, "After the Heroic Style," 83–90.

44. Marx, *Leben und Schaffen,* 312.

45. Kinsky-Halm, 216. For a reproduction of the autograph title page, see Joseph Schmidt-Görg and Hans Schmidt eds., *Ludwig van Beethoven* (Bonn, 1974), 174.

46. Schleuning, *The Fantasia,* 12. Also significant in this connection is C. P. E. Bach's *Abschied von meinem Silbermannischen Claviere in einem Rondo,* discussed by Richards, *The Free Fantasia,* 152–55, and Sisman, "After the Heroic Style," 85.

47. Kramer, "*Gradus ad Parnassum,*" 112.

48. Ibid., 113. Daniel Gregory Mason, too, felt that "the opening movement of Opus 74 already shows [Beethoven] feeling out toward certain of [the late quartets'] most characteristic tendencies:" *The Quartets of Beethoven* (New York: Oxford University Press, 1947), 128. For Beethoven's letter of July 26, see *Ludwig van Beethoven: Briefwechsel; Gesamtausgabe,* ed. Sieghard Brandenburg, ii (Munich: Henle, 1996), no. 392.

49. The quotation from Bloom ["The Breaking of Form," in *Deconstruction and Criticism* (New York: Continuum, 1979), 3] and those preceding it are taken from Kevin Korsyn, "Towards a New Poetics of Musical Influence," *Music Analysis* 10 (1991): 9, 10.

50. Cf. *The Poems of Catullus,* ed. Guy Lee (Oxford: Clarendon Press, 1990), no. CI, 138–41; William Shakespeare, *Julius Caesar,* iii. 2. 80.

CHAPTER SIX

# Aspects of the Genesis of Beethoven's String Quartet in F Minor, Op. 95

*Seow-Chin Ong*

This study of Beethoven's String Quartet in F Minor, op. 95, stems from a first-hand examination of all the known sketch sources for the work and the autograph score. My intent here, however, is not to be comprehensive, but to concentrate on the following specific topics: (a) the chronology and the contents of the sketch sources; (b) the draft of the first movement; and (c) the date of the autograph. Since the composition of the quartet was influenced to some extent by Beethoven's work on the Incidental Music to Goethe's *Egmont,* op. 84, completed just before the composer turned his attention to op. 95, I preface my discussion of the quartet sources with an investigation into the musical affinities between these two very unusual major works.

## I. *Egmont* and the Quartet

The Incidental Music to *Egmont* and op. 95, both were composed in the uncommon key of F minor and completed in close succession in the same year, 1810. These surface details about the two works point to deeper bonds between them, the most striking of which concerns D major, the submediant.

As the key of sizable portions of the music, D major characterizes the second movement of the quartet, significant sections of the two trios of the quartet's third movement, and the penultimate movement of the *Egmont* music. The *Egmont* example is the exclusively orchestral section in the Melodrama that accompanies Liberty's appearance toward the end of the tragedy. Assuming the likeness of Klärchen (Egmont's beloved, who had only recently committed suicide), Liberty arrives in the form of a radiant apparition to the imprisoned Egmont as he sleeps in his cell, awaiting execution.[1] She has come to tell him, as she crowns him with a laurel wreath, that his people will be liberated from their Spanish warlords after his death. Accordingly, then, her music ends with a march, but one with a distinctly gentle touch, characterized in part by delicate arpeggio pizzicati.

The contrast between Liberty's D major in the Melodrama and the ensuing F-major Siegessymphonie is one of rarefied disjuncture defining two different planes of activity, one spiritual and the other more earthly. This contrast is not unlike the effect Beethoven achieved by placing a quietly intense D-major slow movement between two abrasive and highly dramatic F-minor fast movements in the quartet. For despite the fugato breakdown and crisis, identified by Joseph Kerman, in the op. 95 slow movement,[2] this music opens an interior world separating the opening Allegro from the Scherzo.[3]

Elsewhere in the two works, in striking instances in the second group—mm. 235–40 in the recapitulation of the *Egmont* overture, and mm. 49–50 of the op. 95/I exposition—D major emerges suddenly out of D♭ major without any forewarning and, as a result, becomes spotlighted with unusual clarity, even luminosity. Invariably, D major lingers only briefly, like a fleeting apparition, before D♭ major takes hold again. Additional semitone shifts in the two works, which always involve keys closely allied to D, are managed just as abruptly to give a similar expressive effect. These passages may be quickly adumbrated as follows. In the quartet first movement, octaves of A♭, C♯, and F♯ give way in an instant to powerful scales in A major, D major, and G minor in mm. 37–38, 107–8, and 117–18, respectively. In the overture, a short passage in A major in the exposition's second group breaks through the prevailing A♭-major expanse for a brief moment in mm. 92–97, serving as the counterpart to the similar D-major passage in the recapitulation's second group.

We should also mention a couple of other similarities between overture and quartet that are not connected with D major but are, as Kerman has observed,[4] early examples of new procedures. The first is the characterization of the second thematic group in the overture's recapitulation, and the exposition and recapitulation of the quartet first movement, by the submediant major (D♭). Beethoven showed an abiding affinity for that scale degree in the second groups of the first and last movements of large-scale minor-mode cyclic compositions composed after *Egmont* and op. 95. The second is the switch of mode from tonic minor to major at the very end of each work: in *Egmont*'s Siegessymphonie, and in the coda of the quartet finale. Although such a maneuver is not unusual in Beethoven's C-minor works, after *Egmont* and op. 95 it became more common for him to highlight the tonic major in the first or last movement of large-scale minor-mode works that are *not* in C minor.[5]

The most famous precedent for a dramatic change of mode within the composer's oeuvre comes, of course, in the finale of the Fifth Symphony, which Kerman sees as the culmination of several earlier tendencies for "works in C minor to break into C major."[6] In the *Egmont* and op. 95 codas, the shift of mode assumes a surreal quality that is new in Beethoven's handling of what Kerman has called the "minor-major crux."[7] The change of mode is now accomplished very quickly and abruptly, with only the barest of preparations. In contrast to the careful and protracted way in which the minor-to-major resolution is prepared by means of a long, suspenseful link in the last movement of the Fifth Symphony, the Siegessymphonie in *Egmont* negates the minor mode almost in an instant. As for the coda of the quartet finale, music irrepressible in its lightning wit is placed in direct opposition to the agitato that precedes it.[8] (Even with mitigation by the tierce de Picardie in the *ppp* last chord of this agitato, the effect of the mode change in the coda is disruptive and striking.) With the *Egmont* and the op. 95 finale codas, Beethoven scarcely prepared his audience for impending large-scale mode changes. The aesthetic here is not just one of negation but of confrontation, as well—to be sure, more in the quartet coda than in the Siegessymphonie, where the overflowing jubilation still smacks of the headiness of the finale of the Fifth Symphony. The aesthetic of negation and confrontation, not limited to change of mode within the same movement of a piece, is encountered again and again in the late works, especially the last quartets.

A further parallel between the *Egmont* overture and the op. 95 first movement concerns what James Hepokoski has called the "nonresolving recapitulation," a term that suggests a failure of the recapitulation to accomplish its "generic mission of tonal closure."[9] Closure, in Hepokoski's view, is effected by a perfect authentic cadence in the tonic, as secured by the secondary theme in the recapitulation. It corresponds to the similar closure in the exposition that the perfect authentic cadence in the contrasting key provides for the secondary theme.

As Hepokoski has shown, the recapitulation of the *Egmont* overture lacks such closure and therefore is delineated as nonresolving: the secondary theme, placed in D♭ major, has no perfect authentic cadence in F minor.[10] This D♭ major is subsequently clarified as the upper neighbor of the dominant of F, following which Beethoven launched the Siegessymphonie coda, where "the overture's initial F minor [is] both resolved and overturned in jubilant F-major cadences."[11] Indeed, the Siegessymphonie is full of such cadences.

The first movement of op. 95, too, features a nonresolving recapitulation. But the manner in which Beethoven finally resolved the initial F minor is very different from, and arguably more radical than, the example in *Egmont*. The secondary theme in the quartet recapitulation begins in D♭ major (its exposition key!) in m. 89 but changes almost immediately to F major, as if to correct a mistake. It ignores the tonic minor completely, in the interest of preserving its major modality. When it appears that tonic-minor resolution is finally going to happen at the start of the coda at m. 129 (m. 128 is poised with the requisite dominant harmony), the expectation is derailed by the violent and shocking entry of D♭ major in *subito fortissimo*. This extraordinary tonal sabotage kicks off an arpeggio passage of great vehemence, one marked by a string of diminished harmonies. In the midst of all this, Beethoven quickly slipped in the long-awaited F-minor resolution (mm. 137–38; see Example 6.1) but did not immediately sustain the tonic harmony as such.[12]

As if to compensate for this flippant way of handling the tonic resolution, the last measures of the movement present, in an exaggeratedly drawn-out manner, two perfect authentic cadences in succession, the second one stripped down to the dominant and the tonic in bare octaves.

If the similarities between *Egmont* and op. 95 described so far refer mainly to formal, tonal, harmonic, and aesthetic matters, some sketches in the Landsberg 11 sketchbook, SV 65[13] (Biblioteka Jagiellońska, Kraków), and the sketch miscellany called Grasnick 20a, SV 53 (Staatsbibliothek zu Berlin-Preußischer Kulturbesitz) reveal that the two works also share a thematic link, one that cannot be readily traced in the completed scores. Examples 6.2a, 6.2b, and 6.2c are three sketches that Beethoven made for Zwischenakt[14] III.

The sixteenth-note motive in these examples is similar to the principal motive of the first movement of op. 95.[15] The way that Beethoven treated it, in close sequence with chromatic inflections in both the Zwischenakt III sketches and the op. 95 first movement, is also similar, as a comparison of Examples 6.2a, 6.2b, and 6.2c with Example 6.3 shows, although the procedure in the quartet is much more intensely controlled.

*Example 6.1.* Op. 95/I, mm. 136–39.

*Example 6.2a.* Grasnick 20a, fol. 4v, sts. 12/13.

*Example 6.2b.* Landsberg 11, p. 28, sts. 12/13.

*Example 6.2c.* Landsberg 11, p. 28, sts. 14/15.

*Example 6.3.* Op. 95/I, mm. 75–81.

In the final version of the Zwischenakt, the conclusion of which is given in Example 6.4, Beethoven did not retain the motive as it appears in the sketches but modified it in various subtle ways. The original form of the motive has been reassigned to the first movement of the quartet, where it always sounds agitated and unsettled.

This reassignment of the motive from Zwischenakt to the quartet is not inappropriate from a dramatic point of view. Filled with tension from start to finish, the first movement of op. 95 is one of Beethoven's most disquieting pieces of music. In Goethe's *Egmont,* the change of scene from Act III to Act IV, during which Zwischenakt III is to be played, marks a turning point in the drama that introduces a new level of tension in the narrative: the Duke of Alba has arrived in Brussels with his army and has promptly issued an order declaring that anyone talking together in groups of twos or threes in public is guilty of high treason. This sequence of events is reflected in Zwischenakt III. The army's entry into Brussels is represented by a robust C-major march replete with drums, trumpets, and pompous rhythms. The ensuing conclusion in C minor (Example 6.4) relates to the unease brought about by the foreign occupation and the duke's terrifying ban on public conversation. The change from major to minor for this passage creates a dark and ominous atmosphere that anticipates the tension of the opening scene of Act IV, in which the citizens of Brussels, too afraid to speak in normal tones, whisper to one another in a state of fear. It is interesting that in Examples 6.2a and 6.2b (and possibly 6.2c, as well), Beethoven originally intended for the motivic passage to precede rather than follow the march, which continues in the minor mode. The present scheme in Zwischenakt III, however, traces the events of the drama more pointedly and precisely.

*Example 6.4.* Op. 84, Zwischenakt III, mm.100–107.

## II. The Sketch Sources

The extant sketches for Beethoven's op. 95 quartet are contained in five sources, four of which are loose-leaf manuscripts. The Landsberg 11 sketchbook (pages 31–35 and 37–44) and the Grasnick 20a miscellany (folios 8 and 9, a bifolio) have already been mentioned. A full eight-page gathering in the Pierpont Morgan Library in New York, SV 390; another one, owned by Dr. William Dreesmann;[16] and a single folio in the Statens Musikbibliothek in Stockholm, SV 373, constitute the remaining three sources.

According to Alan Tyson, three of the four loose-leaf sources—the Stockholm, Morgan Library, and Dreesmann MSS—once formed part of a homemade sketchbook that Beethoven had made by stitching together as many as twenty-two separate manuscripts ranging from single leaves to eight-page gatherings.[17] These manuscripts contain sketches not only for op. 95, but also for the "Archduke" Trio, op. 97, the music to *König Stephan,* op. 117, and the music to *Die Ruinen von Athen,* op. 113. They are now completely dispersed, and the sketchbook as such no longer exists. Tyson labels it "Sketchbook of 1810–1811" because he believes it was used by Beethoven "in the last months of 1810 and the first eight months of 1811."[18] This time frame needs to be revised in the light of new evidence.

In his reconstruction of this sketchbook, Tyson has postulated (on the basis of matching inkblots in three consecutive single leaves that appear toward the end of the sketchbook as items 17, 18, and 19) that it was stitched together when all the component folios were still unused.[19] This assumption seems incorrect for several reasons. Close examination of items 17 and 18 (I have yet to see item 19) shows that neither the precise locations nor the shapes of the inkblots match up when their pages are placed side by side—an arrangement that requires item 17 to be placed after, not before, item 18, yielding the sequence 18, 17, 19. Furthermore, two manuscripts placed at the front of the sketchbook in Tyson's reconstruction as items 1 and 3 show clear evidence of stab holes piercing either directly through, or extremely close to, sketches that Beethoven must have made earlier when the papers were still unbound.[20] Together with items 2 and 4,[21] items 1 and 3 contain evidence of sketches spilling over the right edge of the staff, extending confidently across the imaginary vertical lines that connect the stitch holes to indicate, without a doubt, that Beethoven was not in the least hampered by any preexisting stitches when he was writing out those sketches.[22] Therefore, like the earlier Landsberg 7 sketchbook, the so-called Sketchbook of 1810–1811 appears to have originated as an afterthought when some of its components had already been used.[23] This conclusion does not contradict Tyson's generalized chronological ordering of the component manuscripts in the sketchbook. The scenario of the composer preparing his loose manuscripts for stitching by putting those already used at the top of the pile, and those still unused at the bottom, is an entirely plausible one. But the chronology can now be refined a little.

Tyson places two of the three op. 97 manuscripts ahead of those for op. 95 in his reconstruction of the sketchbook; he claims that the quartet was still incomplete when Beethoven began work on the "Archduke" and that "Beethoven may have pursued the trio to its completion at the start of [the Sketchbook of 1810–1811] before taking up the quartet again."[24] This claim is based on the hypothesis, shared by Sieghard Brandenburg, that the autographs of opp. 95 and 97 were both "written out three or four years later than the dates that Beethoven inscribed on them."[25] The inscriptions are "1810 im Monath [*sic*] oktober" and "geschrieben im Monat oktober" in the first page of the op. 95 autograph, and "Trio am 3ten März 1811" at the beginning and "geendigt am 26ten März 1811" at the end of the op. 97 autograph. I have argued elsewhere that the op. 97 autograph actually dates from 1811 and not a few years later.[26] In the last section of this chapter, I will argue that the op. 95 autograph may indeed be taken to originate from 1810. With op. 95 completed before op. 97 was begun, it stands to reason that the three op. 95 sketch sources should precede those for op. 97 at the beginning of the Sketchbook of 1810–1811. Thus, the first six items of the Sketchbook of 1810–1811 should occur in the order 4, 3, 5, 1, 2, 15 (item 5 refers to the Dreesmann MS);[27] and item 4 precedes item 3 because its contents were made earlier (see Table 6.1). Also, because items 1–4 were stitched into the sketchbook after they had been used, the same should be true for item 5.

Beethoven's completion of op. 95 before op. 97 also means that the quartet sketches in the Sketchbook of 1810–1811 predate the "Archduke" sketches in the Landsberg 11 sketchbook. This chronology in turn points to the incompatibility of Tyson's time frame of "the last months of 1810" to "the first eight months of 1811" for the Sketchbook of 1810–1811, on the one hand, with the time frame of "winter 1809/1810 to fall 1810" for Landsberg 11, on the other.[28] Because there is no reason to question either the *terminus ante quem* or the time frame for Landsberg 11, the issue here is the *terminus post quem* for the Sketchbook of 1810–1811, which refers essentially to when Beethoven began composing the quartet (as op. 95 is the earliest composition Beethoven worked on in the sketchbook). Although Goethe's *Egmont* premiered on May 24, 1810, the staging with Beethoven's incidental music came only with the fourth performance on June 15, 1810, evidently because the composer was not able to finish his music in time.[29] If we assume that Beethoven did not begin working on his new quartet until the *Egmont* music was finally completed, June 1810 would be the earliest possible date for the Sketchbook of 1810–1811.

## III. An Overview of the Sketch Contents

Of the five sketch sources for op. 95, only the Landsberg 11 sketchbook and Grasnick 20a MS contain work for all four movements of the quartet. Sketches for the fourth movement may be found in the Morgan Library MS, the Stockholm MS, and the Dreesmann MS, and sketches for the third movement appear also in the Morgan Library and Stockholm MSS. It is clear from what has survived in these sources that a substantial number of sketches are now missing. The chronological sequence of Beethoven's work on each of the four movements is shown in Table 6.1. Although

*Table 6.1.* Sketch sources for op. 95.

| *Movement* | *Source* | *Main Contents* |
|---|---|---|
| 1 | a) Grasnick 20a, fols. 8 and 9 | fol. 8r—mm. 1–43.<br>fol. 8v—draft continuation, mm. 44–60; sketches for the development and the end of the movement.<br>fol. 9r—draft continuation, mm. 61–99 (but with the eleven measures of mm. 89–99 conflated into only seven measures); sketches for the development. |
| | b) Landsberg 11, pp. 31 and 32 | fol. 9v—sketches for the development.<br>p. 31—draft (continuation from fol. 9r of Grasnick 20a), mm. 100–141 (roughly); other sketches for the draft.<br>p. 32—draft continuation, mm. 139–49. |
| 2 | a) Grasnick 20a, fol. 9v | concept sketches. |
| | b) Landsberg 11, pp. 33–35 | p. 33—sketches for the opening measures of the movement; fugato time; the transition to the fugato and the beginning of the fugato (roughly mm. 23–51, with the measures on either side of this range).<br>p. 34—sketches for the fugato, including the middle section's extended descending bass line of mm. 64–75; and the final measures of the movement (including the attacca link to the third movement).<br>p. 35—sketches for the fugato and the conclusion of the movement. |
| 3 | a) Grasnick 20a, fol. 9v | concept sketches for the scherzo. |
| | b) Landsberg 11, pp. 34–35 | sketches for the beginning of the movement. |
| | c) Stockholm MS. | recto—brief score draft for Trio I; other sketches for the Trio.<br>verso—sketches for the end of Scherzo II and the end of the movement. |
| | d) Morgan Library MS. | pp. 1–4—score draft for Trio I (mm. 41–102) Library and, in p. 1, a sketch for the end of the movement.<br>pp. 4–6—score draft for Trio II and coda (mm. 142 to end of the movement).<br>p. 7—sketch for the end of the movement.<br>p. 8—sketches for the scherzo and Trios I and II. |
| 4 | a) Grasnick 20a, fols. 8r and 9v | fol. 8r—concept sketch for the second theme.<br>fol. 9v—concept sketches for the introduction to the movement. |

*Table 6.1, continued.*

| *Movement* | *Source* | *Main Contents* |
|---|---|---|
| 4 | b) Stockholm MS., verso | sketches for the introduction leading into the Allegretto. |
| | c) Morgan Library MS., pp. 7 and 8 | sketches for the introduction and first measures of the Allegretto. |
| | d) Dreesmann MS., pp. 1–5 | score draft for part of the introduction leading into the beginning of the Allegretto, roughly mm. 8–39. |
| | e) Landsberg 11, pp. 37–44 | p. 37—sketches for the introduction.<br>p. 38—sketches for the introduction and for the first theme (mm. 16–22).<br>p. 39—sketches for the introduction and beginning of the draft of Allegretto, mm. 8–32.<br>p. 40—draft continuation, mm. 32–51; other Allegretto and coda sketches.<br>p. 41—draft continuation, mm. 51–98; other sketches for the movement.<br>p. 42—draft continuation, m. 99 to the coda, which is incomplete sketches for the coda.<br>pp. 43–44—sketches for the coda. |

work on the various movements overlaps to some degree, there is nevertheless clear evidence to suggest that the composer generally concentrated on one movement at a time, starting with the first.

A composite draft forms the bulk of what has survived in the sketch sources for the opening Allegro con brio. When pieced together from sketches in fols. 8 and 9 of Grasnick 20a and pages 31 and 32 of Landsberg 11, this draft spans practically the entire 151-measure movement (only the final two measures are missing). It reflects an advanced stage of work and mirrors the final version of the music to a great extent. The remaining sketches for the movement in these sources are for the most part directly connected to the draft. There is a conspicuous lack of earlier sketches.

The Allegretto second movement is the most sparsely represented in these sources. The earliest evidence of work on the Allegretto consists of two concept sketches, both later rejected, that Beethoven made in fol. 9v of Grasnick 20a. Like the concept sketches for the third and fourth movements that appear in the same manuscript in fols. 8r and 9v, these sketches were made amid work on the advanced draft of the Allegro first movement, whose impending completion enabled Beethoven to turn to the remaining movements of the quartet. Apart from this very early stage of work and a somewhat later one represented by the sketches in pages 33–35 of Landsberg 11, no other sketches for the Allegretto have survived.

Although they appear as separate entries, some of the Allegretto sketches on page

33 of Landsberg 11 roughly outline the passage from mm. 23 to 51, that is, from the transition to the fugato and continuing to the exposition of the fugato theme in all four voices. Cramped at times with multiple voices in counterpoint, these sketches are often laid out as two-stave score entries, packed with close detail. One should not conclude, however, that they reflect a late stage of work, particularly because the sense of fluent continuity—a common indicator of advanced conception—is absent. Several of the sketches seem to have been made for the purpose of establishing markers for a ground plan for the movement. For example, on page 34, we find sketches that point to some of the prominent features of the second part of the fugato (mm. 65–112): a sketch for the bass line of mm. 65–75; one combining the fugato theme and its inversion in stretto (an idea pursued in mm. 88–96); another sketch combining the fugato theme with an early version of the new sixteenth-note countersubject (entering in m. 78); and so on. These sketches are sometimes very brief—the sketch with the new countersubject, for example, lasts only two measures. Gathered conveniently in these pages, they constitute a pool of ideas to which Beethoven would later return.

As with the Allegretto, large lacunae characterize Beethoven's extant work on the third movement: except for a couple of early sketches, the sketch sources document mostly the later stages of the movement's genesis. The first of these is a concept sketch for the Scherzo's opening (mm. 1–2) in fol. 9v of Grasnick 20a. Already quite close to the final version, this sketch is followed almost immediately on the same page by a revision of the same idea. The leap from here to the type of more advanced work we see in the Stockholm MS, our next sketch source for the movement, is a big one.

The Stockholm MS preserves a very brief quartet score draft of part of Trio I at the top of the recto. Appearing in medias res and with only part of the second-violin and viola lines filled in (with a version of the chorale-like theme that is not retained in the published music), the draft breaks off after only seven measures and continues for another eight as a single line, implying that it was once connected to work that is now lost. The rest of this page, and the first five staves of the verso, are well filled with additional single-line sketches for Trio I (both the G♭-major and D-major sections), the concluding bars of both Scherzo II and Trio II, and the last measures of the movement.

The Morgan Library MS transmits a full-score draft that is much more extensive than the one in Stockholm. The draft begins with the long stretch of mm. 41–102, followed by a second stretch extending from m. 142 to the end of the movement. These sections correspond to the whole of Trio I through the first three measures of Scherzo II, and the whole of Trio II followed by the coda. The gap between m. 102 and m. 142 corresponds to Scherzo II—essentially the reprise of Scherzo I—which Beethoven indicates in the draft with the abbreviation "d.c." (da capo) next to m. 102. A couple of tie marks for the two violins at the start of the draft point to another part of the Scherzo I draft that is now lost. Additional sketches for the two trios, the scherzo, and the conclusion of the movement are found in pages 1, 7, and 8 of the manuscript.

Although the fullness of the open-score draft in the Morgan Library MS represents an advanced stage of work, the more tentative example in the Stockholm MS indicates, by way of contrast, that Beethoven's use of a full-score format in his work was not necessarily reflective of a late phase in the compositional process. Laying out the music in open score, where every voice is immediately clear to the eye, actually gives point to a comment that the composer made to himself in the form of an inscription at the top of page 35 of the Landsberg 11 sketchbook in connection with his work on the second movement on that page: that he should immediately get used to drafting out all the voices just as they are imagined.[30] The comment comes as a significant adjustment to his long-held method of concentrating while sketching mainly on the Hauptstimme, which is laid out almost invariably along a single staff. Thus, whereas the advanced composite draft of the first movement in Grasnick 20a and Landsberg 11, written out before the second movement is composed, appears almost entirely in single-staff continuity, the comparatively less advanced second-movement sketches in Landsberg 11 are laid out, in many instances, in two-stave score featuring four voices. To be sure, the sketching of a quartet in open score was not new to Beethoven. But its new prominence in relation to op. 95 may be taken as indicative of the composer's increasing tendency to think out his music in more contrapuntal terms as he moved gradually and inexorably toward his late style.[31]

The sketches for the finale, more numerous than those for any other movement of the quartet, appear in every one of the five extant sources and may be grouped loosely under two main categories. The first concerns a problem that soon became an obsession for Beethoven: how to write a suitable slow introduction to the Allegretto agitato. The second category comprises a composite draft of the whole movement, as well as associated sketches, on pages 39–42 of Landsberg 11. Although this draft is written mainly as a single-line continuity, it appears to have been made only after the composer had made a score draft of the slow introduction and the first twenty-six measures or so of the following Allegretto agitato in pages 1–5 of the Dreesmann MS. This full-scale reversion to single-line drafting after the determined and impressive attempt to draft out the music in open score in the Dreesmann MS comes as a surprise. But the heavy revising of the slow introduction, the many empty measures in the three lower string parts, and the breakdown of continuity on page 5 of the eight-page manuscript all speak to the composer's apparent frustration over laying out the music in this lavish and expansive manner when most of the voices besides the Hauptstimme had yet to be realized.

The composer worked on the single-line draft in Landsberg 11 on several separate occasions in both ink and pencil, stopping for a time when he became uncertain of the best way to continue. He revised the draft in various ways (adding new voices, clarifying harmonies, inserting dynamic markings, and so on) and made supplementary sketches to address some compositional issues. The draft encompasses essentially the whole movement, but it does not lay out the music in a continuous fashion. Its characteristic open seams stem from the composer's resumption of work without paying close heed at times to how the beginning of a new section might link up with the end of the previous section. Nevertheless, the basic continuity is clear.

## IV. The Draft for Movement I

Beethoven's work on the first movement in the sketch sources, as shown in Table 6.1, consists largely of a draft of the whole movement. Written out over several sittings and consisting of a few separate segments, the composite draft begins in fol. 8r of Grasnick 20a and ends on page 32 of the Landsberg 11 sketchbook. Fols. 8 and 9 of Grasnick 20a together form a bifolio, one that is distinguished from the rest of the op. 95 sketch sources by three distinctive characteristics. It is ruled ten staves to a page instead of sixteen, and its physical measurements of roughly 29 cm by 21.4 cm make it the smallest of all the op. 95 sketch manuscripts. Furthermore, it also has proportionately more pencil sketches than any of the other sources. The bifolio has deep fold lines running down the middle, both horizontally and vertically, to indicate that it had been twice folded, probably for use when the composer was away from his desk. Indeed, some pencil sketches in fol. 9v appear upside down on one side of the vertical middle fold to indicate that the bifolio was still folded when Beethoven made those sketches. The absence of stitch holes also points to the easy portability of this pocket sketch source.

Beginning at the top of fol. 8r, the first segment of the draft stretches from the very first staff of that page through staff 7 of the next page, fol. 8v. This part of the draft neatly corresponds to the exposition of the movement and the first measure of the development (mm. 1–60). It is extremely hard to read: the pencil that Beethoven used was quite blunt, and the writing has become somewhat smudged in places as a result of rubbing against other surfaces over the years. A few supplemental ink entries in this draft segment constitute later revisions.

A new ink section of the draft begins at the top of fol. 9r and continues to the end of staff 7 of the same page. It spans the whole of the development (save the first measure) and part of the recapitulation—up to m. 99 in the midst of the second group. Additional sketches in both pencil and ink that are not part of the draft appear at the bottom of the same page and on much of the next, fol. 9v, where both the upside-down pencil sketches mentioned previously and most of the early concept sketches for the other three movements may be found. These concept sketches, originally in pencil, were later traced over in ink. The tracing provided greater legibility and signaled Beethoven's desire to utilize these sketches, even though that interest did not always hold to the end. The remainder of the recapitulation draft, from m. 100 onward, is recorded in pages 31–32 of the Landsberg 11 sketchbook, first in ink and later in pencil.[32] Some of these pencil sketches Beethoven would later trace over in ink.

It is hardly surprising that the draft of the first movement comes not in one whole unbroken narrative, but as a series of longer continuities and shorter sketches that may be pieced together to form a composite whole. Although its high degree of correspondence to the final version of the music indicates an advanced stage of work, it contains significant deviations that I shall now discuss.

## *Exposition and Recapitulation*

The concluding section of the exposition, mm. 34–59, corresponds to mm. 103–28 of the recapitulation. Each of these passages consists of a repeated cadence-ostinato pairing, organized as follows: mm. 34–42/43–46 and 47–53/54–59; and mm. 103–11/112–15 and 116–22/123–28.[33] Beethoven's manner of juxtaposing the two segments in each pairing is turbulent and terrifying: the cadence is characterized by great harmonic, textural, metrical, and rhythmic upheavals that the ostinato tries to pacify. Examples 6.5 and 6.6 show respectively the two passages as they appear in draft in the exposition and recapitulation.[34]

Immediately evident in Example 6.5 is the presence of three cadence-ostinato pairings instead of two. The additional pairing, which appears near the beginning of the example, extends from the measure following m. [37] to the measure before m. [38], a passage where no measure numbers corresponding to the printed score may be assigned. In this passage, Beethoven accentuates E♭ major, a key not previously encountered in the music, and pits it against A major to create a disjunct, astringent tritone, echoing the very memorable C–G♭ breach that launches the surprise Neapolitan mutation of the first theme in m. 6. By subsequently eliminating E♭ major from this concluding section of the exposition, the composer threw into sharper relief the disjunct tonality between D♭ and D—between the key of the second group and its ♭II enharmonic, the most important subsidiary key of the quartet. The musical argument here, which builds on the pithy Neapolitan shift of F–G♭ in the opening measures of the movement, is thus tightened up and defined more clearly.

The recapitulation draft in Example 6.6, in contrast to the exposition draft, omits the extra cadence-ostinato pairing. The D major of mm. [107–8] and G minor of mm. [118–19]—both of which Beethoven retained to the end—were originally conceived a semitone lower as D♭ major and F♯ major, respectively.[35] In terms of formal symmetry, C♯ major (the ♭VI enharmonic) and F♯ major (the ♭II enharmonic) are by turn the precise counterparts to the exposition's A major (mm. 38–39) and D major (mm. 49–50). But as Tovey has observed, Beethoven made those changes because "the colour value of ♭II has gone. It is hardly distinguishable from ♭VI. Beethoven substitutes the ordinary supertonic, and does not even sophisticate it by making it major. The glare of common daylight is the one thing that can inspire terror at this juncture."[36]

Indeed, ♭II and ♭VI are already familiar sonorities by the time we arrive at the recapitulation, the former as the key of the exposition's second group, and the latter, already in the opening measures, as the very memorable Neapolitan mentioned above. In abandoning them here, Beethoven creates a short cycle of fifths, A, D, and G—while emphasizing D—exclusively in connection with those terrifying scales in the first move-

*Example 6.5.* Grasnick 20a, fol. 8r, st. 8–fol. 8v, st. 6.

st. 2
[38]
[39]
st. 3
[40]
[41]
[42]
[43]
[44]
[45]
st. 4
[46]
[47]
[48]
[49]
[50]
st. 5
[51]
[52]
[53]
[54]
[55]
[56]
od[e]r
[57]
st. 6
[58]

*Example 6.6.* Landsberg 11, p. 31, sts. 1–5.

ment. Thus, when the second movement begins with yet another scale in D, its relationship with the first movement is immediately and unmistakably established.

## *Development*

The draft of the development in Grasnick 20a, fol. 9r, contains remarkably few corrections. Beginning in single-line continuity but switching later to two-stave format, its span of twenty-one measures—mm. [61]–[81]; the first bar of the development, m. [60], is missing—often contains multiple voices, some of which represent, in skeletal form, what Beethoven would later write out in full in the score. Thus, in mm. [66–69] (Example 6.7), the quarter-note markers of the ascending bass line become heavy double-dotted rhythms in the published score, with those in mm. [67–69] brought down an octave for a firmer and deeper resonance, forming an unbroken line with m. [69].

The development in Example 6.7 is less astringent than is the published version, in which the harmonies of C minor in m. [62] and E minor in m. [64] have been replaced by sharp diminished-seventh sonorities.[37] The development has thus purged itself of any hint of other keys besides the F major that launches it and the F minor that caps it when the recapitulation arrives. Consequently, the move from tonic major to tonic minor becomes sharply focused, and the intense manner in which this musical argument is carried out underscores the "serioso" rubric that Beethoven attaches to the work.

The confidence with which the development draft pushes on stands in ironic contrast with the composer's apparent difficulty in launching it; as mentioned previously, the first measure of the development, m. 60, is missing in Example 6.7. Example 6.8, which overlaps with and continues from the exposition draft of Example 6.5, illustrates this omission.

*Example 6.7.* Grasnick 20a, fol. 9r, sts. 1–2.

Toward the end of the exposition draft in Example 6.8, the last cadence-ostinato pairing rests on a low whole-note A♭ (st. 6, m. 58), the fifth of the second group's D♭ major.[38] The two separate sketches in staff 6—with the head motive starting on B♮, and the immediately following series of three whole notes, A♮–B♮–B♮, all of which Beethoven would later cross out, indicate the composer's intent to launch the development in the dominant. These sketches follow his earlier attempt, in the same staff, to begin the development in F, as the figured dominant-seventh chord on C' shows.[39] Two additional sketches on the same page, one beginning toward the end of staff 6 and the other in staff 7 (see also Example 6.8), contain more attempts at a dominant launch: couched in the minor mode in both instances, the entry of the first theme is made more momentous by way of a sharp drop in pitch following a series of powerfully ascending whole notes.

Nevertheless, in a subsequent sketch in fol. 9v, Beethoven revisits F—the tonic minor as opposed to the present major (Example 6.9). But the music shoots toward the dominant almost immediately and with great force, invoking in the process that very memorable scale from the exposition.

A second sketch in fol. 9v (Example 6.10) shows Beethoven recasting Example 6.9 in the dominant (the minor giving way to the major in the same dramatic fashion as before) and making it leaner by four measures. If we imagine this sketch to be in F with the modes reversed at both ends, we would have the tonal framework of the whole development as it now stands.

*Example 6.8.* Grasnick 20a, fol. 8v, sts. 6–8.

*Example 6.9.* Grasnick 20a, fol. 9v, sts. 5–6.

*Example 6.10.* Grasnick 20a, fol. 9r, st. 6.

It seems clear from Examples 6.9 and 6.10 that, regardless of whether the development begins in the tonic or the dominant minor, Beethoven had once meant for the music to head immediately to the dominant major as a point of tension—a strategy not hinted at in the published score. Elsewhere in the same manuscript, in fols. 9r and 9v, a couple of concept sketches suggest that the composer had once thought of bringing back D major, a key already prominent in the exposition, as an area of tension in the development. Thus, Example 6.11 suggests how a developmental procedure in D major begins with the head motive in the cello; and Example 6.12 implies how an ostensible D-major cadence marks off a new section of music in the development. Like the previous plan to launch the development in the dominant, these ideas for D major were never realized.

*Example 6.11.* Grasnick 20a, fol. 9r, st. 9.

*Example 6.12.* Grasnick 20a, fol. 9v, st. 1.

## *Coda*

The coda as we know it makes pointed references to the development in a few significant ways: (1) its two-part structure corresponds strikingly to the same two-part structure of the development: the two first parts, mm. 60–75 and mm. 129–39, are similarly characterized by motivic development and diminished sonorities, and the two second parts, mm. 76–81 and mm. 140–51, feature an ostinato-pedal leading to a tonic cadence; (2) its entry in *subito fortissimo,* with the first theme in the cello accompanied by a sustained chord in the three upper voices, is similar to the development's entry; (3) its length of twenty-three measures is almost identical to the development's twenty-two; and (4) its launch in the surprise key of D♭ major instead of the anticipated F minor parallels the unexpected substitution in the development of the key of F major for the expected D♭ major.

The coda behaves, in other words, like another development; it is shaped not in relation to the exposition but in relation to the development section on which it is loosely based. To compare further these two sections: the long series of eighth-note arpeggios that thrusts the first part of the coda forward with great force and harmonic acerbity may be taken to be an extensive working-out of the series of quarter-note arpeggios at the beginning of the development (mm. 61, 63, 65), and the ostinato-pedal on the tonic, in the form of a repeated head motive in mm. 140–45, parallels the repeated dominant in mm. 76–81 in the development. The capping of the coda with a return of the opening theme in octaves echoes the similar, but much louder, capping of the development at the start of the recapitulation.

Beethoven arrived at a plan for the coda quite late in the course of his work on the movement. In an early sketch in Grasnick 20a,[40] the idea of rounding off the movement with a return of the opening theme was already present, although the composer abandoned it for a time, as we see in the two sketches in Examples 6.13 and 6.14.[41]

Comparison of Example 6.13 with Example 6.14 reveals Beethoven's particular concern with the music's phraseology and the establishment of a perfect authentic

*Example 6.13.* Grasnick 20a, fol. 8v, sts. 9–10.

cadence in the tonic. Example 6.13 plays through a neat pattern of seven two-measure units, 2+2+2+2+2+2+2, from start to finish. In the middle of this configuration (at the start of staff 10), the arpeggios' change of direction from ascending to descending motion comes in tandem with the change of harmony from subdominant to the secondary dominant on F;[42] the corresponding location in the printed score, mm. 137–38, shows an authentic cadence in the tonic. Remarkably, this essential cadence is not indicated anywhere in the sketch; the approach to the tonic via the subdominant five bars before the end is breathtaking in this regard.

The smooth phraseology of Example 6.13 contrasts with the slightly more angular and longer one of Example 6.14: 2+2+2+2+1+2+2+2+2. The one-measure "kink" in the middle of this otherwise even series of two-measure units occurs at the point where Beethoven has now worked in an authentic cadence in the tonic. This cadence corresponds to the one in mm. 137–38 that prefigures the ostinato-pedal beginning two bars later. A similar ostinato-pedal is not indicated in Example 6.14.

In harmonic terms, Example 6.14 is only slightly more intense than Example 6.13, but significantly less so than the final version of the coda. Whereas it takes nine measures for the music to come to a close following the perfect authentic cadence in Example 6.14, the final version of the coda requires fourteen to dissipate the ten-

*Example 6.14*. Landsberg 11, p. 31, sts. 5–9.

sion. Beethoven's revision of Example 6.14 to arrive at something closer to the final version of the music comes soon enough, however: two sketches that may be joined together to form a single continuity show music that is all but identical to the Hauptstimme of mm. 133–49 of the score.[43] This continuity serves to replace part of Example 6.14, but also to extend it to almost the end of the movement. It is the last sketch continuity that Beethoven made for the movement in the extant sources.

## V. The Date of the Autograph

In his letter of May 15, 1813, to Nikolaus Zmeskall, an amateur cellist and one of the composer's closest and oldest friends in Vienna, the composer described himself playfully in the third person as follows: "Beethoven has promised to send the F minor quartet to Count Brunsvik, but he has forgotten to have it copied. So he asked Zmeskall to have the quartet copied at his expense."[44] Op. 95, although completed in 1810, was still not published by 1813 and would not appear in print until December 1816, when it was issued in Vienna by Sigmund Anton Steiner & Co. But Beethoven's letter to Zmeskall makes it clear that an autograph of the work was already in existence at that time, for the source from which the copyist had to work must have been either the autograph itself or a copy made previously from the autograph. Given Beethoven's very difficult hand and complex working methods, it is inconceivable that any copyist would have been able to form a score from the composer's preliminary manuscript of the work, even if such a manuscript had taken the form of advanced score drafts such as Lewis Lockwood speculates to have existed but which have not often survived.[45]

The op. 95 quartet is one of three chamber works written between 1810 and 1812 that underwent unusually long delay in publication. Like the quartet, both the "Archduke" Trio, op. 97, and the Violin Sonata in G Major, op. 96, were issued in 1816, even though they were completed in 1811 and 1812, respectively.[46] Brandenburg and Tyson have claimed that Beethoven lost the original autographs of opp. 95, 96, and 97 before the works were published and that he prepared as replacements the manuscripts now preserved in the Österreichische Nationalbibliothek, Vienna (op. 95, cataloged as Mus. Hs. 16.531), the Pierpont Morgan Library, New York (op. 96), and the Biblioteka Jagiellońska, Kraków (op. 97).[47] Brandenburg's collective date for the putative new autographs is 1814/1815, whereas Tyson believes that the op. 96 autograph was "probably written out in 1815" and that those for opp. 95 and 97 were made "three or four years later than the dates that Beethoven inscribed on them."[48] As mentioned above, I have argued elsewhere that the op. 97 autograph does in fact date from 1811, its year of completion, and not from 1814/1815. It now appears that the op. 95 autograph, too, originates from when the work was completed in 1810 and not some later date.

The op. 95 autograph bears, at the top of its first page, the following two ink inscriptions by Beethoven: "1810 im Monath oktober" and "geschrieben im Monat oktober." The latter inscription (with a more modern spelling of the word *Monat*), which Beethoven had squeezed into the top right corner of the paper for lack of space, appears as part of the dedication of the quartet to Zmeskall. It was almost certainly entered sometime after "1810 im Monath oktober" was already in place. Just when the composer wrote down "1810 im Monath oktober" is less clear, for the rubric appears in a somewhat different script carefully centered at the top of the page. What is clear, however, is that it was probably inscribed at a time when the page was less cluttered with other jottings, such as the famous subtitle "quartetto serioso," which the composer wrote with blunt pencil on yet another occasion. Particularly odd is the emphatic repetition of "im Monat[h] oktober" in two inscriptions that lie so close to each other on the page. It was as if Beethoven was either twice mistaken or was for some reason trying (a little too hard, perhaps) to convince posterity that he had written out the autograph in October 1810 when he in fact did not.

Glued to the bottom left of the inside front cover of the op. 95 autograph is a small white piece of paper that reads, "Restauriet im Februar 1978 durch das Institut für Restaurierung der ÖNB." As the manuscript now stands, every original bifolio and gathering has been cut through along the middle fold to give a total of forty separate individual folios. From these, seven artificial gatherings—the first six with six folios each and the last with four—have been formed and tightly sewn together. All the folios are ruled ten staves to a page.

The papers of the op. 95 autograph are not homogeneous in their paper type. The vast majority of the folios—thirty-six out of forty—are characterized by a watermark similar to paper type 31 for the Landsberg 9 sketchbook in *The Beethoven Sketchbooks* (see Figure 6.1), but fols. 4, 11, and 12 are not (Figures, 6.2, 6.3, and 6.4), and no watermark may be found in fol. 39.[49]

It appear that fols. 11 and 12 had belonged to the same sheet of paper before it was cut, because the missing tips of the letters "A" and "O" in the watermark of fol. 12 reappear in fol. 11, as Figures 6.3 and 6.4 show. (As for the missing tops of the letters "R," "L," "B," and "E," they would have been fairly thin, short horizontal lines that became obliterated when the paper was cut.) Further evidence showing that fols. 11 and 12 were once part of the same sheet is provided by the identical total span (TS) and staff span (SS) measurements shown in Figure 6.5.

Because the autograph contains papers that do not have the same TS and SS measurements even though they may show the same watermark, another way to clarify the structure of the manuscript is by differentiating between those papers that belong to paper type 31 and those that do not, and thereafter categorizing the paper

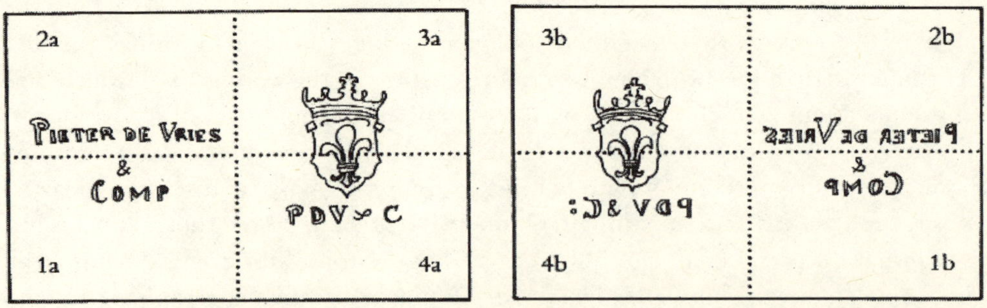


*Figure 6.1.* Paper type 31, Landsberg 9. Reproduced with permission from Douglas Johnson, Alan Tyson, and Robert Winter, *The Beethoven Sketchbooks: History, Reconstruction, Inventory* (Berkeley: University of California Press, 1985), 554.

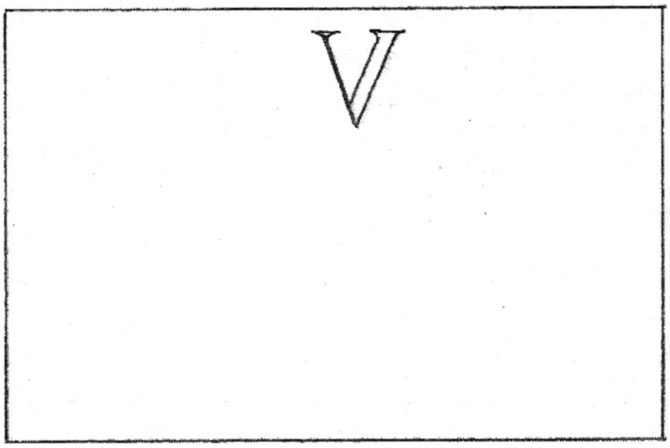

*Figure 6.2.* Watermark of fol. 4.

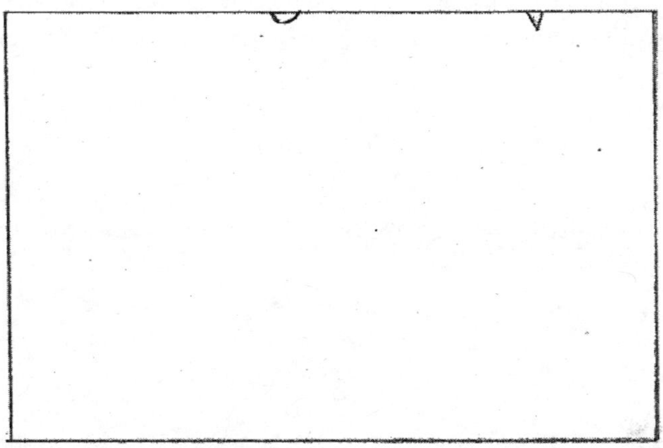

*Figure 6.3.* Watermark of fol. 11.

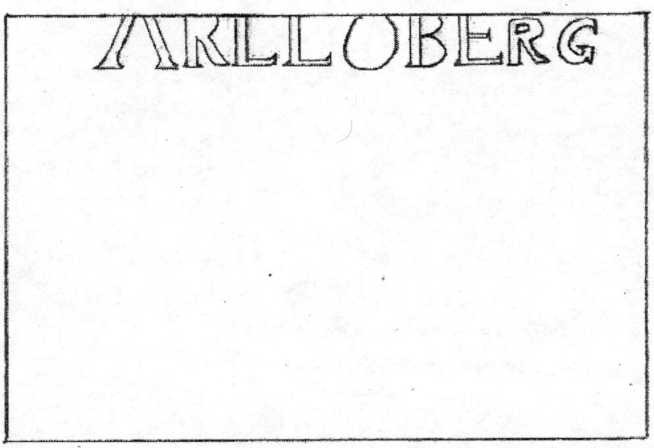


*Figure 6.4.* Watermark of fol. 12.

type 31 folios according to their different SS measurements, as is shown in Figures 6.5, 6.6, and 6.7. To be sure, the variety of TS measurements among the paper type 31 folios is unexpected, and Figures 6.6 and 6.7 clarify that these papers are ruled in two different staff sizes.

The folios in Figure 6.6 are scattered in different places in the autograph, indicating a particularly unusual aspect of the manuscript's makeup—that Beethoven made use of a significant number of loose single leaves (as opposed to the more usual bifolios or sheet gatherings) in the autograph. The pervasiveness of this situation can be seen in the complete list of the autograph's folios in Figure 6.8. Even at an optimistic count, only six intact bifolios—all of which make up just 30 percent of the total number of leaves—may be conjectured to have originally existed.[50] Perhaps Beethoven bought the paper type 31 folios of the autograph as loose remnants (did he pay less for them from the seller on this account?). If so, this would represent a departure from his common practice of buying manuscript paper in standard gatherings.

Although the op. 95 autograph is not made up entirely of papers with the same watermark, it is still a much more homogeneous manuscript than Landsberg 9, the

*Figure 6.5.* Physical dimensions of non-paper-type 31 folios.

| *Folio* | *TS (mm)* | *SS (mm)* |
|---|---|---|
| 4 | 187.5 | 9 |
| 11 | 177.5 | 8 |
| 12 | 177.5 | 8 |
| 39 | 200.80 | 10 |

*Figure 6.6.* Physical dimensions of paper-type 31 folios with bigger staves.

| *Folio* | *TS (mm)* | *SS (mm)* |
|---|---|---|
| 3 | 200.40 | 10 |
| 8 | 200.15 | 10 |
| 9 | 200.30 | 10 |
| 15 | 200.30 | 10 |
| 37 | 200.40 | 10 |
| 40 | 199.00 | 10 |

*Figure 6.7.* Physical dimensions of all other paper-type 31 folios.

TS: 200.50 mm.
SS: 8.5 mm.

*Figure 6.8* Op. 95 autograph folios and their paper types: "31" refers to paper type 31 (Figure 6.1) and "*" indicates paper-type 31 folios with bigger staves.

| Folio | Watermark/ Quadrant | Folio | Watermark/ Quadrant | Folio | Watermark/ Quadrant |
|---|---|---|---|---|---|
| 1 | 31/1b | 15* | 31/1a | 29 | 31/3b? |
| 2 | 31/1b | 16 | 31/4b | 30 | 31/1b |
| 3* | 31/2a | 17 | 31/4a | ┌ – 31 | 31/2a |
| 4 | See Figure 6.2 | 18 | 31/4a | └ – 32 | 31/3a? |
| 5 | 31/4a | ┌ – 19 | 31/2b | 33 | 31/4a |
| 6 | 31/2a | └ – 20 | 31/3b? | ┌ – 34 | 31/3b? |
| 7 | 31/1a | 21 | 31/1a | └ – 35 | 31/2b |
| ┌ – 8* | 31/1b | 22 | 31/2a | 36 | 31/4b |
| └ – 9* | 31/4b | 23 | 31/4a | 37* | 31/3a? |
| 10 | 31/4b | 24 | 31/3a? | 38 | 31/2a |
| ┌ – 11 | See Figure 6.3 | 25 | 31/1a | 39 | No watermark evident |
| └ – 12 | See Figure 6.4 | 26 | 31/3a? | | |
| 13 | 31/1a | ┌ – 27 | 31/4b | 40* | 31/3a? |
| 14 | 31/3a? | └ – 28 | 31/1b | | |

only sketchbook—or, more properly, homemade sketch miscellany—in which paper type 31 also may be found.[51] In its present form, Landsberg 9 consists of a total of thirty-seven folios, the first eight of which record sketches originating from 1818 for the fugue of the "Hammerklavier" Sonata, op. 106. These eight folios were not part of the miscellany as Beethoven used it. The rest of the collection, twenty-seven folios in all, are characterized by folios with varying numbers of staves and display as many as nine different watermarks. All of them contain work on the revision of *Fidelio* from circa February–March 1814, a fact that became the basis for Tyson and Brandenburg's conclusions about the date for the op. 95 autograph.

Because it is a miscellany, the hypothesis that some of the papers of Landsberg 9 may have originated from a time before 1814 cannot be discounted, even though the actual contents of the folios may reflect a later date. It is significant to note, therefore, that the number of leaves of paper type 31 in the op. 95 autograph—thirty-four—is more than twice the count of fifteen for the homemade miscellany. If we take the composer's date of October 1810 for the op. 95 autograph to be correct—and we really have no good grounds to doubt him, especially when the date appears twice in his own hand in the manuscript—then we must further conclude that the paper type 31 leaves in Landsberg 9 were leftovers, pages set aside for later use after the composer had employed the bulk of this paper in the op. 95 autograph a few years earlier.

This scenario of Beethoven using papers dating from a few years earlier when he was working on *Fidelio* in 1814 is, in fact, not unique at all: the now-dispersed sketchbook of 1814–1815, another homemade source containing work on the opera that is almost contemporaneous with Landsberg 9, also includes papers dating from an earlier time—from 1812, according to Brandenburg and Tyson.[52] But one year earlier than this seems much more likely, in view of the fact that the watermarks of these papers are very similar to those found in a set of parts for the "Archduke" Trio that may be firmly dated to 1811. Preserved in the Gesellschaft der Musikfreunde (MS A58a), this set of parts contains editorial markings in Beethoven's hand. They were made by Wenzel Schlemmer, the composer's trusted copyist, except for the first folio of the piano part, which Aloys Fuchs (an erstwhile board member of the Gesellshaft) wrote out to replace the missing original.[53] The watermarks of the parts, and those of a couple of related manuscripts, are illustrated in Figures 6.9–6.14.[54]

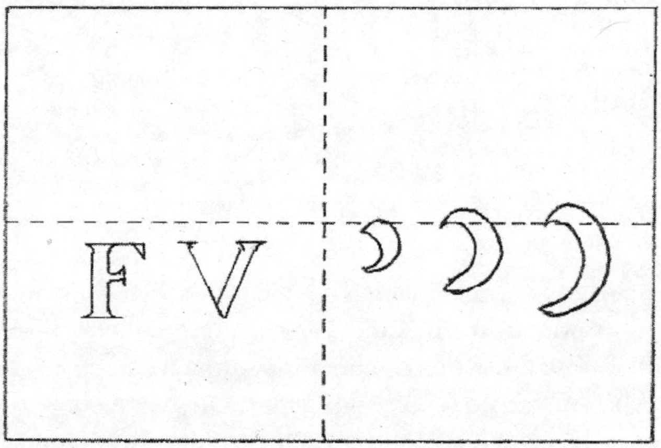


*Figure 6.9.* Watermark of Schlemmer's "Archduke" Trio piano part.

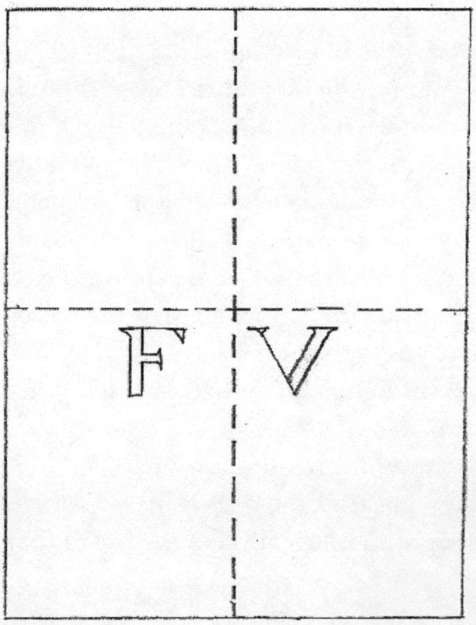


*Figure 6.10.* "FV" watermark from Schlemmer's "Archduke" Trio violin and cello parts.

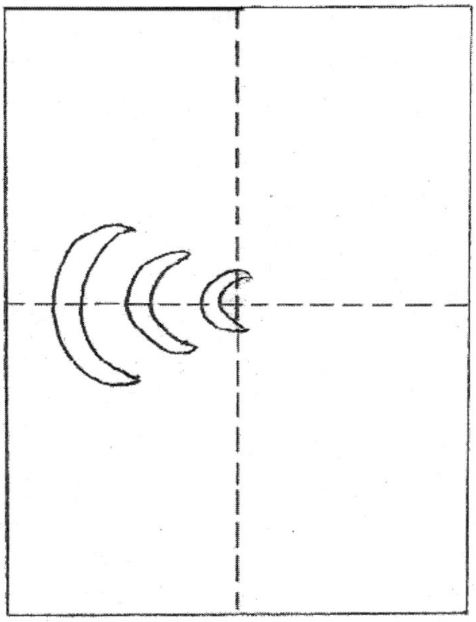

*Figure 6.11*. Three-crescents watermark from Schlemmer's "Archduke" Trio violin and cello parts.

Figure 6.9 shows the watermark of the piano part, which is laid out in *Querformat*, that is, with the horizontal dimensions longer than the vertical (as is the case with many piano scores).[55] The watermarks of the violin and cello parts, both in *Hochformat* (with the vertical length longer than the horizontal), appear as Figures 6.10 and 6.11.[56] Figures 6.9, 6.10, and 6.11 are obviously related to one another; the papers for Figures 6.10 and 6.11, being in *Hochformat*, can each accommodate only one vertical half of the watermark of Figure 6.9. The similarities of Figures 6.9–6.11 to Figure 6.12, the watermark of MS 100 (Bibliothèque Nationale, Paris), a dispersed bifolio from the Sketchbook of 1814–1815, are self-evident.[57]

Related, too, is the watermark displaying a conjoined "FV" in Figure 6.13, the remaining watermark to appear among the folios of Schlemmer's violin and cello parts, and Figure 6.14, the predominant watermark among the remaining dispersed folios of the Sketchbook of 1814–1815 given as paper type 26 in *The Beethoven Sketchbooks*. Significant, too, in this regard, is that among the many watermarks of Beethoven's sketch manuscripts illustrated in *The Beethoven Sketchbooks,* the only other source characterized by a watermark with the letters "FV" besides the Sketchbook of 1814–1815 is the now-dispersed homemade Sketchbook of 1810–1811 that I discussed earlier.[58] We may surmise, then, that in 1814–15, Beethoven stitched together a couple of sketchbooks, Landsberg 9 and the Sketchbook of 1814–1815, from remnant folios salvaged from papers that he had used about four years earlier.

Revising the date of the op. 95 autograph from 1814 to 1810 allows us to refine Tyson's time frame for when Beethoven used the Sketchbook of 1810–1811, and also to propose a new way of reconstructing some of the component manuscripts in that

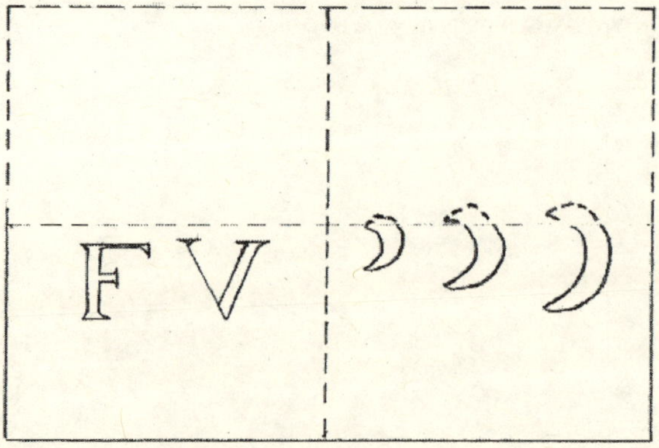


*Figure 6.12*. Watermark of MS 100 (Bibliothèque Nationale).

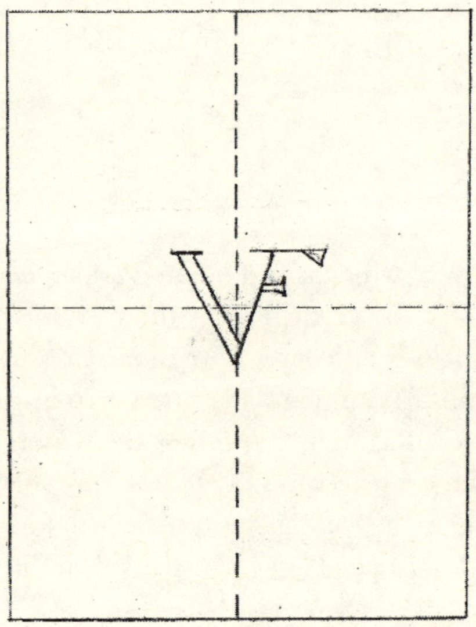

*Figure 6.13*. Conjoined "FV" watermark from Schlemmer's "Archduke" Trio violin and cello parts.

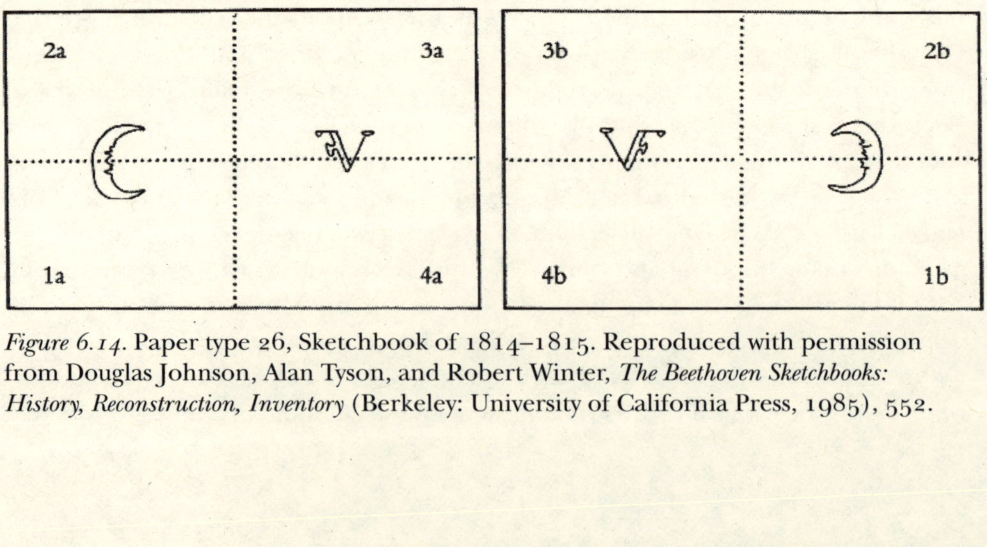


*Figure 6.14*. Paper type 26, Sketchbook of 1814–1815. Reproduced with permission from Douglas Johnson, Alan Tyson, and Robert Winter, *The Beethoven Sketchbooks: History, Reconstruction, Inventory* (Berkeley: University of California Press, 1985), 552.

homemade sketch source. More importantly, it calls into question the view that the quartet is closer than previously recognized to works that Beethoven completed in 1815–16, namely the op. 102 cello sonatas, the op. 101 piano sonata, and the song cycle *An die ferne Geliebte,* op. 98.[59] Certainly, the editorial markings and some of the corrections in the autograph score could have originated from a time closer to its publication date. And differences between the autograph and the Steiner first edition point also to late revisions that Beethoven made to the quartet before it was published. But these considerations do not alter the argument that op. 95 is fundamentally a work of 1810. Beethoven himself had acknowledged the quartet's extraordinary precociousness in his symbolic and highly unusual caution that it was "never to be performed in public."[60] Tempting as it may be, there is no need to explain the work's advanced style by assuming a later date for it.

## Notes

The present research on op. 95 forms part of my work on an edition of Beethoven's Landsberg 11 sketchbook (comprising facsimile, transcription, and commentary) for the University of Illinois Press. I am indebted to Dr. William Dreesmann for his kindness and generosity in allowing me to examine the Dreesmann MS, as well as for his warm hospitality. I am also very grateful to the following individuals for allowing me to study the manuscripts under their care, as well as for invaluable assistance in other ways: Prof. Dr. Krzysztof Zamorski, director of the Biblioteka Jagiellońska, and Mrs. Agnieszka Mietelska-Ciepierska, head of the Music Department; Dr. Ernst Herttrich and Dr. Michael Ladenburger of the Beethoven-Haus; Dr. Helmut Hell, director of the Staatsbibliothek zu Berlin-Preußischer Kulturbesitz, and Dr. Clemens Brenneis; Dr. Otto Biba, director of the Gesellschaft der Musikfreunde; Anna Lena Holm, senior librarian, Rare Collections, Statens Musikbibliothek; J. Rigbie Turner, Mary Flagler Cary curator, Pierpont Morgan Library; John Shepard, Music Division, New York Public Library; and the staffs of the Österreichische Nationalbibliothek and the Bibliothèque Nationale. For making a preliminary study for me of the op. 95 autograph score and of the parts for the "Archduke" Trio, op. 97, written out by Wenzel Schlemmer, I am most grateful to Gregory Dubinsky and to Professor Harald Krebs, respectively. A National Endowment for the Humanities Fellowship and research grants from the American Philosophical Society and the University of Louisville enabled me to travel to the various archives, and I am happy to record here my thanks.

1. Although the music for the Melodrama begins in E♭ major, it is brief and tonally unstable and, while interacting with Egmont's soliloquy on sleep, passes through a variety of keys, including F♯ major, E major, and B major. Tonal stability is achieved only when the music arrives at D major for Liberty's appearance, which occupies by far the greater part of the Melodrama.

2. Joseph Kerman, "Close Readings of the Heard Kind," *19th-Century Music* 17/3 (1994): 209–19.

3. To Kerman, "the confrontation between D major and F minor" is "the most extreme between movements in any Beethoven work, bar none." Kerman takes D major as an "enhancement" of the first movement's second key of D♭, which, in turn, is an "enhanced dominant" taking the place of C, the true dominant. See *The Beethoven Quartets* (London: Oxford University Press, 1967), 175–76.

4. See Joseph Kerman, "Beethoven's Minority," in *Write All These Down* (Berkeley: University of California Press, 1994), 217–37. The tables on pp. 218–19 neatly sum up Beethoven's strategies.

5. Prior to *Egmont* and op. 95, the instances of the practice in the Cello Sonata in G Minor, op. 2 no. 2, and the Piano Sonata in F Minor, op. 57 ("Appassionata"), are exceptions.

6. Kerman, "Beethoven's Minority," 223.

7. Ibid., 228.

8. The coda is twice as fast as the agitato.

9. James Hepokoski, "Back and Forth from *Egmont:* Beethoven, Mozart, and the Nonresolving Recapitulation," *19th-Century Music* 25/2–3 (2001–2): 128.

10. Ibid., 127–36.

11. Ibid., 134.

12. The cello, however, does spot a recurring F in mm. 138–39, which the viola reshapes into a tonic pedal on the head motive in mm. 140–45 in an effort to pin down the music to its tonic.

13. SV numbers refer to the catalog of Beethoven sketch manuscripts compiled by Hans Schmidt in "Verzeichnis der Skizzen Beethovens," *Beethoven-Jahrbuch* 6 (1969): 7–128.

14. The "Zwischenakt" is the interval between segments of the play that is filled by music.

15. This motive was earlier associated with a sketch meant for Zwischenakt IV (Beethoven wrote, "4ter Akt einfallend wäreh[e]nd der Vorhang noch aùf [*sic*]" next to it). The sketch appears in BH 103, side 1, staves 7 and 8 (Beethoven-Haus).

16. The Dreesmann MS, which quietly changed hands a few times in the last decades, was apparently unknown to Schmidt and hence did not appear in his catalog.

17. See the list of manuscripts that make up this sketchbook in Douglas Johnson, Alan Tyson, and Robert Winter, *The Beethoven Sketchbooks* (Berkeley: University of California Press, 1985), 202–3. The Dreesmann MS is the item listed under number 5 as "private collection."

18. Ibid., 206.

19. Ibid.

20. Item 1 is the "Archduke" MS in the New York Public Library (SV 358), and item 3 is the op. 95 MS in the Morgan Library. Thus, the top stitch hole in page 4 of item 1 pierces through previous writing and the last stitch hole of the same page very nearly so, and the last stitch hole in page 6 of item 3 almost pierces through the downward wavy line that is Beethoven's characteristic way of indicating a double bar. The eight pages of item 3 are not actually numbered as such, and the way in which the gathering is currently folded when preserved obscures Beethoven's actual sequence of work. My pagination of the manuscript here restores this sequence; the current first page is page 5 in my pagination.

21. Item 2 is the "Archduke" MS in the Beethoven-Haus (BSk 18), and item 4 is the op. 95 MS in the Statens Musikbibliothek, Stockholm, as mentioned above.

22. These spillovers occur in pages 2 and 8 of the New York Public Library "Archduke" Trio MS, SV 358; pp. 2 and 6 of the Beethoven-Archiv "Archduke" Trio MS, BSk 18; page 6 of the op. 95 Morgan Library MS; and the verso of the op. 95 Stockholm MS.

23. For another example of Beethoven's incorporation of used papers into a sketchbook, see William Kinderman, ed., *Artaria 195: Beethoven's Sketchbook for the Missa solemnis and the Piano Sonata in E major, Opus 109* (Urbana and Chicago: University of Illinois Press, 2003), commentary volume, 27–31.

24. *The Beethoven Sketchbooks,* 206. The third op. 97 manuscript—an incomplete score draft of the trio section of the Scherzo of "Archduke" that Tyson speculates to be a rejected leaf from the autograph—is placed as far down the sketchbook as item 15 because, like items 6–19, it contains work for op. 117.

25. Ibid., 198. See also Sieghard Brandenburg, "Bermerkungen zu Beethovens Op. 96," *Beethoven-Jahrbuch* 9 (1977): 11–25; and "Die Quellen zur Entstehungsgeschichte von Beethovens Streichquartett Es-Dur Op. 127," *Beethoven-Jahrbuch* 10 (1983): 223–24.

26. "The Autograph of Beethoven's 'Archduke' Trio," *Beethoven Forum* 11/2 (2004): 181–208.

27. The "Archduke" sketches are discussed in detail in my doctoral dissertation, *Source Studies for Beethoven's Piano Trio in B-flat Major, Op. 97 ("Archduke")*, University of California at Berkeley, 1995.

28. See *The Beethoven Sketchbooks*, pp. 195 and 206.

29. The second and third performances had come quickly on May 25 and 28, respectively. The unusually large gap of eighteen days separating the third from the fourth performance was probably due to the extra time needed for including Beethoven's music in the play.

30. "Sich zu gewöhnen gleich das ganz alle Stimmen wie es sich zeigt im Kopfe zu entwerfen."

31. Landsberg 11 also contains several other examples of Beethoven's engagement with contrapuntal procedures. These include exercises devised for self-instruction, as well as extensive copies, in pages 69 and 70 of the sketchbook, of Bach's *Chromatic Fantasy and Fugue*, BWV 903.

32. The two broken halves of a tie link the C'''' in m. 99 of the recapitulation, the last measure of the ink draft in fol. 9r of Grasnick 20a, with the same pitch in m. 100, which begins the Landsberg 11 draft at the top of page 31.

33. I borrow the cadence-ostinato terminology from Kerman, *The Beethoven Quartets*, 171.

34. Bar numbers in parentheses correspond to those in the printed score.

35. For the D-major scale, Beethoven initially inscribed "cis dur" in m. [107] to signify C♯ major. Thereafter, he spelled out the scale enharmonically as D♭ major before indicating, by writing out "d [dur]" and the first three notes of the scale (the staff was by this time already crowded by previous writing), that he intended to change it to D major. The D-major scale in full appears in pencil in staves 12–13 of the same page as part of a longer sketch for the same music.

36. Donald Francis Tovey, *Beethoven*, ed. Hubert Foss (Oxford: Oxford University Press, 1973), 107. See also Carl Dahlhaus, "Zum Begriff des Thematischen bei Beethoven Kommentare zu opus 95 und opus 102,1" in *Beethoven '77*, ed. Friedhelm Döhl (Zürich: Amadeus Verlag, 1979), 57–59.

37. The harmonies in the rest of the draft are largely retained in the published score.

38. This sketch, marked "od[e]r" and signifying the end of the exposition, is a version of the same idea, stated an octave higher in staff 8, which Beethoven had previously tagged with an encircled "X" referent. The first two bars of the sketch in staff 8 were crossed out because they duplicated mm. [55] and [56] in the draft (see Example 6.5). A matching encircled "X" referent, which Beethoven apparently forgot to insert into the draft, should have been placed just before m. [57].

39. The "7" below the note is redundant, and the "♯" above indicates a sharpened third, i.e., E♮. No matching counterpart may be found for the "X" referent that lies above the barline next to this figured C'.

40. Fol. 9r, staff 8.

41. Written in ink in the last two staves of fol. 8v of Grasnick 20a, Example 6.13 was probably made at the time when Beethoven was drafting out the development in ink in the next page, fol. 9r (much of the rest of the work for the quartet in Grasnick 20a is in pencil). Example 6.14 is a later effort, made when the composer had switched manuscript to Landsberg 11.

42. The viola head motive could also signal the start of the tonic pedal that now begins in m. 140.

43. The first of the two sketches begins in staff 15 of page 31 of Landsberg 11 and continues in staves 12, 14, and 16 of the following page. The second sketch follows immediately in staff 16 of page 32. Although double bar lines mark the end of the first sketch, there is no doubt that Beethoven meant for the two sketches to form a single continuity when he placed them side by side in this way. This continuity entails eliminating the cadential last bar of the first sketch.

44. Emily Anderson, ed. and trans., *The Letters of Beethoven,* vol. 1 (London: Macmillan, 1961), 417 (letter 422). Original text of the letter appears in Sieghard Brandenburg, ed., *Ludwig van Beethoven: Briefwechsel Gesamtausgabe,* vol. 2 (Munich: G. Henle, 1996), 348 (letter 650). Beethoven actually wrote, "Quartett aus E-Moll," which, as Brandenburg points out, is evidently an error.

45. See the following writings by Lockwood: "On Beethoven's Sketches and Autographs: Some Problems of Definition and Interpretation," *Acta Musicologica* 42 (1970): 32–47; "The State of Sketch Research," in *Beethoven's Compositional Process,* ed. William Kinderman (Lincoln: University of Nebraska Press, 1991), 9–10; and the review of Barry Cooper, *Beethoven and the Creative Process* (Oxford: Clarendon Press, 1990), in *Notes* 48/3 (1992): 850.

46. The reasons behind the publication delay of op. 97 are discussed in my article "The Autograph of Beethoven's 'Archduke' Trio." Opp. 96 and 97 actually appeared in parallel editions by Steiner in Vienna and Birchall in London. Beethoven had also sought to publish op. 95 in England through the advocacy of two London residents: first, Charles Neate, a member of the Philharmonic Society in London, and later the impresario Peter Salomon. Both attempts came to naught. The first English edition of op. 95 appeared in an inauthentic edition issued by Clementi, most likely in the early months of 1817. See Alan Tyson, *The Authentic English Editions of Beethoven* (London: Faber and Faber, 1963), 95–96.

47. See *The Beethoven Sketchbooks,* p. 198, and Brandenburg, "Bermerkungen zu Beethovens Op. 96" and "Die Quellen."

48. Brandenburg, "Die Quellen," 223–24, and Johnson, et al., *The Beethoven Sketchbooks,* 198.

49. Watermarks shown are drawn freehand and not to scale. The watermarks of both fol. 4 (Figure 6.2) and the bifolio formed by joining fols. 11 and 12 together (Figures 6.3 and 6.4, as described elsewhere in this chapter) vary somewhat from those given for the same folios as watermarks 63 and 66, respectively, by Karin Breitner in Ingrid Fuchs, ed., *Ludwig van Beethoven: Die Musikautographe in öffentlichen Wiener Sammlungen* (Tutzing: Verlegt bei Hans Schneider, 2004). Two observations may be made here. First, watermarks are sometimes very faint and hard to see, which is why they may be deciphered differently by different investigators. What is certain, however, is that the watermarks of fol. 4 and the bifolio are both unique in the manuscript. Second, fol. 4 is only a single quadrant, and Breitner's precise identification of it as quadrant 2a in the complete watermark 63 is not corroborated by any evidence in the Op. 95 autograph.

50. In Figure 6.8, definite and conjectured bifolios are indicated by continuous and dotted line brackets, respectively. The identifications of the watermark quadrants in this figure vary in some respects from those given by Karin Breitner in Ingrid Fuchs, ed., *Ludwig van Beethoven: Die Musikautographe,* 211, where measurements of the physical dimensions of the various folios sometimes differ marginally from those given above in Figures 6.5, 6.6, and 6.7. These differences in measurement may have resulted from both the calibrations of the rulers used and how the measurements were made.

51. *The Beethoven Sketchbooks,* 220–23.

52. Ibid., 235–40.

53. These parts were probably made by order of the archduke (who was acceding to Beethoven's request), which is why they became part of the archduke's library; see Brandenburg, *Ludwig van Beethoven: Briefwechsel Gesamtausgabe,* vol. 2, p. 183 (letter 491) and Anderson, *Letters of Beethoven,* vol. 1, pp. 316–17 (letter 301). See also my "Autograph of Beethoven's 'Archduke' Trio," and Brandenburg, "Die Beethovenhandschriften in der Musikaliensammlung des Erzherzogs Rudolph," in *Zu Beethoven: Aufsätze und Dokumente,* vol. 3, ed. Harry Goldschmidt (Berlin: Verlag Musik, 1988), 168. Contrary to Brandenburg's report, the two string parts of the set are not missing, but are preserved together with the piano part in a bundle.

54. For Figures 6.9–6.13, mirror images constitute the complementary molds.

55. The paper, ruled eight staves to a page, measures about 229 mm by 320 mm, with a TS of 181 mm and SS of 8.5 mm.

56. The papers of both the violin and cello parts are ruled ten staves to a page and measure approximately 326 mm by 230 mm with a TS of 246 mm and SS of 10 mm.

57. Paris MS 100 is ruled sixteen staves to a page. Measuring roughly 226 mm by 324 mm, it is in *Querformat* with a TS of 181 mm and SS of 8.5 mm. As a bifolio, its watermark is necessarily incomplete, and the missing portions are indicated by dotted lines in Figure 6.12. It has been severely mutilated: a gaping trapezial hole now appears in fol. 1, where a (presumably) coveted portion of staves 7–10 has been removed.

58. *The Beethoven Sketchbooks,* 201–6 and 553 (paper type 27). One folio (pages 23 and 24) of the Landsberg 9 miscellany has a watermark with a "VF" monogram that may be related to the "FV" and "VF" found in some of the papers in the Sketchbook of 1810–1811 and the Sketchbook of 1814–1815. Another folio (pages 51 and 52) from Landsberg 9 has a watermark characterized by three crescents that is very likely related to Figures 6.9, 6.11, 6.12, and 6.14. See ibid., 222.

59. Brandenburg, "Die Quellen," 223–24.

60. See Anderson, *The Letters of Beethoven,* vol. 2, 606 (letter 664), and Sieghard Brandenburg, *Ludwig van Beethoven: Briefwechsel Gesamtausgabe,* vol. 3, 306 (letter 983). If Schindler is right, the work was first performed publicly in May 1814 in the Prater by Schuppanzigh's quartet. See Anton Schindler, *Beethoven as I Knew Him,* ed. Donald MacArdle, trans. Constance Jolly (New York: Norton, 1972), 171.

CHAPTER SEVEN

# "So träumte mir, ich reiste . . . nach Indien"

## Temporality and Mythology in Op. 127/I

*Birgit Lodes*

"Aus Gott floß alles rein und lauter aus."
—Beethoven's *Tagebuch,* no. 63a

It has been claimed that in his late works Beethoven created passages, and sometimes whole movements, in which the sense of an acting self at the core of the conception is replaced by the expression of an ideal state or transcendental, utopian vision. Critics have usually concentrated in this context on movements expressing a utopian transcendence that follows music depicting the struggling self. Examples from the late period include the last movement of the Ninth Symphony, the twofold sequence of Adagio and transcendental Allegro fugue at the end of the Sonata op. 110, and the two-movement design of the final Sonata, op. 111.

Beethoven's op. 127 expresses that kind of floating, tensionless, utopian state already in its first movement. I argue that in this quartet, Beethoven undercut the directional, dynamic qualities of a sonata-form Allegro, which is such a suitable form for telling a unique, teleological story, and he instead sought to convey what we might deem "mythic time." This movement can indeed be read as a myth, spiraling around the fundamental question of a cosmos, deity, or fate governing an enduring human essence that can only partially, at most, mold its own life, but that is part of an ongoing, cyclic *Weltgeschehen.* In this context, I suggest that our understanding of Beethoven's late works in general may be enriched by taking into account the idea of myth and mythology.

"Myth" is a much-discussed category in recent literary theory, especially since the writings of Claude Lévi-Strauss,[1] which brought about tremendous inflation and frequent degradation of the term *myth*. Nevertheless, it seems to me that in the present case there are compelling reasons, historical and ideological, to invoke the term.[2]

At the outset of the nineteenth century, *myth* resonated deeply with many German-speaking intellectuals. In 1800, Friedrich Schlegel proclaimed a "New Mythology,"[3] intensifying a trend that had begun several decades earlier with Johann Gottfried Herder and Karl Philipp Moritz. In 1767, Herder had been one of the first to discover the heuristic possibilities of mythology, which, because of its sensuous concreteness, opened perspectives and enabled discoveries that could not be attained by rationalistic methods. Moritz, in his *Götterlehre* of 1791, stressed the poetic structure of myths, whereas Schlegel saw myths as a rich fund of ideas and subjects for artistic use and as a special aesthetic category that promoted a mediation between Enlightenment reason and prelogical forms of thought. As Schlegel's ideas were quickly taken up by writers and thinkers, foremost among them Friedrich W. Schelling,[4] the idea of "myth" became a popular and compelling topic at the beginning of the nineteenth century.[5]

That Beethoven, too, was caught up by that fascination is revealed in many ways, but perhaps most clearly by entries in his Tagebuch,[6] or diary (see Figure 7.1). In this document, written during the years 1812–18, and thus spanning the period of transition between his middle and late styles, we find ample evidence of Beethoven's preoccupation with not only Greek and Roman mythic literature, but also with texts by Johann G. Herder, a key German figure in mythopoetic writings, and with publications on the then recently fashionable Indian and Brahman myths. (Myths from primitive cultures, exhaustively examined by Lévi-Strauss and Clifford Geertz, were hardly known at the time.) Beyond this documented awareness of ancient Indian or Greek myth, we can surmise that Beethoven may also have known about Schlegel's aesthetic vision of the importance of mythology, as the conversation books record several discussions about Schlegel, who was then living in Vienna.[7]

Before delving further into the subject of myth and mythology, however, let us first examine the music of op. 127. Regarded from the perspective of the sonata-form procedure and aesthetics, several features of the first movement of this quartet are especially unusual and have drawn comment from scholars:

* The movement opens with a two-part idea that contains a strong contrast: a six-measure majestic chordal Maestoso (2/4) is followed by a more subjective and flowing Allegro (3/4). The rising *forte* impetus of the Maestoso contrasts with the falling *piano* Allegro lines.
* The function of this composite idea seems deliberately ambiguous. It represents either a combination of slow introduction and first theme,[8] or a compound theme. The Maestoso returns twice (the second time shortened), in two different keys.
* The second theme (beginning in m. 41) offers little contrast to the first. Its key is the mediant minor (that is, G minor in relation to E♭ major), creating a very unusual

*Figure 7.1.* Beethoven's readings in mythology. Derived from Maynard Solomon, ed., *Beethovens Tagebuch* (cf. note 6). Numbers refer to this edition.

### WRITINGS ON INDIAN, BRAHMAN, AND EGYPTIAN MYTHS

Johann Friedrich Kleuker and Johann Georg Fick, *Abhandlungen über die Geschichte und Alterthümer, die Künste, Wissenschaften und Literatur Asiens,* 3 vols. (Riga, 1795-97); trans. of Sir William Jones and others, *Dissertations and Miscellaneous Pieces Relating to the History and Antiquities, the Arts, Sciences, and Literature, of Asia* (London, 1792)

- Vol. 3, pp. 412–15, for no. 62
- Vol. 3, p. 415, for no. 65
- Vol. 1, p. 355, for no. 94d; trans. of Sir William Jones, "On the Chronology of the Hindus," *Asiatick Researches,* 2 (1790), p. 115

Johann Friedrich Kleuker, *Das brahmanische Religionssystem im Zusammenhange dargestellt* (Riga, 1797); Supplement to Kleuker/Fick

- Pp. 34–35 for no. 61a    P. 37 for no. 61b
- Possibly pp. 35 and 174ff. influenced Beethoven's formulations in no. 63a
- P. 212 for no. 94c; transl. of Paulinus a Sancto Bartholomaeo, *Viaggio alle Indie Orientali* (Rome, 1796); trans. by William Johnston as *A Voyage to the East Indies* (London, 1800), p. 265n
- P. 214 for no. 95

Georg Forster, *Robertson's historische Untersuchung über die Kenntnisse der Alten von Indien* (Berlin, 1792); trans. of William Robertson, *An Historical Disquisition Concerning the Knowledge Which the Ancients Had of India* (Dublin, 1791)

- P. 307 for no. 64a and b; conflation (with omission) from two passages from the *Bhagavad-Gita*
- P. 337 for no. 93b

*Bhagavad-Gita*

- Chap. 3, line 7, for no. 64a, and chap. 2, lines 47–50 (part of l. 49 omitted), for no. 64b: probably copied from Forster/Robertson
- Possible inspiration for no. 63a

### ANCIENT GREEK AND ROMAN MYTHOLOGY AND LITERATURE

#### *Greek*

Johann Heinrich Voss (trans.), *Homers Odüssee* (Hamburg, 1781); Beethoven's annotated copy today in DSB, Autograph 40.3

- P. 95 for no. 74    P. 387 for no. 169
- P. 373 for no. 170

Johann Heinrich Voss (trans.), *Homers Ilias* (Hamburg, 1793); Beethoven used the reprint Vienna, 1814.

- Vol. 2, p. 424, for no. 26
- Vol. 2, p. 357 (not p. 356, as he himself notates), for no. 49

Gottlob Benedict von Schirach (trans.), *Biographien des Plutarch,* 10 vols.

- Vol. 3 (Berlin and Leipzig, 1777), *Philopoemen,* p. 484: par. 11, lines 2–3, for no. 96
- Vol. 5 (Berlin and Leipzig, 1778), *Sertorius,* p. 193: par. 6, line 3, for no. 150

Plato, *Republic*

- Cf. no. 87

#### *Roman*

Ovid, *Epistulae ex Ponto*

- Book 4, letter 10, line 5, for no. 125

Ovid, *Tristia*

- Book 5, letter 1, line 59, for no. 136

Pliny, *Epistulae*

- Book 3, letter 9, lines 3–4, for no. 113
- Book 3, letter 21, line 6, for no. 114

### GERMAN MYTHOPOETIC WRITINGS

Johann Gottfried Herder, *Blumen aus morgenländischen Dichtern gesammelt*; in *Zerstreute Blätter,* vierte Sammlung (Gotha, 1792)

- P. 11 for no. 5    P. 27 for no. 6
- Pp. 98–101 for no. 57    P. 102 for no. 58
- P. 103 for no. 55 and no. 56

Johann Gottfried Herder, *Vermischte Stücke aus verschiedenen morgenländischen Dichtern,* in *Sämmtliche Werke: Zur schönen Literatur und Kunst,* vol. 9, ed. Johann von Müller (Tübingen, 1807)

- P. 196 for no. 59

tonal relationship),[9] and its motives and phrase structure are highly akin to the Allegro section of the first theme.

* There is no dramatic emphasis at the moment of recapitulation. On the contrary, Beethoven blurred the precise location and harmonization of the recapitulation's beginning. This procedure is not singular in Beethoven's works, but it is done here in a particularly conspicuous way; the most powerful *fortissimo* reappearance of the Maestoso is pushed back into the development (perhaps that moment should be called the beginning of the recapitulation?) and appears in the submediant major (m. 135), whereas the contrasting Allegro theme begins smoothly on the second degree (m. 167).
* Throughout the movement, the composer avoids the dominant, the key ingredient of tonal contrast and structuring.

How do these features affect the movement's musical architecture? In choosing a barely contrasted second theme, and by deemphasizing the entry of the recapitulation, Beethoven smoothed out the typical tension and dynamism of a sonata-form movement. The avoidance of the dominant has a similar effect; indeed, it is possible to see this idea as underlying both of the features just mentioned. At least one writer has gone so far as to suggest that the avoidance of the dominant represents the fundamental challenge Beethoven sought to conquer in this movement.[10] Those who subscribe to the idea that a musical analysis begins with the question "To what compositional question does this piece give an answer?" would probably find this a reasonable proposition.

Yet I doubt that Beethoven was seized solely by the idea of solving such a compositional riddle. Instead, I would argue, his choices had to do with a desired artistic effect. He weakened some of the most striking characteristics of sonata-form dynamics in order to create a movement that was as undynamic and undirectional as possible, and in so doing he created a piece of music that displays a temporal structure remarkably different from his middle-period works.

If we accept the notion that the dynamics of sonata form are strongly compromised in this movement, we must ask what holds the movement together and whether other formal traits operate in it. One of the key features we would expect in a late work by Beethoven is motivic integration. Characteristically, there are several motives that appear for the first time in the opening six measures of the piece and that determine the motivic material of the movement and even the entire quartet.[11]

The Allegro theme, to be played "teneramente," "sempre piano e dolce," is, if not in character, then in construction, closely related to the Maestoso theme. Structurally, the basic rising line (E♭ to C) of the Maestoso is opposed by a falling one (C to E♭) in the Allegro. The first four-measure phrase only reaches B♭ (m. 10; cf. m. 5), the second, G (m. 14; cf. m. 3). The varied repetition in mm. 15–18 does not further the goal, but in the fourth and final section, the uppermost line encompasses the entire range from C down to E♭ (mm. 19–22), raised an octave. Similar observations have led Daniel Chua to the conclusion that the Allegro part of the theme (mm. 7–22) is a palindrome of the Maestoso.[12] Chua's argument is reinforced by the fact that at the beginning of the Allegro, the first violin constitutes the mirror (retrograde inversion) of the last pitches in the uppermost voice in the Maestoso (see Example 7.1), flowing from the sustained pitch C[2]. Other ways of seeing the motivic connection include deriving the motive of the first violin in m. 7 from the bass line in mm. 5–6, or, as Cooke suggests, from the pitches F–B♭–G in the first violin in mm. 4–5.[13]

The beginning of the Allegro theme is inconceivable without the foregoing Maestoso measures, since it emerges out of the subdominant harmony reached by the Maestoso. Characteristically, the Maestoso and the Allegro music are inseparably glued together. From m. 6 to m. 7, the moment of their encounter, every voice sustains its pitch, the second violin and the viola are tied over the bar line, the harmony and dynamic level are maintained, and even the Allegro's legato articulation is anticipated in the last measure of the Maestoso. The effect is a special one that also touched Beethoven's contemporaries, as an entry by his nephew Karl in a conversation book reveals: "The transition to the theme (at the beginning) really pleased [Beethoven's] brother."[14]

The notion that motives govern not only the thematic substance on a local level but also determine a movement's formal architecture is typical of Beethoven's late style. The most far-reaching large-scale unfolding of motives seems to concern the keys in which the opening Maestoso reappear later in the piece.

As David Epstein has shown, the semitone motive B♭–B–C that appears for the first time in mm. 5–6 in the Maestoso, links the phrases in mm. 10f., 14f., and 18f. (Examples 7.2a and b) and recurs various times in the following measures (cf. mm. 28 and 30–31, first violin; mm. 29–30 and 31–32, cello). This motive also governs the long-range linear progression from the second theme to the C-major Maestoso and determines the important key centers G minor–G major–C major (Example 7.2c). It is furthermore the background line of the upper voice, guiding the harmonic progression from m. 125 up to the tonicization of C major in m. 135 (Example 7.2d).[15]

However, Epstein does not point out that the same progression, transposed up a fourth (E♭–E–F), governs the harmonic progression C minor (m. 103 within the development) –C major–F minor (m. 167, beginning of the recapitulation; see Example 7.3). This specific transposition can be seen as a reflection of the opening harmonic gesture of the very first Maestoso: I–IV.

On a local level, this progression is spread across mm. 108–10 (see Example 7.4a

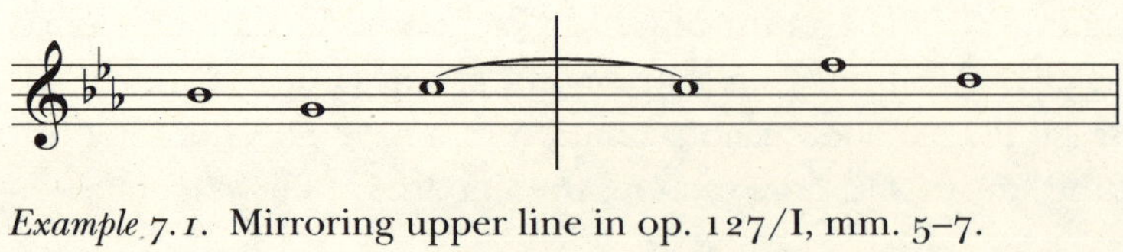

*Example 7.1.* Mirroring upper line in op. 127/I, mm. 5–7.

*Example 7.2a–d:* Op. 127/I: The connecting device B♭–B–C. (From David Epstein, *Beyond Orpheus,* 216–17).

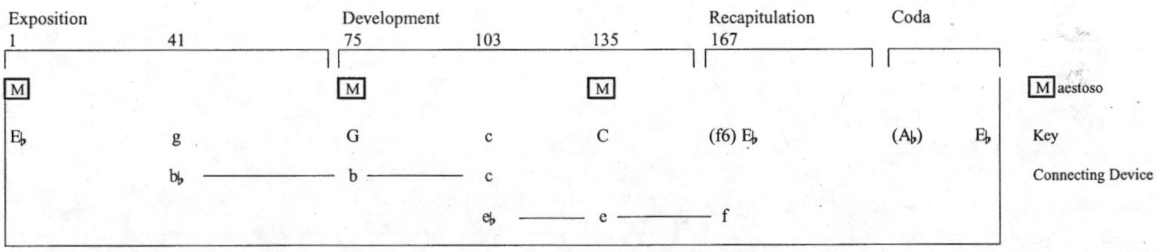


*Example 7.3.* Op. 127/I: The connecting devices B♭–B–C and E♭–E–F on a structural level.

in the second violin), where a C-major chord is introduced in passing by way of the E♮. In the immediate context, this event creates a degree of harshness (see the cross-relation with the first violin) that foreshadows the sudden outburst of the C-major Maestoso at mm. 133–47, which likewise originates in C minor (m. 113) and leads to F minor (mm. 150–53 and mm. 166f.). Characteristically, the motive (E♭–E–F) is not neglected later in the movement but is retained locally in the recapitulation at two conspicuous places. First, as shown in Example 7.4b, it appears in the "cadential theme" that ends the first theme, as a result of the transposition of the added modulation toward the subdominant (see E♭–E–F in m. 194, first violin; mm. 195–96, cello and first violin). Second, it appears in the varied recapitulation of the second theme, in which the transposed and untransposed versions of the half-tone motive occur simultaneously (mm. 211–13 and mm. 219–21; see Example 7.4c). Hence, this motive determines the keys of the second theme and the two returning Maestosi and, transposed by a fourth, shapes the harmonic course of the development section. Furthermore, the motive's impact is felt in the later movements.

The first Maestoso prefigures the keys of the later Maestosi in another way, as well. The successive appearances of the Maestoso in E♭, G major (mm. 75–80), and C major (mm. 135–38) are foreshadowed in the sustained pitches E♭$^1$–G$^1$–C$^2$ in the upper voice of the first Maestoso.[16] Indeed, Daniel Chua sees the movement's structure encapsulated in the initial contrasting Maestoso-Allegro:[17] in the same way that the first Maestoso expands powerfully from E♭$^1$ to C$^2$, then sustains that C$^2$ as a bridge to the

*Example 7.4.* The transposed connecting device (E♭–E–F) on a local level.

*a.* Op. 127/I, mm. 107–13.

*b.* Op. 127/I, mm. 193–98.

*c.* Op. 127/I, mm. 211–14 and mm. 219–22.

ensuing Allegro with its descent from $C^2$ back to $E\flat^1$, the movement's overall architecture rests on the unfolding of the Maestoso on a grand level (that is, recurring on G and on C), the prolongation of the C-major chord (mm. 135–66 as an expansion of m. 6), and a stepwise descent from C to E♭ beginning with the recapitulation. Chua does not mention, however, that the stepwise local preparation of the $C^2$ at the beginning of the recapitulation in the foregoing mm. 147–66 ($E^2$–$F^2$–$G^2$–$A\flat^2$–$B\flat^2$–$C^3$) recalls the stepwise ascent in the first Maestoso measures, split between the first violin and the cello ($E\flat^1$–F–$G^1$–A♭–$B\flat^1$–$C^2$).[18] The interrelation of the two passages is underlined by the fact that in both cases the ascent proceeds stepwise and stretches the interval of a sixth (major in the Maestoso, minor in the development), with every new pitch filling just one musical entity (a measure in the Maestoso, a four-measure group in the Allegro). Also pointing to their interrelation is the peak C that is reached in both cases before the beginning of the Allegro theme (m. 6 and m. 166, respectively), during which the dynamic level is reduced.

Beethoven has therefore established a network of connections on different levels in the opening Maestoso measures. At least two different processes of motivic "unfolding" are at work, guaranteeing a logical building of the movement on a level beyond that of the thematic foreground. These processes are not congruent with the sonata form; instead, they undermine it. Both networks involve the appearance of the Maestoso, which powerfully articulates the form, whereby neither the return at the beginning of the development in G major, nor the one within the development in C major, can be explained solely by principles of sonata form: G major is "the point of furthest remove,"[19] which is usually not the point at which the development is begun, and C major prepares the second scale degree in E♭ major instead of the tonic. Daniel Chua observes that Beethoven's motivic network is so powerful that it "stretches sonata form 'out of shape,'"[20] and he calls this a sign of "madness." Nicholas Marston, among others, has rightly expressed surprise at Chua's point of view, because networks such as these, paramount in Beethoven's late work, are traditionally regarded as a manifestation of order.[21] Thus the question remains as to why Beethoven chose this specific kind of motivic network and unfolding in op. 127, and what kind of expressive goal he wished to convey thereby.

In approaching this issue, it is useful to note that the subsurface motivic connections function as a web of crisscrossing threads. These connections are not confined to directional procedures tying the piece together; they also allow for manifold foreground possibilities for structuring time.[22]

When I hear or play this music, I find it striking that, apart from the three Maestosi, it conveys a unique quality of relaxed and lyric floating, of flowing in a seemingly timeless space. Several compositional means combine to create this impression. In the Allegro, by virtue of the sequence in the first violin and—above all—the rhythm in the cello, the triple meter is clear almost from the very beginning, yet at the same time, the 3/4 meter is far from being as well articulated as it would be in, say, a dance movement. It conveys neither the feeling of a dialectical sonata-allegro nor that of a folk-like song movement, something its high degree of periodicity might seem to imply.[23] Instead, the theme is a contrapuntal complex, somewhat similar to a Fuxian species exercise. The over-the-bar ties of the middle voices lend a certain lightness, or what we might call "lyric flow," to the theme, a quality that also characterizes many later passages. This flow is supported by harmonic means, as well. There are few strong V–I articulations, almost all leaps are filled in with stepwise motion (see, e.g., mm. 9–10, mm. 13–14, mm. 17–18, and mm. 21–22), and the stepping tenths of the outer voices support the flowing, smooth impression.

If we examine the Allegro theme as a whole, we soon realize that the music does not display the directionality so often characteristic of sonata movements. The theme is not formed as a "Satz," with its inherent directional potential.[24] Instead, the four-measure unit is repeated three times in slightly varied form, creating sixteen measures composed of two corresponding eight-measure groups, each in turn formed by two corresponding four-measure units. Checks and balances are at work here. Every one of these four-measure units moves from IV to I. It is as if the Allegro theme were

*Ludwig van Beethoven, Streichquartett Es-dur Opus 127*, ed. Emil Platen, Henle Studien-Edition, HN 9740,
Printed with the kind permission of Henle Verlag.


*Example* 7.5. Op. 127/I, mm. 1–92.

*Example 7.5, continued.*

*) Siehe *Bemerkungen*. *) See *Comments*. *) Cf. *Bemerkungen* ou *Comments*.

carried by its own inertia—as if it were an object turned over and around to be viewed in different shades of light.

Ulrich Siegele and Joseph Kerman have both commented on the rigidity of the four-measure units throughout the exposition.[25] These fixed units contribute to the feeling that there is no pronounced hierarchy among theme, bridge, or cadential materials. The bridge and cadential materials strongly relate to the themes, and they are also structured consistently in four-measure units, the only two exceptions in the exposition being a pair of added two-measure groups at the end of the first theme (mm. 30–31) and at the end of the exposition (mm. 73–74), respectively. This constant flow of four-measure units yields the impression of a constantly moving time-wheel, spinning around itself.[26]

Related to this impression is Beethoven's construction of the themes. Despite the fact that the second four-measure phrase of the second theme (mm. 41–56) differs markedly from the first phrase (more so than in the first theme), Beethoven adhered to the principle that the eight-measure phrase of the theme is repeated in variation, thus forming a sixteen-measure unit. After the opening Maestoso of the development, a sense of flow similar to the exposition develops.[27] The four-measure unit, now moving from IV to I in G major (mm. 81–84), returns several times, each time seemingly randomly changed in its outlook. In the second unit, the quarter-note motive is inverted and prolonged (mm. 85–88), coupled with the other voices. In the next unit (mm. 89–92), this same version of the quarter-note motive is played by the second violin and viola in octaves while the reduced version (dotted half notes) appears in descending form in the first violin and cello instead of following the contour of the other instruments. Finally, in the last unit (mm. 93–96), material from this first theme is infused by the more chromatic material of the second half of the second theme (see the motive in the cello), accompanied by the eighth-note figure first heard in mm. 81–82 in the middle voices, now repeated. Thus Beethoven does nothing other than combine nondirectional motives (which amount to diatonic lines) within fixed four-measure-units.[28]

The second sixteen-measure span (mm. 97–112) is structured similarly (aside from the two-measure canonic beginning and a two-measure prolongation, mm. 97f. and 107f., respectively), and closes with practically the same cadential formula as the first one (cf. mm. 95f. and 111f.). From m. 121 onward, the stable four-measure units are continued. Their regularity is abandoned only at the intrusion of the C-major Maestoso, where a unit is truncated (mm. 133–34). Following this Maestoso, the rest of the development is once again articulated in stable four-measure units, as are the recapitulation and the coda.

The main musical techniques applied in the development are variation, voice exchange, canon, new combinations of existing building blocks, and other contrapuntal procedures—nonpropelling devices altogether. Moreover, the four-measure units are hardly ever developed in a directional sense, through either prolongation or shortening. And except for the prominent Maestoso, it is almost impossible to detect a thematic hierarchy. As Kerman has noted, "a process of continuous free variation seems to supplant traditional developmental energy in this movement."[29] The result is that the development does not convey a directional sense; instead, the music is—as in the exposition—carried by its own inertia.

As we have seen, Beethoven made several compositional choices that defused much of the characteristic tension of sonata form. Other features also contribute to this lack of directionality. At the core of the first theme stands one of the most tensionless chord progressions imaginable: the move from tonic to subdominant (m. 6; the first nontonic chord sounding on a downbeat) back to tonic. This rather innocuous harmonic combination is important for the whole movement, and the subdominant (or other harmonizations of the upper-voice pitch C) will figure prominently throughout the piece.[30]

The movement's main source of tension lies in the repeated Maestoso sections. Despite the fact that there is an internal logic as to why Beethoven employed the Maestoso in C major, it is a static rather than a dynamic procedure, articulated in recurring blocks that are not integrated, developed, or otherwise elaborated. The Maestoso, with its massive *forte* chords, retains its separate identity throughout the piece; it symbolizes something gigantic that is contrasted, but not calmed, by the flowing *piano* texture of the Allegro.

Harmonically, the Maestosi in the development section are not provided with directional preparation. Although the first, in G major (mm. 75–80), is preceded by a dominant D, there is no real modulation to G major (see Example 7.5). Because G minor was the tonic for more than twenty measures (beginning with the second theme, m. 41), it is only a question of resolving the dominant not to the minor, but to the major, the typical semitone shift that would normally imply a further move to C. To understand the passage's tremendous power, it is necessary to gaze farther back in the movement. One of the prevailing characteristics of the exposition's Allegro is that every four-measure unit closes on the local tonic, something that imparts a repetitive, cyclic feeling rather than one of musical progression (see mm. 10, 14, 18, 22, 26 [somewhat], 31, 36). This feeling changes, however, with the emergence of the second theme, which establishes a clear ending for the first time after a four- or eight-measure unit. Because any such ending must at the same time be a beginning, an overlapping continuation emerges. The dominant preparation (m. 40) that precedes the second theme hints that the phrases will overlap from now on. It is a subtle hint, because the bass already touches the G, but it is one nonetheless underscored by a *crescendo.* Note that the sense of arrival could also have been carried out by the Maestoso in G major—it would fit perfectly at m. 41![31] After arriving on the local tonic at the fourth measure (m. 44), as is expected, the second four-measure-phrase's ending remains open on the dominant in the eighth measure (m. 48), which is stressed by a lively rhythm and by a *subito piano,* preceded by a *crescendo.* And in the varied repetition of the eight-measure phrase, the crescendo is even prolonged until the very end of the phrase, whereas the resolution to the local tonic in m. 57 is subdued once again.

The voices then present a closed two-measure cadence that begins and ends on the local tonic. This cadence is followed by an articulation of the same phrase three times in a row (mm. 57–58, 59–60, 61–62) with exchanged parts ("Stimmtausch"), but the third time, the one with the largest ambitus, a *crescendo* opens up to a different two-measure unit that finally leads to a true cadence in G minor: the first tonic reached decisively after a four- or eight-measure unit. (Notice how the first violin changes rhythmically the motive played before by the viola, mm. 57–58, the cello, mm. 59–60, and the second violin and viola, mm. 61–62.) This event is not without consequence. The sound reverberates, first *forte,* then *piano,* before the dominant returns, hesitantly in *piano,* and the low pitches are displaced in the cello to the high register (m. 68).[32] Beethoven then asserted G major powerfully through sudden *fortes* and through a leap of more than two octaves in the cello. What could have been a simple modal shift from G minor to G major is completely changed in its effect. Again there is a reverberation, almost exactly as in mm. 66–68, but in this case there is no resolution. Instead, a void ensues. After another timid attempt on the dominant (m. 74), G major, missed before, now enters with even more force, a force that derives not from resolution but from surprise, as we hear the chordal Maestoso theme.

This situation is deepened with the next and final Maestoso, this time in C major (mm. 135–38). After an extended regular sequence of four-measure units, in which, starting in m. 121, the Maestoso's loud volume and long harmonic blocks are already adumbrated, the C that was clearly reached as a dominant in mm. 133–34 is cut off after only two measures, giving way to the powerful Maestoso in a tonicized C major. Again, the Maestoso is not reached as the organic outcome of what had preceded but instead is presented as something surprising and new—a fresh starting point. Hence, in both instances the Maestoso is not prepared as much as asserted boldly after a fissure. Both times, the Maestoso steps forth mightily after a passage that had developed something of a directional sense (cadencing after the square unit in the first case; modulating with V–I sequences in the second) but was then cut off.

In using the compound Maestoso-Allegro theme as a formal signpost[33] at the beginning of the exposition and development, Beethoven chose a very clear means of formal articulation. The simplest version would have been to have the Maestoso return at the beginning of the recapitulation in the tonic, but his solution is much more unusual. The Maestoso returns before the end of the development in the key of the submediant, C major.

The transition back to the Allegro theme is achieved in an extraordinary manner (see Example 7.6). After the intrusion of the Maestoso in C major, the voices move in double counterpoint at the octave with three different motives.[34] The motive in the first violin (mm. 141–42, stemming from mm. 8–9) is repeated an octave lower in the viola, then again in the second violin. The same principle occurs in the accompanying figure (m. 142 [with upbeat] in the cello, m. 144 again in the cello, m. 146

in the first violin) and in the figure running parallel to it in thirds or sixths (m. 142 [with upbeat] in the second violin, m. 144 in the first, and m. 146 in the viola). We hear the same music three times, only with changed roles and an increase in range each time. Afterward, the field is even more stable. From m. 147 up to m. 167, the beginning of the recapitulation, there is no change in the motivic material. The four voices propel the rhythm ♩♩♩ together,[35] the first violin in an eighth-note version,[36] until the end of this passage. The recapitulation is harmonically prepared, but in an astonishing way. The second degree (F minor) is prepared by its own dominant (mm. 162–66), but every possibility of creating a meaningful event out of this progression

*Example 7.6.* Op. 127/I, mm. 132–71.

*Example 7.6, continued.*

is systematically undercut. The F-minor chord enters two beats early (on two and three of m. 166), thus paralleling the two previous occurrences of the Allegro theme (mm. 7 and 81), where the harmony was also reached before the theme began. Likewise, every harmonic change in the preceding passage occurs in the fourth measure of every four-measure phrase (see mm. 150, 154, 158, and 162).[37] Any sense of arrival is undercut by the displacement of the harmonic and the dynamic articulation. The harmonies hinted at are F minor (II) in m. 150, then A♭ major (IV) in m. 158, thus portraying a vacillation between two similar possibilities that had been placed side by side in the first measure of the first Allegro.[38] Despite the fact that a reiteration of V–I patterns can have an extremely goal-directed impetus (especially in Beethoven's work), they appear here in an exceptionally controlled demonstration of this cadential nucleus, with its directional powers subdued.

To sum up the formal processes at work in this movement, Beethoven consciously avoided normal sonata-form hierarchies. Except for the Maestoso, he aligned and combined thematic material of similar character. Keys and themes were partially determined by motivic material that occurred in the very first measures. This motivic treatment operates in the background and is not a dynamic process. The result of these interlocking phenomena (sonata architecture and motivic network) is a static form, which was chosen, I would suggest, not merely as a compositional experiment but in order to convey the sense of a nondirectional, mythical conception of time.

This compositional strategy, unprecedented among the first movements of

Beethoven's string quartets, may reflect an aspect of Beethoven's broadened perspective on life, transcendence, nature, and art.

As the title of his essay states, Maynard Solomon has recently discerned "A Sea Change in Beethoven's Spiritual Outlook" from about 1812 to the first phases of his involvement with the late works.[39] Citing examples from Beethoven's *Tagebuch* and letters, Solomon came to the conclusion that the Beethoven who would once have grab[bed] fate by the throat[40] had changed into a person who felt a deep submissiveness to fate, who admired the true and eternal light of a godhead, who was attracted to a life of silent contemplation, who considered retreating from the world and living like a monk to attain a state of grace, who was prepared to admit his faults, and, finally, who saw his art as a spiritual means that would elevate him above "normal" people and enable him to partake of the endless, flawless, timeless, all-encompassing state of transcendence.[41]

This new dimension in Beethoven's outlook must be seen in connection with his longing and search for contact with the Christian deity during times of trial and depression. The search first emerged when he realized he would suffer lifelong deafness, and it resurfaced during the years of struggle over his nephew. Both phases saw the composition of religious works: the songs on texts by Christian Fürchtegott Gellert, the oratorio *Christus am Ölberge,* and the C-Major Mass in the earlier phase, the Missa solemnis at the end of the second. To the second phase, too, belong plans for compositions on Ancient (Greek and Indian) myths. For example, in 1818 Beethoven noted in the sketches for a new symphony: "im Adagio Text griechischer Mithos Cantique Eclesiastique—im Allegro Feier des Bachus."[42] He thought of setting texts by Homer to music, as scansion marks in his *Tagebuch* reveal.[43] As we know from a letter by Joseph von Hammer (later "Hammer-Purgstall") of February 24, 1819,[44] he was even eager to set an Indian text of religious character for choir, a plan left unrealized because of time constraints.[45] Yet Beethoven did set a highly myth-inspired text, Schiller's "Freude schöner Götterfunken, Tochter aus Elysium," in the Ninth Symphony. It is conspicuous that in the traces remaining from Beethoven's study of transcendental matters there seems to be little distinction made between the Christian God and mythic godheads—that is, between the monotheistic character of Christianity and the polytheistic character of myth. Beethoven's perspective apparently reflects the widely held idea, especially among the early Romantics and Schelling, that Christianity itself was a myth among myths.[46]

Thus it is not surprising that in his Tagebuch, Beethoven wrote down excerpts from ancient Indian, Egyptian, Greek and Roman, and Christian sources alike. Several of the essays Beethoven copied from draw explicit parallels between the different worlds;[47] some of them might stem from Masonic circles.[48] (It should be noted that Beethoven had been familiar with some ancient Greek and Roman sources since his childhood in Bonn.)[49] Whereas this interest certainly gained new facets and a new intensity during the phase of writing the Tagebuch,[50] his specific preoccupation with Eastern thought was, from all we can tell, new at the time he wrote the Tagebuch.[51]

If one scrutinizes Beethoven's entries from mythological and mythopoetic writings in his Tagebuch (see Figure 7.1), the following main ideas can be distilled:[52] Beethoven was taken by the notion that every being was determined by God or fate, and, as Solomon points out, he felt very submissive to that fate.[53] Thus he jotted down, "Show your power, Fate! We are not masters of ourselves; what has been decided must be, and so be it!" (no. 73); "Fate gave Man the courage to endure to the end" (no. 26), from Homer's *Iliad;* and finally, "The chief characteristic of a distinguished man: endurance in adverse and harsh circumstances" (no. 93a).[54] In this context, Beethoven developed the idea that it would be desirable to retreat from worldly life and live instead solely for his art (cf. the Romantic image of the "Peasant Hut," so well described by Solomon).[55] He was also aware that he would be able to take part in timelessness and infinity through his art, so he copied from Homer's *Odyssey:* "Sacrifice once and for all the trivialities of social life to your art, O God above all! For eternal Providence in its omniscience and wisdom directs the happiness and unhappiness of mortal men" (no. 169). From another source he copied: "Everything that is called life should be sacrificed to the sublime and be a sanctuary of art. Let me live, even if by artificial means, if only they can be found!" (no. 40).[56] A passage he took from a letter of Pliny may reveal how central this notion was to him: "Nevertheless, what greater gift can be conferred on a man than fame and praise and eternal life?" (no. 114).[57]

Secondly, Beethoven's excerpts from Brahman and Egyptian writings reflect a special interest in the timelessness of the godhead, a fact not brought forth by Solomon.[58] This becomes evident through entries such as "For God, time absolutely does not exist" (no. 94d), or "[As] God is immaterial, He is above all conception; as He is invisible, He can have no form; but from what we behold of His works, we may conclude that He is eternal, omnipotent, omniscient, and omnipresent" (no. 93b).[59] Beethoven is also reported to have kept inscriptions about the Veil of Isis on his desk during his later years, the second of which reads: "I am everything that is, that was, and that shall be. No mortal man has lifted my veil."[60]

That the concept of time was a topic of special concern to Beethoven can be seen in the inclusion of references to divine timelessness and, by contrast, to the temporality of the human condition. From Plutarch he excerpted and underlined Sertorius's observation that "the most precious thing for a man who wants to accomplish important things" is to possess time (no. 150).[61] He apparently also thought about the notion that the subjective experience of time can vary substantially: "No time passes more quickly, rolls by faster, than when our mind is occupied or when I spend it with my Muse" (no. 31).[62]

Preoccupation with mythological issues, Eastern and Western, evidently played an important role for Beethoven. Even if the excerpts written down at a certain time cannot serve as "proofs" or psychological scripts for his exact thoughts, they can nevertheless convey a sense of the issues on which he ruminated during the years of the evolution of his late style. For all we know, Beethoven did not subscribe to any of the documented ideas blindly or dogmatically, but he approached them from the perspective of an educated, enlightened human being. The musical fruits growing from these thoughts ripened over the years, and the first movement of op. 127 is one of the lush experimental gardens where we can encounter them.

Which connections might we draw specifically between the structure of the first movement of op. 127 and that of myths?

* According to Claude Lévi-Strauss, binary oppositions are necessary for the structure of "primitive" or mythic thinking: thinking in binary oppositions is a fundamental element of how human beings comprehend the world.[63] The immediate sequence of Maestoso and Allegro at the outset of op. 127 can be understood as such a binary opposition. We can take it as a point of departure for interpreting the first movement as if it were a myth, following the further occurrences of the Other (the Maestoso) in relationship to the opposite Allegro during the course of the piece.[64]
* Beethoven's use of a developed motivic network is a central means for guaranteeing coherence within op. 127/I. Myth, according to Peter Gendolla, is "a framework . . . that makes it possible to grasp the unique present and an abiding unity at the same time, holding fast to a momentary event as the embodiment of an everlasting essence."[65] Neither the "everlasting essence" nor the motivic network is bound to linear time.
* The motivic constellations in op. 127/I act as motivic units that materialize in many different ways and on many different levels. In a similar way, myths stand for a central phenomenon cast in many different guises. There is no one individual story. "Myth tells of . . . no single narrative, but much more of potentiality, a structure that can be endlessly repeated in multiple ways."[66] Although Beethoven constructed a highly individualized movement in op. 127/I, the music behaves in a way that creates a certain feeling of randomness. The same motives recur again and again, slightly varied, combined, or moved to other voices. We gain the impression that some of them could be omitted without doing much harm to the course of the music.
* The joining of themes and motives in op. 127 consists in good part of nondirectional combinations linked to one another with seemingly casual freedom. As in a myth, a directional "development" is not what counts. As in a myth, Beethoven put musical cells together, sometimes with, sometimes without readily apparent cohesion, a procedure that is intensified by the frequently nondirectional harmony. In a myth it is very common that an Other, which humans do not necessarily understand, interrupts events surprisingly.
* The piece's temporality seems akin to a myth. That notion, however, should be examined in greater detail.

In analyzing the first movement of op. 127, one discovers that its aesthetic conception is very different from first movements that primarily follow the logic of a dialectical process and are profoundly goal oriented. Beethoven composed this movement as if time would not vanish. The core of the musical architecture is grounded in a careful balancing of thematic groupings that do not express a teleological direction.

One of the central characteristics of myth is its cyclic time structure, which is fundamentally different from the more linear time normally assumed in Western civilization.[67] Mythic time is a cyclic and infinite one that is determined by the eternal change of day and night or other natural or cosmic events. Beethoven was confronted with this different concept of time in his mythical readings.

It might be helpful to examine a passage on the subject by William Jones from his *On the Chronology of the Hindus* (1788), which we know Beethoven read at least in excerpts (see Figure 7.1).[68] Jones began his "dissertation" with a long passage, actually the first chapter, from one of the oldest Sanskrit tracts, *On Religious and Civil Duties,* taken, as it is believed, from the oral instructions of Menu, son of Brahmà, to the first inhabitants of the earth.

> The sun causes the division of day and night, which are of two sorts, those of men and those of the Gods; the day for the labor of all creatures in their several employments; the night for their slumber. A month is a day and night of the *Patriarchs,* and it is divided into two parts; the bright half is *their* day for laborious exertions, the dark half *their* night for sleep. A year is a day and night of the Gods, and that is also divided into two halves; the day is when the sun moves toward the north, the night when it moves toward the south. Learn now the duration of a night and day of Brahmà, with that of the ages respectively and in order. Four thousand years *of the Gods* they call the *Críta* (or *Satya*) age; and its limits at the beginning and at the end *are,* in like manner, as many hundreds. In the three successive ages, together with their limits at the beginning and end of them, are thousands and hundreds diminished by one. This aggregate of four ages, amounting to twelve thousand divine years, is called an age of the Gods; and a thousand such divine ages added together, must be considered as a day of Brahmà: his night has also the same duration. The before-mentioned age of the Gods, or twelve thousand of their years multiplied by seventy-one, form what is named here below a *Manwantara.* There are *alternate* creations and destructions of *worlds* through innumerable *Manwantaras:* the Being supremely desirable performs all this again and again.' Such is the arrangement of infinite time, which the *Hindus* believe to have been revealed from Heaven.[69]

Time, as described in this Brahman instruction, is structured by natural occurrences: day, month, year. Every occurrence is split into halves: day–night; waxing moon–waning moon (within the month); sun moving north–sun moving south (within the year), and so on. There is perfect balance. Later on, the calculations get unintelligibly complex and lead to the "Manwantara," the highest conceivable unit of time, which can be constructed in innumerable ways, so that everything is becoming infinite. But the "Being supremely desirable performs all this again and again."

In my view, we can sense this kind of temporal conception when listening to the opening movement of op. 127. This is not the only such example, but as a first movement a remarkable instance in which the composer was apparently guided by the notion of mythic time. The Allegro parts of op. 127/I consist almost exclusively of constant four-measure units, which are neither prolonged nor shortened, but repeated, combined, or varied. These units seem to act like a basic category for perceiving time, like days, months, seasons, or years. Hardly any of them comes alone, but each is balanced by a corresponding unit. It is as if Beethoven adhered to a law that set out a fixed space, in this instance, a four-measure unit, to be filled with music that was often, but never quite, the same, and that might also be of a different character. As we never know what the next day will be like, we also do not know which music we will hear in the next unit. We do know, however, that there will be a next unit, of a given length. Furthermore, after having read some of the books about India from which Beethoven copied, the mellifluous character of the first movement inescapably reminds me of the reputedly soft character of the people of ancient India.[70]

The movement opens in a completely different way. In contrast to the clear four-measure units of the Allegro, the Maestoso chords do not allow the listener to grasp a sense of meter. Michael Steinberg reports that he could not understand Beethoven's rhythm and meter in virtually any of the performances of the piece he heard, and although this lack of comprehension might partly be due to players not coming to grips with the notated rhythm, it occurs not completely by chance.[71] The chord progressions and dynamics suggest units of 5/8 and 3/8 in a twofold change, and only at the very end is a 4/8 meter audible, although it is unstable even then, because of the foregoing ambiguities, not to mention the trill in the first-violin part. Despite the majestic character of the chords, we discern that time in a directional sense does not exist. We are rather left within a space without temporal calibration. Concerning its timing, the opening passage is not tangible, not earthbound. Moreover, each time the Maestoso returns throughout the movement (mm. 75–80, mm. 135–138), it occurs unexpectedly. Typically, events that cannot be explained by logic or experience—catastrophes such as periods of drought—are predominant themes in myths.[72] Myths are able to offer a framework for events that escape human control. Mythic time is open for the unforeseeable.

The impression that in the first movement of op. 127 the laws of a logically and dynamically structured sonata-form movement give way to a mythical, circling, somewhat static structure can become even more palpable if we compare op. 127 to an earlier work: the first movement of the *Eroica*.

"The most overwhelming effect the Revolution had on its contemporaries was indeed an entirely new mode of experiencing 'time'."[73] Reinhold Brinkmann argues that this "new mode of temporal experience" is reflected in Beethoven's works after 1800, among them, historically most decisive, the Third Symphony.[74] Drawing from a wealth of contemporary sources and from scholarly studies on the topic, Brinkmann paints a picture of the feeling for temporality circa 1800, which he sees as characterized by "(1) radical temporalization itself and its intensification through acceleration; (2)

the direction of the temporal axis toward progress, in effect, the moment of finality within this mode of thought; and (3) the belief in the beginning of a new, superior age as the result of both."[75]

Proceeding from the premise that "in the temporal art of music, the experience of time, of a new—in this context—revolutionary structural use of time, assumed a central role,"[76] Brinkmann characterizes the *Eroica* as a

> temporalization of musical form. . . . The term does not refer to accelerando, increase in tempo (though this can be a means of temporalization, albeit a rather superficial external one), but rather to the simulation of acceleration by the compositional fleshing out of the process. . . . Compositions of the form-as-process variety address both path and goal. As for the path, the usual descriptive models refer to composing thematically and to quasi-logical extension, i.e. 'developing variation.' More important still seems the concept of form as a chain of events which invariably refers beyond itself, a chain of events that does not conclude but progresses, continually pressing forward, in which the processes create a dynamic experience of time. The goal of a form oriented in this way lies at the end of the work, or even beyond the work itself. Finality is its organizing principle; all symphonies organized as processes are 'finale symphonies.' In the radically constructed process form, repetition becomes problematic.[77]

As already indicated, these features are certainly not at all the ones that prove characteristic for the first movement of op. 127. Instead, the music indulges in repetitive structures (despite the fact that there is no written repeat mark), and the phrases conclude but do not progress or press forward. Quite contrary to the *Eroica* movement, a sense of nondirectional movement prevails.

We should now leave the plane of generalization, looking at several specific passages in both pieces side by side. There are common features that invite a comparison, after all, because both movements are in E♭ major, both in 3/4, and for both the tempo indication reads "Allegro" (in the symphony, "molto e con brio" is appended, but it is played probably at about the same tempo as the quartet movement).[78] In the following I will focus on those passages Brinkmann singled out in his analysis of op. 55: the opening; the end of the development and the start of the recapitulation; the end of the recapitulation and the beginning of the coda; and finally the end of the movement.

The symphony opens with two short chords that "define tonality, meter, tempo, orchestra, musical space, and the intense 'tone' of the whole." Something similar can be said about the Maestoso chords in the string quartet, yet they, in contrast to the harsh opening of the *Eroica,* define neither meter nor tempo. The continuation is also very different. Whereas in the Allegro of the string quartet the theme descends from a high point and closes, closes, closes, and closes, in the *Eroica* the main theme is built up from below, from the dynamic level of *piano,* and new, unsettling elements rise in every of its three appearances, so that it never completes a Classical period but presses constantly forward; characteristically, all three thematic phrases begin on the tonic but end openly on the dominant. Whereas in the *Eroica* the theme strives forward ("from the start the entire main part of the exposition was itself a 'transition'—exemplary proof of a radical strategy of development, driven by a 'new irrevocable propulsive force'"),[79] in the string quartet the first theme closes and advances only by means of an increase in range and dynamics. In the *Eroica,* the themes are developed in a new manner every time they appear, whereas in op. 127 they are merely varied (mm. 15–22 are a variation of mm. 7–14; mm. 49–56 a variation of 41–48), but never developed. In op. 127, the remaining techniques applied in the exposition and in the development, such as voice exchange, canon, and inversion, are also of a nondirectional character, which again is the exact opposite of the progressive techniques in the *Eroica.*

The beginning of the recapitulation in the *Eroica* (m. 398) is crystal clear, as it is preceded not only by a long dominant preparation, but also by the very conspicuous "false" horn entrance in the tonic and by the entrance of the whole orchestra, *forte* and *fortissimo,* on the dominant. The main theme then starts afresh with new developments. In the string quartet, however, the beginning of the recapitulation is blurred and we hardly notice the moment the main Allegro theme slips in. Furthermore, the recapitulation of op. 127 does not intend "to drive the formal process emphatically forward."[80] Rather, Beethoven "seems certainly to have meant to soften the recapitulation. The feeling is altogether different from the emphatic, forceful, or triumphant recapitulations in most of the previous quartet first movements."[81]

Whereas some scholars have discussed the coda of the first movement of the *Eroica* as a paradigm of the heroic drive pervading the whole movement, scarcely anyone has written more than a few words or phrases about the coda and the ending of the first movement of op. 127; perhaps the coda of op. 127/I seems too simple to attract analysts' attention. However, with the extreme achievements in Beethoven's middle-period codas in our consciousness, we should be suspicious, asking what made him write a coda so revolutionary in its waning tenderness. From my point of view, this coda is as telling and consequential for the prevailing tenor of the whole movement as is the coda in the *Eroica.*

Let us start again by outlining common features. In both movements the recapitulation ends with loud hammering chords on the tonic (op. 55: mm. 547–50; op. 127: mm. 231–32, 235–36; see Example 7.7) and the coda begins with a shortened version of the main Allegro theme, sounding three times in different instruments and on various pitches (op. 55: E♭ major–D♭ major–C major, mm. 553ff.–557ff.–561ff.; op. 127: starting out from E♭''–E♭'–C', mm. 241f.–243f.–245f.). Major differences lie in the treatment of the first thematic return and the continuation of the coda. Whereas the coda of op. 55 takes its departure from the tonic (m. 551), introduced by a short diminished-seventh chord (over a pedal point E♭ in the basses), op. 127 moves on from the last and deflated dominant chord in m. 240 to a diminished chord on the third beat so that the theme can start out, as in the exposition (m. 7), from the subdominant.

And the continuation? In op. 55, after the third occurrence of the head of the theme, a grand process of modulation starts in m. 565, using material of various themes until in m. 631 the tonic is finally reached again after an extended dominant preparation. Characteristically within this process, most of the four- or eight-measure units (sometimes expanded) open up to a (local) dominant, so that the units project beyond themselves (see, e.g., G6/5 in mm. 569–72, C6/5 in mm. 577–80, B♭7 in mm. 587–88, 591–92 or 629–30).

In op. 127, the music continues in a completely different manner: After the third occurrence of the head motive, the second measure is cut off and repeated (m. 247; m. 248 an octave higher). The whole four-measure phrase is then repeated twice (mm. 249–52 in the first violin, mm. 253–56 in the second violin), and the last measure is repeated and transposed (mm. 257–58).

Of special importance for our investigation, and contrary to the events in the *Eroica*, are the following:

* From mm. 245 to 256 we hear the same music three times in a row, but with the parts lying in different voices (except for the cello, which sticks to its role, and the voice sounding first in the second violin is slightly varied each time).
* Each of these units moves from either II to I or from V to I, thus not projecting forward as in the *Eroica*, but closing. (The only exception is m. 244, where the entry of the next phrase on the II—cf. the beginning of the recapitulation in m. 167—is prepared.)

*Example* 7.7. Op. 127/I, mm. 231–82.

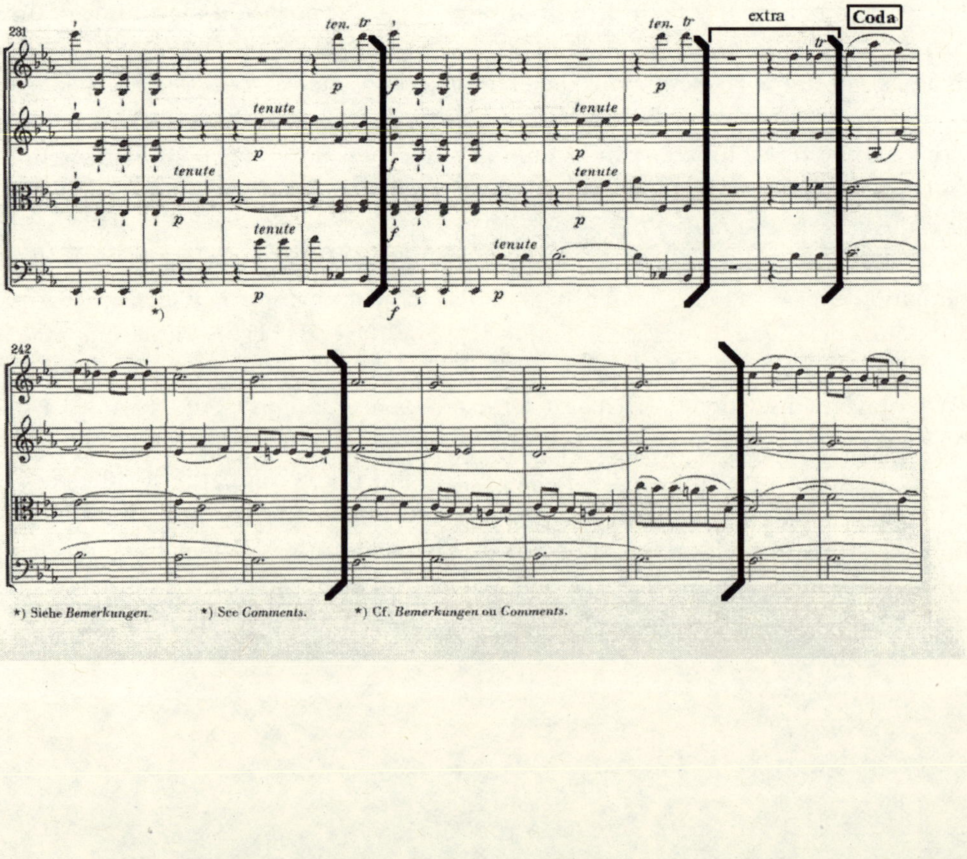

extra
251
cresc.
259
p
cresc.
267
p dolce
dim.
274
dim.
p
pp

* Because none of these tonics is in root position, we may describe their "closing" as a state of suspension or of "hanging in the air." In harmonizing the same melodic figure, starting from C in every single measure (viola in mm. 245–48, first violin in mm. 249–52, second violin in mm. 253–56), once with the dominant, once with the tonic, Beethoven undercut a sense of arrival. The V–I changes largely lose their directional quality. It is only in the prolongation of the last four-measure unit, in mm. 257–58, that the harmony comes down to a tonic in root position, but Beethoven took care to push it (and the preceding dominant) back to the last beat of the measure, again weakening any sense of arrival.

The principle of E♭ major sounding at the end of the four-measure units is also not relinquished in the following eight measures (mm. 259–66), where this key is reinterpreted as the dominant to A♭ major. Thus, in contrast to the *Eroica,* the only dominant chords used at the end of four-measure units (mm. 244, 262, and somewhat, in m. 266) lead astray from the tonic, and all the real dominants (B♭) are domesticated, locked up within the four-measure phrases.

Especially telling for the profoundly different styles of the first movement of the *Eroica* and the first movement of op. 127 are the endings of these pieces. In the *Eroica,* the so-called main theme reenters at m. 631 in the horn, changed into an eight-measure phrase that consists of four measures of tonic and four measures of dominant (again not a periodic theme!). This melodically and harmonically open-ended final version of the theme is repeated three times.[82] During this "climactic peroration," the "central event in the coda," various parameters (dynamics, instrumentation, range) increase and create a tremendous surging effect.[83] We partake in a continuous process of intensification. The piece's grand ending must be achieved by a nonthematic, emphatic reiteration of the dominant, resolving, again outside the square phrases, into the tonic. The movement's close occurs on a large-scale downbeat. In op. 127, too, the main thematic material returns (m. 267ff.), but there, all the units do not open up, and instead close on the tonic. As we now realize, throughout the coda almost every four-measure unit ends on the tonic—a crazy plan! How, then, is it possible to achieve a satisfying ending to the piece? Beethoven did not do much about this: he simply reinforced the dominant (two changes V–I, each a measure long) and used the well-known eighth-note motive in a modified closing form (mm. 279–82).[84] Basically, he did not close the movement differently from how he ended the main theme in m. 22. The theme does not reveal its history at the very end; it is just a little more meager, having lost some of its energy.

Remarkably, in the very last measures of op. 127/I, Beethoven reduced the dynamics and the number of voices. Throughout the coda, a *piano* dynamic prevails until the final *pianissimo* last measures. What a difference in comparison to the ending of the first movement of the *Eroica,* where more and more instruments enter, the music gets louder and louder, and at the very end we are swept away by a celebration of harmony and sound: "It is the orchestra as such, the collectivity and its unfolding, that functions as the agent and goal over 800 measures of this gigantic movement."[85]

In the *Eroica,* the tonic is reached after the eight-measure units. The goal of the movement projects beyond itself: "The movement virtually could go on forever. Its telos is the future."[86]

In both movements, the prevailing gesture crystallizes at the very end. As Dahlhaus has rightly stated, "the thematic figure remains at the end of the movement what it was from the beginning: a function of the formal process, a sign of the passage of time, a vehicle of temporality."[87] In the *Eroica,* whose main theme never was a fixed shape but rather a continuous process of transformation gaining more and more energy, this "main theme" transforms for the last time into an opening gesture (I–V) leading into a majestic and forceful ending that projects beyond itself. In op. 127, the prevailing character of the main theme, its coming back to an end, is utilized. The gesture of the coda in the *Eroica* is one of projecting, of forward-driving energy. In op. 127, the gesture is one of reducing, of cowering. The music vanishes into nothing, without dramatization. The coda of op. 55/I has been interpreted as the glorious victory or the posthumous glory of the hero (the theme) that was constantly acting and developing throughout his journey (the movement).[88] The coda of op. 127/I can be understood, I suggest, as the (natural and therefore totally unspectacular) dissolution of an individual energy in the ongoing *Weltgeschehen*—as in a myth.[89]

To the four exemplary passages looked at in some detail following Brinkmann's analysis, I wish to add a further unequal parallel between op. 55 and op. 127, one that is lodged in their treatment of silence.[90] The climactic point in the enormous development of the *Eroica* movement is the accented silence in measure 280. This climax of the development is generated by an intense rhythmic process involving accented, syncopated dissonances; so unrelenting is this rhythmic fragmentation and compression that the thematic material is virtually dissolved into nothing at about that point when the recapitulation would normally be expected. Here Beethoven introduced an apparently new theme in the remote key of E minor. In op. 127, on the other hand, it is the silence of the incomplete, stammering cadences at the end of the exposition and recapitulation that open a meaningful gap. The expectant pause that anticipates the first return of the Maestoso in G major, marking the beginning of the development, "connects" the two interdependent parts of the binary opposition that lies at the heart of the whole movement. In the coda, the gap is not filled in this way, yet the temporal structure is provocative, and instead of the whole measure of rest that marks the beginning of the coda, the movement might already have ended in the same spacing as the final chord. Without needing another literal return of the Maestoso, the music still seems touched by its memory.

The distinct types of construction in the first movements in the *Eroica* and in op. 127 respectively are palpable in more general features, too; for example, Beethoven relied heavily on the tension between dominant and tonic in the *Eroica,* whereas he largely avoided it in op. 127. The developmental character of the whole movement in the symphony is juxtaposed to a highly moment-oriented movement in op. 127 (including the development, where static strategies prevail), and in op. 127 any process of cutting off ("Abspaltung"), any acceleration of harmonic or motivic pace is avoided, quite contrary to the procedures in the *Eroica*.

The different "stories" of the two movements, revealing themselves in so many details, build upon two very different usages of time. Corresponding to Brinkmann's argument that the first movement of the *Eroica* reflects the new temporal consciousness of the French Revolution, especially the feeling of a radical acceleration and directionality, I would argue that op. 127 expresses an alternative to that feeling, a temporal consciousness that embraces circularity, the actual moment, and openness to the Other.

We should remind ourselves that the time when Beethoven wrote his op. 127 quartet was very different from when he wrote his *Eroica* Symphony. The hype and hopes of the revolution were buried; the Congress of Vienna (1814–15) had resulted in a reordering of Europe, guided by the eighteenth-century idea of a balance of powers with which to guarantee peace. A feeling of political and social stagnation and frustration prevailed. At that time, an interest in the Other, in ancient, medieval, and Eastern thought and religion, became more and more popular, as did an interest in myth. And as we have seen, Beethoven himself had evidently developed a somewhat different outlook since his "revolutionary" years.

These contemporary currents contributed to Beethoven's experimentation with alternatives to the former predominant temporalization of acceleration and directionality as he searched for ways to express another experience of temporality through his music. In any case, the first movement of op. 127 expresses a temporal experience fundamentally different from the one expressed in the first movement of the *Eroica.* Given the conspicuous standing of op. 127 within Beethoven's output, as the first string quartet after a hiatus of fourteen years, and its shared E♭-major tonality with the *Eroica,* a work often seen as the main representative of his so-called "heroic" style,[91] it even seems possible that Beethoven conceived op. 127/I deliberately as a work setting forth a different concept of structuring time as mythic, nonlinear temporal experience, as opposed to the historic, linear approach that dominated his middle-period works.[92] We might even consider it an active "protest against linear temporal consciousness."[93]

So far I have indicated general parallels between the architecture of the first movement of op. 127 and that of myths, concentrating on the perspective of mythical time. I now wish to suggest the possibility of hearing this work as a concrete myth. The beginning of op. 127 sets up a binary opposition: a majestic Maestoso is opposed to a lyric, flowing Allegro; a *forte* with *sforzati* accents gives way to *piano e dolce,* as chords stand against lines, an unclear meter (written 2/4) is followed by clearly defined four-measure (3/4) units, and a rising impetus is opposed to a falling one. As we have seen, these different musical characters are structurally interrelated, rather as if the Allegro theme receives its energy from the Maestoso, rolling downward from C (m. 7) to, ultimately, E♭ (m. 32), whereas the Maestoso climbed up from E♭ to C. Special importance is attached to the moment the two entities come together, expressed through Beethoven's employment of the trill and reduced dynamics as an instant of what we might call "excited tranquility."[94]

Typical for a myth, according to Lévi-Strauss, would be the binary opposition of Heaven and Earth, or of transcendence and the human being.[95] According to my understanding of his music, clues to Beethoven's ultimate meaning in these passages point exactly in that direction. The tempo marking "Maestoso" is striking because Beethoven had used this marking in only a few other works. One finds it, apart from op. 127, in the slow introduction of op. 111; the beginning of the overture "Zur Namensfeier," op. 115; nos. one and fourteen of the Diabelli Variations; and otherwise only in vocal compositions, some of them referring to a secular majesty, as in the following works:

> *Fidelio:* the entry of Don Fernando [minister of state], *"Un poco maestoso,"* within the Finale: "Des besten Königs Wille . . ."
>
> *Der glorreiche Augenblick,* op. 136: in no. 2, Recitativo of the leader of the people: "maestoso ma un poco mosso," then "maestoso ma meno mosso:" "Der Kaisermantel ist's . . ." (the emperor is stepping forward; sudden shift to E♭ major); in no. 3: "Der Heros, der den Fuß aufstellet . . ."; "Der Herrscher an der Spree Strand . . ."; "Der Wittelsbacher, dessen Land und Schild . . ."
>
> *Kantate auf den Tod Kaiser Josephs II,* WoO 87: in no. 3, Aria, "Andante maestoso": "Da kam Joseph mit Gottes Stärke . . ."
>
> *Kantate auf die Erhebung Leopolds II zur Kaiserwürde,* WoO 88: in no. 5, Coro, "Un poco allegro e maestoso"; "Heil! Heil! Heil!"

Many examples, however, refer to a sacred godhead: The first use is in the Gellert lied *Die Ehre Gottes in der Natur,* op. 48 no. 4, where it appears in German as part of the marking "Majestätisch und erhaben." It occurs again in the oratorio *Christ on the Mount of Olives,* op. 85, locally in the Introduzione (mm. 68–73), where the music creates an analogy for God's power and the judgment; and again as the marking over the last movement, where the text reads: "Welten singen Dank und Ehre dem erhab'nen Gottessohn." It reappears in Beethoven's late vocal works, as in the Gloria of the *Missa solemnis* at the "Quoniam tu solus sanctus" ("Allegro maestoso") and the Ninth Symphony, as part of the tempo indication of the first movement, "Allegro ma non troppo, un poco maestoso," and then at portions of the Finale ("Andante maestoso") at the words "Seid umschlungen, Millionen! Diesen Kuss der ganzen Welt! Brüder! überm Sternenzelt muß ein lieber Vater wohnen," and finally, as "Maestoso," at a short section to the last words of the choir, "Tochter aus Elysium, Freude schöner Götterfunken," almost at the end of the piece.

Beethoven's use of the term "Maestoso" is thus restricted almost exclusively to the context of the sublime and powerful divine, which on account of the divine right of kings (expressed clearly in WoO 88 no. 1) is also reflected in the passages referring to secular majesties. Thus it seems reasonable to infer that this connotation is likewise cloaked in an instrumental appearance in op. 127, especially because the forceful chordal nature of the passage proves similar to the other passages.

The association of the opening Maestoso with a godhead or the principle of a sublime transcendence accords with the other musical features of these measures, as well. Beethoven did not specify an actual tempo, thus avoiding any association between the godhead and temporality—think of the notion scribbled in the Tagebuch that, "For God, time absolutely does not exist" (no. 94d). Also, E♭ major is generally known as the key for the "Numinose."[96] As William Kinderman has shown, Beethoven had used an E♭-major chord as a referential sonority symbolizing God in both the Credo of the *Missa solemnis* and the choral finale of the Ninth Symphony, the latter work completed immediately before the composition of op. 127.[97] Another famous example of a Beethovenian musical representation for God, not headed "Maestoso," but instead marked "Allegro sostenuto. Mit Andacht," appears in the Kyrie of the Missa solemnis (see Example 7.8).

We surely cannot help but hear the majestic invocations of "Kyrie" as a musical sign for God, as Warren Kirkendale has argued.[98] Like the Maestoso chords in op. 127, these threefold *tutti* chords are loud (*forte/fortissimo*) and are placed outside the meter (with the entrance "before the beat"). It seems as if with these chords Beethoven wished to create a musical analogy to the realization that the greatness of God remains intangible and unimaginable.[99]

I regard the Maestoso chords at the very beginning of op. 127 as follows: A moving force, possibly the godhead, mightily makes its appearance and sets things into motion. It reveals a harmonic space and basic set of pitches and exposes several motives that will be important in this movement and throughout the entire quartet—a work that shows an extraordinary degree of coherence, as various writers have noted.[100] This coherence extends further, or points beyond to all of the late string quartets, if we are willing to accept the reasoning of Deryck Cooke.[101]

A concrete meaning for the other sphere, the Allegro, is harder to explicate. By analogy to the music in the *Missa solemnis,* where the calls of "Kyrie" are immediately opposed to the human sphere,[102] and where both realms are the work's basic building blocks,[103] and following the notion that the typical opposition in a myth occurs between the transcendent and the human, I tend to associate the second part of the binary opposition in op. 127/I with the human sphere. When we conceive the binary opposition as spheres encompassing the godly versus the human, then the excitement in the moment of contact between the spheres (m. 6) becomes comprehensible. In myth, as opposed to Christian belief, transitions from the godly to the human are possible. The human being can flow from the energy that the godhead has given to him or her.

When in op. 127/I the "human" Allegro theme emanates smoothly from the "divine" Maestoso chords without articulating time in an individual way, the music seems to convey a state of being that draws its energies wholly from the godly sphere,

*Example 7.8.* *Missa solemnis,* Kyrie, mm. 21–33, piano reduction.

a realm that does not struggle within time, but that is enveloped with such security that questions of worldly timing almost seem to vanish. This might be regarded as symbolic for the feeling of being "timeless" in having had contact with the godhead. Because it is an ideal human state, it might even assume the connotation of the perfect art. In being embraced by transcendence, there is no need for individual action. In this sense, the first movement of op. 127 can be read as the myth of a godhead ruling powerfully and safely so that the world, including humanity, feels sheltered.

Although any attempt to relate biography and music—human outlook and musical content—closely to each other must be considered profoundly problematic, the "sea change in Beethoven's spiritual outlook" distilled by Solomon from Beethoven's entries in his Tagebuch, among other sources, may provide a valuable background for our understanding of the first movement of the string quartet op. 127. As we have seen, the notion of submissiveness to fate or to a godhead became very important for Beethoven. If one reads further in the books Beethoven had at hand, his vision, which we usually have to deduce from brief entries, becomes ever more palpable. For example, on page 337 of Georg Forster's *Historische Untersuchung über die Kenntnisse der Alten von Indien* (Berlin 1792), right above the Brahman definition of God quoted by Beethoven ("[As] God is immaterial . . .") we find the following: "Thou who art worthy of our praise! For thou must hold me, like a father his son, the friend his friend, and a lover his beloved." The notion of "inner peace," moreover, most likely belongs in this context, as well. Inner peace, as Ambrosius von Lombez described it in his then famous book *Über den innern Frieden,* is the positive impact of God upon the individual, a peace not won but bestowed. This is probably the kind of peace Beethoven had in mind (apart from outer, worldly peace) when he pleaded in the Agnus Dei of the *Missa solemnis* for "inner and outer peace."[104]

"All things flowed clear and pure from God," Beethoven wrote in his Tagebuch (no. 63a), and that is the message I hear in the opening Allegro of op. 127/I.[105] All things flow clear and pure from the Maestoso. That idea is compatible not only with the Christian God but also with the idea of emanation encountered by Beethoven in his readings in Indian myth. He noted for example in his Tagebuch, from Kleuker, *Das brahmanische Religionssystem:* "He, the Mighty One, is present in every part of space . . . You are the true, eternally blessed, unchangeable light of all times and spaces . . . You sustain all things."[106] (See Figure 7.1 for the full reference to Kleuker's work.) From Forster's *Historische Untersuchung* comes this example: The Brahmans "took the Deity as a life-giving fundamental being dispersed through the whole creation, and as a common soul that invigorates every part of it."[107] Here is another passage Beethoven took down in his Tagebuch, this time from Kant:

> It is not the chance confluence of the <Lucretian> atoms that has formed the world; innate powers and laws that have their source in wisest Reason are the unchangeable basis of that order that flows from them not by chance but inevita-

> bly . . . When in the state of the world order and beauty shine forth, there is a God. But the other is not less well founded. When this order has been able to flow from universal laws of Nature, so the whole of Nature is inevitably a result of the highest wisdom.[108]

The consequence of such thinking is that it is not necessary for the individual to take life into his or her own hands. Although Beethoven was well aware that life in Western civilization would not always work that way,[109] he still hoped he would be able to lead a life for his art in which "Tranquility and freedom are the greatest treasures" (Tagebuch, no. 126; source unknown).[110] And he considered silence to be an ideal, as opposed to worldly actions and conversations.[111]

These are the thoughts I associate with the emanating Allegro in relaxed flux, which is certainly one of the least rhetorical or "speaking" movements Beethoven ever wrote. In drawing attention to this parallel, I do not argue that Beethoven's changed outlook and his involvement with Eastern myth and religion allowed him only to compose in a specific way, but that it opened up new aesthetic possibilities that he would occasionally utilize in his music.

Beethoven was by no means alone at this time in his preoccupation with emanation and its artistic realization. Friedrich Schlegel, for example, who believed he had found the prototypical idea of an emanate God in India, meant to exemplify in his fragmentary novel *Lucinde* (1799) the Romantic notion of, as one writer put it, "unity in multiplicity [*Allheit*]: it is in God, and both the self and the world are emanations of God."[112] The distinction between a Christian and a mythological godhead was to a great degree irrelevant for Beethoven and his contemporaries, and the idea of "emanation" apparently existed alongside the concept of the unique incarnation of the Christian God.

If the binary opposition of two contrasting musical phrases tightly relating with each other at the beginning of the movement can be heard as part of a myth about the relationship between the transcendental and the human, the question must be asked, "How does the myth proceed?"

First of all, the "godly" Maestoso embodies the motives that spread out as a network over the whole movement and quartet. "The Deity, who appears in many forms, continues one immutable essence," wrote Sir William Jones in his "Chronology of the Hindus."[113] The immutable (sub)motivic essence in this movement appears in many different forms. But as the godhead is, as Beethoven noted, omniscient and all-encompassing, the motivic network secures the all-encompassing coherence of the piece. On this basis, many different foreground actions can develop.

The "divine" first Maestoso also determines the keys of the subsequent Maestosi (in G major and C major). Tellingly, the human sphere, despite the fact that it can develop energies that lead close to the godly sphere (see mm. 66–74 and 121–34), can never actually reach up to it. There always remains a fissure. The godly sphere enters surprisingly, from outside the human realm, but as it passes tightly and smoothly into the human sphere, new energies begin to flow.

In emanating smoothly from the godly sphere, the human realm takes on different existences. In some measures of the development, particles from different "human" themes are combined, as different states of being are tested. In so doing, this human part finally releases great energy, but it will not be able to reach the Maestoso. Instead, the godly sphere again makes its own powerful statement but is stopped after four measures (m. 139) on a symbolically significant chord; the magic transition to the human sphere, until now a simple one-measure trill figure, is prolonged for more than twenty measures. Its completion infuses the further course of the movement.

The key reached by the final Maestoso, C major, bears a special connotation outside the world of op. 127: in Haydn's Creation, for example, the "light" breaks out in a grand C-major chord. And in Beethoven's own oeuvre, the progression C minor–C major is strongly associated with the metaphor *per aspera ad astrum.*[114] Thus it is probably not by chance that C major is precisely the key Beethoven reached with the last appearance of the godly sphere, all the more so since "light," as Solomon points out, is the association Beethoven was very much attracted to when taking notes from his mythical readings concerning transcendence.[115]

Last but not least, according to Kinderman, is that the final chord reached by this Maestoso in C major, a first-inversion C-major triad with a $G^3$ in the first violin that is further developed in the slow movement, belongs to a network of sonorities that serve as symbols for the divine in the *Missa solemnis* and the finale of the Ninth Symphony.[116] Thus the keys and sonorities reached by the Maestoso in the further course of the piece confirm the association of the Maestoso with the godly sphere. In light of the fact that Beethoven might have been guided to the Eastern world by Freemasonic thinkers, his choice of key (E♭ major), of three loud rising tonic chords at the beginning, and of the threefold occurence of the Maestoso, culminating in C major, might even have a special Masonic connotation.[117]

Referring to the *Missa solemnis* and the Ninth Symphony for the sake of comparison, it is necessary to point out that, despite the fact that their architecture is infused by the idea of an almighty, intangible godhead in the heavens that cannot be reached nor comprehended by humans on earth, the dimension where the divine sphere flows or emanates into the human is largely missing.[118] We encounter frequently a shift in perspective from the individual to the Other in Beethoven's compositions, including in the *Missa solemnis* and the Ninth Symphony, either in the sense of a (devotional, spiritual, Masonic?) journey, a passage from darkness to illumination (as Solomon has proposed, citing various examples from Beethoven's late works),[119] or in the sense of an abrupt switch into a dream world and back again (to which Karol Berger has drawn attention).[120] In op. 127, however, the Maestoso—the divine power—sets the Allegro—the individual—into motion. In this sense, the quartet reflects a striking shift in perspective.

"While just slumbering I dreamt that I was travelling to very distant parts of the world, even to Syria and, in fact, to India and back again, and even to Arabia; and finally I came, indeed, to Jerusalem," wrote Beethoven on September 10, 1821, to Tobias Haslinger.[121] In his dream, Beethoven visited exclusively countries and places with an ancient high culture or even a legendary holiness. He stressed the distance of all these places "nicht weniger nach . . ." (three times) "endlich . . . gar nach . . . ," naming them in due geographical order: Syria, India, and from there back again to Arabia and Jerusalem. The farthest point in his dreamed travel, which he certainly understood in a spiritual, not a physical, sense, was India.

Obviously, Beethoven's attraction to India lay partly in its being at the farthest thinkable remove. India serves as the extreme point of reference, as the destination from which he took his return journey. But India was not such an uncommon choice. At the beginning of the nineteenth century it was on everybody's mind as the intriguing cradle of humanity and as a fascinating Other.[122] People were able to understand this culture only in a limited way, but they were all the more fascinated by it because it offered alternatives to Western ways of thinking. In the end, a spiritual involvement with ancient India left considerable traces in European culture.

The fact that Beethoven did some reading of Indian sources has been known for quite some time, but until the very recent writings by Solomon (see note 39), no one, to my knowledge, has questioned whether Beethoven's occupation with Indian and Brahman thought might have left traces in his oeuvre. Although I do not support a Schering-like approach, advancing the thesis that Beethoven set any individual Indian story to music,[123] I do suggest that in his contact with the spiritual world of the ancient Indians, his mind opened for alternatives to Western categories of thinking, especially those concerning the structuring of time and the human attitude toward transcendence or fate. In this sense, op. 127/I, as I perceive it, is a key work in his musical and spiritual development. In exploiting concepts of structuring a movement that depart from the dynamics of a "Western" sonata form, Beethoven certainly did not go mad, but he tried to capture in his music a different, largely spiritual aesthetic that was not easy for people to understand then, or even today.[124] Behind the lyrical and smooth surface, we encounter a highly challenging, unsettling work.

As if programmatically, Beethoven chose the opening movement of the first of the late quartets to serve as a vessel for the experiment. No other work seems to offer such a concentration of features that find a common background when referred to the idea of Eastern myth. In its singular departures from the norms of even his later musical language, op. 127 opens a window on a previously unexplored aspect of Beethoven's artistic world. Not all of his later music is constructed as nondirectional or cyclic, in the manner of op. 127/I, but in this quartet movement, Beethoven opened up a new dimension of expression, one to which he could always return, if he wished.

## Notes

An abbreviated version of this paper was read in German at the "Colloquium zur Kammermusik," Schloß Engers, November 16–17, 2001. The full-length version will appear in the conference report in German translation. I wish to thank Andreas Dorschel, Heiko Jung, Bill Kinderman, and Joshua Rifkin for their inspiration and sound advice in mythological and analytical matters, and for countless improvements to my English.

1. Especially his *La pensée sauvage* (Paris, 1962) and *Mythologiques*, 4 vols., (Paris, 1964–71), translated into various languages; important impulses were given earlier by Ernst Cassirer, *Sprache und Mythos: Ein Beitrag zum Problem der Götternamen* (Leipzig, 1925).

2. See, for example, Manfred Frank, *Der kommende Gott: Vorlesungen über die Neue Mythologie* (Frankfurt am Main, 1982), 76–80.

3. "Rede über die Mythologie," in *Friedrich Schlegel, Kritische und theoretische Schriften*, ed. and with commentary by Andreas Huyssen (Stuttgart, 1978), 190–201; first printed as part of "Gespräch über die Poesie," in *Athenäum: Eine Zeitschrift von August Wilhelm und Friedrich Schlegel*, vol. 3, St. 1 (Berlin, 1800), no. IV, 58–128, vol. 3, St. 2, no. II, 169–87.

4. See Schelling's *Über Mythen, historische Sagen und Philosopheme der ältesten Welt* (1793), in *Schellings Werke*, ed. Manfred Schröter, Erster Hauptband: Jugendschriften 1793–1798 (München: C. H. Beck and R. Oldenbourg, 1927; reprint 1958), 1–43; evidence that Beethoven was probably acquainted with the thoughts and writings of Schelling is given in Otto Baensch, *Aufbau und Sinn des Chorfinales in Beethovens neunter Symphonie, Schriften der Straßburger Wissenschaftlichen Gesellschaft an der Universität Frankfurt/M.*, Neue Folge, 11. Heft (Berlin and Leipzig: Walter de Gruyter, 1930), 87–88.

5. For a comprehensive scholarly study, see Helmut Buchholz, *Perspektiven der Neuen Mythologie. Mythos, Religion und Poesie im Schnittpunkt von Idealismus und Romantik um 1800, Berliner Beiträge zur neueren deutschen Literaturgeschichte* 13 (Frankfurt am Main: Peter Lang, 1990).

6. The best editions are Maynard Solomon, "Beethoven's Tagebuch," in Solomon, *Beethoven Essays* (Cambridge, Mass.: Harvard University Press, 1988), 233–95 (English only); and, slightly revised, including a facsimile of Anton Gräffer's copy (the original is lost but for two pages): Solomon, *Beethovens Tagebuch*, ed. Sieghard Brandenburg (Mainz: Hase and Koehler, 1990) (German only); the entries have identical numbers in both editions.

7. Cf. *Ludwig van Beethovens Konversationshefte*, ed. Karl-Heinz Köhler et al. (Leipzig: VEB Deutscher Verlag für Musik, 1968–), vol. 1, pp. 169, 200, 352; vol. 2, p. 348 (this conversation took place early February 1823, that is, at about the same time Beethoven began working on op. 127: Beethoven's brother Johann brought along Schlegel's translation of a story from the ancient Indian *Mahabharatà*, given to him by Count Moritz Lichnowsky); vol. 3, p. 23 (probably referring to F. Schlegel); vol. 4, pp. 237, 245, n. 491; no others in vols. 5–11, which cover the period from mid-December 1823 until Beethoven's death. On the impact of the Schlegel brothers on Beethoven, see John Daverio, "Manner, tone, and tendency in Beethoven's chamber music for strings," in *The Cambridge Companion to Beethoven*, ed. Glenn Stanley (Cambridge: Cambridge University Press, 2000), 147–64, esp. 151–52.

8. This aspect is discussed by, among others, Klaus Kropfinger, "Zur thematischen Funktion der langsamen Einleitung bei Beethoven," in *Colloquium amicorum Schmidt-Görg*, ed. Siegfried Kross and Hans Schmidt (Bonn: Beethoven-Haus, 1967), 197–216; and Birgit Lodes, "Beethovens individuelle Aneignung der langsamen Einleitung: Zum Kopfsatz des Streichqartetts op. 127," in *Musica* 49 (1995): 311–20.

9. I know of only one other such case in Beethoven's oeuvre: the last movement of the Seventh Symphony. I am grateful to Nicholas Marston for reminding me of this example.

10. Ulrich Siegele suggests that Beethoven himself posed the task to exclude the fifth degree and that he consequently used every other diatonic scale degree except the first (that is II, III, IV, and VI) equally often; see Siegele, *Beethoven: Formale Strategien der späten Quartette*

(Munich: text + kritik, 1990), 63; see also Joseph Kerman, *The Beethoven Quartets* (New York: Alfred A. Knopf, 1967), 239.

11. See e.g. Basil Lam, *Beethoven String Quartets,* vol. 2 (London: BBC, 1975), 12–13; Deryck Cooke, "The Unity of Beethoven's Late Quartets," in *Music Review* 24 (1963): 30–49, esp. pp. 34–5; David Epstein, *Beyond Orpheus: Studies in Musical Structure* (Cambridge, Mass.: Harvard University Press, 1979), 216–17. The motive chosen differs from author to author. Daniel Chua refers to these various motives and proposes that all of them together govern the movement in various combinations; see *The "Galitzin" Quartets of Beethoven* (Princeton: Princeton University Press, 1995), 31–32.

12. Chua, *The "Galitzin" Quartets,* 29–31, 36.

13. Cooke, "The Unity of Beethoven's Late Quartets," 34.

14. "Der Übergang ins Thema, (am Anfang) gefällt dem Herrn Bruder so gut," *Ludwig van Beethovens Konversationshefte,* vol. 8, 261. (English translation by Robert Adelson, see n. 122 in this article.) The entry (and another by Karl in vol. 7, p. 192) indicates that contemporary listeners took the Allegro theme only (without the Maestoso) as the first theme.

15. Epstein, *Beyond Orpheus,* 216–17.

16. Lodes, "Beethovens individuelle Aneignung," esp. 316–17; cf. Chua, *The "Galitzin" Quartets,* 37.

17. Chua, *The "Galitzin" Quartets,* 38–39; I do not agree with all the details in his graph on p. 39, but I share the main idea.

18. On mm. 1–6, see William Kinderman, "Streichquartett Es-Dur op. 127," in *Beethoven: Interpretationen seiner Werke,* ed. Albrecht Riethmüller, Carl Dahlhaus, and Alexander L. Ringer (Laaber: Laaber Verlag, 1994), vol. 2, 278–91, here p. 283.

19. V of VI, according to Leonard G. Ratner, *The Beethoven String Quartets. Compositional Strategies and Rhetoric* (Stanford, Calif.: Stanford Bookstore, 1995), 195.

20. Chua, *The "Galitzin" Quartets,* 40.

21. See Marston's review of Chua's *The "Galitzin" Quartets of Beethoven* in *Music & Letters* 78 (1997): 281–83.

22. Cf. Carl Dahlhaus, *Ludwig van Beethoven und seine Zeit* (Laaber: Laaber Verlag, 1987; 3rd ed. 1993), especially 245–62.

23. Kerman, *The Beethoven Quartets,* 205.

24. The theme is a "Periode," not a "Satz"; concerning these (not uniformly applied) terms, see Erwin Ratz, *Einführung in die musikalische Formenlehre. Über Formprinzipien in den Inventionen J. S. Bachs und ihre Bedeutung für die Kompositionstechnik Beethovens* (Wien: Österreichischer Bundesverlag für Unterricht, Wissenschaft und Kunst, 1951), 22–25; or Clemens Kühn, "Form," in *MGG* 2, *Sachteil* vol. 3 (1995), cols. 607–43, esp. cols. 627–28.

25. Siegele, *Beethoven: Formale Strategien,* esp. 60–63; Kerman, *The Beethoven Quartets,* 205.

26. It is not that Beethoven had never before experimented with composing time structures of that kind. However, such procedures were typically characteristic of a slow movement, not of a first movement: Carl Dahlhaus describes a somewhat comparable case in the second movement (Larghetto) of the second symphony (*Ludwig van Beethoven,* 120–22).

27. Beethoven worked on the development until very late in the compositional process, during his labors on the autograph score; see Sieghard Brandenburg, "Die Quellen zur Entstehungsgeschichte von Beethovens Streichquartett Es-Dur Op. 127," in *Beethoven Jahrbuch* 10 (1978/81): 221–75, esp. p. 274. I have refrained from studying the sketches and autograph of the movement, as Dr. Martina Sichardt (Berlin) is currently preparing a book-length study on the sources for op. 127.

28. The directional half-step motive B♭–B–C, or transposed E♭–E–F is used in the development as in the exposition, primarily to paste the four-measure units together (see mm. 84, 88, transposed to D–D♯–E; see mm. 96 and 112 for variants, echoed in mm. 113 and 115) or it is employed in the cadencing measures 13–16 of each 16–measure unit.

29. Kerman, *The Beethoven Quartets,* 206.

30. See especially the motion in the cadential theme toward the subdominant in m. 198 or the important role of C minor and C major in general in the development.

31. I am indebted for this observation to Michael B. Weiß, who pointed it out in a graduate seminar (winter semester 1997–98) held by Lewis Lockwood at the University of Munich.

32. Note the slightly changed articulation in the new Henle edition (Henle: HN 9740, ed. Emil Platen, see Example 7.4; it corresponds to the score of the Complete Edition, *Beethoven Werke,* Abt. VI, Bd. 5, Streichquartette III).

33. For use and meaning of the term, see Lodes, "Beethovens individuelle Aneignung," 313.

34. Siegele, *Beethoven: Formale Strategien,* 49.

35. It was introduced in the cello in m. 123, then taken up by all the voices in mm. 133–34, and is connected to the first Allegro theme (see esp. the slurred form in m. 85–88, first violin).

36. This motive is taken from the third measure of the first Allegro theme; cf. also m. 146, second violin.

37. The *forte* measures undoubtedly mark the first measures of a four-measure unit (cf. also mm. 65–72). The articulation of the passage is not consistent in the sources: The new Henle edition (see Example 7.4) suggests an articulation of 2 + 2 measures (with the latter only having a short first note) for mm. 147–58 (see the editorial comment by Platen on p. 54).

38. IV, then II on first and second beats; interestingly, Beethoven did not place an explicit IV in mm. 11 and 15 (the music retreats on an undecided third with the pitches A♭ and C only); in m. 19, the last reiteration of the phrase, the situation is as in m. 7: IV, then II.

39. Solomon, "Late Beethoven: A Sea Change in His Spiritual Outlook," paper read at the conference "Biographie und Schaffensprozess bei Beethoven. Grundlagen—Tendenzen—Perspektiven," Berlin, 1999; I thank Professor Solomon for sending me his manuscript prior to publication; my thoughts owe much to this contribution, as well as to his earlier editorial comments on Beethoven's Tagebuch. Since then, Solomon's ideas have appeared in several studies from which I quote: Solomon, "Beethoven, Freemasonry, and the Tagebuch of 1812–1818," in *Beethoven Forum* 8 (2000); 101–46, reprinted slightly revised as "The Masonic Thread" and "The Masonic Imagination," in Solomon, *Late Beethoven: Music, Thought, Imagination* (Berkeley: University of California Press, 2003), 135–58 and 159–78; Solomon, "Prologue: A Sea Change," in *Late Beethoven,* 1–10. Solomon perceived mythic aspects in Beethoven's Ninth Symphony in his "The Ninth Symphony: A Search for Order," in Solomon, *Beethoven Essays* (Cambridge, Mass.: Harvard University Press, 1988), 3–34, notes pp. 303–7. Solomon's most recent contributions to possible musical parallels of Beethoven's "Sea Change," as laid out in various chapters of his book (esp. chapters 4, 6, 9, and 10), were not known to me when I developed my ideas about op. 127. My thoughts have followed a somewhat different path than Solomon's, stressing other aspects and concentrating on a work Solomon himself did not discuss in the context of Beethoven's "Sea Change."

40. "ich will dem schicksaal in den rachen greifen, ganz niederbeugen soll es mich gewiß nicht"; Beethoven in a letter to Franz Gerhard Wegeler, November 16, 1801, no. 70 in Sieghard Brandenburg, ed., *Briefwechsel Gesamtausgabe* [hereafter referred to as *BG*] (Munich: Henle, 1996–), vol. 1, p. 89.

41. Solomon, "The Masonic Imagination," 170; "Sea Change," passim.

42. Gustav Nottebohm, *Zweite Beethoveniana: Nachgelassene Aufsätze* (Leipzig: C. F. Peters, 1887), 163.

43. For a compilation of the evidence, see Solomon, *Beethovens Tagebuch,* 134.

44. ". . . als mich heute H. Schick mit dem Wunsche Eurer Wohlgeborn einen indischen Chor religiösen Sinns zu sezen bekannt machte. Da meine Absicht bei dem dramatisch bearbeitetem indischen Gedichte hauptsächlich dahin gieng das religiöse System der Hindus dichterisch und gefühlvoll wie es ist darzustellen, so dürfte sich vielleicht Etwas darinnen finden, daß Ihrem Wunsche entspräche," *BG,* no. 1290, vol. 4, pp. 243–44: not in Anderson, but in Theodore

Albrecht, ed., *Letters to Beethoven and Other Correspondence* (Lincoln, Neb.: University of Nebraska Press, 1996), no. 199, with incorrect date.

45. Beethoven, who had just decided to compose the *Missa solemnis* for the inauguration of Archduke Rudolph as archbishop (see letter from March 3, 1819, in *BG*, no. 1292, vol. 4, p. 245), had to send the material back (*BG*, no. 1291, vol. 4, pp. 244–45; Emily Anderson, ed., *The Letters of Beethoven* [London: Macmillan, 1961], no. 206, with wrong date), thanking Hammer-Purgstall while indicating that he wished to come back to the plan at a later point.

46. See Hans Maier, "Mythos und Christentum," in *Richard Wagner—Der Ring des Nibelungen: Ansichten des Mythos*, ed. Udo Bermbach and Dieter Borchmeyer (Stuttgart: J. B. Metzler, 1995), 143–55, esp. p. 152; this is also the time of romantic conversions to catholicism (Schlegel's conversion is even reflected in Beethoven's conversation book; see *Beethovens Konversationshefte*, 1, 352–53); cf. also Novalis in 1800 about "the possible mythology . . . of Christianity and its earthly manifestations" ("die mögliche Mythologie (Freyes Fabelthum) des Xstenthums, und seine Verwandlungen auf Erden"). Quoted in Maier, "Mythos und Christentum," 151; from Novalis, *Schriften*, vol. 3: *Das philosophische Werk* II, ed. Richard Samuel (Stuttgart, 1960), 666.

47. See Forster, *Historische Untersuchung* (full title in Figure 7.1), 305, 308, 324–28 (among others).

48. Solomon, "The Masonic Thread," 148: "Almost every issue of the weighty Viennese *Journal für Freymaurer* featured an extended article or monograph on one of the mystery religions—Pythagorean, Eleusian, Etruscan, Osiric, Hebraic, Mithraic and Zoroastrian, Cabirian, Brahman, and Dionysian." See also Solomon, "The Masonic Imagination," 166: Beethoven's "attention to Eastern ways of thought is strongly suggestive of Masonic preoccupations, for intellectuals of the period came to Eastern thought in all its manifestations through the Masonic literature and by way of the supposedly oriental rites practiced by the Freemasons in their exotic temples."

49. For a useful survey of the many traces of Beethoven's knowledge of Greek and Roman literature and myth, see Günter Fleischhauer, "Beethoven und die Antike," in *Bericht über den internationalen Beethoven-Kongreß 10.-12. Dezember 1970 in Berlin*, ed. Heinz Alfred Brockhaus and Konrad Niemann (Berlin: Verlag Neue Musik, 1971), 465–82, and Reinhard Witte, "Beethoven, Homer und die Antike," in *Das Altertum* 48 (2003): 3–54.

50. Many of the contemporary traces are in one way or another connected to the education of his nephew Karl, e.g., Beethoven's recorded intention to buy August Heinrich Petiscus' *Der Olymp, oder Mythologie der Aegypter, Griechen und Römer*; see a letter from 23.8.1823 in *BG*, no. 1735, vol. 5, p. 219; compare a letter to his nephew Karl, who had probably asked for the (expensive, but very popular) book (Berlin, 1821); see *BG*, no. 10, vol. 5, p. 221. There are also many reports of Beethoven reading his ancient favorites until the very end of his life.

51. Cf. Walther Schubring, "Beethovens indische Aufzeichnungen," in *Die Musikforschung* 6 (1953): 207–14, and, more recently and reliably, the various remarks in Solomon's studies.

52. The translations stem from Solomon, "Beethoven's [*sic*] Tagebuch," passim; the German is taken from Solomon, *Beethovens Tagebuch*, passim (see n. 6 for full references). For the identifications of Beethoven's sources, I rely on Solomon's comments.

53. Solomon, "The Masonic Imagination," 167–70.

54. "Zeige deine Gewalt[,] Schicksal! Wir sind nicht Herrn über uns selbst; was beschlossen ist, muß seyn, und so sey es dann!——" (source unknown); "Den ausduldenden Muth verlieh den Menschen das Schiksal—"; "Die große Auszeichnung eines vorzüglichen Mannes. Beharrlichkeit in widrigen harten Zufällen" (source unknown).

55. Solomon, "Some Romantic Images in Beethoven," in *Haydn, Mozart, & Beethoven: Studies in the Music of the Classical Period: Essays in Honour of Alan Tyson*, ed. Sieghard Brandenburg (Oxford: Oxford University Press, 1998), 253–81, esp. 274–75; revised in: Solomon, *Late Beethoven*, 42–71.

56. "Opfere noch einmal alle Kleinigkeiten des gesellschaftlichen Lebens deiner Kunst, o

Gott über alles! denn die ewige Vorsicht lenkt allwissend das Glück oder Unglück sterblicher Menschen." "Alles[,] was Leben heißt[,] sey der Erhabenen geopfert und ein Heiligthum der Kunst, laß mich leben, sey es auch mit Hilfsmitteln[,] wenn sie sich nur finden! ————"

57. "Wiewohl[,] was kann man einem Menschen größeres geben, als Ruhm und Lob und Unsterblichkeit?"

58. Solomon focuses instead on the idea of a spiritual journey by Beethoven, which he relates to Masonic thinking and ritual. This aspect shall not concern us further here.

59. "Zeit findet durchaus bey Gott nicht statt." (no. 94d); "*Gott ist immateriel*[,] *deßwegen geht er über jeden Begriff;* da *er unsichtbar ist, so kann er keine Gestalt haben. Aber aus dem, was wir von seinen Werken gewahr werden, können wir schließen, daß er ewig, allmächtig, allwissend, allgegenwärtig ist.*" (no. 93b; words in italics are underlined in the manuscript).

60. "Ich bin, was da ist. // Ich bin alles, was ist, was war, was seyn wird, kein sterblicher Mensch hat meinen Schleier aufgehoben." For a possible context and Beethoven's source for this quotation, see Solomon's essay "The Masonic Thread," 147, from which I borrowed the translation.

61. "A Man's Most Precious Possession [Beethoven's heading]// Sertorius did not mind the appearance of dishonour that occurred, and he maintained that he would merely buy time, which is the most precious thing for a man who wants to accomplish important things." "Das kostbareste für einen Mann [Beethovens Überschrift]. Sertorius achtete auf den *Schein des Schimpfes*[,] *der dabey war*[,] nicht, *und behauptete*[,] *er kaufe nur die Zeit, die das kostbareste für einen Mann sey, der wichtige Dinge ausführen wolle*" (words in italics are underlined in the manuscript).

62. "Deine Zeit vergeht geschwinder, rollt schneller um, als die wo wir unsern Geist oder ich mich mit meiner Muse beschäftige" (source unknown).

63. Cf. Lévi-Strauss, *Mythologiques.*

64. As is well known, there are quite a few cases, especially in Beethoven's late works, where the narrative course is developed from a binary opposition. However, no one thus far has attempted to link this feature to the concept of myth. Martin Geck invokes the relationship for a work of the "new path" in his "Das wilde Denken: Ein strukturalistischer Blick auf Beethovens op. 31, 2," in *Archiv für Musikwissenschaft* 57 (2000): 64–77. I thank Professor Geck for sending me the manuscript prior to publication.

65. "ein Schema . . . , das es ermöglicht, Einmaliges und Dauerndes zusammenzudenken, das momentane Ereignis als Beweis einer unvergänglichen Substanz festzuhalten." Peter Gendolla, *Zeit. Zur Geschichte der Zeiterfahrung. Vom Mythos zur "Punktzeit"* (Köln: DuMont Buchverlag, 1992), 9.

66. Ibid., 16. "Der Mythos erzählt . . . keine einmalige Geschichte, vielmehr eine Potentialität, eine Struktur, die in vielfacher Gestalt unendlich wiederholt werden kann."

67. From the vast literature concerning the question of individual and historical concepts of "time," especially helpful for my questions, were the following: Rudolf Wendorff, *Zeit und Kultur: Geschichte des Zeitbewußtseins in Europa* (Opladen: Westdeutscher Verlag, 2/1980); Wolf Lepenies, *Das Ende der Naturgeschichte: Wandel kultureller Selbstverständlichkeiten in den Wissenschaften des 18. und 19. Jahrhunderts* (München and Wien: Carl Hanser Verlag, 1976); and Gendolla, *Zeit.*

68. Of course, we cannot rule out completely the possibility that Beethoven took the mythical excerpts from a single review article and not from the various original sources (as he is known to have done in comparable cases). Because no such article is known so far, however, I proceed from the assumption that he actually knew the books.

69. William Jones, "On the Chronology of the Hindus," 280–82 (Beethoven copied in his Tagebuch a passage from page 285). Jones, after pages and pages of retelling old Indian scriptures and trying to calculate the different ages (he had a very strong mathematical interest), comes to the following conclusion: "The *three first* ages of the *Hindus* are chiefly *mythological,* whether their mythology was founded on the dark enigmas of their astronomers or on the

heroick fictions of their poets; and, that the *fourth,* or *historical,* age cannot be carried farther back than about two thousand years before Christ" (319).

70. Forster describes the Indians as a people, "das sich mehr durch die Sanftheit seiner Neigungen, als durch die Erhabenheit seines Geistes auszeichnet."-"Obgleich die Sitten der Indier, von der Zeit her, da sie den westlichen Völkern zuerst bekannt wurden, wegen ihrer Sanftheit berühmt sind, scheinen sie doch in einem entfernteren Zeitalter den Sitten anderer Nationen ähnlich gewesen zu seyn" (Forster, "Historische Untersuchung," 308, 327).

71. Michael Steinberg, "Notes on the Quartets," in *The Beethoven Quartet Companion,* ed. Robert Winter and Robert Martin (Berkeley: University of California Press, 1994), 219–20.

72. For a concise discussion of this phenomenon and its negligence in the writings of Lévi-Strauss, cf. Arie de Ruijter, *Claude Lévi-Strauss* (Frankfurt and New York: Campus Verlag, 1991), 119–20.

73. Reinhold Brinkmann, "Die Zeit der *Eroica,*" in *Musik in der Zeit—Zeit in der Musik,* ed. Richard Klein, Eckehard Kiem, and Wolfram Ette (Weilerswist: Velbrück Wissenschaft, 2000), 183–211; I quote from the English version, translated by Irene Zedlacher: "In the Time of the *Eroica,*" in *Beethoven and His World,* ed. Scott Burnham and Michael P. Steinberg (Princeton: Princeton University Press, 2000), 1–26, here p. 8.

74. Brinkmann, "In the Time," pp. 8 and 203–4. For a congenial but independent view of the temporal structures in the *Eroica,* proceeding from Adorno's comments, see Richard Klein, "Prozessualität und Zuständlichkeit. Konstruktionen musikalischer Zeiterfahrung," in *Abschied in die Gegenwart: Teleologie und Zuständlichkeit in der Musik,* ed. Otto Kolleritsch, *Studien zur Wertungsforschung* 35 (Wien and Graz: Universal Edition, 1998), 180–209.

75. Brinkmann, "In the Time," 12.

76. Ibid., 16.

77. Ibid., 16–17.

78. For other E♭-major chamber music works, especially the ones with a rather lyrical first movement (op. 27 no. 1, op. 31 no. 3, op. 70 no. 2, and op. 74), see the article by Nicholas Marston in this volume. The "lyric" character of these movements is still considerably different from the cyclic one of op. 127/I. Regarding tempi, even Rudolf Kolisch, who puts the two movements into separate categories, suggests tempi not too distant from each other (𝅗𝅥. = 60 for the symphony; ♩ = 168 for the string quartet); cf. Rudolf Kolisch, *Tempo und Charakter in Beethovens Musik, Musik-Konzepte* 76/77 (Munich: Text + Kritik, 1992), 53, 65, and 100; the essay is the revised version of Kolisch, "Tempo and Character in Beethoven's Music," in *The Musical Quarterly* 29 (1943): 169–87 and 291–312.

79. Quotations in this paragraph from Brinkmann, "In the Time," 18.

80. Ibid., 19.

81. Kerman, *The Beethoven Quartets,* 208.

82. Scott Burnham, *Beethoven Hero* (Princeton: Princeton University Press, 1995), pp. 19 and 53–55.

83. Lewis Lockwood, "*Eroica* Perspectives: Strategy and Design in the First Movement," in Lockwood, *Beethoven: Studies in the Creative Process* (Cambridge, Mass.: Harvard University Press, 1992), 118–33, here p. 128; originally published in *Beethoven Studies* 3, ed. Alan Tyson (Cambridge: Cambridge University Press, 1982), 85–106.

84. The eighth-note figure in the first violin is taken from the main Allegro theme (mm. 9 and 13). At the many places where it is used throughout the movement, this motive keeps its characteristic whole tone between the first two pitches, thereby leading either to the fifth or to the third of the harmony in the following measure. Only in the coda did Beethoven introduce a truly closing variant of this motive, with a semitone between the first two notes, the first time leading to II (m. 244), the other times somewhat hidden through parallel motion and followed only by a retarded tonic (mm. 257–58 and 269). Therefore, it is only half true to speak of a "closing motive," as did Siegele in *Formale Strategien,* 56–57.

85. Brinkmann, "In the Time," 21.

86. Ibid., 20.

87. Ibid.

88. See Burnham, *Beethoven Hero,* 18–19, for programmatic explanations of the coda by different authors. Concerning the equation of theme and protagonist, see Burnham, p. 8, among others.

89. Fear of death is a historical, not a mythic experience. It presupposes nonrecurring uniqueness; see Gendolla, *Zeit,* 16, 24.

90. I am grateful to Bill Kinderman for this observation.

91. Concerning the difficulties with the concept and the terminus "heroic style," see Lewis Lockwood, "Beethoven, Florestan, and the Varieties of Heroism," in *Beethoven and His World,* ed. Scott Burnham and Michael P. Steinberg, 27–47, and esp. 36–44.

92. Aspects of nonlinearity in Beethoven's late music, albeit in a somewhat different sense, are stressed also by Jonathan D. Kramer, who does not, however, draw the parallel to Beethoven's readings or thoughts about life; see Kramer, "Multiple and Non-linear Time in Beethoven's Opus 135," in *Perspectives of New Music* 11 (1973): 122–45; revised version in *The Time of Music: New Meanings, New Temporalities, New Listening Strategies* (New York: Schirmer, 1988), 123–36. For other recent studies on temporality in Beethoven's late compositions, see Eckehard Kiem, "Der Blick in den Abgrund: Zeitstruktur beim späten Beethoven," in *Musik in der Zeit—Zeit in der Musik,* ed. Richard Klein, Eckehard Kiem, and Wolfram Ette, 212–31; see also David B. Greene, *Temporal Processes in Beethoven's Music* (New York/London/Paris: Gordon and Breach Science Publishers, 1982).

93. Such is the title of a chapter (ch. 13c: "Protest der Romantik gegen das lineare Zeitbewußtsein") in Wendorff, *Zeit und Kultur,* 357–76. "Da das romantische Zeitgefühl nicht auf das Handeln ausgerichtet ist, besteht auch nicht die Tendenz, möglichst viele Inhalte in das Leben hineinzuzwingen und es deshalb zu höherem Tempo zu beschleunigen. Die zukunftsgerichtete Willenhaftigkeit fehlt, und so gibt man sich der Empfindung des Langsamen gerne hin" (362).

94. Or in the words of Paul Bekker, "The trilling first violin loosens the solemn earnestness in a released smile."-"Die trillernde 1 Violine löst den feierlichen Ernst in ein befreiendes Lächeln." *Beethoven* (Stuttgart and Berlin: Deutsche Verlags-Anstalt, 1922), 526.

95. Cf. Lévi-Strauss's analysis of 813 American myths in *Mythologies:* They all deal with the question of transition between nature and culture, mediated by the human battle for the celestial fire; for a critical perspective, see Gerhart von Graevenitz, *Mythos: Zur Geschichte einer Denkgewohnheit* (Stuttgart: J. B. Metzler, 1987), esp. 100.

96. Ludwig Finscher, "Mythos und musikalische Struktur," in *Richard Wagner—Der Ring des Nibelungen: Ansichten des Mythos,* 27–37, here p. 29.

97. William Kinderman, "Beethoven's Symbol for the Deity in the *Missa solemnis* and the Ninth Symphony," in *19th Century Music* 9 (1985): 102–18; and "Beethoven's Compositional Models for the Choral Finale of the Ninth Symphony," in *Beethoven's Compositional Process,* ed. William Kinderman (Lincoln: University of Nebraska Press, 1991), 160–88. Kinderman also draws attention to parallels between op. 127/II and the Benedictus of the *Missa solemnis,* last but not least in the key structure; see pp. 117 and 183, respectively; see also by the same author, "Tonality and Form in the Variation Movements of Beethoven's Late Quartets," in *Beiträge zu Beethovens Kammermusik: Symposion Bonn 1984,* ed. Sieghard Brandenburg and Helmut Loos (Munich: Henle, 1987), 135–51, esp. 145–50; and *Beethoven* (Oxford: Clarendon, 1995), 238–52, 279–83, 288–90.

98. Kirkendale, "New Roads to Old Ideas in Beethoven's *Missa Solemnis,*" in *The Musical Quarterly* 56 (1970): 665–701, esp. 666–67, reprinted in German as "Beethovens Missa solemnis und die rhetorische Tradition," in Ludwig Finscher, ed., *Ludwig van Beethoven: Wege der Forschung 428* (Darmstadt: Wissenschaftliche Buchgesellschaft, 1983), 52–97.

99. See Lodes, "Probing the Sacred Genres: Beethoven's Religious Songs, Oratorio, and Masses," in *The Cambridge Companion to Beethoven,* ed. Glenn Stanley (Cambridge: Cambridge University Press, 2000), 218–36 and 332–34, esp. 229.

100. See, for example, Hugo Riemann, *Beethoven's Streichquartette* (Berlin, 1903), 118–20. Riemann argued that the main themes of the quartet derive from the opening Maestoso. See also Kerman, *The Beethoven Quartets,* 238–39, and Kinderman, "Streichquartett Es-Dur," 282.

101. Cooke, "The Unity of Beethoven's Late Quartets," 34: "The six introductory bars provide the thematic source of the set of five quartets."

102. An individual solo voice answers every loud call while the woodwinds provide a stepwise, calm background, at a dynamic level of *piano.*

103. Especially in the Gloria and Credo, as William Kinderman and I have shown; cf. my article "'When I try, now and then, to give musical form to my turbulent feelings . . .': The Human and the Divine in the Gloria of Beethoven's *Missa Solemnis,*" in *Beethoven Forum* 6 (1998): 143–79; and Kinderman, "Beethoven's Symbol for the Deity," and "Beethoven's Compositional Models for the Choral Finale of the Ninth Symphony."

104. Lodes, "Probing the sacred genres," 234.

105. "Aus Gott floß alles rein und lauter aus. Werd' ich nochmals durch Leidenschaft zum Bösen verdunkelt[,] kehrte ich nach vielfacher Büßung und Reinigung zur erstern erhabenenen[,] reinen Quelle, zur Gottheit zurück,—— und—zu Deiner Kunst." (*Beethovens Tagebuch,* no. 63a. According to Solomon (*Beethovens Tagebuch,* 151), those are probably Beethoven's own words, perhaps inspired by Kleuker, *Das brahmanische Religionssystem,* pp. 35 and 174ff., or by the *Bhagavad-Gita;* in my opinion, however, it might also be motivated by Forster, *Robertson's historische Untersuchung,* 339–40 (we know that he read p. 337); see Figure 7.1 for full references.

106. " . . . Er der Mächtige ist in jedem Theile des Raumes gegenwärtig. . . . Seine Allwissenheit ist von eigner Eingebung[,] und Sein Begriff [begreift] jeden andern [.—] von allen viel begreifenden Eigenschaften ist die Allwissenheit die Größte . . . —für sie gibt es keine *dreyfache Zeit, keine dreyfache* {anstatt von: "andere"} Art des Seyns. Sie ist von allen unabhängig[.] O Gottheit[,] du bist das wahre[,], ewig selige[,], unwandelbare Licht aller Zeiten und Räume. . . . Du allein bist der wahrhafte *Bhagavan* {anstatt von: "Seelige"} [,] die das Lesen aller Gesetze, das Bild aller Weisheit [—] der ganzen Welt gegenwärtig [—] trägst Du alle Dinge, *Sonne, Aether, Brahma*" (no. 61). "Geist der Geister die durch jeden Raum [und] durch die endlose Zeit dich verbreitend. über die Schranken des emporkämpfenden Gedankens erhaben. Dem Aufruhr befiehlst Du zur schönen Ordnung zu werden. Ehe Himmel waren, warst Du. [. . .] O! Leite meinen Geist[,] o hebe ihn aus dieser schweren Tiefe durch Deine Kraft entzückt[,] damit er furchtlos streb' aufwärts in feurigem Schwunge. Denn Du, Du weist allein, Du kannst allein begeistern.-" (no. 62). The italicized words are added from Beethoven's sources; they are missing in the copy. Cf. Solomon ("The Masonic Imagination," n. 1 on p. 286): "One must take into account clear evidence that the [Tagebuch] text was censored during the copying process to mask several references to Brahman religion, among them the words and phrases 'Brahm,' 'dreyfache Zeit,' 'Bhagavan,' and 'Sonne, Aether, Brahma' (no. 61); 'Yog' (no. 64); and 'Sah' Brahm nur seinen Geist' (no. 65)."

107. "So hielten sie die Gottheit für ein lebendigmachendes, durch die ganze Schöpfung verbreitetes Grundwesen, für eine allgemeine Seele, die jeden Theil derselben belebe. Jedes intellektuelle Wesen, vorzüglich die Menschenseelen, waren, nach ihren Gedanken, abgerissene Theile von diesem großen Geiste" (Forster, *Historische Untersuchung,* 339–40).

108. *Beethovens Tagebuch,* no. 105 [a] and [b]; taken from Immanuel Kant, *Allgemeine Naturgeschichte und Theorie des Himmels* (1755), reprint Zeitz 1798, p. 108 and pp. 121–22 respectively: "Nicht der ohngefähre Zusammenlaut der Atome des Akkords hat die Welt gebildet; eingepflanzte Kräfte und Gesetze[,] die den weisesten Verstand zur Quelle haben, sind ein unwandelbarer Ursprung derjenigen Ordnung gewesen, die aus ihnen nicht von ohngefähr[,] sondern nothwendig fließen müssen, [. . .] wenn in der Verfassung der Welt Ordnung in

Schönheit Wetterleuchten; so ist ein Gott. Allein[,], das andere ist nicht weniger gegründet[,], wenn diese Ordnung aus allgemein Naturgesetzen hat herfließen können, so ist die ganze Natur nothwendig eine Wirkung der höchsten Weisheit[.]-"

109. In a letter to Carl Friedrich Peters, he was concerned about Karl's financial future and wrote: "His future must also be provided for, since we are neither Indians nor Iroquois who, as everyone knows, leave all to the Lord God." Anderson, *Letters of Beethoven,* vol. 2, no. 1083, p. 952; "Es muß auch für die Zukunft auf ihn [Karl] gedacht werden, da wir weder Indianer noch Irokesen, welche bekanntl. dem Lieben Gott alles überlaßen, sind." *BG,* no. 1473 (vol. 4, p. 500); letter of June 26, 1822, to Carl Friedrich Peters in Leipzig. Very similar to Beethoven's draft of a letter to Prince Nikolaus Galitzin in St. Petersburg (*BG,* no. 2003, vol. 6, p. 96) concerning the payment for the commissioned quartets, including op. 127: "da wir nun einmal keine Iroquesen sind, die bekanntlich <derg>das wohl der ihrigen der bloßen Zukunft u Gott anheim stellen." (Anderson, *Letters of Beethoven,* vol. 3, no. 1405. p. 1225, erroneously translates: "we are not great Princes [recte: not Iroquois] who, as we know, merely leave the welfare of their subjects to the future and to God.")

110. "Ruhe und Freyheit sind die größten Güter."

111. "Five years of silence is required of future Brahmans in the monastery": "5 jähriges Stillschweigen sind den künftigen Braminen im Kloster aufgelegt." (Tagebuch, no. 94c).

112. Carl Enders, *Friedrich Schlegel: Die Quellen seines Wesens und Werdens* (Leipzig, 1913), 351, quoted in Amos Leslie Willson, *A Mythical Image: The Ideal of India in German Romanticism* (Durham, N.C.: Duke University Press, 1964), 204.

113. Jones, "On the Chronology of the Hindus" (1790), 283 (see Figure 7.1); Beethoven copied his Tagebuch entry no. 94d from p. 285.

114. This is, of course, only one type of expression of the instrumental possibilities of a minor-major type; cf. Joseph Kerman, "Beethoven's Minority," in Sieghard Brandenburg, ed., *Haydn, Mozart, and Beethoven: Studies in the Music of the Classical Period: Essays in Honour of Alan Tyson* (Oxford: Oxford University Press, 1998), 151–74.

115. Solomon, "The Masonic Imagination," 165–67.

116. See Kinderman, *Beethoven,* 290.

117. Many of the Masonic pieces are in E♭ major (the three flats reflecting the meaningful number three); C major is symbolically considered the pure key (cf. Jacques Henry, *Mozart Frère Maçon. La symbolique maçonnique dans l'oeuvre de Mozart* [Aix-en-Provence: Editions Alinea, 1991], 41–44). Lewis Lockwood was the first to associate the rising Maestoso chords of op. 127 (and of other E♭-major compositions) with the three chords opening Mozart's *Zauberflöte;* see Lockwood, *Beethoven: The Music and the Life* (New York: W. W. Norton, 2003), 446, and n. 16 on p. 544).

118. One of the very few exceptions occurs remarkably in the Credo of the *Missa solemnis* to the text "et descendit." When talking about composing the *Missa solemnis* in a letter of February 18, 1823, Beethoven characteristically described this "constantly looking *upwards*" as the "greatest happiness." Anderson, *Letters of Beethoven,* vol. 3, no. 1139, p. 1002; "bey so vielem *nach Oben* sehen, das Glücklichste des Menschen" *BG,* no. 1571, vol. 5, p. 47.

119. Cf. e.g. Solomon, "The Shape of a Journey: The 'Diabelli' Variations," in *Late Beethoven,* 179–97; "The Masonic Thread,", esp. 154–57; "Intimations of the Sacred," 198–212; and all articles in Solomon, *Late Beethoven: Music, Thought, Imagination* (Berkeley: University of California Press, 2003).

120. Karol Berger, "Beethoven and the Aesthetic State," in *Beethoven Forum* 8 (2000): 17–44.

121. Anderson, *Letters of Beethoven,* vol. 2, no. 1956, p. 922; translation adopted, cf. Maynard Solomon, "The Dreams of Beethoven," in *American imago* 32 (1975): 113–44, here p. 122, reprinted in: Solomon, *Beethoven Essays* (Cambridge, Mass.: Harvard University Press, 1988), 56–76, notes pp. 314–9. "-während ich nun schlummerte, so traümte mir, ich reiste sehr weit[:]

nicht weniger nach Siryen[,] nicht weniger nach Indien—wieder zurück nicht weniger nach *arabien,* endlich kam ich gar nach Jerusalem" *BG,* no. 1439, vol. 4, p. 447. Beethoven, in this letter to Tobias Haslinger, continued that a canon, "O Tobias," associated via the Holy books in Jerusalem, among them the Apocryphal *Book of Tobit* (in German "Tobias"), presented itself while he was dreaming, and he wrote down the dream when awake the other day. ". . . die Heilge stadt erregte den gedanken an die Heilgen Bücher[.] kein Wunder, wenn mir nun auch der [Mann]Name Tobias einfiel." Haslinger later would be the first publisher of op. 127. For a psychoanalytical interpretation of this dream, see Solomon, "The Dreams of Beethoven," 133–38.

122. The "cradle of humanity" is Herder's famous designation; August Wilhelm Schlegel called it "die Pflanzschule des Menschengeschlechts" (cf. Willson, *A Mythical Image,* 201).

123. Arnold Schering (1877–1941) was a scholar known to indulge in overextended and often programmatic interpretations of Beethoven's works.

124. The (mostly negative) reception of the quartet in its early performances is documented, among other places, in Beethoven's conversation books; cf. Robert Adelson, "Beethoven's String Quartet in E Flat Op. 127: A Study of the First Performances," in *Music & Letters* 79 (1998): 219–43.

CHAPTER EIGHT

# Plenitude as Fulfillment

## The Third Movement of Beethoven's String Quartet in B♭, Op. 130

*Robert Hatten*

The Andante con moto ma non troppo of Beethoven's op. 130 is an unusual movement in an unusual quartet of six movements with an alternate finale. Its unique expressive meaning can best be understood in terms of four aspects: its relationship to the other movements of the quartet, its treatment of an original topic as premise, its tropological exploitation of a hybrid form and genre, and its many rhetorical shifts in level of discourse. Together, these four arenas of creative innovation support a coherent expressive argument for the movement, suggesting how Beethoven extended the Classical style to embody an immediacy of expression akin to the unfolding of conscious experience. My interpretation of the movement, then, will not only address the expressive motivations behind atypical structural and formal events, but will also help explain why Beethoven might have departed from sonata form so radically in this movement.

The evidence for expressive relationships between movements begins with the creative process itself. There are two extensive (and competing) accounts of the lengthy and fascinating compositional history of Beethoven's String Quartet in B♭, op. 130. Each has something to contribute to my interpretation of the Andante movement, with respect to Beethoven's decision to include four inner movements before the finale. It will be helpful to begin with a brief summary of Barry Cooper's account, which occupies an entire chapter of his *Beethoven and the Creative Process.*[1] After completing the weighty first movement in B♭ major and the short Presto in B♭ minor, Beethoven abandoned several sketches for a slow movement in D♭ that would eventually become the Cavatina and quickly wrote the Andante, also in D♭, in its place. The finale, originally conceived as a much lighter and shorter movement, gradually evolved into a fugue and then expanded into the monumental *Grosse Fuge*. The mammoth proportions of this finale led Beethoven to reconsider the middle of the cycle, and he added another dance–slow movement pair to help balance the design. For the dance movement Beethoven chose the Alla danza tedesca he had originally considered using as the fourth movement of op. 132 and transposed it from A to G major. And the slow movement evolved from earlier sketches into the Cavatina, now in E♭ major. Later, at the urging of Karl Holz and with a "financial inducement" from his publisher, Matthias Artaria, Beethoven composed the substitute finale that—according to Cooper—may have been closer to his original conception before the fugue called forth two more inner movements.

Klaus Kropfinger offers a different version of the compositional genesis of op. 130, emphasizing the crucial evidence in the sketches that Beethoven conceived of a fugal finale from the beginning.[2] In the de Roda sketchbook, fol. 14r (May–September 1825), the words "le[t]ztes Stück des Quartetts in B-dur" precede a sketch of a theme that at one point is labeled "Fugha." Already on fol. 6r Beethoven had sketched the opening of the first movement, appending the words "Le[t]ztes Quartett [of the Galitzin set] mit einer ernsthaften und schwergängigen Einleitung" ("Last quartet with a serious and weighty introduction"). Together, these bits of evidence suggest that Beethoven conceived of the work from the start as framed by two potentially weighty movements. Kropfinger makes a strong case for the cumulative integration of a conceptual cycle, an integration that the original finale completes.[3] He notes that Artaria's financial incentive, which led Beethoven to decide on composing a new finale after only one day's consideration, was actually offered several months after the initial performance of the work, and that Beethoven's decision in no way negated his initial conception, but in part reflected realities associated with Artaria's marketing strategies for the quartet (he had already decided to publish the fugue separately in a piano transcription of the entire quartet).[4] In a later article, Kropfinger finds further reason to appreciate, if not prefer, the second finale, including a motivic/rhythmic resemblance between bars 2–3 of the Cavatina and 5–6 of the second finale; the similarity implies that the second finale may be ironically reversing the seriousness of the Cavatina.[5] The idea is suggestive, and I will explore possible rhetorical associations between inner movements of the quartet as part of a larger expressive strategy in the quartet.

If Beethoven originally conceived of op. 130 in terms of a typical four-movement cycle, one might suppose that in expanding to six movements he was moving toward a more relaxed organization akin to a suite. However, his design for the inner movements clearly suggests two *pairs* of contrasting movements, corresponding to the traditional model of scherzo–slow movement, but doubled. This logical inner expansion of the traditional four-movement cycle would have served not only to balance the weightier outer movements but also to project the first movement's dialectic of contrasting affects across the cycle as a whole. Consider the analogous movements of each pair. The "scherzo-like" movements feature a contrast between the relaxed Alla danza tedesca (IV), marked Allegro assai but heard in a leisurely one to the bar, and the highly intense Presto (II). The "slow" movements feature a contrast between the profound Adagio of the Cavatina (V) and the genial Andante of the third movement. Within each "scherzo–slow" pair, Beethoven also foregrounded oppositions: the Andante third movement "responds" rhetorically and expressively to the Presto second movement, and tellingly, this pair of movements is sharply separated from the following pair by the highly disjunctive tonal shift from D♭ major to G major for the Alla danza tedesca fourth movement.

Beethoven's choice of tempo for the third movement, Andante con moto ma non troppo, as well as his expressive indication of *Poco scherzoso* for the potentially tragic opening (itself a reference to the lament that opens the first movement), signals an unusual, and perhaps hybrid, movement. Indeed, the Andante is soon inflected by the rhythmic energy of a lighter, easygoing scherzo. The sixteenth-note walking bass with which the leisurely first theme gets under way in m. 3 (Example 8.7a, mm. 3–4) may be compared to similar textures in two middle movements from the piano sonatas (Examples 8.1a and b). The Andante tempo of the quartet movement falls midway between the Largo appassionato of op. 2 no. 2 (clearly a slow movement in 3) and the Scherzo: Allegretto vivace of op. 31 no. 3 (clearly a scherzo in spirit, but with an overlaid lyric line and duple meter). Op. 31 no. 3 pairs a Scherzo with a Menuetto, but the Menuetto alludes to the missing slow movement by means of its lyrical opening strain. The Andante third movement of op. 130, on the other hand, might be viewed as a trope at the level of genre, in that it creatively fuses the playfulness and rhythmic drive of a scherzo with the tunefulness of an Andante.

What further evidence might support an interpretation of paired movements? With its initial gesture in the first violin, the Andante alludes to the lament opening of the first movement (Example 8.2a), and it also appears to respond, speculatively, to the B♭ minor of the Presto (Example 8.2b) before shifting gears tonally and rhythmically into D♭ for a first-theme group. The play of B𝄫 versus A♮ in mm. 1 and 2 (Example 8.7a) is notated to imply vii°7/D♭ in m. 1 and vii°$^{6}_{5}$ of B♭ minor in m. 2, but the listener who is not also performing the work would probably hear both B𝄫 and A as leading tones in B♭ minor, thereby prolonging the key of the Presto. When the A♮ in m. 2 is expressively reversed to A♭ (*dolce*) at the end of the measure, the sigh relaxes into a contented D♭ major (note the "collapsing" parallel tenths in the viola and cello that respond to the A♭'s "yielding" effect).

Lawrence Kramer has introduced a trope he calls "expressive doubling" to help interpret a relationship between movements in four Beethoven piano sonatas that have only two movements (opp. 54, 78, 90, and 111).[6] According to Kramer, in these sonatas the second movement provides contrast and significantly responds to the first movement, dialectically interpreting its problematic issues by transposing them to "a higher or deeper plane, a more brilliant or profound register."[7] How might one adapt Kramer's concept to interpret the relationship between the paired inner movements of op. 130? The Andante expressively doubles the Presto's obsessive drive by counterposing a leisurely pace suggestive of the workaday world. An interpretation at this stage might claim that the Andante comments on the abnormal intensity of the Presto by proposing a more humane alternative. There is more to the expressive doubling, however, than a speculative opposition of expressive states based on contrasting tempi. As Lawrence Kramer writes, "whatever conflicts or instabilities appear in the lower term of the doubling tend to be carried over into the higher term."[8] Indeed, the Presto experiences a series of dramatic reversals in its transition from the trio back to the scherzo proper (Example 8.3), and the Andante expressively doubles this idea with its own series of reversals and deferrals, distractions and interruptions,

*Example 8.1.* Comparison of themes with staccato bass line.

*a.* Beethoven, Piano Sonata in A Major, op. 2 no. 2, II.

*b.* Beethoven, Piano Sonata in E♭ Major, op. 31 no. 3, II.

*Example 8.2.* Derivation of the Andante's opening sigh (a) and link with the Presto (b) in Beethoven, String Quartet in B♭ Major, op. 130.

*a.* first movement, opening theme.

*b.* Second movement, closing measures.

*Example 8.3.* Dramatic reversals in the transition to the return of the Presto of op. 130.

that affect the otherwise contented forward progress of its texture. These various disruptions demand closer analysis and interpretation.

But first consider the following pair of movements. The Cavatina is already linked with the subsequent fugal finale by means of the common tone G.[9] Can it also be construed as an expressive doubling of the previous Alla danza tedesca? Perhaps not as obviously as the Presto and Andante pair, because there is no linking transition. Nevertheless, there are indicators that support an explicitly framed opposition. Each movement is based on an imported topical genre; the Ländler-like "deutscher Tanz," a low-style peasant dance, contrasts with the high-style vocal genre of the Cavatina (Examples 8.4a and b). Both genres draw on simplicity as a means of achieving their expressive effects. Like the previous pair, these two movements each have disruptive episodes, but they relate more closely to each other, in that the disruptions are both fragmentary and to some degree dissociative.

The coda of the German dance features a disorienting permutation of isolated solo measures (Example 8.5a), turning what might initially have suggested an echo of the cadence into a complete retrograde of the four isolated motives of the second phrase (one in each instrument), followed by a normal ordering of the first phrase of the theme, also parceled out in solo motives. The Cavatina features the parenthetical *Beklemmt* ("oppressed, *Angst*-laden") recitative, in which the first violin as soloist projects an emotional collapse in a rhythm suitably dissociated from the accompanying strings (Example 8.5b).

*Example 8.4.* Framed opposition between the fourth and fifth movements of op. 130.

*a.* Opening theme, Alla danza tedesca.

*b.* Opening theme, Cavatina.

*Example 8.5.* Dissociative events in the fourth and fifth movements of op. 130.

*a.* Permutation of measures of the theme near the end of the Alla danza tedesca.

*b. Beklemmt* episode in the Cavatina.

Finally, the opening themes of each movement feature "sighing" and broken-off articulations, whereas the Presto and Andante themes feature textural continuity within their main themes. The striking gestural character of the Alla danza tedesca, in which the articulations of the odd measures suggest wistful sighs, is complemented by traces of empfindsamer broken declamation in the Cavatina (the literal sigh figure in m. 3 is "choked" off and the second violin fills the emotion-laden gap). In terms of expressive doubling, the Cavatina might thus be understood as responding to the dance's relatively surface expression with a greater depth of emotional intimacy; but the dance is touching in its own way, with gentle yet undeniable yearnings that also suggest a deeper purport.

As for the Presto and Andante movements, there is further compelling evidence for their expressive pairing. The Andante alludes to the Presto theme—somewhat skeletally, to be sure—in bars 81 and 83 (compare Examples 8.6a and b). The significance of this spectral echo will emerge from a closer analysis of the Andante's other disruptions and their implied shifts in level of discourse. The main themes of the two movements (Examples 8.6a and 8.7a) also support an interpretation of expressive doubling. The Presto features a motivic third emerging from a sequential stepwise descent. The Andante sequences its thirds in a stepwise ascent. This opposition may

*Example 8.6.* A thematic link between the second and third movements of op. 130.

*a.* Opening theme of the Presto.

*b.* Spectral echo in the Andante (mm. 1–4 echoed in m. 81 and m. 83).

be interpreted dialectically as a pessimistic descent (in the Presto) countered by an optimistic ascent (in the Andante). Furthermore, the contrasting tempi support an expressive opposition between obsessive irritation in the more dynamic Presto and naive, good-hearted optimism in the Andante proper.

Textural evidence for expressive doubling arises from both movements' density of activity, suggestive of the clockwork topic proposed by Leonard Ratner. Ratner cites three examples from the third movement of op. 130 as topical representations of a clock-like mechanism in which "the wheels appear to have a highly eccentric motion, at times running completely wild."[10] I think the function of such textures in this movement is part of a larger textural strategy, motivated by a concern for what I will call "plenitude," conceived as both premise and topic for each movement. Expressively, plenitude implies saturation or repleteness, and as such, the prototypical state of plenitude would be one of suffused, contented fulfillment. An exemplary treatment of plenitude as premise is found in the Adagio of the Ninth Symphony, and indeed, the transcendent effect of diminutions in Beethoven's late variation sets is based on a progressive strategy of textural saturation. But plenitude need not be tied to a particular affective state; the obsessive Presto conveys a dysphoric plenitude, expressively doubled by the euphoric plenitude of the Andante. As part of a compositional premise, plenitude may be understood as a desired goal achieved by processes that lead to the ultimate saturation of texture, and fulfillment—perhaps even apotheosis—in the case of a theme. As a topic, the relative textural, registral, and activity-level saturation characteristic of plenitude is present in the opening themes of both Presto and Andante, Examples 8.6a and 8.7a, and is also supported by the hint of perpetual motion in each theme's consistency of rhythmic texture.

The processes that contribute to plenitude include the following, most of which appear in the opening eight measures of the Andante (see circled letters in Example 8.7a):

a. Phrase and motivic construction by (varied) repetition of thematic/textural units, often featuring textural inversion. Measures 1–2 are constructed as 1+1, mm. 3–6 as 2+2, and mm. 7–8 as 1/2+1/2+1/2.
b. Diminutional variation procedures (these occur later in the movement). Diminutions add rhythmic complexity and density to the texture; compare the extra activity when the theme returns in m. 38.
c. An expressive crux (m. 7) characterized by "fulfillment" and tending toward stasis; varied repetition of a marked motivic/textural idea as if for pure enjoyment (compare the Andante moderato sections from the Adagio of the Ninth Symphony).
d. A sense of "timelessness" as extended continuities override sharp formal articulations (e.g., the evaded cadence in m. 8).

To create a more dramatic expressive genre from this premise, Beethoven countered the timeless suffusion of textural and temporal plenitude by means of a wide range of disruptive strategies. As with other topical premises—for example, the heroic struggle to achieve victory—this progress toward ultimate fulfillment is impeded and deflected to create a dynamic trajectory. But some of the disruptions also imply what I have called "shifts in level of discourse,"[11] in that the sudden reversal suggests a self-reflexive response or shift in consciousness on the part of a single agent, rather than an external agency antagonistic to the progress of a protagonist. Such shifts may also imply a Romantic ironic comment on the prevailing musical discourse, subverting or dismissing that which is seen as too self-indulgent, or too naive, or simply in need of a midcourse correction.

Interestingly, some of these disruptive strategies are motivated by the very temporal extensions and irregularities that result from working out the premise of desired plenitude. When continuities overly prolong states of fulfillment, they may begin to imply states of distraction, diffusion, wandering, or winding down from euphoria into a state of depression. Other, more confrontational strategies highlight *discontinuity* by means of reversals, deferrals, sudden recognitions, redirections, and projections that may in turn be positive rechargings of expressive energy that has become diffuse, as well as negative displacements of euphoric states that cannot hold. Whatever the disruptive strategy, the fulfillments of plenitude are thereby made to appear fragile, and hence more valuable, as they are subject to eventual decay or displacement. Beethoven broke new ground stylistically in his treatment of disruptions and shifts in levels of discourse. The temporal/textural premise of plenitude itself—so different from the more directed, progressive energies and forceful breakthroughs of his heroic style—also opens a new expressive field. Euphoric fulfillments are disrupted at the very point we might begin to believe they would go on forever, or they are allowed to stutter and decline as their energies dissipate. The result can be seen to represent, or enact, something akin to a reflective stream of consciousness or desire.

The following analysis examines in detail the remarkable sequence of disruptions and digressions, noting their role in undercutting or deflecting the blissful experience of plenitude (excerpts from the score of the movement appear in Examples 8.7a through d).

1. (Mm. 1–10) The first theme gets fully under way in m. 3, reaches an expressive crux in m. 7, and luxuriates in its *subito piano* yet expansive arrival in the dominant, A♭ major, by treating a half-bar idea to two varied repetitions. This is the first expressive crux in the movement. An expected cadence in A♭ in m. 8 is bypassed harmonically, and the rhythmic sequencing extends until a quiet cadence regains the tonic (see Example 8.7a).
2. (Mm. 10–13) The cadence figure is then subject to clock-like *pizzicato* imitation and remodulation to A♭, only to be displaced by a theme that, although clearly in A♭, does little more than cadence. After variations on its cadential melodic descent, the discourse becomes diffuse and a sudden V7/IV serves to inject new energy.
3. (Mm. 13–17) Another cadentially oriented theme ventures forth in the cello. It is echoed in increasingly thick textural variation (plenitude without expressive fulfillment) until its diffused stasis is more forcefully disrupted in m. 17 (see Example 8.7b) by an unexpected $V^6$ of F, which I have elsewhere analyzed as a "recitative chord"—a dislocating major $^6_3$ that suggests the "paragraph break" of a recitative. Beethoven imported these $^6_3$ recitative chords into nonoperatic music to cue a sudden shift in discourse, often entailing a more intimate or direct expression by the implied agent.[12]
4. (Mm. 17–19) But instead of spawning a new theme, as had the previous interruption, this sudden seizing of the dramatic reins engenders a rhythmic figure that is distracted by reiterated cadential gesturing. The tonic never solidifies, however, and the reactive passage merely prolongs the disruptive V of F. Wedge-like intensification in m. 19 is sharply displaced by an isolated D♭ (as expressive flat-$\hat{6}$), posed like a question or a warning ("nicht diese Töne"?) and functioning as a pivot for the return to an idealized state, as represented by the main theme (see Example 8.7b).
5. (Mm. 20–25) Resolving to C, the D♭ has indeed triggered a return to the main theme, but in brighter C major, not F, which complements the greater saturation of texture (a canonic imitation at the fifth begins on the second beat) and enhances its sense of plenitude. This reprise of the main theme, the only idea thus far with sufficiently marked expressive character to qualify as a central focus for the discourse, then embarks on a journey through a series of keys. The theme is both developed (fragmentation and sequence in m. 21 and m. 23) and characteristically varied (new textural setting in mm. 22–23) as it leads, progressively and texturally intensified, to a new expressive crux (again in the dominant, A♭ major) marked Cantabile, beginning in m. 26 (see Example 8.7c).

6. (Mm. 26–38) Plenitude is fulfilled with this thematic arrival. The descending melodic second is reminiscent of the expressive crux in m. 7, made more thrilling here by acceleration or diminution and more replete by its elaboration into a fully achieved melodic phrase. Texturally and registrally the passage is saturated, and the decorative grace-note turns unmistakably mark the euphoric character of the arrival. A varied repetition hints at return with its modulation to D♭ in m. 30, but the melodic cadential trill is again disrupted, in m. 31, by $V^4_2$ of ii. This disruption, *subito pp,* merely serves as a cutback to enhance the ongoing fulfillment of the theme and its plenitude. Continuous sixteenths lead to an even more decorative version of the second expressive crux; the exquisite scalar ascents and their sequential treatment (mm. 32–35) extract still more pleasure from this thematic fulfillment. Just when it appears that the euphoria might be prolonged indefinitely, a premonitory flat-$\hat{6}$–$\hat{5}$ in A♭, recalling the sighs of mm. 1–2, falsely prepares the tonal return of the main theme in D♭.
7. (Mm. 38–63) The main theme returns with further diminution in the accompaniment, as though replete with the pleasures of the previous section, and the literal return of material (with appropriate tonal resolution) marks a sonata recapitulation. After the extended cadence back to D♭, the pizzicato imitative echoes are transposed down a fifth and the subsidiary, "cadential" themes are resolved to D♭. The interruptive recitative chord is now $V^6$/B♭, and flat-$\hat{6}$ leads to F instead of C, but surprisingly, what appeared to be the beginning of a development section is faithfully recapitulated, as well. The second expressive crux returns in D♭, but this time it is truncated to make room for a truly transcendent elaboration.
8. (Mm. 64–67) Just as before, the varied repetition of the second crux moves down a fifth, here from D♭ to the subdominant G♭. But the melodic cadential trill in m. 65 is suspended by a fermata, and instead of an interruption by V/ii, a cadenza-like treatment of the ascending scale returns us to the *first* expressive crux (from m. 7), now in the subdominant, and with a sense of transcendent return to what had already been the expressive goal of the first theme. But this time the first expressive crux cadences on schedule (last beat of m. 67), normalizing the previous two phrase extensions and saving cadential evasion for a later surprise.
9. (Mm. 68–73) The pizzicato imitative echoes of the original transition do not herald a new theme here; instead, they get "stuck" in a clockwork stasis and then appear to suffer a "slippage" as a partly chromatic sequential descent slides to a diminished-seventh reference to the ambiguous opening two bars (mm. 71–73). The enharmonically conceived diminished seventh at first resolves to the black hole of V/d, emblematic of the depths to which depression has wound down from transcendent bliss. Another attempt is made, but the progression to V/D♭ is not secured by a subsequent tonic chord. When a third try replicates the A♮ of m. 2 without the softening reversal to A♭, it signals a further treatment of the dysphoric (see Example 8.7d).
10. (Mm. 74–76) The main theme returns, but it is subjected to a circle-of-fifths sequence that allows the poignancy of the introductory sighs to infect the optimistic cast of the theme, which is now reversed by a continuously chromatic melodic descent.
11. (Mm. 77–79) The less-disruptive passage used to evade cadences in mm. 28 and 31 is used here in an attempt to regain positive orientation—almost willfully, as if one were trying to convince oneself. The gambit is not successful, however.
12. (Mm. 80–84) A sudden cadential evasion to V/ii, as in m. 31, sets up a state of suspended animation and the most spectacular shift in level of discourse thus far. The

circle-of-fifths sequence with which Beethoven created the chromatic slippage in the return of the main theme at mm. 74–75 may have suggested a parallel with the sequential Scherzo theme. Here, the clockwork effect returns in slow motion with a bass line that echoes the previous movement's theme, in both mm. 81 and 83, and the spectral recollection suggests a consciousness haunted by its less-euphoric past.

13. (Mm. 84–88) The extreme displacement of mm. 80–84 is ultimately resolved by a brief transition in m. 84 that regains the positive and energetic realm of the second expressive crux for an even more fully saturated closing four bars (mm. 85–88). Plenitude has the last word; despite the motivic liquidation in m. 86, the texture continues to increase in density, and by m. 87 all the voices are in thirty-second notes. Even the elegant arpeggiation of the final tonic (m. 88) features registral saturation in a last reverberation of the idealized state of plenitude.

This account of strategies of plenitude and counterstrategies of disruption has used sonata form as a referential frame and point of departure. The recapitulation involves resolution down a fifth of material heard earlier in the movement, and the music from the fermata in m. 65 to the end could be analyzed as an extensive coda. More problematic for a sonata-form analysis are the following:

1. The move to the dominant occurs too soon, and the crux of the main theme in m. 7 is in A♭. The dominant key is cadentially evaded in m. 8 and then regained in m. 10 without any dominant prolongation that would strongly articulate a second theme arrival.
2. The lack of clear articulation of the end of the exposition. However, both the recitative chord (m. 17) and the premonitory flat-$\hat{6}$ (m. 19) are disruptive cues indicating that the forward progress of an exposition has been thwarted, and the return of the main theme in a new key (m. 20) suggests the fresh momentum of a development section.
3. The placement in the "development" section of a second expressive crux in A♭, expressing fulfillment (m. 26ff.), and its appearance in D♭ not long after—the modulation to D♭ occurs within the varied repetition of the theme in mm. 29–30, and its sequential treatment begins in D♭ (m. 32ff.). This euphoric expressive crux may thus be recapitulated down a fifth without any threat to the resolutional status of the return section, which would not be the case if the material were more dissonant (as in a typical development section).

The form of this movement may owe much to sonata, but these unusual features suggest that an expressive interpretation may be more to the point in capturing the relevant dramatic trajectory. The following summary outlines the expressive argument of the movement:

The main theme (m. 3) embodies the premise of the movement with its sturdy, optimistic, stepwise ascent from the doldrums of the initial sigh gesture, enfolded in a textural plenitude that reaches fulfillment with the first expressive crux in m. 7. The enjoyment of that arrival is not really earned; rather, it appears as a moment of spiritual insight, and its reiterated half-bar idea is akin to a reverberation in consciousness. The attempt to maintain this idealized state is ultimately frustrated, and even the attempt to pin it down with a definite cadence is undercut. Much of the remain-

*Example 8.7.* Beethoven, op. 130, III, Andante con moto ma non troppo.

*a.* mm. 1–10.

*b.* mm. 16–20.

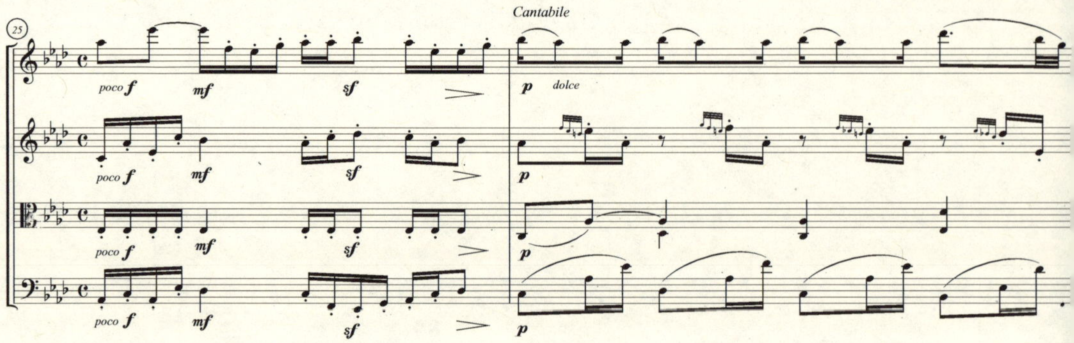


*Example 8.7, continued. c.* mm. 25–26.

*d.* mm. 67–75.

der of the movement may be read as a series of attempts to regain what has been briefly experienced, and the "development" does indeed "will" itself toward an ecstatic opening-out that becomes its climax of plenitude (mm. 26ff.). The "recapitulation" also replicates much of the development down a fifth, allowing us to reexperience that ecstatic opening, and trumping it expressively by means of a cadenza-like fermata and transcendent return to the original expressive crux (mm. 65–67). A series of slippages creates drama in the coda, where depression threatens to displace transcendence. But even the spectral recall of the Presto—in a melancholic frame that suggests not only the suspension of time but also its omnipresence as clockwork—cannot derail the final peroration of the second expressive crux in its glorious plenitude.

## Conclusion

Traditional formal articulations have a properly dramatic function in sonata form conceived as a dramatic scheme. What Beethoven explored in his late style, as I have demonstrated elsewhere, are alternative sites of drama that often override or subvert the traditional structural sites of a conventional form.[13] In this movement, the play of continuity versus discontinuity takes center stage and sonata form recedes to the background. As formal schema is negotiated by expressive genre, and lyricism is troped by scherzo-like playfulness, the unique expressive synthesis of the movement begins to emerge.

At a larger formal level, the expressive doubling of Andante and Presto movements reflects the troping in the first movement between Adagio/slow-introduction sighs and Allegro fanfares. The dialectical engagement and intercutting of themes based on contrasting gestures is the central premise of a dissociative opening movement that strives to achieve integration, as Kerman notes in his perceptive analysis.[14] The first movement's disruptions are principally due to the action of intercutting between these two seemingly incompatible ideas, each contending for control of the discourse in the opening of the movement and at the junctures of development and coda. The coda achieves thematic closure with what Kerman calls the "forced wedding of the *adagio* and *allegro* themes,"[15] as Beethoven attempted to synthesize and, through voice-leading connections, stitch together a kind of resolution to the conflict between these two ideas, despite their ultimately irreconcilable tempi and meters. It is in the coda that a masterful, if elusive, trope is achieved.

Disruptions in the Andante, however, are understood more as shifts *away* from the perceived dissolutions of fulfillment, as first occurs after the expressive crux in mm. 7–8 is liquidated in mm. 9. As shifts in level of discourse, these various discontinuities imply a self-conscious subjectivity or agency—musing upon loss, reacting with determined energy, or spiraling down into depressive obsession. The shifts of discourse in the Andante suggest a sequence of emotional states that are not only experienced but also subsequently engaged by self-reflection and reactive feelings—in other words, the mixing of thought and emotion characteristic of fully human consciousness. Irony at times emerges from the play of self-consciousness and its dismissals: either simultaneously (the *poco scherzoso* undercutting of self-pitying sighs) or successively (the recitative-chord disruption that brings wandering distraction up short). There is an intriguing tension in the movement between two possible ways of losing one's path—either by extended euphoria that may lose its sense of directed motion and dissolve in thematic liquidation, or by various modes of distraction that may lead to depression or melancholy. And ironically, continuity may be marked either as euphoric fulfillment or dysphoric obsession.

In forging the language of his late style, Beethoven often relied more on the expressive associations available from key relationships in the tonal system, rather than the generative tonal schema of sonata form as currently theorized. In the Andante we have seen how sonata form yields to the idiosyncratic development of a new thematic topic (plenitude), conceived within the trope of slow movement and scherzo styles, and broken up by self-reflexive shifts in level of discourse. Beethoven's speculative treatment of plenitude as premise, however, goes far beyond a surface play with clockwork textures. The various disruptions of that surface reveal a deeper quest in which plenitude as contentment or fulfillment soon begins to represent an elusive state of spiritual bliss—that which emerges without being earned, is experienced without being consummated, and dissolves simply because it cannot be sustained. The poignancy in this movement is not that of typical tragedy, but—as in the Alla danza tedesca, and even more devastatingly in the Cavatina—the evanescence of that which is most deeply felt and cherished.

## Notes

1. Barry Cooper, *Beethoven and the Creative Process* (Oxford: Clarendon, 1990), 197–214.

2. Klaus Kropfinger, "Das Gespaltene Werk Beethovens Streichquartett Op. 130/133," in *Beiträge zu Beethovens Kammermusik* (Symposium Bonn 1983), ed. Sieghard Brandenburg and Helmut Loos (Munich: Henle, 1987), 305, and "Streichquartett B-Dur Op. 130," in *Beethoven: Interpretationen seiner Werke,* vol. 2, ed. Albrecht Riethmüller, Carl Dahlhaus, and Alexander L. Ringer (Laaber: Laaber, 1994), 304.

3. Kropfinger, "Das Gespaltene Werk," 316.

4. Ibid., 301–3.

5. Kropfinger, "Streichquartett B-Dur," 315.

6. Lawrence Kramer, *Music as Cultural Practice, 1800–1900* (Berkeley: University of California Press, 1990), 22.

7. Ibid., 30.

8. Ibid., 31.

9. Richard Kramer ("Between Cavatina and Ouverture: Opus 130 and the Voices of Narrative," *Beethoven Forum* 1 [Lincoln: University of Nebraska Press, 1992], 178–84) notes that the doubled Gs at the end of the Cavatina enhance the rhetorical and narrative function of the quadrupled Gs that announce the Ouverture of the *Grosse Fuge* finale. This linkage supports expressive doubling, in that a reversal in intensity marks a shift to another realm of discourse, one that for Kramer turns the Cavatina into "an act of fantasy" (p. 181). For an in-depth analysis of expressive meaning in the Cavatina itself, see Hatten, *Musical Meaning in Beethoven: Markedness, Correlation, and Interpretation* (Bloomington: Indiana University Press, 1994), 203–23.

10. Leonard Ratner, *Classic Music: Expression, Form, and Style* (New York: Schirmer, 1980), 391.

11. Hatten, *Musical Meaning in Beethoven,* 174–88.

12. Ibid., 15.

13. Ibid., 24.

14. Kerman, *The Beethoven Quartets* (New York: Norton, 1966), 305–13. See also the insightful analysis by William Kinderman in *Beethoven* (Oxford: Oxford University Press, 1995), 299–303, and my own interpretation in *Musical Meaning in Beethoven,* 134–45.

15. Kerman, *Beethoven Quartets,* 312.

CHAPTER NINE

# The Genesis of the Countersubjects for the *Grosse Fuge*

*William E. Caplin*

The idea that a musical work—as a whole or in part—may be seen as a "solution" to some compositional "problem" is commonplace in music analysis and criticism. So widespread is this interpretive trope that the nature of the problem itself can range from the most concrete detail of harmony, rhythm, or voice leading to highly general issues of large-scale form and aesthetic effect. In some cases, the problem can be seen as any one of numerous routine procedures occurring regularly in connection with a given genre: in every sonata exposition, for example, there arise the problems of how to achieve a convincing modulation to the new key, how to create sufficient thematic contrast in the subordinate group, or how to manipulate expositional material within the framework of the development, to mention only some of the most obvious. In other cases, however, the problem seems to be more idiosyncratic to the work and can even be identified as a predicament of the composer's own making. When Beethoven began his Ninth Symphony with a "journey out of the sphere of the inaudible into that of the audible," as William Kinderman has put it, he created the problem of how this gesture, which is entirely unrepeatable—can, in fact, be "recapitulated" in accordance with the norms of sonata form. His solution—the "dramatic reinterpretation of the opening material"—is as unique as the problem that spawned it.[1]

The world of the fugue presents the composer with a host of similar problems, both routine and potentially singular. One entirely conventional problem for any fugue is the creation of melodies that can effectively counterpoint the fugue subject itself. When such a melody appears against the subject on several occasions or more, it is customarily termed a *countersubject.* Typically, the solution to finding successful countersubjects involves fashioning a melody that both contrasts with and complements the subject. Such contrast usually occurs through the use of distinctly different motives, whereas complementation often entails the rhythmic filling-in of durational gaps presented by the subject.

Normally we have no idea whether the creation of a given fugal countersubject may have been difficult or not, as we rarely have evidence revealing the progress from problem to solution. Such cannot be said, however, for Beethoven's most famous fugue—the *Grosse Fuge,* originally intended as the finale to the B♭ Quartet, op. 130. For here we possess substantial documentation suggesting that finding suitable countersubjects seems to have become a problem elevated beyond the merely routine. The more than fifty surviving sketches lead to the speculation that a difficulty with the subject itself may have inhibited the ready formation of countersubject material. The fugue subject possesses certain harmonic and melodic peculiarities that could impede the creation of interesting and coherent contrapuntal settings. And the two main countersubjects Beethoven ultimately used in the fugue represent different solutions to the compositional problems posed by the subject. Examination of many of the sketches reveals how Beethoven grappled with these difficulties and eventually found his two successful solutions.

In the course of working on the finale of the op. 127 Quartet in E♭, Beethoven jotted down the theme shown in Example 9.1a, which appears on folio 27 recto in the Berlin sketchbook autograph 11, bundle 2.[2] As Peter Stadlen has hypothesized,[3] Beethoven returned to this sketch while considering the finale of op. 130, and on the facing folio (26 verso) he transposed the theme into the key of B♭ (Example 9.1b).[4] He then compressed it from eighteen notes to eight (Example 9.1c). By combining the first measure of 9.1b with the second and third measures of 9.1c, Beethoven created what eventually became the subject for the *Grosse Fuge* (Example 9.1d). No further sketching survives for this theme, so he seems to have come up with the idea fairly easily. As often discussed, the theme obviously relates to others from Beethoven's later period through its emphasis on the upper tetrachord of the harmonic minor scale (see Examples 9.2a–d).

What distinguishes the subject of the *Grosse Fuge,* however, is that the harmonic minor tetrachord arises within the supertonic region, C minor, as shown in Example 9.3. This highlighting of the supertonic has significant consequences for the implied harmonic rhythm of the subject. The most natural harmonization is I–V/II–II–V–I. But the secondary dominant of II embraces four of the subject's eight notes, and following this emphasis on II, the concluding V–I progression comes almost as an

*Example 9.1a.* Aut. 11/2, f. 27r/1.

*Example 9.1b.* Aut. 11/2, f. 26v/4a.

*Example 9.1c.* Aut. 11/2, f. 26v/4b.

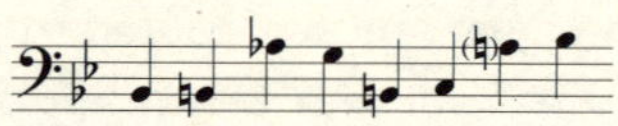

*Example 9.1d.* Op. 133, fugue subject.

*Example 9.2a.* Op. 132.

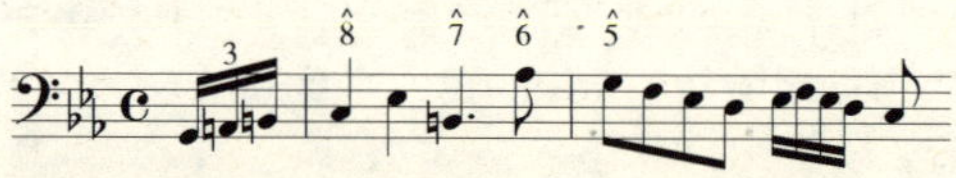

*Example 9.2b.* Op. 111.

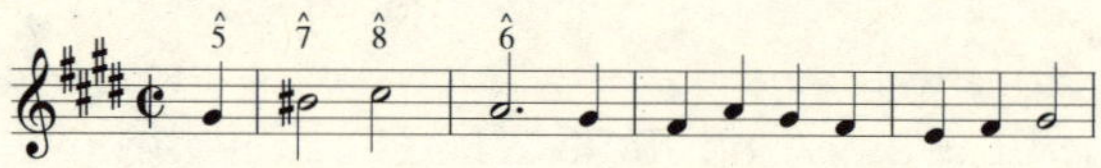

*Example 9.2c.* Op. 131.

*Example 9.2d.* Op. 131.

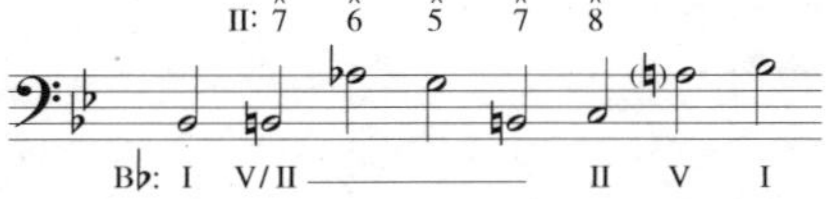


*Example 9.3.* Op. 133, fugue subject.

afterthought. The harmonic rhythm, of course, is highly unbalanced, especially for an idea that regularly returns throughout the movement. Thus we might recognize here a compositional "problem" requiring a solution, presumably one that would regularize this asymmetrical feature.

Another characteristic of the subject is its prominent leaping motion. Within the tonal space of an octave, the melody regularly skips between the lower and upper regions. The resultant compound melody thus reduces the possibilities of composing an independently melodic countersubject, one whose notes would not be frequently colliding with those of the leaping subject, thereby giving rise to empty octaves in the counterpoint. An obvious solution to this problem would be to confine the countersubject to the three notes of the middle region that are not sounded by subject, namely, D, E♭, and F. Indeed, the countersubjects in a number of the early sketches often wander aimlessly around these pitches, as if the melody were being constricted by the leaping subject. Beethoven eventually discovered how to expand the range of the countersubject lines, but these three pitches from the middle region remain to form the background structure of both countersubjects. In addition, Beethoven used the two notes D and E♭ as the sole counterpoint in the Allegro molto e con brio passages of the fugue, where the subject is played quickly in 6/8 meter (see Example 9.4).

In short, once Beethoven had chosen this particular fugal subject, he would have to invent a countersubject whose inherent harmonic rhythm is relatively regular and whose contour complements the leaping motion in the subject. Given these restrictive conditions, it is remarkable that he created not just one, but two countersubjects for use in the final form of the work (see Examples 9.5a and 9.6a).[5] Although the countersubjects each have an individual style and character, they are related in a number of ways. The rhythm of each features uniform durational patterns in a four-

Allegro molto e con brio

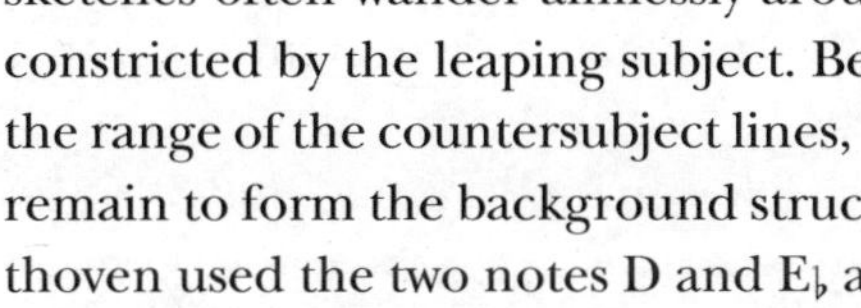


*Example 9.4.* Op. 133, Allegro con brio measures.

to-one setting against the subject. The two melodies employ a considerable amount of immediate note repetitions. Both begin and end in different registers, and their melodic range is almost the same, extending from a low D to a high A♭ or G. And finally, their underlying melodic frameworks present a stepwise descent from the fifth scale-degree to the third. Yet despite these many similarities, the countersubjects are not mere variations of each other; rather, their internal motivic and harmonic organizations differ fundamentally.

As shown in Example 9.5a, the first countersubject is bipartite in structure, with the second half being a modified sequential repetition of the first. Each half is likewise divided into two ideas: the large leaps that embellish the repeated notes, and the stepwise descent. The harmony consists of the same progression of chords implied by the fugue subject alone. But given the symmetry of the melodic lines, the harmonic rhythm is more balanced, such that the secondary dominant of II resolves at the third measure where the subject moves to G, and the dominant appears at measure four to embrace C and A of the subject. Indeed, this harmonization is made explicit in the first full-voiced setting within the fugue (shown in Example 9.5b). But one detail does not fit into this neatly symmetrical design: the second B of the subject finds no place in the C-minor harmony of m.3 of Example 9.5a. So Beethoven made certain adjustments that mitigate the effect of the nonharmonic B. First, he employed a rarely used transformation of the subject, one that some eighteenth-century theorists termed *interruption*.[6] As a result, the B does not sound until the fourth beat of the measure, at which point it creates a consonance against the G in the countersubject. Second, m. 3 is not an exact sequence of m. 1, for the upper E♭ leaps down an octave, rather than a tenth, in order to avoid a clash between a low C in the countersubject and an immediately following B in the subject, as seen in Example 9.5c. Finally, in subsequent subject entries where the harmony is more complete (see again Example 9.5b), the B moves as an appoggiatura immediately to the C, thus reducing even further the dissonant clash. (See the circled notes.)

Example 9.5d presents a melodic analysis of this first countersubject. As noted before, the background melodic structure (shown in line 1) is restricted to a descent of the three middle-region notes, F, E♭, and D. At a middleground level (line 2), Beethoven succeeded in creating a broader, independent melody that does not produce any octave collisions with the leaping subject. The foreground (line 3) is achieved simply by embellishing this middleground melody through note repetitions and the large leaps.

For the second countersubject (Example 9.6a), Beethoven discovered a different solution to the problems inherent to his fugal theme. Because of the slower tempo, the harmonic implications of the second B can no longer be masked. So Beethoven set this note and the following C to the progression V/II–II. He avoided overemphasizing the secondary dominant, however, by also resolving this harmony when the A♭ moves to G at m. 3. Thus a fairly steady harmonic rhythm is achieved by twice using the progression V/II–II. As a result of this harmonic repetition, a sequential, bipar-

*Example 9.5a.* Op. 133, countersubject no. 1.

*Example 9.5b.* Op. 133, mm. 38–42.

*Example. 9.5c.* Reconstruction.

*Example 9.5d.* Melodic analysis of countersubject no. 1.

tite organization of the motives, such as that found in the first countersubject, is not so easily accomplished. And so Beethoven matched the internal harmonic repetition with an exact motivic repetition, shown by the brackets.

Example 9.6b presents the melodic structure of the second countersubject. Note how the internal harmonic-motivic repetition also finds expression at the background level as the motion from F to D is interrupted at the E♭. A second F is then prolonged by the stepwise descent to the lower register, after which the E♭ quickly moves to the concluding D. With such an expansive melodic sweep, we would expect the countersubject to come directly into contact with the leaping subject at some point, and indeed, the two parts meet on the note C, as circled in Example 9.6b. But the potentially weak effect of this octave, coming as it does just before the end, is offset by the powerful contrary motion of the two lines.

We have now seen how from a problematic fugue subject Beethoven masterfully shaped two countersubjects, each with a distinct emotional character and melodic structure. Let us now turn to the sketches and follow some of the paths that lead eventually to the final forms of the two countersubjects.

*Example 9.6a.* Op. 133, countersubject no. 2.

*Example 9.6b.* Melodic analysis of countersubject no. 2.

There already exist important discussions of the early sketches to the *Grosse Fuge*, including contributions by Nottebohm, de Roda, Kropfinger, Cooper, and Marston.[7] Scholars have been especially concerned with the never-ending controversy over Beethoven's decision to detach the fugue from the op. 130 quartet and the writing of a substitute finale. And so they look to the sketches in order to reconstruct Beethoven's intentions regarding the nature of the original finale: Was it initially meant to be a weighty fugue that would counterbalance the powerful opening movement, as Klaus Kropfinger argues?[8] Or was it intended to be of more "modest dimensions" and of lighter character, as Barry Cooper has asserted?[9] These scholars do agree, though, that interpreting the sketches is challenging on a number of accounts, for they hardly show a directed effort toward one clear goal. Rather, they present numerous sidetracks, dead ends, and cross implications.[10] In this sense, these sketches resemble to some extent the kinds of compositional discontinuities that mark the end product, the *Grosse Fuge* itself.

One problem is establishing a compositional chronology of the sketches, especially because Beethoven employed several sketch formats simultaneously. The majority of the surviving sketches are found in the Berlin pocket sketchbook, autograph 9, bundle 5.[11] Most of the other sketches appear in the standard-sized "de Roda" and "Kullak" sketchbooks, which Beethoven was using at the same time as autograph 9.[12] One additional sketch for the first countersubject appears, completely out of place, in the much earlier autograph 11, and the most advanced sketch for that countersubject is found in a single folio from the Wegeler collection from Koblenz.[13] Because the pocketbook sketches present a strong sense of continuity from what appears to be the earliest efforts to fairly advanced stages, I have used this sequence to create the basic chronology, and I place the remaining sketches in relation to those of autograph 9 according to both philological and stylistic evidence.

In general, the sketches can be organized into three groups. Two of these are obviously associated with the countersubjects used in the fugue; a third group is made up of what I call "primitive" sketches, some of which are devoted to working out obvious contrapuntal settings, whereas others are nonfugal in nature. I begin with the group of primitive sketches and then turn to the two groups that show a more direct relation to the final countersubjects.

Before examining the primitive sketches individually, I want to consider some general issues pertaining to the group as whole. Some of these sketches clearly lay the groundwork for the final countersubjects. But we must be cautious about viewing too many of them in this light. In the first place, we will see later that Beethoven conceived the general character and style of countersubject no. 2 prior to writing most of these sketches. Second, some of them need not necessarily be understood in relation to either of the countersubjects; instead, they may have been leading toward a completely different countersubject, one that was never realized as such. Third, some of the sketches contain ideas that do not even suggest the genre of fugue, but rather point to other styles suitable for a finale movement. Indeed, these sketches could be regarded as evidence that Beethoven may have early on intended, or at least strongly considered, a nonfugal finale for the quartet. But these nonfugal sketches can also be interpreted in another way. We know that in the final version Beethoven wrote many passages that are largely homophonic in texture (such as the one shown earlier in Example 9.4). So we must still hold on to the possibility that he may have originally conceived of the finale in terms of fugue yet might have nonetheless sketched early on some nonfugal ideas to be inserted within that genre.

Let us now turn to the individual sketches. Example 9.7 is the first to use the newly found theme derived from the melodies in Example 9.1. And as in those earlier sketches, Beethoven set the lower voice in eighth notes, thus suggesting a somewhat fast tempo, especially with the upper voice in the slower quarter-note rhythm. The only characteristics of the simple counterpoint in the upper voice that point toward later developments are the continuous rhythmic pattern and the general melodic descent. (Though nothing in this sketch suggests fugue, I will nonetheless identify the melodic material in the lower voice as the "subject" for the sake of convenience, a practice that I will continue in the remaining sketches, even those that are clearly nonfugal.)

Immediately next to this sketch, Beethoven wrote the setting shown in Example 9.8. Now the rhythm of the subject has become quarter notes, suggesting a somewhat slower tempo, especially in relation to the eighths and sixteenths in the upper voice. When that voice is sounding against most of the subject, it consists of just two notes—D and E♭—notes that we earlier identified as ones that would not conflict with the leaping subject and that eventually are used to form the background of both countersubjects. If the upper line seems constricted by the subject, the former be-

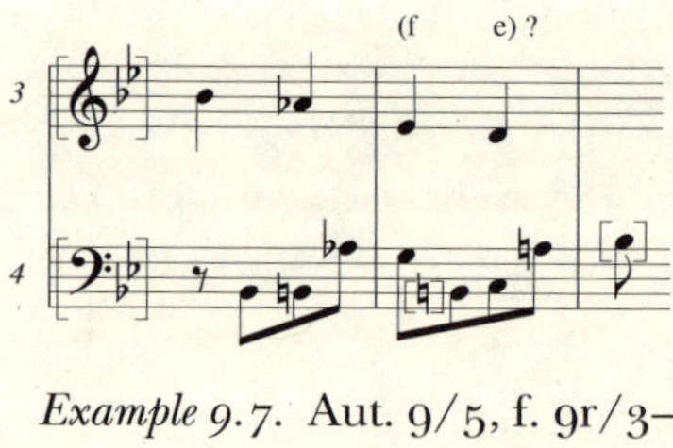


*Example 9.7.* Aut. 9/5, f. 9r/3–4.

*Example 9.8.* Aut. 9/5, f. 9r/3–4.

gins to break free and develop its own melodic and rhythmic interest as the subject draws to an end.

As we will see, the contrapuntal line in a number of the following sketches often acquires greater interest and coherence in those places where it is not actually sounding against the subject. Though the materials of this sketch do not particularly suggest a fugal context, one detail points in that direction. The turn to F major at the end of the counterpoint, as expressed by the E♭, could be taken as a sign that an "answer" version of a fugal subject might shortly appear.

The next sketch (Example 9.9a) is entirely homophonic in texture and thus not at all suggestive of a fugue. Though this very early sketch is unrelated to any of the other surviving ones, it nonetheless alludes to a passage that Beethoven wrote in the coda of the *Grosse Fuge* (Example 9.9b).

Sketch 9.10a brings for the first time several features that point directly to the first countersubject, namely, the use of A♭ in the contrapuntal voice and a clear bipartite organization, as signaled by the return of the opening sixteenth-note motive. But an interpretation of this sketch is made difficult because of the crossed-out m. 3: it is not clear whether Beethoven wrote the entire upper voice as a five-measure unit and then crossed out the third measure, or whether he crossed out m. 3 immediately upon writing it and then wrote a substitute m. 3 (what stands here as the fourth

*Example 9.9a.* Aut. 9/5, f. 10r/4–5.

*Example 9.9b.* Op. 133, mm. 690–702.

measure), continuing the melody to make a four-measure unit. In Examples 9.10b and 9.10c, I have reconstructed the results of both scenarios.

The presumption that Beethoven crossed out m. 3 and then replaced it with the following measure is supported by the considerably better counterpoint in m. 3 of Example 9.10c compared with 9.10b, whose clunky octave on the second quarter-note beat is decidedly weak. But the alternative notion, that Beethoven may have initially conceived of version b, despite its poorer counterpoint, remains plausible, especially in light of some later sketches in which the contrapuntal line is extended well beyond the end of the subject.

A set of four sketches now follows in which Beethoven tries out the subject against generally continuous triplets in the contrapuntal line (see Example 9.11). The first, fragmentary attempt (9.11a) largely meanders around the interior pitches of D, E♭, and F. But the next sketch (9.11b) is quite coherently organized: the contour is well controlled, and the counterpoint avoids any dissonant clashes. Though this setting seems fine in itself, Beethoven continued to try out additional possibilities. The beginning of the counterpoint in sketch 9.11c is the same as the previous attempt, but toward the end, he toyed with the idea of letting the line descend into a lower register. He cut off the music, however, just where the leading tone is doubled. In the next sketch (9.11d), he again pursued the idea of a downward plunge, this time by beginning with A♭, the highest note of the contrapuntal line. He then pushed the melody down to the low D, in a manner that strongly resembles the end of the second countersubject. But this sketch also relates to countersubject no. 1 through its bipartite, sequential organization, as shown by the brackets. Also, we find the problematic clash of the subject's second B within a clearly implied C-minor harmony projected

*Example 9.10a.* Aut. 9/5, f. 10r/6.

*Example 9.10b.* One reconstruction.

*Example 9.10c.* Alternate reconstruction.

*Example 9.11a.* Aut. 9/5, f. 11r/3.

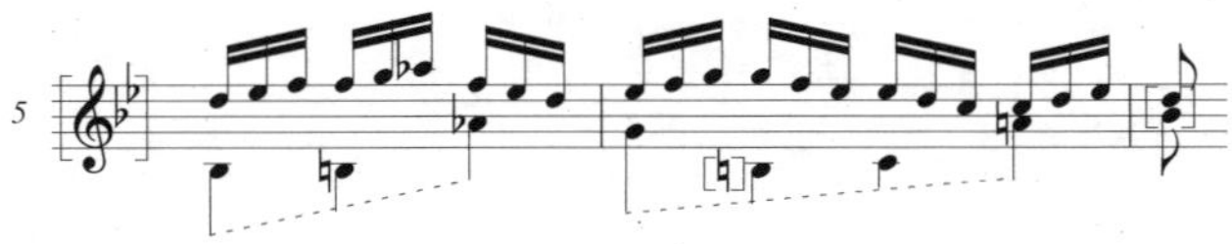

*Example 9.11b.* Aut. 9/5, f. 11r/5.

*Example 9.11c.* Aut. 9/5, f. 11r/6.

*Example 9.11d.* Aut. 9/5, f. 11v/1–2.

by the counterpoint, just the situation that lingers on in the final version of the first countersubject.

The set of sketches shown in Example 9.12 brings back the two-to-one rhythmic setting and features descending sequential repetitions, shown by the brackets. The first sketch brings a melody that is coherent and well organized, but the counterpoint that it creates against the subject is weak.[14] Example 9.12b is slightly better in this respect, but then, the counterpoint does not even begin until the middle of the subject. Like the previous one, this sketch brings descending sequential repetitions that extend beyond the end of subject. Closely related to this sketch is Example 9.12c, which appears in the de Roda sketchbook, the standard-sized desk sketchbook that Beethoven was using at the same time as the pocket sketches of autograph 9. On stylistic grounds we might believe that this de Roda sketch may have actually preceded 9.12b from autograph 9, owing to its more primitive counterpoint and less effective sequential organization.

The final sketch in this group (9.12d), also from de Roda, sees Beethoven attempting to use the "Ode to Joy" theme from the Ninth Symphony against the *Grosse*

*Example 9.12a.* Aut. 9/5, f. 11r/5.

*Example 9.12b.* Aut. 9/5, f. 11v/3.

*Example 9.12c.* De Roda, f. 35r/8.

*Example 9.12d.* De Roda, f. 35r/12.

*Fuge* subject, though with less-than-satisfactory results. That he tried this combination of themes is not so unusual, however, for the melodic line in Example 9.12a already hints at the "Joy" theme, which itself features the sequential descent common to all of the sketches in this group. In these four sketches we can also observe that the contrapuntal lines stretch well beyond the end of the subject, thus suggesting that Beethoven found it easier at this stage to form a coherent upper-voice line independent of the constraints of the subject itself.

The next two sketches, shown in Example 9.13, come from the de Roda sketchbook. The counterpoint here seems especially primitive, as if the sketches had been written before most of the others examined so far. The two melodies exhibit a restricted range, simply meandering around the interior pitches D, E♭, and F, and lack any sense of internal motivic organization. Yet they appear together with the de Roda sketches of Example 9.12 (c and d), and thus they would seem to follow all of the earlier sketches of autograph 9. Here is a good case of the difficulties these sketches present in trying to reconcile the documentary evidence with that of style.

The next two sketches from autograph 9 are given in Example 9.14. With respect to their melodic content, they refer back to the earlier sketch shown in Example 9.10a;

*Example 9.13a.* De Roda, f. 35r/10.

*Example 9.13b.* De Roda, f. 35r/16.

but their clear descending sequential organization also links them up with those in Example 9.12. The first sketch, 9.14a, has no obvious fugal implications, suggesting instead a possible rondo finale theme. Beethoven tried to place the subject in the lower voice but gave up after only two notes. As my extrapolation shows, any further use of the subject would result in an unacceptable counterpoint. The next sketch, however, works fairly well. Beethoven took melodic fragments from the prior sketch and set them over the complete subject in the bass. If we fill in the gaps in the melody with material from sketch 9.14a, the resulting counterpoint is entirely satisfactory. The bipartite organization and implied harmonic rhythm strongly relate to countersubject no. 1. Indeed, the resulting melody of Example 9.14b strongly resembles the middleground structure of that countersubject (see Example 9.5d, line 2).

The remaining primitive sketches to be considered are nonfugal in nature. The first two, based on some common melodic features, seem to form a small set (seen in Example 9.15). Each is the next sketch in order from the de Roda sketchbook and autograph 9, respectively. Example 9.15a is shaped as one of the classical homophonic theme types—the sentence.[15] It begins with a four-measure idea in tonic, repeated

*Example 9.14a.* Aut. 9/5, f. 13r/2.

*Example 9.14b.* Aut. 9/5, f. 13r/6.

immediately in a dominant version. The continuation phrase that follows sees the entrance of the subject in the lower voice, while the upper voice is restricted to the middle-region pitches D, E♭, and F. Sketch 9.15b begins like the continuation phrase of the previous example but then sequences upward, in a manner unlike all of the previous sketches. Though nothing in this sketch suggests that Beethoven was writing a fugal countersubject, the melodic line nonetheless points the way to countersubject no. 1 through the dotted-eighth/sixteenth-note rhythms and the suggestion of a march, the "topic" of the large first fugue of the *Grosse Fuge*.[16]

The final two primitive sketches (Examples 9.16 and 9.17) have little relation to the others. Example 9.16 appears in part 2 of autograph 11, a sketchbook that, as discussed at the very beginning of this essay, precedes all of the others. For this reason, this sketch probably was written down at some later date after work in this sketchbook had otherwise been discontinued.

Example 9.17, on the other hand, appears early in the Kullak sketchbook, the one that Beethoven took up after completing work in de Roda. The appearance of the subject in this sketch clearly points to the homophonic passage seen earlier in Example 9.4. But both the counterpoint and the inversion of the parts also reminds us of Example 9.11d.

*Example 9.15a.* De Roda, f. 36r/7–6.

*Example 9.15b.* Aut. 9/5, f. 15v/1–2.

*Example 9.16.* Aut. 11/2, f. 30r/7.

*Example 9.17.* Kullak, f. 2r/4–5.

Let us now turn to the group of sketches that relates directly to the first countersubject. Beginning with the set shown in Example 9.18, Beethoven finally fixed upon the dotted rhythms and the four-to-one setting that prefigure the final version.

Although the melodies become more expansive, they lose at first the bipartite structure and the balanced harmonic rhythm achieved in some of the earlier sketches. Thus, the countersubjects in Example 9.18 circle around the middle region, displaying little sense of motivic coherence. An interesting feature of Beethoven's compositional process can be observed here nonetheless. In Example 9.18a, the bracketed figure "x" that effects the ascent to A♭ is set against the first B in the subject. In sketch 9.8e, Beethoven placed a variant of this same idea against the opening B♭ instead. Likewise, motive "y" in 9.18b, which is found over the opening B♭, is shifted in 9.18d to B in order to condense the melody. Another instance of this shifting technique occurs in some later sketches. Looking ahead to Example 9.20b, we can observe that figure "z," which contains the chromatic inflection E♭–E, is set against C in the subject. In sketch 9.21a, this same idea is placed over the preceding B instead. One has the impression that Beethoven independently conceived of melodic fragments for the countersubject and then experimented to see how well they could integrate with the subject at various points. Finally, a brief comment on Example 9.18c: I have included this example here because it appears together with the others in the sketchbook. But the sketch is entirely chaotic and shows the kind of mess that Beethoven could get into even at this fairly late stage in the formation of the countersubject.

In the next group of three sketches, Example 9.19, Beethoven explored a new opening gesture. Each melody begins with a high B♭ and then descends using a leaping motive "a," which had already been introduced in the previous Example 9.18e. In the first sketch, Example 9.19a, the descent is already completed at the end of measure two, after which the leaping motive is discontinued and the melody circles aimlessly around pitches from the middle region. In 9.19b, the descent is extended more gradually to the end of the phrase. Yet here, too, the "a" motive is quickly abandoned, and the second half of the melody remains rather flaccid. Finally, in 9.19c, Beethoven used the leaping motive more systematically throughout the entire descent, imparting greater uniformity to the countersubject.

*Example 9.18a.* Aut. 9/5, f. 17v/1–2.

*Example 9.18b.* Aut. 9/5, ff. 17v/6–18r/1.

*Example 9.18c.* Aut. 9/5, f. 18r/2–3.

*Example 9.18d.* Aut. 9/5, f. 18r/4–5.

*Example 9.18e.* Aut. 9/5, f. 18r/6.

*Example 9.19a.* Aut. 9/5, f. 18v/3.

*Example 9.19b.* Aut. 11/2, f. 30r/8.

*Example 9.19c.* Aut. 9/5, f. 19r/1.

Related to this last set of sketches are three from de Roda, shown in Example 9.20, in which the first two begin on G rather than B♭. The third sketch in this set is left largely incomplete, but its beginning on F points to the next set, as well as to the final version of the countersubject, whose basic melody begins on that pitch (following the leap from the low D).[17]

*Example 9.20a.* De Roda, f. 37r/1.

*Example 9.20b.* De Roda, f. 37r/1.

*Example 9.20c.* De Roda, f. 37r/6.

In Example 9.21a, Beethoven altered the opening motive and developed this idea more extensively in 9.21b. In this last sketch, he has again figured out how to give the countersubject a clear two-part sequential structure and a regular harmonic rhythm. Furthermore, he has captured in full the basic middleground melody of the countersubject's final form (added above the sketch), which was only implied in the earlier sketch 9.14b. Left unsolved, however, is the integration of the subject's second B, which sorely conflicts with the motive in the upper part. In Example 9.21c, Beethoven varied the previous melody by giving it a uniform rhythmic flow and thus brought it even closer to the final version. But as the revision of m. 2 shows, he decided instead to break the rhythmic continuity with the long E♭, in order to make more evident the essential bipartite organization of the countersubject.

On the same page as the previous sketch are found two incomplete sketches (Example 9.22) that seem somewhat less advanced than the preceding ones. Of interest in both, however, is that they break off just after Beethoven had written parallel fifths in the counterpoint.

With Example 9.23, Beethoven returned to a gesture that he had earlier abandoned—the opening high B♭ with the "a" motive descent. The sketch might seem to

*Example 9.21a.* Kullak, fol. 1r/12–13.

*Example 9.21b.* Aut. 9/5, fols. 22r/6–22v/2–1.

*Example 9.21c.* Aut. 9/5, fol. 23r/4–5.

*Example 9.22a.* Aut. 9/5, fol. 23r/2.

*Example 9.22b.* Aut. 9/5, fol. 23r/6.

*Example 9.23.* Aut. 9/5, fol. 23v/6.

be out of place in the sketchbook, but one important detail clearly relates it to the previous example, 9.21c: the dotted-quarter E♭ in m. 3. articulates a two-part structure that is missing from all of the earlier sketches that begin with the high B♭.

The next sketch, Example 9.24, appears at first to be even more primitive than the last: it contains only one leap, and the second part of the melody does not correspond to the first part. Yet this sketch does mark an advance toward the final form, insofar as Beethoven returned to an opening on F with repeated notes and discarded the idea of using a dotted quarter note in m. 3 in favor of maintaining rhythmic motion throughout the repeated E♭s.

Having returned to the idea of a uniform rhythm for the countersubject, Beethoven then had to find another way of expressing more clearly the two-part structure. His ultimate solution, the use of large leaps in measures one and three, finally appears in Example 9.25, the sketch that most closely resembles the actual countersubject used in the fugue. An interesting detail in this sketch is found in the upper voice at the beginning of m. 2. Notice that Beethoven seems to have originally planned a stepwise descent from the high A♭, just as in the final form. But he rejected this idea, as evidenced by the crossed-out G, and instead embellished the descent with

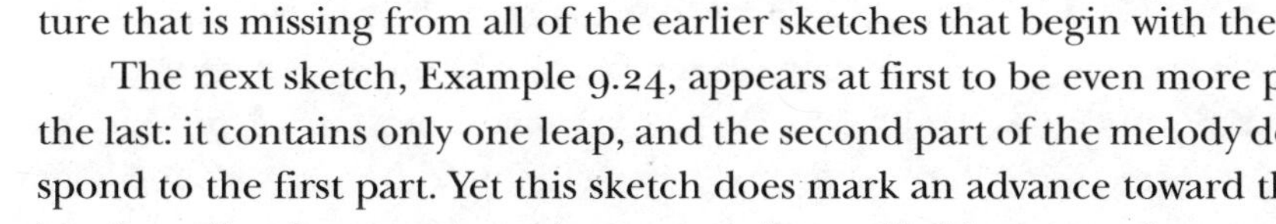

*Example 9.24.* Aut. 9/5, fol. 24r/1.

the leaping "a" motive, which he had recovered in Example 9.23. At some point, of course, Beethoven changed his mind again and returned to the stepwise descent for the version of the countersubject eventually used in the fugue.

Unlike the first countersubject, whose main characteristics appeared only after considerable preliminary sketching, the genesis of the second countersubject presents a completely different story. In fact, the evidence suggests that we must take seriously the opinion put forth by Klaus Kropfinger, and reaffirmed by Barry Cooper, that Beethoven had formulated the basic material of what was to become the second countersubject before his even having "rediscovered," so to speak, the fugue subject itself.[18] For the very first sketches arise in autograph 9 prior to any appearance of the subject. Example 9.26 contains the two sketches in question. Note that the steady sixteenth-note rhythm, the overall contour, and the melodic shape of both the opening and closing gestures immediately bring to mind the final version of countersubject no. 2. Yet the melodies are accompanied by a syncopated bass line that has no relation to the fugue subject. Indeed, with their implied basic harmonization of I–V–I, these melodies cannot be placed against the subject without creating unacceptable dissonances.

Immediately after writing these melodies, Beethoven introduced the subject into his sketching process and produced the "primitive" sketches already examined in Examples 9.7–9.10. He then set out to adapt the melodies of Example 9.26 to the constraints of the subject. His first attempt (Example 9.27a) shows that he immediately encountered difficulties. Unlike the sketches we have seen so far, this one reveals extensive revisions and alternative ideas that yield four different versions. The first version, which I have placed on the staff directly above the subject, reproduces many of the melodic elements from those in Example 9.26. The first layer of revisions, shown in the next staff above, seems to be designed to correct a number of prob-

*Example 9.25.* Wegeler, fol. 2v/10–11.

*Example 9.26a.* Aut. 9/5, fol. 8v/2–3.

*Example 9.26b.* Aut. 9/5, fol. 9r/1–2.

lems. First, the initial four-note descending pattern in the upper register E♭–D–C–B (bracketed in the score) differs from the prior patterns, so Beethoven revised it to F–E♭–E♭–D. Second, the final descent in the first version seems to begin too early, such that the B and C of the subject collide with the Cs and B of the upper part. In the revision, Beethoven recaptured the upper G and allowed the descent to occur through a largely uninterrupted scalar passage, similar to what happens in the final countersubject. As a result of both revisions, Beethoven eliminated the Bs from the contrapuntal line. With only one later exception, this note finds no further place within the second countersubject sketches, or, for that matter, in the final version. But Beethoven seems not to have been satisfied with this scalar descent, and in a further revision, he introduced a large leaping motive that strikingly anticipates similar gestures appearing in later sketches for countersubject no. 1 (and, of course, in its final version).

Another countersubject sketch in autograph 9 (Example 9.27b) brings two versions. The difference between them is essentially one of register: in the first version, Beethoven allowed the melody to leap up a seventh so that when the line descends, it can restore the opening register. But in the revised version, shown in the staff above, Beethoven eliminated the leap, so that when the line descends towards its end, the lower register is opened up for the first time. As we can recall, this is exactly what happens in the final version of countersubject no. 2. Two other features are notable in this sketch. First, Beethoven introduced A♭ as an upper goal of the melodic line. We will see that most of the remaining sketches feature this pitch, one that we know to be prominent also in countersubject no. 1. Eventually, however, he purged this note in the final version of countersubject no. 2, for reasons that I will propose later. Sec-

*Example 9.27a.* Aut. 9/5, fol. 10v/1–3.

*Example 9.27b.* Aut. 9/5, fol. 10v/6.

ond, Beethoven directly repeated the motive F–E♭–E♭–D introduced in the previous sketch. This use of a literal internal repetition is, as discussed earlier, a significant characteristic that differentiates countersubject no. 2 from countersubject no. 1.

Example 9.28 includes sketches that are situated together in de Roda. On purely musical grounds, they give the impression of being distinctly less advanced than the sketches we have just examined from folio 10 of autograph 9. But as regards compositional chronology, they appear in the immediate proximity of counterpoint no. 1 sketches (shown earlier in Example 9.20), which themselves are clearly associated with folios 17–19 of autograph 9. This disparity between stylistic and documentary evidence makes it difficult to interpret the intent and significance of these sketches. The three-to-one rhythmic setting in Examples 9.28a and 9.28c is especially hard to understand: it is not clear at all why Beethoven would at this point have reconsidered the basic rhythmical relation of countersubject to subject, especially when he immediately preceded Example 9.28c with the four-to-one version of 9.28b. I will offer one possible explanation for these triplet settings shortly, but first let us examine some other characteristics of these sketches. In 9.28a, we see another case of how the breakdown to the lower register can seem to appear too early, such that the counterpoint over the B and C in the subject is poor. In sketch 9.28b, Beethoven avoided the problem of the final descent by ending the melody in the same register in which it begins. But this creates a melodic line that meanders around a relatively restricted range. This version does bring the internal repetition (shown by the brackets), but the resulting counterpoint, especially over the subject's B and C, is as awkward as ever. In sketch 9.28c, Beethoven tried another way of creating interest through register shift, this time breaking up the melody into two parts. The counterpoint against the problematic B and C is better, but the melodic line at this point becomes stagnant with the threefold statement of the G–F–E♭ motive.

Curiously, the bipartite organization created by the register shift clearly points in the direction of countersubject no. 1; it seems unlikely, though, that Beethoven was trying to reconceive the nature of the first countersubject at this point in his sketching. So perhaps we can speculate that in these three-to-one rhythmic settings Beethoven was trying to forge a "third" countersubject, or else a contrapuntal line for some other undetermined function, a melody that would synthesize features from both the first and second countersubjects. A related sketch arising somewhat later in autograph 9 (see Example 9.29) is interesting in light of this speculation, for once again we find a triplet version of countersubject no. 2 material. But rather than being set against the subject, the melody is supported by a bass line that brings the roots of the implied

*Example 9.28a.* De Roda, fol. 36v/1–3.

*Example 9.28b.* De Roda, fol. 37r/3.

*Example 9.28c.* De Roda, fol. 37r/4–5.

harmonies of the subject along with the regularized harmonic rhythm found in countersubject no. 1. Here we might believe that Beethoven was turning back to earlier sketches from de Roda in order to fashion a melodic line for use in a more homophonic section of the fugue. Note that once the subject was no longer present, Beethoven returned to using a B in the melody and eliminated the upper A♭ in favor of G as the highpoint, both of these being features found in the original countersubject ideas of Example 9.26, sketches also made without the presence of the subject.

The final set of sketches for countersubject no. 2, Example 9.30, are found in the first folio of the Kullak sketchbook, the one that follows de Roda. The three sketches here share a four-to-one rhythmic setting and generally follow the basic outline of the final countersubject, though each handles the issue of register in a different way. Sketch 9.30a brings a leap to the higher register toward the end of the line, similar to what we saw in the first version of Example 9.27b. Sketch 9.30b has the same contour as the final countersubject, beginning relatively high, ascending even higher, and then plunging down to the lower register at its end. Sketch 9.30c, however, returns to Beethoven's earliest idea, namely, starting low at first but then quickly leaping up to the higher register, only to descend to the original register at the end of the line. Clearly, he had not yet settled on how he would handle this issue, and indeed, a remnant of this latter option finds its way into a nonfugal passage in the actual work (see Example 9.30d). Regarding melodic and contrapuntal organization, sketches 9.30a and 9.30b resemble closely the final version, especially in how they begin and end; sketch 9.30c, however, starts its descent too early and thus breaks off before even reaching its goal.

We have now reached the end of the surviving sketches for countersubject no. 2. Looking back, we can see that the sketch that most closely approaches the final version actually appeared relatively early in the compositional chronology, namely the second version of Example 9.27b. Here, the opening eight notes and the final ten are identical to the end product; moreover, Beethoven introduced the idea of an internal repetition halfway through the melody, though not in a manner that clarifies the harmonic rhythm or deals effectively with the second B of the subject. At some point, undocumented in the sources, Beethoven hit upon the specific melodic configuration that could be repeated in such a manner as to solve both of these problems. He actually got close to that figure in sketches 9.30a and 9.30b (see the brackets with asterisks). By changing the second E♭ in that motive to F, he would find the figure that

*Example 9.29.* Aut. 9/5, 23v/2–3.

permits a regularized harmonic rhythm and a good counterpoint against the subject's B (see Example 9.31). But then in order to repeat this motive exactly, he would have to eliminate the high A♭, which was featured so prominently in the sketches up to this point, and restore G instead, a note that had appeared in this location in Beethoven's original melodic conception, the nonfugal melodies of Example 9.26.

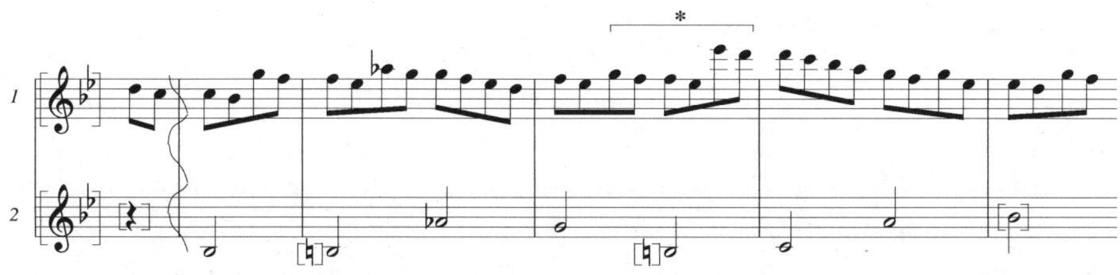

*Example 9.30a.* Kullak, fol. 1r/1–2.

*Example 9.30b.* Kullak, fol. 1r/15–16.

*Example 9.30c.* Kullak, fol. 1v/1–2.

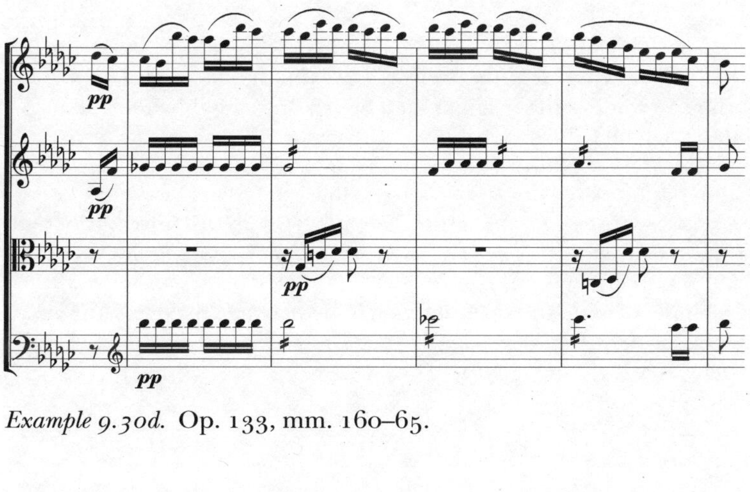


*Example 9.30d.* Op. 133, mm. 160–65.

*Example 9.31.* Op. 133, countersubject no. 2.

In a number of classic essays on the Beethoven sketches, Lewis Lockwood challenges what he perceives to be the "prevailing view" of Beethoven's compositional process, which sees the composer gathering together primitive melodic fragments and gradually building up larger and more sophisticated thematic units. As an alternative, Lockwood offers the following interpretation, based on the sketches to the song *Sehnsucht:* "One might . . . be persuaded that Beethoven had in mind from the beginning one or more fixed points in the conceptual scheme, and that against these fixed points he proceeded to develop variant possibilities, emphasizing different dimensions of the final scheme."[19]

From this perspective, it is not hard to view the subject of the *Grosse Fuge* as another kind of "fixed point," for as we have seen, Beethoven held firm to the problematic melodic and harmonic profile of his subject throughout the sketching process. But perhaps it is just because of the difficulties associated with this fixed point that the genesis of the countersubjects, especially the first, reveals an arduous progression from the relatively primitive to the advanced. In other words, the "prevailing viewpoint" and Lockwood's alternative position can perhaps both be used to reveal how the composer struggled to find solutions generated by the problems of his fixed point, the fugal subject itself.

## Notes

This essay derives from research first undertaken within a graduate seminar on sketches to the *Grosse Fuge* led by Professor Philip Gossett at the University of Chicago in 1973. Support for travel to Bonn and Berlin to examine the original sketches was provided by the Faculty of Graduate Studies and Research, McGill University.

1. William Kinderman, *Beethoven* (Oxford: Clarendon, 1995), 267, 270.

2. For more information on this sketchbook, see Douglas Johnson, Alan Tyson, and Robert Winter, *The Beethoven Sketchbooks: History, Reconstruction, Inventory* (Berkeley: University of California Press, 1985), 299–305; see also *Ludwig van Beethoven: Autographe und Abschriften,* ed. Hans-Günter Klein (Berlin: Merseburger, 1975), 59.

3. Peter Stadlen, "Possibilities of an Aesthetic Evaluation of Beethoven's Sketches," in *Bericht über den internationalen musikwissenschaftlichen Kongress Bonn 1970,* ed. Carl Dahlhaus, et al. (Kassel: Bärenreiter, 1971), 111–17.

4. Folio 26v also contains a sketch (systems 5 and 6) for the first movement of op. 132 in A minor. The chronological relationship between this A-minor sketch and the "Thema" sketch in E♭ on fol. 27r (Ex. 9.1a) remains unclear. See Stadlen, "Possibilities," 112, 114; see also Barry Cooper, *Beethoven and the Creative Process* (Oxford: Oxford University Press, 1990), 211.

5. For greater ease of comparison, the second countersubject is transposed from G♭ major to B♭, the key in which it was originally conceived.

6. Warren Kirkendale, *Fugue and Fugato in Rococo and Classical Chamber Music,* rev. and exp. 2nd ed., trans. Margaret Bent and the author (Durham, N.C.: Duke University Press, 1979), 262–63.

7. Gustav Nottebohm, "Sechs Skizzenhefte aus den Jahren 1825 u. 1826," in *Zweite Beethoveniana: Nachgelassene Aufsätze* (Leipzig: C. F. Peters, 1887), 5–6; Cecilio de Roda, "Un Quaderno di autografi di Beethoven del 1825," *Rivista Musicale Italiana* 12 (1905): 734–67; Klaus Kropfinger, "Das gespaltene Werk: Beethovens Streichquartett Op. 130/133," in *Beiträge zu Beethovens Kammerkmusik: Symposium Bonn 1984,* ed. Sieghard Brandenburg and Helmut Loos (Munich: Henle, 1987), 296–35; Cooper, *Beethoven and the Creative Process,* 209–14; Nicholas Marston, "Review Article: Beethoven's Sketches and the Interpretative Process," *Beethoven Forum* 1 (1992): 232–35. See also Richard Kramer, "Between Cavatina and Ouverture: Opus 130 and the Voices of Narrative," in *Beethoven Forum* 1 (1992): 165–89.

8. Kropfinger, "Das gespaltene Werk," 313–14.

9. Cooper, *Beethoven and the Creative Process,* 211, 213–14.

10. Kropfinger, "Das gespaltene Werk," 313.

11. Johnson et al., *Beethoven Sketchbooks,* 426–49.

12. Ibid., 306–12; 313–17.

13. Identified as SV 331 in Hans Schmidt, "Verzeichnis der Skizzen Beethovens," *Beethoven Jahrbuch* 6 (1969): 104.

14. Sketch 12a appears on fol. 11 recto among the sketches of Example 9.11; I have included it in Example 9.12 because of the many features it shares with the other sketches of this set.

15. See William E. Caplin, *Classical Form: A Theory of Formal Functions for the Instrumental Music of Haydn, Mozart, and Beethoven* (New York: Oxford University Press, 1998), 9–12.

16. Leonard Ratner, *Classic Music: Expression, Form, and Style* (New York: Schirmer Books, 1980), 269.

17. Though sketches 9.20a and b seem clearly to begin with G, we might wonder whether Beethoven actually intended an F, as in most of the remaining sketches for countersubject no. 1.

18. Kropfinger, "Das gespaltene Werk," 309–10; Cooper, *Beethoven and the Creative Process,* 211. Recall that the subject was first sketched in connection with the op. 127 quartet (see note above).

19. Lewis Lockwood, *Beethoven: Studies in the Creative Process* (Cambridge, Mass: Harvard University Press, 1992), 110–11.

CHAPTER TEN

# Opus 131 and the Uncanny

## *Joseph Kerman*

Grotesque and wild! it has invincible energy.
You want to bark like a dog.
—John Dalley[1]

### I

Theodor Adorno's take on the category of Beethoven's late style was unencumbered by chronological scruples. Adorno's major statement on this topic, which was central for his music criticism, treats the *Missa solemnis* of 1822 as a "Late Work without Late Style," to cite the lapidary chapter title in *Beethoven: The Philosophy of Music,* the recent anthology of his writings on the composer compiled by Rolf Tiedemann. And in the copious notes for his unfinished Beethoven book, we hear of many other "late works without late style." They include the finale of the Quartet in C♯ Minor, op. 131, as well as the finale of the Quartet in A Minor, op. 132.

Probably Adorno found too much in the op. 131 finale that resonated with the symphonic style of Beethoven's heroic period. This was Adorno's antithesis of the late style. Features such as the strenuous development section, the enhanced recapitulation, and the delirious drive to the final cadence—these would have reminded him of the masterworks in the Scott Burnham canon. It is true that op. 131 does not end heroically in the major mode, with affirmation, or tragically in the minor, with defiance. It ends with plagal accents of pathos, albeit with the addition of a sudden *fortissimo* whiplash in the last bars. But Adorno knew his Beethoven backwards and forwards, and he knew that for the young composer such endings had been a regular cliché. Most early Beethoven works in C minor conclude with a plagal hush, rocking back and forth between F-minor and C7 sonorities, and one of them even adds a whiplash (the Quartet in C Minor, op. 18 no. 4). Placing all this under the banner of disruption, alienation, and critique might well have made Adorno uncomfortable.

This essay maintains that Adorno was wrong, and that op. 131 deserves a place of honor in the late style as he conceived it.

## II

The crux of the matter is the finale—a sonata-form movement of some kind, undoubtedly, though commentators have struggled with its idiosyncrasies.[2] The second key area, E major, barely prepared and certainly not confirmed, accommodates a lyrical, half-improvisatory theme that makes maximum contrast with the first-group material. William Kinderman would probably call it a "parenthesis," as in the Piano Sonata in E Major, op. 109.[3] The "development" starts with a rondo-like statement of the first theme in the subdominant. The recapitulation duly tilts toward the subdominant, and the lyrical theme actually returns in the Neapolitan key, D major, before sinking into C♯ major. D major was of course a major issue in the quartet's opening movements. Then there comes a long, eventful, stormy coda which cedes, however, to a plagal hush in two stages prior to what I referred to as a whiplash, for a final tierce de Picardie scored for maximum volume.

The body of this essay consists of a review of the vicissitudes of the movement's first two themes, themes that precede the "parenthesis" in the second key area. We will start with the second of them, at bar 22, still in the first key area and marked *piano* (see Example 10.1c). This is the famous theme that recalls or, I would rather say, retrieves the opening fugue.

Much about it is already disorienting. Apart from the peculiarity of so subdued a response to so emphatic a beginning, there is the anomaly of a new theme introduced so early in a Beethoven finale. Although precedents can be found, this certainly doesn't happen very often. And a clear, indeed blatant, functional reference to the theme of another movement: this *never* happens. It is an assault on the expectations of the competent listener.

So much of an assault that some competent listeners have refused to believe their ears. "It may or it may not be of symbolic significance that Beethoven makes some use of the fugue theme in this last movement," wrote J. W. N. Sullivan, "but the character of the theme, as it occurs here, is entirely changed, and any symbolic significance it may have is not obvious."[4] Yet Sullivan at least saw the manifest change of character as a problem, unlike most who have written about op. 131. Other critics seem to have been so struck by the very fact of thematic transformation here that they have nothing to say about its quality. Sometimes they are struck dumb by the "unity" it is thought to establish.

*Example 10.1.* Quartet in C♯ minor, op. 131, finale, beginning.

Central to this change in character, in any case, is the augmented second resulting from the rearrangement of the first notes of the fugue subject. Robert Winter, in his groundbreaking study of the sketches for op. 131, has many good things to say about this rearrangement—"scrambling," he calls it[5] (Reti called it "introversion")—yet even Winter seems more interested here in process than product, for he fails to focus on the interval itself: a wayward, not to say farouche sound that never occurred as a linear element in the fugue itself, never once. In the finale, the second violin immediately answers the first with a loose and aborted canon in inversion, featuring an augmented fourth. The conjunction of augmented second and augmented fourth nags at our ears again and again as the music proceeds (see Example 10.1).

Equally striking is the theme's rigidity. Recall that grave, expressive, fluid fugue subject: after curtailing it—after cutting off two notes—as well as scrambling it, Beethoven was left with a pair of stiff two-bar segments with a half-cadence at the end. He expanded this residue into one of those simple, self-repeating, closed eight-bar phrases that turn up so often in the late music. Beethoven's "doublets" (my own term for these phrases) are not only simple, they are simplistic; most of them evoke naive country dances or nursery songs, as indeed several do in the scherzo movement of op. 131. They reminded Adorno of the *Sprüchlein* from fairy tales, and he cited one: *"Knusper, knusper Knäuschen, wer knuspert an mein'm Häuschen":* "Fee, fi, fo, fum, I smell the blood of an Englishman." They "have something of the ogre about them," said Adorno.[6]

Other features to be noted about this theme are the continuation of the trochaic beat from the first theme in the viola, which makes me think of a more famous viola in *Iphigenia in Tauris;* the battering away at the leading tone on so many of the downbeats; the turn figure in quarter notes, with its altogether-too-obvious inversion; and, in the repetition, the collapse of the texture into bare octaves and weird contrapuntal inversions (Example 10.1d). That's at least one feature that ought to have given Adorno pause. The willful dynamic markings are another.

On the evidence, then, this music has been meticulously crafted to make it aberrant, eccentric, grotesque. What do the commentators say? About half of the suspects that one can round up speak of a lament, somber, deeply mournful, profound gloom, and the like,[7] while the other half register nothing about its affect or quality at all. A recent writer, Stephen Rumph, breaks ranks and speaks of trivialization and travesty—something that would not be out of character for the composer of the Turkish music in the Ninth Symphony.[8] Something like an op. 131 quadrille. Still, that does not seem quite right. The sort of distortion Beethoven transacted here can either amuse us or unsettle us, and this listener, at least, is not laughing or smiling. The adjective that works for me is *uncanny.* This music has something of the ogre about it.

## III

The uncanny doublet theme returns three times later in the movement, once in the recapitulation and twice in the coda. It becomes progressively closer to the fugue subject that it has retrieved. It also becomes less and less uncanny, because of changes in melody, harmony, and texture, and because each time it appears, it sits differently vis-à-vis the first theme or first-theme material. The original blank—and, once again, uncanny—juxtaposition of the two themes gives way to unexpected conjunctions of great richness and expressivity.

### *Recapitulation*

Here the first theme appears with new figuration and a marvelous new thematic element—a cantus firmus figure in whole notes, C♯–A–G♯, answered by G♯–F♯–E (see Example 10.2). New, except that its pace has been prepared in the development section, and its pitches sound familiar . . . abstracting, as they do, the much-discussed four-note *Urmotiv* of the late quartets. In the immediate context, the heavy arrival of

*Example 10.2.* Quartet in C♯ minor, op. 131, finale, mm. 182–201.

the cantus firmus onto the pitches A–G♯ echoes the same arrival in the original doublet theme. Clearly, then, if the latter is now to be recapitulated, it cannot remain in the tonic key. It turns instead to the subdominant, a good place to go if the "parenthesis" is going to visit in the Neapolitan.

The move could not be simpler—a deceptive cadence using a V/iv chord (actually V9/iv, a direct recall of the pathos-laden ending of the Adagio quasi un poco andante movement that introduces the finale). The cantus firmus answer having now worked its way up to the treble, it softens into the major mode so that F♯–E♯ in the figure G♯–F♯–E♯ can elide with the first two notes of the transposed doublet melody, F♯–E♯–D–C♯.

The rather obvious modulatory ploy has been made functional. And many little things combine to deepen the morose, cranky quality of the original doublet into something closer to pathos. The doublet's opening step F♯–E♯ acquires a new sense as a rhetorical intensification of the same step heard just previously; it feels like a vocal gesture, a catch in the voice responding to an expansive new stretto of the cantus firmus in the cello. There is a real surge of feeling at this place, a breaking of constraints, for by relaxing the rigid proportions of the doublet, Beethoven allows us to hear a six-bar phrase at the start of it, rather than four. Meanwhile the trochaic backbeat in the viola dissipates; the doublet's opening note becomes a nonharmonic tone, rather than a firm tonic; and the stark octaves of the inverted canonic answer are toned down into thirds and tenths. Although the doublet still follows on the heels of the main theme without any transition, as in the exposition, the sequence is altogether smoother. The themes engage.

## *Coda (1)*

The coda of this work evinces superlatives; one commentator pronounces it the greatest of all Beethoven codas. The body of it consists of two more-or-less parallel heroic surges, both met by the doublet theme in successive transformations (see Examples 10.3 and 10.4).

When the first surge is halted—momentarily—by what promises to be a full (sixteen-bar) return of the doublet, the latter enters an octave higher, hastily, distractedly, with new counterpoints and melting new harmonic details pivoting around a high cello G♯. It has now shed its grotesque canonic answer, as well as the backbeat. Beethoven does bring the answer back, but only to resolve it in a famous *unisono* passage that restores a few more pitches from the original fugue subject. He breaks the doublet phrase down and extends it, drawing it into the world of the main theme, the world of invincible energy and the barking of dogs. Iambic accents derived from the canonic answer complement and relieve the trochees that have been battering us up to now: another masterly detail.

## *Coda (2)*

The second surge of the coda has reached a huge climax and has started to make the necessary cadential noises—and suddenly has collapsed (Example 10.4).

Perhaps the music that responds to this collapse counts as a development or a transformation of the doublet theme, rather than a "return" to it. In any case, it functions like Fortinbras prior to the final tucket (or whiplash). It resolves, absorbs, mourns, and does what it can to restore the *status quo ante:* that is, the state of play in the quartet's first movement.

For by now, most of the aberrant features have fallen away. The inverted canonic answer and the backbeat are both gone, liquidated earlier in the coda, as we have seen, as are the jarring quarter notes and the doublet structure itself. The theme is reduced down to a single motive, the key motive, the motive featuring the augmented second. And reduction allows the theme to be developed and expanded—a welcome outcome, after we have heard it so many times locked into the doublet: 2 bars + 2, 2 bars + 2. We now hear 2 + 2 + 5 + 9 (and no terminal cadence, either). As reduced and developed and then expanded, I think the theme effectively regains the fluidity and the calm of the first-movement fugue subject. Over the course of the finale, a doublet in *alla breve,* with a march beat back of it in the viola, reaches its last transformation as an open form in *Ritmo di due battute,* an approximation of the weary pace of the quartet's first movement, Adagio ma non troppo e molto espressivo. This transformation, with its spectral octaves, comes as an expressive revelation.

Also regained is the fugue's notorious bias toward the subdominant, which Winter writes about so well. This bias was removed early in the finale when the doublet scrambled the fugue subject so as to stress the dominant pitch, G♯, rather than A. Beethoven had called for dominant sounds even earlier: the Adagio/andante movement in G♯ minor and a modulation to G♯ minor in the following Allegro theme. Now, approaching the end of the work and developing the key motive as a sequence, he settles the melody first on the dominant (G♯), then on the subdominant (F♯). The subdominant is reinforced very beautifully: the third leg of the sequence reaches up an octave, so that it can sink down the scale through a whole tenth, down to F♯ once again. Resolving that farouche interval B♯–A, this long downward scale, together with its repetition, recaptures not only the fluidity of the first movement, but I think also its gravity and its almost surplus expressivity. Beethoven is not playing with the pitches of the fugue subject here. He is restoring the sorrow of the fugue.

New intermovement echoes help this process along. A pair of long, shuddering diminished-seventh chords in mm. 363–66 flash back to the liquidation of the fugue subject in the first movement, just before the transition to the second movement (see Example 10.5). William Kinderman draws attention to this in the course of a trenchant discussion of op. 131 in his *Beethoven.*[9] The original doublet theme referred to the pitch content and rhythm of the fugue subject; these diminished chords refer to its affect.

*Example 10.3.* Quartet in C♯ minor, op. 131, finale, mm. 275–96.

*Example 10.4.* Quartet in C♯ minor, op. 131, finale, mm. 344–67.

*Example 10.5.* Quartet in C♯ minor, op. 131, first movement, mm. 113–17; finale, mm. 363–69.

And inasmuch as they refer to the conclusion of the fugue, rather than its beginning, the finale music now bears the emotional weight of the fugue's total trajectory.

To my ear, also, though this may be disputed, the melodic sequence recalls the main recurring episode in the fugue and the feeling of melancholy or lassitude that this episode brings with it at each of its appearances (see Example 10.6).

In sum, although the relationship between the main theme of the finale and the doublet theme is initially one of uncanny juxtaposition, this quality no longer holds for later encounters. In the recapitulation, the doublet seems definitely to respond in some way to the main theme, and to respond with new emotionality. In the coda, on the other hand, a desperate doublet attempts to ward off an onslaught and is

*Example 10.6.* Quartet in C♯ minor, op. 131, first movement, mm. 21–24, 46–49, 106–10; finale, mm. 350–54.

shattered for its pains (a narrative reading is hard to evade or resist here, I should think, which in any case I would not wish to do). Yet later in the coda, when the main theme fades, the doublet, or what so beautifully remains of the doublet, is still there to pick up the pieces.

## IV

Let us now turn to the first theme of the op. 131 finale and trace *its* various appearances over the course of the movement. This theme, too, is less straight-arrow than it is usually taken to be (Example 10.1).

The anapestic opening bars may be transparent enough. But the same cannot be said for the following trochaic melody. Although usually described as marchlike (Romain Rolland called it Beethoven's *"chant d'assaut, son Marseilleise à cheval"*),[10] any melody with *eight* rhythmically identical incises is following its own quirky agenda. In a march, regular rhythms incite vitality; these rhythms seem lifeless, like the robotic clank of the *Grosse Fuge*. Tovey called this theme "tragically sardonic."[11] To me there is something especially uncanny about the way the accompaniment adheres to the melody—the lower instruments almost sound like a harsh sonorous extension of each individual melody pitch, a sort of downward organ mixture.

The modulation to the dominant in bars 9–13 is hard to credit in a composition that has programmatically avoided dominant modulations up to this point—especially hard, perhaps, because it proceeds so formulaically, by way of a cliché used in a number of early C-minor compositions.[12] And the new key collapses; the return to the tonic comes too soon, by means of an all-but-mechanical sequence. Then a Neapolitan articulation overcompensates, in the quite astonishing aporia of bars 17–21 (Example 10.1b). The music panics, slamming on the brake so hard that the accompaniment comes unstuck, as does the harmony.

A new grace-note articulation appears at bar 47; I take this as a further crack in the theme's facade but will bypass this detail to speak of the recapitulation.

Here the theme appears with new figuration and with the new or new-old cantus firmus figure (visible in Example 10.2), which invests the complex with great power. But meanwhile, the trochaic theme itself destructs. The modulation to the dominant, which gave it its character, simply disappears. Tovey appreciated the grand and spacious quality of the swings between I and V that replace the original dynamic I–v–I.[13] Yet the swings can also sound rather automatic. Walter Riezler was on the mark: "It is as though the tension of the opening theme were being reduced by degrees."[14] From this point on, the main theme appears only in rhythmic shards.

The most superb of them come at the climax of the coda (see Example 10.7): the trochees, rearing up under the downward scale and stretching through a seventh, their maximum span, retrace the move to the dominant that originally energized the theme and then disappeared from the recapitulation. The climax of the coda acknowledges its failure, in a vision of what has been and cannot be again.

*Example 10.7.* Quartet in C♯ minor, op. 131, finale, mm. 312–27.

The following cadential action includes another famous *unisono,* of rushing D-major scales—an uncanny feature if ever there was one (right after Example 10.7). No doubt this passage confirms the Neapolitan thrust of the work as a whole, if anyone still feels a need for confirmation, but it does little to settle the finale. "Cadences [at this point] only serve to establish C sharp minor as the home key, not to confirm it or close it," Leonard Ratner has observed. "The cadences in measures 332 and 336 are far too short to serve the role of closure, while the cadence in measures 340–341 occurs in the middle of what promises to be a symmetrical period."[15]

In this unstable situation, and given this history of instability, collapse is perhaps not entirely unexpected—collapse of the one element of the main theme that has retained its integrity up to now, the anapest motive. The suppression of this motive, shown in the first line of Example 10.4, opens up a unique, unconstrained space for the doublet theme in its final transformation. Instead of background trochees stressing every half note, we now have anapests that do not even stress, just adumbrate every whole note.

With the first theme enervated, Beethoven empowers the doublet theme with new resources of development or transformation, so that it can re-enter and review the world of the opening fugue . . . as I have tried to show. I say "re-enter and review" that world, rather than "regress to" that world, because I feel that the trajectory of the finale is fully acknowledged. It is acknowledged all the way from the anapests at the beginning of the exposition to the climax of the coda; the two long descending scales at that point are echoed and resolved by the two long descending scales in the later passage (see Examples 10.4 and 10.7). Those were *fortissimo;* these are *piano.* One can hear these voicing both a reproach and condolence after the cadential surge that failed. Adorno's word would be *critique.*

Because descending *fortissimo* whole-note scales, shown in Example 10.7, invert whole-note scales that storm heroic heights in the development section, one can see the critique extending to the rhetoric of heroism more generally. (Another referent may be bars 25–28 in the previous Adagio quasi un poco andante movement, another long plunge involving a sequence.) Critique also extends to the source of power in the recapitulation, the cantus firmus figure C♯–A–G♯. It is now cast into a limbo of misgiving and pathos by the whole-note ostinato figure on the last page of the quartet, C♯–F♯–E♯—which is no longer answered. The music winds down to Poco adagio. Only here, as Kinderman points out, do those critical long As with their diminished chords achieve resolution.

Thus the recall of the very end of the quartet's opening Adagio comes in the same tempo. The disparity between the original slow fugue subject and the faster recall of it in the finale, what one could call the "global tempo dissonance" of this extraordinary composition, is resolved along with the harmonic dissonance.

## V

Beethoven's String Quartet no. 14 in C♯ Minor, op. 131, is a unique piece. It begins with an Adagio (not quite unique in this respect: we will not forget that other piece in C-sharp minor). It begins with a fugue. Its movements run continuously, from the controversially labeled No. 1 to No. 7, a condition that encourages explicit, egregious echoes between them. These culminate in the recall of No. 1 in No. 7, the retrieval of the fugue into the finale, the topic of this whole chapter up to now.

And more is unique: this is a minor-mode composition destined to end unassertively (for surely the final *fortissimo* fails to convince. It hardly tries.) Most commentators say it ends tragically. Most seem to sense a deep sadness in the opening fugue—"the saddest thing ever said in notes," according to Wagner—and then a kaleidoscope of lighter experiences in major keys, some of them not only light but humorous and quirky. Then sadness deepens into tragedy when the piece reverts at last to the minor. The turning point comes with the *fortissimo* G♯ octaves after the scherzo. After this savage call to reckoning, the composer takes his time before resolving G♯ to the work's first cadence in C♯ minor, time filled with memories of minor-mode afflictions. In the finale that emerges from this momentous launch, sonata action drives the quartet for the first time, as in the "Moonlight" Sonata, as is often observed.

This finale is also often compared to the finale of the Quartet in E Minor, op. 59 no. 2, for fairly good and in any case obvious reasons. Yet the blazing conclusion in the minor mode of the earlier work stands at the opposite pole from what happens in op. 131. Indeed, the coda promises the same sort of defiant apotheosis, but it fails to deliver. What happens is much more equivocal.

The real drama in this music develops late and works independently of contrasted key areas and harmonic resolutions. According to the present reading, two themes both introduced in the initial tonic key area emerge from a continuing series of transformations as counterforces. At the end, after the cadential surge developed out of the main theme collapses, the doublet (or the material of the doublet) survives. It guides the music back to the subdominant and stirs new memories of the first movement. I am very high on this passage, as you gather. It seems to me to achieve a remarkable sense of consummation, an authentic return at the end of the quartet to the ethos of the great fugue that began it.

In short, this is one of those late Beethoven sonata movements that accommodates a counter-narrative—in this case, a counter-narrative that ultimately prevails. We are not dealing only with the dynamic of sonata form in its classic state, whatever that is, or sonata form with "deformations," as James Hepokoski would say. We are dealing with that and something else, too. An analogy would be the Quartet in E♭ Major, op. 127, where the initial Maestoso cuts across sonata-form norms and in effect undercuts the recapitulation. (Daniel Chua, a critic much beholden to Adorno, writes well about this.) Beethoven's undercutting of sonata form was an important aspect of the critique Adorno found central to the late style. So I say he was wrong to exclude the finale of op. 131 from the late style. Tovey and his epigones are no help, either, when they eulogize this quartet under the banner of "normality."

Of course op. 131's counter-narrative differs entirely from op. 127's, and of course the critique of sonata form proceeds differently than in other familiar cases, such as in op. 130 or 132. But although only a dummy would try to press the point, to me the critique does seem more explicit in op. 131, and more vivid, inasmuch as Beethoven evokes the heroic accents of the symphonic style so deliberately within the movement itself. The opening anapestic exclamations echo the wake-up call of the Fifth Symphony and the E-Minor Quartet. The trochaic march is merely the most severe example of another well-worked Beethovenian topos. The inexorable climb in the development section and the roaring triumph of the recapitulation—all this is not only deliberate, it is hyperbolical. As for the coda, Wagner said it best: "The dance of the whole world itself, wild joy, the wail of pain, love's transport, utmost bliss, grief, frenzy, riot, suffering; the lightning flickers, thunders growl: and above it the stupendous fiddler who bans and bends it all, who leads it haughtily from whirlwind into whirlpool, to the brink of the abyss . . ."[16]

## VI

The argument of this essay on "Opus 131 and the Uncanny," which might more usefully have been entitled "Opus 131 and Exorcism of the Uncanny," is open to an obvious objection. If the finale (indeed, the work as a whole) is to be read as enacting the retreat from sonata teleology in favor of circularity, why, it may be asked, does this take place by way of an *uncanny* thematic manipulation? It is hard to bring up the uncanny without bringing in Freud, and critics of a psychoanalytical bent could probably pick up op. 131 and run with it. Less agile, I can do no more than stumble over the obvious pitfalls. For example, one could have Beethoven anticipating Freud by arranging for a "repressed" fugue theme to surface as the uncanny doublet—but only on the basis of a questionable concept of repression in this music. As the fugue theme comes to mind as soon as the doublet is heard, it can hardly be said to be repressed, only forgotten for a while. In any case, "repression" applied to the fugue is particularly problematic since the first movement of op. 131 forgoes closure. In retrospect, it can be heard signaling its own recall. To perceive repression in the four-note *Urmotiv* of the late quartets, rather than the fugue theme, would be more intuitive, but in that case the whole finale should register as uncanny from bar 1 on, and it does not. Such initiatives seem to me facile and of next to no hermeneutic promise.[17]

I have no answer to the question. You can ask the artwork that sort of question, if you have to, but the artwork will not answer. (No tact, no hermeneutics.) A context for the whole issue is well known: Beethoven often proceeded to the desired culmination of his works circuitously, with something uncanny, humorous, or even freakish along the route. The classic case is no doubt the Fifth Symphony. E. T. A. Hoffmann—master of the uncanny, for Freud—called the double-bass fugato in the third movement *unheimlich* and spoke of "fear which constricts the breast" at the return of the opening material in pizzicato, and "the terror of the extraordinary, the fear of spirits" at the timpani pedal. (In the finale, though, Hoffmann was not similarly moved by the return of "the simple theme of the Menuett.")[18]

Familiar, all-too-familiar examples in the late music are the Turkish march in the Ninth Symphony, the pastiche of popular ditties in the second movement of the Piano Sonata in A♭, op. 110, and the terrific explosion in the scherzo of the Quartet in F, op. 135, to which I propose adding the finale of op. 131 as a further example. No doubt the place in the symphony is less uncanny than *grotesque*—John Dalley's word—and the place in the string quartet less uncanny than wild. A truly uncanny moment is later in the sonata, when one of the ditties from the second movement turns up again in the finale in a double diminution.[19]

## Notes

1. David Blum, *The Art of Quartet Playing: The Guarneri Quartet in Conversation with David Blum* (New York: Alfred P. Knopf, 1986), 230. Blum rushed up to the Guarneri Quartet after they had played op. 131 and asked them for their immediate reactions. Dalley is the quartet's second violinist.

2. For example, Manfred Hermann Schmid in the formidable *Beethoven: Interpretationen seiner Werke,* ed. Albrecht Riethmüller, Carl Dahlhaus, and Alexander L. Ringer (Laaber: Laaber, 1994): "Im Finale des cis-Moll-Quartetts durchdringen sich drei Formaspekte. Themendualismus und Konfliktzuspitzung prägen den Satzcharakter in Sinne des Sonatenprinzips, die Reihungsanlage mit einem beherrschenden, nicht abshüttelbaren thema stammt hingegen aus dem Rondo, die harmonische Disposition aus der Fuge" (vol. II, p. 323).

3. William Kinderman, *Beethoven* (Oxford: Clarendon, 1995), 219.

4. J. W. N. Sullivan, *Beethoven: His Spiritual Development* (New York: Knopf, 1927), 243.

5. Robert Winter, *Compositional Origins of Beethoven's Opus 131* (Ann Arbor, Mich.: UMI Research Press, 1982). The *locus classicus* for scrambling in late Beethoven is of course the end of the Alla tedesca movement of op. 130; on op. 135 see also Daniel Chua, *Absolute Music and the Construction of Meaning* (Cambridge: Cambridge University Press, 1999), 283–84, where Chua makes much of the scrambling of "Es muss sein" in the first theme of the finale (D–F–

C) into the nonsensical "muss sein es" of the second theme (F–C–C–D, originally A–E–E–F♯)—a doublet phrase, almost a twin of the present case.

6. Theodor W. Adorno, *Beethoven: The Philosophy of Music; Fragments and Texts,* ed. Rolf Tiedemann, trans. Edmund Jephcott (Stanford, Calif.: Stanford University Press, 1998), 191.

7. Jacques Lonchampt, *Les Quatuors à cordes de Beethoven* (Paris: Broché, 1987), 171; Philip Radcliffe, *Beethoven's String Quartets* (London: Hutchinson, 1965), 191; Daniel Gregory Mason, *The Quartets of Beethoven* (New York: Oxford University Press, 1947), 264; Joseph de Marliave, *Beethoven's Quartets,* trans. Hilda Andrews (London: Oxford University Press, 1928), 321 (paraphrasing Theodor Helm, *Beethovens Streichquartette: Versuch einer technischen Analyse dieser Werke im Zusammenhange mit ihrem geistigen Gehalt* (Leipzig: E. W. Fritzsch, 1885), 261: "tief schmerzlichen Klage"). Words that I threw into the pot years ago were *pathos* and *bile:* see Joseph Kerman, *The Beethoven Quartets* (New York: Alfred A. Knopf, 1967), 343, 203.

8. Stephen Rumph, *Beethoven after Napoleon: Political Romanticism in the Late Works* (Berkeley and Los Angeles: University of California Press, 2004), 131.

9. Kinderman, *Beethoven,* 322.

10. Romain Rolland, *Beethoven: les Grandes époques créatrices,* vol. 5 (Paris: Éditions du Sablier, 1943), 260.

11. Donald Francis Tovey, *The Mainstream of Music and Other Essays* (New York: Oxford University Press, 1949), 293.

12. Such as the finales of op. 18 no. 5 and opus 37. An early C-minor work with more serious connections to the finale of op. 131 is the String Trio in C Minor, op. 9 no. 3, as has often been observed. In the first movement, the passage in the coda with the opening theme C–B–A♭–G in even notes (dotted quarters in 6/8 time) treated as a descending sequence resembles the end of the quartet so closely as to suggest conscious modeling. There is even a new figuration that is vaguely similar. This movement seems to provide the earliest example of Beethoven's characteristic enhanced recapitulations with a new continuous figuration, as in opp. 57, 93, etc., and op. 131; and in this recapitulation, the first idea of the second group returns in the Neapolitan key, D♭. The finale of op. 9 no. 3 offers another forecast of the quartet: the coda includes a grandiose *fortissimo* on the Neapolitan, followed by a back-and-forth passage pressing hard on the subdominant.

13. Tovey, *The Mainstream of Music,* 293.

14. Walter Riezler, *Beethoven,* trans. G. D. H. Pidcock (London: Forrester, 1938), 240.

15. Leonard Ratner, *The Beethoven String Quartets: Compositional Strategies and Rhetoric* (Stanford, Calif.: Stanford Bookstore, 1995), 257.

16. Richard Wagner, *Prose Works,* vol. 5, trans. William Ashton Ellis (London: K. Paul, Trench, Trübner 1896), 97–98.

17. I had repressed Freud—I am grateful to a participant at the Victoria conference whose question sent me back to volume 17 of *The Complete Psychological Works* (London: Hogarth, 1955), 217–52.

18. *Beethoven: Symphony No. 5 in C Minor,* Norton Critical Score, ed. Elliot Forbes (New York: Norton, 1971), 159–60

19. Another point brought forward by William Kinderman in *Beethoven,* 229.

CHAPTER ELEVEN

# Beethoven's Last Quartets

## Threshold to a Fourth Creative Period?

*William Kinderman*

The progressive and innovative, yet richly historical orientation of Beethoven's last string quartets poses challenges to interpretation that have not yet been met. One part of this challenge is captured in Carl Dahlhaus's claim that in these works, "the distinction between past, present, and future fades and becomes unimportant." Dahlhaus continues, "Nothing could be more mistaken than to extract what is archaizing in Beethoven's late quartets—[for example] the 'Lydian mode'—and what is modern—the abstract nature of the four-note figure that roams through them, like a harbinger of the twentieth century—and set them up in mutual opposition."[1] Indeed, a special synthesis of old and new, of retrospective and futuristic tendencies, comes to fruition in a movement like the *Grosse Fuge,* or Great Fugue, the original finale of the B♭ Major Quartet, op. 130. On the one hand, this movement looks back to Haydn's fugal finales of his op. 20 quartets and to Beethoven's early studies with Albrechtsberger; Beethoven pursued here the unfashionable traditional idiom of the fugue with exhaustive vigor, as Warren Kirkendale has stressed.[2] On the other hand, the eighty-year-old Igor Stravinsky praised the Great Fugue as "the most perfect miracle in music," adding that "it is also the most absolutely contemporary piece of music I know, and contemporary forever . . . Hardly birthmarked by its age, the Great Fugue is, in rhythm alone, more subtle than any music of my own century . . . I love it beyond everything."[3] Yet if Stravinsky celebrated the Great Fugue for its modernism, for being "pure interval music,"[4] one recent writer characterizes the work as "a logical narrative of destruction" that prefigures the decline of the Enlightenment "into barbarism," as "techniques of reason become those of tyranny."[5] The music that provokes such divergent reactions merits closer examination.

More than a generation ago, Martin Cooper described Beethoven's stylistic evolution as a "gradual reorientation of a complete, mature personality" whose artistic quest centered on a search for a "unity lying behind the diversity of the phenomena of human existence."[6] Such a notion of "unity" has roots both in the Beethoven sources and in the aesthetics of his day and should be clearly distinguished from the allegedly "tautological" unity cited in recent years by some critics of musical analysis. Aesthetic thinkers such as Friedrich Schiller and E. T. A. Hoffmann did not embrace a totalizing concept of an artistic unity embodied in a structural matrix. What they did espouse was a concept of the artwork as a synthesis of the rational and sensuous, of structure and expression. For Schiller, whose thought resonates closely with Beethoven's music, the central goal of the successful artwork and its performance was located in what he described as the "play drive" (*Spieltrieb*), a capacity combining thought and feeling, and drawing alike on the "form drive" (*Formtrieb*) and "sensuous drive" (*Sinntrieb*) in human nature.[7] This rich synthesis gave pride of place to an improvisatory dimension, which has not received enough recognition in some recent scholarship about Beethoven's aesthetics.[8]

Like Schiller, Beethoven recognized in art an ethical component tied to the idea of freedom. In a letter from July 1819 to his patron and student the archduke Rudolph, he wrote characteristically about the need for "freedom and progress . . . in the world of art as in the whole of creation."[9] To refer to his own artistic goal in this context, Beethoven coined the term *Kunstvereinigung*, or "artistic unification," a notion that is connected to the aging composer's intense assimilation of Handel and Bach during his last decade. A striving toward *Kunstvereinigung* is in no way confined to his assimilation of Baroque models, however, and the context of this letter invites an interpretation giving equal recognition to Beethoven's insistence on infusing his works with the new poetic sensibility. Beethoven's entire career may be viewed as embodying such a progressive unification of artistic means. In the same letter to the archduke, Beethoven continued that "refinement in manners has opened many new things to us" and he warned his royal pupil "not to subject himself to the accusation of one-sidedness." In the same vein, in 1826 he told Karl Holz, in reference to the last quartets, "Art demands of us that we shall not stand still," adding, "Thank God there is less lack of fantasy than ever before."[10]

A celebrated stylistic shift in Beethoven's career occurred, of course, at the threshold to the so-called "heroic" period during 1801–4, the period of the two Fantasy Sonatas, op. 27, the Piano Sonatas, op. 31, the Variations on Original Themes, op. 34 and op. 35, and the *Eroica* Symphony. Yet this evolution is not simply a case of an artist setting out to be more original at any one particular moment in history. Beethoven's "heroic" period arose out of a confluence of historical, stylistic, and personal factors, and close examination of the music reveals deep continuities with Beethoven's earlier and later works. But if the self-professed "new path" of 1802 was not entirely new, it was certainly long: the expression attributed to Hippocrates, "*ars longa, vita brevis*" (art is long, life is short) was a favorite dictum of Beethoven, one he repeatedly set as a canon many years later. The innovative tendencies of Beethoven's art were nourished by the primacy of improvisation or "fantasieren" in his compositional practice—a restless, spontaneous attitude toward artistic creation that was by no means confined to his music for piano. Ferdinand Ries reported that Beethoven once planned a concert tour in which Ries was to play Beethoven's piano concertos and other completed works, whereas "Beethoven himself wished only to conduct and to improvise" (*phantasieren*).[11]

The evolution of Beethoven's "third period" or "late" style after 1812 was a very gradual process about which no clear critical consensus exists. In assessing the position of the five late quartets in Beethoven's evolving style, I shall focus especially on the second, third, and fourth of these works in order of composition, the Quartets in A Minor, op. 132, in B♭ Major, op. 130 (in its original version), from 1825, and in C♯ Minor, op. 131, from 1826. Various authors, beginning with Paul Bekker, have described these works as a triptych, in view of their obvious thematic resemblances.[12] These three quartets represent Beethoven's boldest experiments with the formal design of a multimovement composition going beyond the conventional framework of four movements. In various ways, these works seem to push toward a new threshold in Beethoven's creative development. The B♭ Quartet, in particular, is a pathbreaking yet enigmatic and controversial piece. Joseph Kerman has described the B♭ Major Quartet as Beethoven's "most dissociated composition" and its original finale, the Great Fugue, as the most "vitally problematic work, doubtless, in the entire literature of music."[13]

A striking dimension of these works lies in their temporality, and especially the presence in this music of nonlinear as well as linear temporal succession. The linear or deterministic aspect of Beethoven's works is a familiar aspect of his style, but the nonlinear features deserve more recognition. Jonathan Kramer has drawn attention to nonlinear qualities in the first movement of Beethoven's last Quartet in F Major, op. 135. He focuses on the strong tonic cadence heard already in bar 10 of the opening Allegretto, as well as the disconnection of this gesture from the immediate continuation, and he probes the paradoxical implications of an "actual ending" of the piece in "gestural time" heard just as it begins.[14] Actually, Beethoven had a longstanding interest in nonlinear temporal relations, or in what might be termed "temporal multiplicity," but his experimentation in this direction reached a climax in the trilogy of quartets under consideration here, opp. 132, 130/133, and 131.

Examination of the nonlinear aspects of his music may help to address a quandary about one conspicuous quality of the last quartets, and particularly parts of opp. 132 and 130/133: the contrast-ridden surface of the music, and its sometimes puzzling junctures and apparent discontinuities. In assessing this phenomenon, Theodor

W. Adorno argued that the aging Beethoven saw through the Classical style as classicism, exposing its affirmative or festive aspects to a critique that puts into question the unity of subjectivity and objectivity that sustained his own earlier style.[15] However, one problem in Adorno's view is that "affirmative or festive aspects" do not in fact disappear from Beethoven's late style, neither in the *Missa solemnis* and Ninth Symphony nor in the last sonatas and quartets.[16] To intensify Adorno's attitude by regarding the "quartets as critiques," as does Daniel Chua, easily yields a one-sided if not distorted picture.[17] As we shall see, the use of contrast in late Beethoven is not *simply* disruptive—it is often constructive on another, perhaps higher, level. Important here is the coexistence in his music of nonlinear and linear time, corresponding to philosophical concepts of being and becoming. Nonlinear time in Beethoven can be manifested in nonadjacent connections of various kinds; we will explore several examples below. The assessment of these issues invariably depends on the musical context and requires more detailed attention from both historical and analytical perspectives. It is helpful, also, to review aspects of the compositional genesis of these works, serving as that does to point us toward connections and interrelationships of which we might otherwise remain unaware.

## Quartet in A Minor, Op. 132

The network of interrelationships that connects the five late quartets to one another is by no means confined to the four-note motivic configuration mentioned by Dahlhaus. In fact, that motivic pattern, which highlights the semitones from the leading note to the tonic and from the lowered sixth degree to the dominant, surfaces in sketches for the slow introduction to a projected piano sonata for four hands that Beethoven never completed; the motivic material and sequential pattern, transposed from C minor to E♭ major, found its way into the scherzo of the first of these quartets, the Quartet in E♭ Major, op. 127 (Examples 11.1a and b). This sketch, from about August 1824, reveals that the basic intervallic configuration so prominent in the last quartets arose during Beethoven's reflection on another project altogether, in a different key. The topos in question stems from the Baroque, and it was familiar to Beethoven in part from some of Mozart's C-minor works, such as the Fugue for two pianos K. 426, which Beethoven had copied out in score many years earlier.

Studies of Beethoven's manuscripts have helped clarify various affinities between these quartets, particularly affinities connected to their extension beyond the conventional classical framework of four movements. As Sieghard Brandenburg has shown, Beethoven already envisioned such an expansion of the formal design during his composition of op. 127.[18] During the process of composition, this quartet was envisioned in as many as six movements, including a character piece in C major, entitled "La gaieté," planned at one point as the second movement, as well as a slow introduction to the finale in the key of the Neapolitan, E major. In the end, Beethoven retained the four-movement form in op. 127, but his flirtation with such an ex-

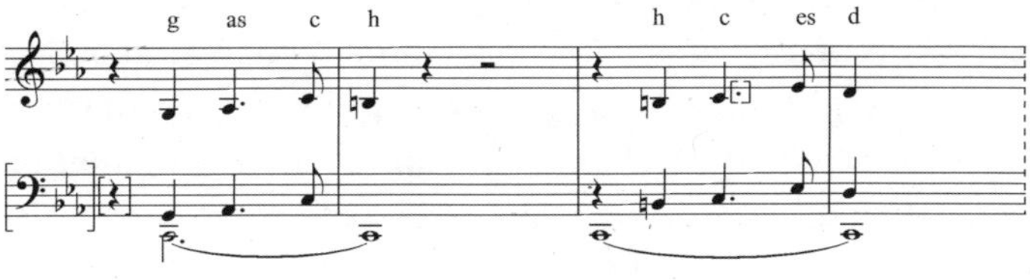


*Example 11.1a.* Autograph 11/2, fol. 5v.

*Example 11.1b.* Quartet in E♭ major, op. 127, III, mm. 2–4.

pansion of the narrative chain of movements bore fruit in the following trilogy of quartets, in A Minor, op. 132, B♭ Major, op. 130, and C♯ Minor, op. 131. (Despite its misleading opus number, op. 132 was the second in order of composition.) The A-Minor Quartet is usually regarded as having five movements, but Beethoven himself regarded it as having six, because he counted the recitative transition to the finale as a separate movement.[19] The B♭-Major Quartet employs a six-movement design, including the multisectioned fugal finale, whereas the unique design of the C♯-Minor Quartet embraces seven movements. Yet we now know from studies of the autograph manuscripts and sketchbooks that each of these pieces was originally conceived on a still larger scale. In different ways, Beethoven ultimately limited the size of each of these huge works by rearranging or abridging his material.

The A-Minor Quartet, op. 132, was initially larger because of its inclusion of the Alla danza tedesca movement in penultimate position, which was replaced only at the autograph stage by the concise marchlike intermezzo, the Alla Marcia, assai vivace.[20] The following Quartet in B♭ Major absorbed the Alla danza tedesca (which was transposed for this purpose from A major to G major), yet the piece as a whole was eventually curtailed through Beethoven's removal of the *Grosse Fuge* ("Great Fugue") in favor of the substitute finale. Even the C♯-Minor Quartet, op. 131, was to have been capped by a resolving section in D♭ major at the end of the finale—material that Beethoven withheld from this quartet but that formed the nucleus for the Lento assai in that key in his final Quartet in F Major, op. 135.[21] Thus, in writing each of these works, Beethoven conceived material that spilled over beyond the composition immediately at hand. His fertility of invention refused to be contained within the boundaries of the singular work.

The incorporation of the Alla danza tedesca as the fourth of six movements of op. 130 marked a decisive development in the genesis of the A-Minor and B♭-Major quartets. To judge from the sketches, Beethoven may have remained undecided for several months about what movement would follow the great slow movement of op. 132, the "Heiliger Dankgesang eines Genesenen an die Gottheit, in der lydischen

Tonart" ("Holy Song of Thanks of a Convalescent to the Godhead, in the Lydian Mode"). The "Dankgesang" was composed at Beethoven's summer lodgings in Baden near Vienna in May of 1825, following his sustained period of illness beginning in mid-April. By July, op. 132 was finished in the autograph, in a version with the Alla danza tedesca as its fourth movement. Only in August did Beethoven settle on a six-movement plan for the following Quartet in B♭, in which the Alla danza tedesca found its new home.

Another connection of this kind exists between rejected thematic material for the finale of the Ninth Symphony and the finale of the A-Minor Quartet. Beethoven repeatedly weighed the option of an instrumental finale, even while he was composing the choral finale of the symphony.[22] In turn, the abandoned theme for a "finale instromentale" in the Ninth was transposed from D minor to A minor and incorporated into the quartet as the main theme of its rondo finale. The parallel can be extended: Like the choral finale of the Ninth, the final movement of op. 132 is introduced by a passionate recitative-transition. A violin recitative is heard here above tremolo textures in the other strings, suggesting an almost operatic setting. The most poignant phrases stress a descending semitone figure that rises sequentially at the breathless, destabilizing *accelerando* passage, with a crescendo from *pianissimo* to *fortissimo* within just two measures. This climactic gesture could hardly be more extreme: a piercing, syncopated diminished-seventh chord with the first violin on high F yields at the Presto to a cadenza-like fall through three octaves before it resumes the earlier recitative texture, which had been torn asunder by the force of this dissonant interjection (Example 11.2b).

This passage represents a turning point within the narrative design of the whole quartet, linking the first and last movements. Near the outset of the opening movement, at the first juxtaposition of the contrasting tempi Assai sostenuto and Allegro, Beethoven had already exposed the F–E relationship in a strikingly similar way; Kerman has fittingly referred to the gesture as a "scream."[23] The ♭6–5 scale step is fundamental to the emblematic four-note configuration played in the cello in the first moments of the piece (Example 11.2a). The A-Minor Quartet shows its Janus face at once, as the understated flatness of the contrapuntal cantus firmus yields without transition to this painfully impassioned continuation. The mysterious objectivity of the slow music is pitted against the emotional force of the Allegro.

In tonal music, unstable tones, or dissonances, are inherently more expressive than consonances. Consonances provide the stable framework against which dissonances make their mark. In this sense, musical structure finds its very raison d'être in relation to the tensional pressure that is exerted against it. An old rule of thumb in the voicing of dissonances specifies that these should be played more loudly than consonances, because the "passions should be generally aroused by dissonances."[24] This principle was subsumed into Beethoven's entire treatment of contrasts and dynamics in his music, but the beginning of op. 132 offers a particularly striking example.

At the shocking Allegro interruption in m. 9, the first violin swoops through two octaves in a driving rhythm, outlining a diminished-seventh chord, and the gesture is underscored by the intensification to *forte* and the strong downbeat after the double bar. The controlling idea of the violin gesture is the semitone step F–E, which involves a consistent treatment of register. In the last measure of the Assai sostenuto, the first violin plays these notes as a rising semitone, as the faster pacing in quarter notes is introduced. The crescendo marking in this measure is easily misunderstood, since it does not connect directly to the dynamic level of *forte* in the next measure—the sharp contrast remains largely unmediated, and a real transition is not accomplished. Here, as often in his later works, Beethoven was concerned with nonadjacent connections, whereby even powerful contrasts can be subsumed into larger continuities. At the end of the second bar of the Allegro, after the cadenza-like "scream," the first violin returns to these same pitches as the falling semitone F–E in the same register. The dynamic level here of *piano* corresponds with the intensity of sound at the earlier

*Example 11.2a.* Quartet in A Minor, op. 132, I, beginning.

*Example 11.2b.* Quartet in A Minor, op. 132, transition to beginning of finale.

crescendo from *pianissimo*. Thus the two-measure violin flourish is essentially parenthetical, with the resumption of the musical discourse occurring as the crucial semitone is recaptured.[25]

To regard such passages as emblematic of "shattered subjectivity," as does Susan McClary, seems wide of the mark, since so many audible features of the music bridge its disruptive contrasts.[26] The prolonged E in the first violin in the third measure of the Allegro corresponds in its extended duration to the long notes of the Assai sostenuto; the repeated figures stressing the falling half-step F–E in dotted rhythm in mm. 14–15 recall the descending half-steps heard in all the voices in that section. By later placing an Adagio measure before a recall of the "scream" in the first violin at m. 22, Beethoven restated the pairing of contrasting tempi, while the violin elongates the F–E semitone as two whole notes in mm. 23–24. To understand such "unpredictable shifts of musical thought" as part of "an ultimately integrative process," as does Robert Hatten, is not to denature the music.[27] On the contrary, it is as if an enlarged subjectivity enabled us to confront shock and dislocation without any sacrifice of the integrity of the artistic form. Although the piercing violin gesture assumes unusual importance in the first movement, its reincarnation at the threshold to the finale surpasses these passages in intensity (see Example 11.2b). The syncopated *fortissimo* in all four instruments employing double stops and with the first violin on high F goes beyond the similar interjections in the first movement. Beethoven even employs an *accelerando* here, as well as a crescendo from *pianissimo* to *fortissimo*. Here again, the F–E semitone is the crux of the matter, and modulations in preceding phrases of the recitative help bring this long-range pitch relationship sharply into relief. Unlike in the first-movement passages, however, Beethoven has left the dissonance on F unresolved in the two higher registers before the music, regaining composure in the middle register, broadens to Poco adagio. The highest F at the Presto outbreak as well as the F on the downbeat at the resumption of the recitative texture four bars later are both left hanging; the pitch of resolution, E, is denied. At the Poco adagio, at last, the semitone figure emerges as the outcome of this extreme passage.

Then, in the ensuing Allegro appassionato, which is played *attacca*, these same pitch relations are recaptured in the same registers (see Figure 11.1). The second violin takes from the first the F–E semitone, now treated as an ostinato, and Beethoven has emphasized the point by including two bars of accompaniment before the expressive main theme begins to unfold in the first violin (Example 11.2b). As the theme is restated an octave higher, this semitone figure migrates upward as well, initially reiterating the F–E scale step before shifting to other scale degrees. After each of the eight-bar phrases of the theme is restated, the continuation pits the highest F against E in consecutive two-bar phrases, starting in measure 35. Beethoven here has recalled the first movement in his recitative-transition and allowed this passage to take on special importance in the narrative design of the whole quartet. Motivic echoes of the dissonant F–E scale step of the recitative sound throughout the closing Allegro appassionato. These remind us that in the quartet Beethoven has inverted the

*Figure 11.1.* The F–E semitone in the Presto and finale theme of op. 132.

function of the recitative in the Ninth: Instead of opening up utopian possibilities, this recitative forces a renewed confrontation with the music of pathos that was already heard in the opening gestures of the first movement.

This brief but weighty passage of recitative, with its catastrophic climax and transition to the Allegro appassionato, is seldom rendered adequately in performance. Particularly challenging is the need to convey convincingly the expressive duplication of the unresolved hanging Fs in the Presto, the distillation of the F–E relation at the Poco adagio, and the assimilation of this motive into the accompaniment and the melody of the rondo finale. The psychological process of transition demands a rigorous shaping of the small motivic units, in order that these be heard in relation to one another, even when they are not directly juxtaposed in the temporal unfolding of the music. Here, as often in Beethoven's works, but especially in his later music, a close attention to such nonadjacent connections is essential.

The serious, and even agonizing, expressive character of the A-Minor Quartet was probably a factor in Beethoven's choice of the Alla Marcia, assai vivace to serve as a contrasting buffer zone between the "Heiliger Dankgesang" and the recitative and finale. We know when Beethoven seems to have first considered this juxtaposition of movements. In a musical sketch entered into a conversation book on May 27/28, 1825, he wrote the end of the "Dankgesang," marked "Dor[isch]" ("dorian"), followed by the Alla Marcia on the reverse of the same page.[28] Yet in other sources from this period, such as on the very first page of the "Moscow" sketchbook, entries for the "Heiliger Dankgesang" are juxtaposed instead with the Alla danza tedesca, which is written in the key of A major.[29] Beethoven weighed these two alternatives. After having first decided to use the Alla tedesca in op. 132, he changed his mind and restored the Alla Marcia. It has been suggested that Beethoven was motivated here by a desire for metric contrast: the second and last movements and parts of the third movement are in triple time, as is the Alla tedesca, whereas the movement chosen is a march, in duple time.[30] In this context, his emphasis on dotted rhythms recalls the marchlike motivic figures of the first movement, whereas the prominent descending step in alternate measures also links this subject to the main theme of the rondo finale. Figure 11.2 shows several of the conspicuous motivic relations shared between the first, fourth, and fifth movements of op. 132.

Recognition of the shared affinities between the outer movements of op. 132 helps us to reassess the narrative design of the quartet as a whole, in which the

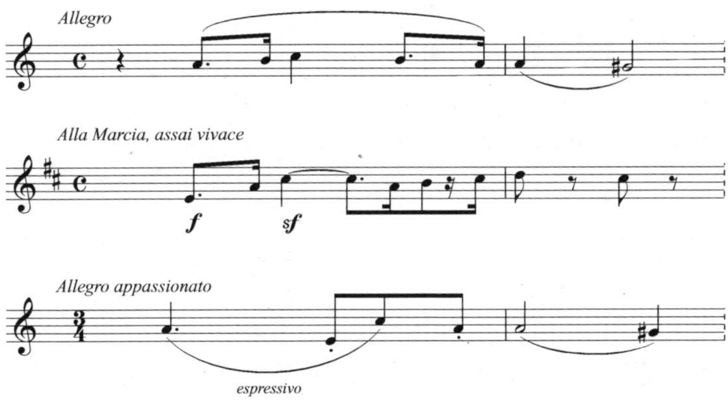


*Figure 11.2.* Motivic relations in the Quartet in A Minor, op. 132.

"Heiliger Dankgesang" assumes such a prominent position. The shocking $F^3$ at the Presto is undoubtedly a gesture of negation and despair targeted at specific earlier passages in the quartet. As Greg Vitercik has observed, this is the same high F as is heard at the conclusion of the "Heiliger Dankgesang." As Vitercik puts it, this "wrenching F''' [= $F^3$] in the first violin . . . recalls, as in a nightmare, the breathlessly poised F''' of the last measure of the 'Dankgesang.'"[31] The "Dankgesang" movement consists of a five-part form: three sections based on the lydian chorale in duple meter are wrapped around two lively, highly decorated tonal sections marked "Neue Kraft fühlend" ("Feeling new strength"). Of the five phrases making up the lydian cantus firmus, it is the first that strongly emphasizes the E–F semitone that we have discussed in the outer movements. The last section of the form of the "Dankgesang," moreover, is based just on this first phrase. Significantly, the passage leading to the climax of this Molto adagio emphatically restates the opening phrase in the highest register (Example 11.3). The enormous intensification of sonority in this passage, fortified by canonic imitations of the accented notes of the hymn, contributes to the impact of music "beside whose strength the *Neue Kraft* pales," in Kerman's formulation.[32]

It is revealing in this connection to compare the design of the A-Minor Quartet with one of the most impressive of Beethoven's middle-period works in the minor mode, the Piano Sonata in F Minor, op. 57 ("Appassionata"). Donald Francis Tovey described this sonata as Beethoven's only work to maintain a tragic solemnity throughout all its movements.[33] Its tragic character is connected to the use of a tonal plan with conspicuous parallels to op. 132. Whereas the turbulent outer movements are in F minor, the contemplative slow movement is a set of variations on a serene, chorale-like theme in D♭ major, marked Andante con moto. The motivic semitone figure D♭–C assumes outstanding importance in the outer movements, in conjunction with a character of tragic strife. This half-step dissonance is a counterpart to the F–E semitone relation that is so decisive in the quartet. In both pieces, moreover, Beethoven employed the flat sixth degree as the tonality for a lyrical theme in the first movement

*Example 11.3.* Quartet in A Minor, op. 132, III, climax of final Molto adagio section.

and as the tonic of the slow movement in the middle of the entire work. (In op. 132, of course, this slow movement is set not in F major, but in the lydian mode, an F mode without B♭). Thus the expressive polarity at the heart of each composition exploits a 6–5 semitone relation as a source of dissonance and pathos, as well as the instability of an internal tonic in a flat-sixth relation to the overall minor tonic key.

In accordance with this compositional strategy, both works contain a particular moment of tragic reversal, when the serenity or spirituality of the slow movement is shattered. In the "Appassionata," the reversal occurs at the end of the Andante con moto, at the harmonic substitution of an arpeggiated diminished-seventh beneath the cadential D♭ in the treble, which might, under other circumstances, have closed the movement. The autonomy of the variation movement is thus annihilated, as D♭, the tonic note of the slow movement, now becomes a crucial dissonance in the context of F minor, recalling a similar treatment in the first movement. Beethoven even derived the principal theme of the finale by composing out in sixteenth notes the diminished-seventh chord as a sinuous line that descends by thirds into the lowest register before reaching a structural downbeat on low F. This structural downbeat marks the true beginning of the finale, after the *Schreckensfanfare* ("terror fanfare") of the chords and the descending transitionary passagework, but it is from this passagework that the figuration of the finale proper is drawn.[34]

In the Quartet in A Minor, the corresponding moment of catastrophic setback comes at the *fortissimo* outbreak in the recitative preceding the finale. Yet, unlike in the "Appassionata," this negating gesture is set at a distance from its target—the ethereal final passages of the "Heiliger Dankgesang"—separated as these are from the recitative by the Alla Marcia, assai vivace. This circumstance points to the greater complexity of the quartet compared to the sonata. One aspect of the complexity lies in the role of modal contrast in the work, particularly the placement of the second and fourth movements, as well as the coda of the finale in A major. The polarity of major and minor in op. 132 is emphasized through Beethoven's decision to maintain A as tonic in four of the five movements of the quartet. Several audible long-range connections between movements are bound up with this modal contrast. The exquisite sound texture of the Presto coda recalls the trio of the second movement, and its stress on F in the cadential phrase recalls once more not only the ostinato accompaniment of the main theme of the finale but the expressive poignancy of this note in the first movement. The inflections of pain in the opening Assai sostenuto are not entirely forgotten, and even the prominent tonal stress on F throughout the quartet—from the second subject of the first movement to the lydian "Dankgesang"—resonates faintly in this telling melodic detail.

Another challenging aspect of op. 132 is the design of the "Heiliger Dankgesang" itself, especially its split into the radical duality of the lydian hymn and Neue Kraft fühlend. In an insightful essay, Kevin Korsyn has observed how aspects of "feeling new strength" are assimilated into the final modal section to support the climactic passages we have discussed, enabling the lydian music to attain closure for the first time. Yet he ultimately regards it as a matter of interpretation whether this interpenetration be regarded as a "coalescence . . . [or] a mere coexistence of opposites." Korsyn asks: "Does Beethoven fuse opposites or simply narrate the impossibility of their convergence?"[35]

The same question could be asked of other contrasts in this quartet. The notion of a Classical resolution of tensions is put to the test here, as it will be in different ways in the following quartets. Adorno claimed in this regard that "something in [Beethoven's] genius, probably the deepest thing, refused to reconcile in the image what is unreconciled in reality."[36] Yet Beethoven actually went far toward "reconciling what is irreconcilable" through his handling of the "Heiliger Dankgesang" in the lydian mode together with the animated, dance-like tonal sections marked "feeling new strength." If these drastically opposed idioms are at first juxtaposed, suggesting two independent beginnings, they are also partly integrated in the final section. Regarding the quartet as a whole, one difference of interpretation lies in the extent to which listeners acknowledge what Kerman describes as "the creation of a psychological progress perhaps more arresting than in any other work."[37] Daniel Chua, for instance, perceives substantial relationships between the parts of the quartet, asserting that "what happens in the last three movements of the work is nothing less than an expansion of the first 30 bars of the quartet into 661 bars; the fusion of the movements and the fissures in their contrast trace exactly the same semiotic, harmonic, thematic, and gestural patterns presented at the beginning."[38] Yet after making this rather ambitious claim, he insists at the same time that the work "negates Enlightenment thinking itself" in delivering a "devastating critique" that contains "no psychological linear progression."[39] A problem with this argument lies in its denial of a psychological dimension in the narrative design of the music. Expression and structure are not in contradiction here, as more balanced discussions of the quartet have recognized.[40]

A comparison can be made with the Piano in A♭ Major, op. 110, composed in 1820–22.[41] Like op. 132, the genesis of the sonata was connected to Beethoven's recovery from sickness, in this instance an even more prolonged illness.[42] Both works display powerful binary oppositions that are associated with sickness and revitalization, death and life. Beethoven's title "Holy Song of Thanks to the Godhead from a Convalescent" implies a serious loss of life energies on the part of the grateful convalescent, and related gestures elsewhere in op. 132, such as the recitative preceding the finale, show that a sense of foreboding is not confined to the slow movement. As Kerman has stressed, a quality of anguish or suffering seems deeply embedded in the quartet. In the finale of the sonata, a counterpart to the pairing of lydian "Dankgesang" and "New Strength" is embodied in the duality of the Arioso dolente and fugue. Mournful stanzas of the Arioso in the minor mode are juxtaposed with the hopeful, aspiring music of the fugue, whose subject features a series of rising perfect-fourth intervals set in the major. After the first fugal section is abruptly broken off, the lament returns in an even more despairing version in the remote key of G minor. This second presentation of the Arioso dolente, with its sighing vocal rhetoric reminiscent of Pamina's "Ach ich fühl's," in the same key, seems destined to end, as does that aria, in unmitigated despair. Only at the last possible moment does the miraculous turning point occur, like an evasion of death: at the final framing cadential gesture in G minor, Beethoven has substituted the unexpected and, in the immediate context of the arioso, even incongruous sonority of the major (m. 5 of Example 11.4). That event signals the beginning of an extended transition, whereby the fugue subject returns in inversion, and only very gradually, through a process of contrapuntal and rhythmic development, does the music recapture the tonic key and ultimately reach a climax of lyric euphoria in the high register.

This transition in op. 110 might also have carried the inscription "Feeling new strength"; Beethoven wrote a similar message above the music: "nach u. nach sich neu belebend" ("gradually coming anew to life"). In fact, op. 110 and op. 132 are not alone in absorbing into music such a dialectical expression of the polarity between death, as a termination of striving and outcome of depressive forces, and life, as a vitalization of energies culminating in joyful abandon. This symbolic dimension sur-

*Example 11.4.* Sonata in A♭ Major, op. 110, III, end of second arioso section.

faces in Beethoven's instrumental music at least as early as the Piano Sonata in D Major, op. 10 no. 3, and it is found in major works, including the *Eroica* Symphony, the *Egmont* music, and the *Missa solemnis,* among others.[43] The duality stands at the very center of Beethoven's only opera, *Fidelio,* where it was emphasized through the expansion in 1814 of Florestan's aria in the dungeon, where the prisoner, close to death, is sustained through his delirious vision of the "angel of freedom," Leonore.

Of all his instrumental works in this vein, the Quartet in A Minor contains perhaps the most challenging narrative design, one whose implications can be cautiously explored. In answer to Korsyn's question, Beethoven seems in the "Heiliger Dankgesang" to narrate the possibility of a *partial* convergence of opposites, achieving thereby the revitalization of the implied subject. And although the despairing recitative retracts this promise, the finale ultimately restores it. The passage leading to the coda hammers out the crucial F$^3$ on downbeats, with the theme in the cello in a high, strained position, as the tempo accelerates to Presto. This extraordinary passage becomes the gateway to an A major never previously attained.

Here may lie the reason why the second and fourth movements—the two dance movements in the major—"are experienced in a curious and unique way as subsidiary," as Kerman says. Some commentators have noted a flatness or static quality in the second movement, the Allegro ma non tanto, and Vitercik writes about its "obsessive clarity" and "endless permutations" of the counterpoint of mm. 5–6 such that "the mesmerizing insouciance of these repetitions comes dangerously close to trivializing that counterpoint, reducing it to the level of a parlor trick."[44] Furthermore, the trio of this movement, with its innocent tone, block-like sectional construction and collage-like reuse of scraps of music Beethoven wrote thirty years earlier, is just as provocative as the Alla Marcia, assai vivace in standing aloof from the serious character of the other three movements. The second and fourth movements in A major are handled in a somewhat parodistic manner, and the coda of the finale is reserved as the true destination for the psychological progress of the work as a whole. In his later years, Beethoven was especially interested in such techniques of parody, and his music with rustic connotations, such as the musette in the trio of the second movement, can harbor deeper meanings. In its texture, meter, and key, this musette anticipates the coda of the finale of op. 132. Here, too, the Piano Sonata in A♭, op. 110, offers a parallel. Its second movement, a humorous scherzo-like Allegro molto, alludes to a folk song on "Ich bin lüderlich, du bist lüderlich" ("I am dissolute, you are dissolute"). That very passage is recalled near the end of the fugal finale of op. 110, where a texture of double diminution helps point the way toward the closing passages of resolution. In both works, an energy drawn from the commonplace helps enable the positive conclusion in the tonic major. Beethoven seems to convey thereby that an openness to experience is an indispensable condition for the sustaining vision of fulfilled life.

## Quartets in B♭ Major, Op. 130/133, and C♯ Minor, Op. 131

As we have seen, the Quartet in A Minor shows points of contact with certain earlier works by Beethoven, particularly the Ninth Symphony and the Piano Sonata in A♭ Major, op. 110. At the same time, it displays particularly innovative qualities of nonlinear temporality. Even immediate, dramatic gestures—such as the violin "scream" at the Presto preceding the finale, seem to be embodied in a formal network that stretches over the work as a whole, and the timing of such events is not always coordinated with their expressive meaning in a singular continuity. Yet conflicts and gaps in this music need not be understood as "devastating critique"; they can assume a range of significance that reaches beyond their immediate context. Special devices—such as the controlled use of the highest register—help to articulate long-spanned connections between movements. In yet another way, the parodistic character of the second and fourth movements broadens the aesthetic scope of the work. Boldest of all is how Beethoven captured a remote or timeless ethos in the lydian hymn of the "Dankgesang," yet the impulse is not antiquarian but essentially modernistic; older models are sought in order to be tested and strained to their limits.

In approaching the Quartet in B♭ Major, we shall focus on the original version of this work with the *Grosse Fuge* as finale.[45] Without recounting in detail the circumstances that led to the composition of a new finale, we should note that this was no straightforward substitution, as with the replacement of the Andante favori as slow movement of the "Waldstein" Sonata, the reassignment of the finale of the Violin Sonata in A Major, op. 30 no. 1, to the "Kreutzer" Sonata, or the substitution of the march-like fourth movement of the A-Minor Quartet, op. 132, for the Alla danza tedesca that Beethoven redeployed in turn as the fourth movement of op. 130. An analogy might also be made to the severing of the magnificent overture Leonore No. 3 from *Fidelio,* but the case of the *Grosse Fuge* remains unique.

There are good reasons for regarding the original version of the B♭ Quartet with the Great Fugue as the most definitive one, and it is this form of the work that pushes most strongly toward new aesthetic perspectives. Of all Beethoven's compositions, the original B♭ Quartet is perhaps the most heavily end-weighted, with a diverse series of shorter and lighter movements followed by a colossal fugal essay. One commentator has even suggested an analogy to the sequence of free and strict pieces from the Baroque, such as Bach's preludes and fugues, whereby the fugal finale balances all of the preceding five movements.[46] Without the rest of the quartet, moreover, the Great Fugue is effectively orphaned, and the beginning of its elaborate Ouvertura loses point. The *Grosse Fuge* is a finale in search of the work with which it has now, in modern performances, often been reconciled.

While he was composing op. 132, in May 1825, Beethoven made the notation on fol. 6r of the "de Roda" sketchbook, "letztes Quartett mit einer ernsthaften und schwergängigen Einleitung" ("last quartet with a serious and weighty introduction"), which can refer only to op. 130, the last of the three quartets included in the commission from Prince Galitzin. Eight pages later, on fol. 13v, amid the first sketches for the slow introduction to the first movement of op. 130, and while he was still working on the finale of op. 132, Beethoven made an entry for "letztes Stück des quartetts in B" ("last movement of the quartet in B♭") including the notation "Fugha" ("fugue"). As Klaus Kropfinger has stressed, this evidence implies that Beethoven was concerned from an early stage in the genesis of op. 130 with a complex and ambitious project.[47] However, it was not until August 24, 1825, that Beethoven informed his nephew and Karl Holz that the new quartet would have six movements, and he added in the letter to his nephew that the piece would be "completely finished in at most 12 days."[48] His prediction was overly optimistic, and the quartet continued to occupy him until December of 1825.

According to Barry Cooper's evaluation of the sketches, Beethoven's plans for the quartet remained unsettled for a time after the first two movements had been sketched, and the fourth and fifth movements—the Alla danza tedesca and Cavatina—were included only after the fugue had begun to assume large dimensions.[49] By about late August, Beethoven evidently began to work on the Cavatina and fugue simultaneously. The sketches show that Beethoven only gradually altered the intervallic structure of the Cavatina to incorporate some of its striking melodic features, whereas the main fugal subject had been devised earlier, while he was at work on the E♭ Major Quartet, op. 127. One guiding factor in his labors was surely the thematic motto heard at the outset of the entire quartet, in Adagio tempo, which prefigures musical events in the work as a whole (Example 11.5). For instance, Beethoven recalled this opening, with its falling semitones from B♭ to A♭, when he introduced the change of key to D♭ major for the third movement, the Andante. Rudolph Reti even proposed that the outer notes of the motto—G and E♭—are coordinated with the *keys* of Beethoven's fourth and fifth movements, in G major and E♭ major, respectively.[50] Despite a difference in tonality, the rising sixth B♭–G and third G (A♭)–B♭ that begin the Cavatina also display an audible motivic kinship to the notes of this opening motto. The Adagio molto espressivo of the Cavatina develops a lyric strain that was latent in the Adagio ma non troppo in the first movement.

That this opening Adagio is more than a slow introduction is made clear from its return in later passages of the first movement, including the repetition of the exposition of the sonata form. Beethoven's initial idea was to juxtapose just the first four measures of the Adagio with the Allegro in running sixteenth notes. This is essentially the procedure carried out later in the exposition (mm. 21–24) and in the coda, which is based entirely on this pair of contrasting themes.[51] The contrapuntal passage Beethoven added to lengthen the initial Adagio was by no means the only major revision he made during the compositional process. As Elena Vjaskova has observed, the astonishing development section of the first movement was originally conceived on very different lines, as a double fugato reminiscent of the first movement of the Piano Sonata in C Minor, op. 111.[52] In revising these early plans, Beethoven introduced elements of whimsy and unpredictability—qualities not absent from the movements to come. At the beginning of the development section as we know it, he repeatedly juxtaposed short fragments of the music in the two contrasting tempos. The continuation then brings an uncanny motivic dialogue played against an ostinato in the middle voices that is derived from an appoggiatura figure in the Adagio (Example 11.6). This dialogue highlights both the head motive from the Allegro, with its rising fourth, and a variant of the lyrical second subject, with its initial ascending interval now widened to an octave and the continuation compressed into

*Example 11.5.* Quartet in B♭ Major, op. 130, I, beginning.

eighth notes instead of quarters. These motives communicate in a weirdly inconsistent fashion, reserving the right to disappear at will into the ostinato background. The lyrical octave ascent in the cello in the third measure of the Allegro seems to influence the rising head motive in the first violin three bars later, where the fourth is expanded to an octave. Just after the change in key signature to G major, the corresponding bass entry is blended into the ostinato figure. Curiously, the direction of resolution of these motives into the ostinato background can initiate an inversion in the direction of the prevailing appoggiatura figure: the F♯–G ostinato of mm. 11–12 thus becomes G–F♯ three bars later. Such relationships heighten the effect of temporal stasis—the trance-like suspension characteristic of this remarkable episode—which reveals one possible synthesis of apparently incompatible themes.

Beethoven reserved his supreme exercise in paradox for the coda. After recalling the beginning of the Adagio ma non troppo in slightly varied form, he dovetailed the Allegro and Adagio phrases into each other to form a new continuity (Example 11.7). The chromatic ascent derived from the original Adagio passage is extended in the series of Adagio excerpts before finding a further continuation in the Allegro tempo of the cadential passage. These interdependent Adagio and Allegro sections, which make up the coda, are held in perfect balance, and Beethoven's manipulation of the music in contrasting tempos creates a mutually interlocking parenthetical structure. The excerpts interrupt one another and are themselves interrupted. It becomes difficult, if not impossible, to say what is actually "parenthetical" under such circumstances. The apparent contradiction is transcended in the achievement of the composite theme.

For all the mercurial, unpredictable qualities of op. 130, we can discern pairings of movements: the swift, bagatelle-like Presto in B♭ minor serves as a foil to the opening movement, whereas the Alla danza tedesca in G major complements the profound Cavatina in E♭ major. A sharp sense of disjunction, on the other hand, divides the exquisite Andante con moto ma non troppo from the Danza tedesca. This Andante, marked "Poco scherzando," is filled with felicitously textured sonorities; elsewhere in this volume, Hatten has aptly described its character using the notion of "plentitude." Nowhere is its delicious dwelling in sonority felt more strongly than in the theme, marked "cantabile" and "dolce," that is heard at the ends of sections, recurring for the last time four bars before the end. This *dolce* theme consists of cadential inflections, while the first violin plays repeated appoggiatura figures, which sound on the tonic as the falling step E♭–D♭ (mm. 61, 85). The resulting quality of indulgent repetitiveness, or expressive plentitude, is bound up with the fascinating conclusion to the movement (Example 11.8).

Immediately before the close, Beethoven has interrupted the musical unfolding with a brief but surprising pause marked by a fermata over a sixteenth rest. This remarkable gesture suggests an invitation to sensuous continuity, subverting the linear temporality of the music in favor of its nonlinear essence. Because the leisurely *dolce* theme has previously filled this very gap, the sensitive listener may spontaneously

*Example 11.6.* Quartet in B♭ Major, op. 130, I, development, mm. 104–27.

*Example 11.7.* Quartet in B♭ Major, op. 130, I, coda, mm. 214–end.

Example 11.7, continued.

imagine it as the continuation: that is surely the point of the pregnant pause. An endless elliptical loop is thus embedded within the movement, reinforcing its character of plentitude. We are invited to linger, to replay the Andante in memory by indulging our recollection of earlier occurrences of the dolce theme. With gentle wit, Beethoven allows the actual ending after the fermata to come as an abrupt bump, as if it were not a true ending. This play with the expectations of the listener facilitates the otherwise tenuous link to the ensuing Danza tedesca, with its tonal shift across the tritonal gap from D♭ major to G major. In part, Beethoven may have chosen the key of G major because he associated it with the character of a German dance: close thematic parallels connect this movement to the Presto alla tedesca of his Piano Sonata in G Major, op. 79, as Ludwig Misch has observed.[53] A melodic emphasis on G connects the Danza tedesca with the Cavatina, and this note joins the Cavatina in turn to the overture of the Great Fugue.

During 1826, Beethoven's last year of full creative activity, the B♭ Quartet was discussed, rehearsed, performed, and even engraved in its original version with the Great Fugue as finale. The first rehearsal of the quartet took place on Tuesday, January 3, 1826, in Beethoven's apartment, with many further rehearsals following before the premiere of the work took place in a concert on March 21. The conversation books used by the deaf composer during these weeks are astoundingly informative about the B♭ Quartet, and especially about the fugue. In them, Beethoven's violinist friend Karl Holz told the composer that "everything will go easily, except for the fugue," and that this "last movement must be practiced at home," for which reason the players needed to take the parts with them.[54] Several entries refer to the difficulty of the Great Fugue, and on one occasion, Schuppanzigh quipped that "Holz has fallen asleep, since the last movement has made him *kaput*."[55] Various other topics were discussed, including destructive forest fires in Canada,[56] but the recurrent theme was the formidable challenge of the *Grosse Fuge,* especially involving the bowing, clarity, and ensemble of the sections in swift tempo involving triplets and leaps in register. Holz commented in this vein that the difficulties would be overcome with practice, and that "the novelty of playing such passages makes at first for greater obstacles than are really there."[57] In a conversation book from more than a half year later, September 1826, Holz told Beethoven, "You could have easily made 2 [works] out of the B♭ Quartet."[58] This remark was presumably connected to Beethoven's decision to write a new finale, as urged by the publisher with Holz's support; Beethoven's first sketches for the substitute finale date from about this time. In a general way, of course, Holz's comment touches on a conspicuous feature not only of op. 130, but of all of the middle three of the late quartets. These works expand the cycle of movements beyond the conventional framework that had, with few exceptions, served Beethoven adequately throughout his career.[59] Formal expansion beyond the four-movement framework is a remarkably consistent feature of this group of works.

In some respects, the original version of the B♭ Quartet is even more expansive than the C♯-Minor Quartet, since it presents five contrasting movements preceding

*Example 11.8.* Quartet in B♭ Major, op. 130, end of Andante con moto ma non troppo, beginning of Alla danza tedesca.

the fugue and it culminates in a big, multi-sectioned finale that itself contains distinct formal divisions set apart from one another through changes in key and character. As Beethoven noted at the head of the score, the Great Fugue is "sometimes free" and "sometimes strict"; its two strict, robust fugal sections in B♭ and in A♭ alternate with freer fugato or scherzo-like sections, and Beethoven also employed an elaborate network of premonitions and reminiscences of themes. The most comparable formal design among Beethoven's other works is probably the choral finale of the Ninth Symphony. Like the choral finale, moreover, the Great Fugue opens with a transitional introduction, here dubbed "Ouvertura," which not only anticipates themes to come but is connected as well to the preceding movement, the Cavatina.

A study by Richard Kramer has focused on the threshold from the Cavatina into the Great Fugue, and the peculiar paradox it entails: as he observes, the initial gesture of the Overture of the Great Fugue is deprived of meaning when the fugue is separated from the rest of the quartet. For the emphatic octaves on G that launch the Overture represent a drastic reinterpretation of the gentle, lingering, fading G heard as the highest pitch at the close of the moving, lyric Cavatina in E♭ major. As Kramer writes, this G that opens the Overture "has more to do with the Cavatina than with the fugue."[60] And Beethoven of course retained the idea of a prominent G at the beginning of the substitute finale, as well, employing an octave bass pedal that surely influenced Schubert at the beginning of the finale of his own last great work in B♭ major, the final piano sonata, D. 960, composed just two years later.

The relation between the Cavatina and fugue merits close examination. Kramer regards this linkage as a moment of intermovement narrativity, confined to "a brief interval of narrative discourse between *Cavatina* and fugue."[61] This insight can be expanded. For Kramer, the emphatic G that opens the Overture "seems to assert that the *Cavatina* is fictional" and "casts the *Cavatina* into the past."[62] Here, as at the analogous juncture at the beginning of the transition to the choral finale of the Ninth Symphony, there is a sense of overcoming, or perhaps even of negating, what has preceded, though not so emphatically as in the Ninth Symphony, where the "terror fanfare" is sounded with shocking dissonance at the threshold of the finale. Whether the Overture asserts "that the *Cavatina* is fictional" is questionable. These musical events suggest a transformation based on an inward-outward dichotomy, as the lyric beauty and self-possession of the intimate Cavatina yield to wider-ranging, powerful forces of contrast and dramatic development.

Intense scrutiny has been given to the four-note intervallic cell, mentioned by Dahlhaus, which involves two semitones separated by a larger interval, and which surfaces in the first and last movements of the A-Minor and C♯-Minor Quartets, as well as in op. 130 and the Great Fugue.[63] At the outset of the Overture of the Great Fugue, the pattern begins on a sustained G and pushes upward to an accented G♯ (Example 11.9). This rising semitone is balanced by the ensuing upward leap of a diminished seventh to F and the falling semitone to E, before Beethoven's recapturing of the accented G♯, which then ascends another half-step to A. The basic pattern consists of

*Example 11.9.* Great Fugue, op. 133, opening fugal subject.

the four notes G–G♯–F–E, and as this motive is treated in sequence a half-tone higher, Beethoven shaped the outcome in telling ways. First, he compressed the sequence rhythmically, so that what had occupied more than five measures is heard in just three bars. At the point of rhythmic compression, the texture is altered by the use of rests and by the brilliant flourish of the trill on the upper G in m. 10. Furthermore, the sequence of the four-note motive departs from the model, inasmuch as the final semitone does not move downward but instead ascends. Hence the pattern G–G♯–F–E is answered by G♯–A–F♯–G, and the entire thematic statement spans a full octave.

Surprisingly, the audible motivic kinship between the Cavatina and this fugue subject has received scant attention. According to Holz, Beethoven said "that the *Cavatina* was composed in the very tears of misery, and that never had one of his own pieces moved him so deeply, and that merely to relive it in his feelings always cost him a tear."[64]

Example 11.10 shows the beginning of the Cavatina (see also the facsimile of Beethoven's autograph manuscript in the frontispiece); the end of the movement, together with the Overture of the Great Fugue, is shown as Example 11.11. A sensitive analysis of the Cavatina has been offered by Robert Hatten in his book *Musical Meaning in Beethoven.*[65] As Hatten observes, the fifth and sixth measures of the melody represent a climactic "expressive interpolation" in the thematic structure, reaching what he describes as an "apex" and "crux" that imply hopeful ascent and tragic reversal. The central importance of this melodic peak and gap is underscored by Beethoven's *crescendo* and *decrescendo,* and by his rhythmic enhancement and echoing of this phrase in the second violin and viola when it recurs in 21–22. Then, after the glimpse of the abyss contained in the "Beklemmt" ("oppressed") section, with its stammering recitative-like gestures, the Cavatina melody returns, restating the climactic melodic contour of the falling sixth and semitone F–A♭–G in measure 54. In the final section of the Cavatina, Beethoven once more emphasizes these melodic pitches, with the approach through E♭ to the high F stated three times in measures 58, 59, and 62, now in a rhythmic pattern paralleling the opening of the Cavatina, which itself features a rising major-sixth interval to the crucial half-tone step G–A♭. These expressive gestures in the final section are underscored by the dynamic inflections of *crescendo* and *decrescendo.* So fervent are these lyrical impulses that they spill over to undermine the serenity of the cadence in E♭ heard in measures 64–65, as the second violin echoes the first. Earlier, at the end of the first thematic statement (mm. 8–10) or at the close of the first section of the Cavatina (mm. 39–40), the melody had completed a linear descent to the tonic degree E♭. Now, however, in the very last mea-

**Cavatina**

Adagio molto espressivo

*Example 11.10.* Quartet in B♭ Major, op. 130, beginning of Cavatina.

sure, Beethoven has stressed the upper E♭, recalling its linear connection to the E♭–F figure heard two bars before, and he has asserted once more the falling half-step A♭–G that was so prominent in earlier passages. In so ending the Cavatina, Beethoven avoided resolving the melody to the tonic and instead emphasized the semitone A♭ falling to the third degree, G, the pitch that serves in turn as the ensuing point of connection into the overture of the Great Fugue. By denying the Cavatina firm closure, Beethoven exposed the fragility and vulnerability of this personal utterance to what might come.

At the outset of the Overture to the Great Fugue, as in some other pivotal passages of his later works, Beethoven used elements of retrograde writing.[66] He reversed the dying fall F–A♭–G from the Cavatina, boldly reasserting these same pitches in

*Example 11.11.* Quartet in B♭ Major, opp. 130/133, end of Cavatina and overture of Great Fugue.

Meno mosso e moderato.
Allegro.
sempre pp
Fuga.

massive accented unison *fortissimo* octaves, but with the first violin in the same register as in the Cavatina. The pitches G–G♯–F can thus be heard as enharmonically equivalent to the falling motive from the Cavatina, and the reversal in direction of these notes can be perceived as a vital part of the change in character. The unfolding of this fugal subject on G also incorporates the identical intervallic pattern up a half-step as G♯–A–F♯, before the theme culminates in brilliant trills on the upper-octave G. The melodic climax of the moving Cavatina, with its reflective, inward sentiment, is transformed and superseded in the dramatic, extroverted announcement of the fugal subject.

By virtue of the dominating role of the fugue subject throughout the original finale, this motivic connection ensures a close relation between the Cavatina and the *Grosse Fuge* as a whole. It also helps explain an aspect of the Overture that has often puzzled listeners and critics: the appearance of the fugal themes in reverse order from their working-out in the main part of the movement. As we have seen, the emphatic unison version is initially played in G precisely on account of its relation to the preceding Cavatina, whereas the ensuing scherzo-like variant compresses and reshapes these very same pitches into a new rhythmic pattern. A sequence of this idea reaches the dominant of F, the key in which the Meno mosso e moderato is heard. The ensuing "gapped" version of the subject with rests, played *pianissimo,* prefaces the following double fugue, in which this "gapped" subject is used. This is the first of the thematic segments to be stated in B♭ major, the tonic key of the *Grosse Fuge.* Tonally, the Overture has a transitional function, but thematically it offers a series of hierarchical derivations from the decisive opening unison statement. The initial statement, too, has a double aspect, because it foreshadows both the A♭ fugue subject with its trill and also the massive unison texture of the version that ushers in the triumphant resolving passages in B♭ major at the end of the work.

In his book *The "Galitzin" Quartets,* Chua describes the Overture as comprising "gestures of disintegration [that] are incorporated into the work, to fracture the entire form," whereas the whole fugue is regarded as a "narrative of destruction."[67] The poverty of such attitudes seems to stem above all from an unwillingness to appreciate the richness of musical relationships transcending a strict linear sequence. For instance, the opening *fortissimo* unison statement of the fugue subject does several things at once. It energetically transforms substance drawn from the Cavatina while foreshadowing both the A♭ fugue and coda of the *Grosse Fuge,* it serves as the reservoir out of which the scherzo variant and other fugal versions are shaped, and it is also tangibly related to the thematic motto heard at the very outset of the quartet. To a considerable degree, the appreciation of this single gesture entails contemplation of the entire design. This is music for the memory, calling for an awareness of nonadjacent connections and nonlinear time. In this musical environment, sharp contrasts or structural inversions do not automatically signal a destructive critique, but on the contrary, they point toward an enhanced context of meaningful relations. The composite theme in the coda of the first movement, joining segments of the contrasting Adagio and Allegro ideas; the provocative pause just before the close of the Andante, inviting endless mental replay of the delicious pre-cadential cantabile theme; the delightful retrograde presentation of four measures in the Alla danza tedesca—all of these remarkable passages are oversimplified if regarded as a predictable narrative of dissolution.

A more promising critical approach would affirm Beethoven's affinity with some early Romantic currents. It is possible that the authentic modernism of Beethoven's later music is lodged especially in his capacity to maintain his commitment to classical principles even while pressing forward to seemingly embrace diversity and chaos, irony and paradox. In 1825, a reviewer of Beethoven's A-Minor Quartet, op. 132, concluded that he was dealing with a "musical Jean Paul."[68] A self-reflexive mode of musical writing, joined with a propensity for wit and comedy, was unmistakably present already in Beethoven's early music, but this dimension of his art reached a climax in his post-heroic phase, especially in the 1820s. A major monument to this tendency is his most extended piano work, the Diabelli Variations, completed in 1823. Jean Paul's analysis of "humoristic totality" in his *Vorschule der Aesthetik*, from 1804, reads almost like a program for the Diabelli Variations, in that he described a dialectical interaction between the Great and the Small, with each canceling the other and being canceled in turn.[69] In Beethoven's case, the Small—a publisher's banal waltz he described as a "cobbler's patch"—found its place beside the Great—the cycle of thirty-three transformations that last almost an hour in performance—through an aesthetic attitude that did not hesitate to "invert the sublime"—Jean Paul's definition of humor. Ironically, Beethoven incorporated Diabelli's ditty most fully by not only ennobling and transforming it but by exaggerating its shortcomings and redundancies and indulging in caricature, by poking fun at the "cobbler's patch." Paradoxically, however—and this is the real point—it is only through such means that Beethoven was able to shape the work as a well-rounded whole. A tension between the Great and the Small is the central compositional idea.

One complaint about Beethoven's challenging works had long been his alleged overindulgence in fantasy; the critic August Wendt in 1815 found it unfortunate that most of Beethoven's sonatas and symphonies were spoiled by the formlessness of the fantasy.[70] For his part, Beethoven fully accepted this accusation and could even parade it himself in jest, as when he ironically wrote on the autograph copy of the C♯-Minor Quartet for the publisher Schott that the work was "put together out of various pilferings of one thing and another." He was later obliged to reassure the nervous publisher that his comment had been a joke.[71]

Actually, the fantasy had long represented for Beethoven a means for imposing coherence based on nonadjacent connections and a more evolutionary model for a multimovement work. One of his compositional models for the C♯-Minor Quartet was surely his own sonata "quasi una fantasia," op. 27 no. 2 from 1801, the so-called "Moonlight" Sonata, his only other sonata-style work in this key. What these works share is the idea of starting not with an Allegro but with a slow movement, whose thematic material is much later reincarnated in a fully developed sonata form in a rapid tempo in the finale. In the opening Adagio sostenuto of op. 27 no. 2, a static texture of repeated arpeggios is heard over a descending bass in octaves. In the final movement, Beethoven has reinterpreted this placid texture by spreading the ascending arpeggios over the entire keyboard and anchoring them by heavy syncopated chords. The substance of the opening movement is thus drastically reinterpreted as the dreamy tentativeness of the first movement is transformed into dramatic action.

Op. 27 belongs, of course, to that cluster of works that marks the formation of Beethoven's stylistic shift after 1800. An approach often suggestive of improvisatory techniques, employing fragmentary or tentative beginnings and material in contrasting tempi, surfaces as well in works such as the first movement of the "Tempest" Sonata, op. 31 no. 2. But if fantasy style played a significant role in the evolution of Beethoven's second-period or "heroic" style, it remained at least as important in later years. Relevant in this context is the 1970 study by Paul Mies on *Die Krise der Konzertkadenz bei Beethoven* ("The Crisis of the Concerto Cadenza in Beethoven"). Mies locates a signpost to Beethoven's later style already in 1809, in conjunction with his necessary retreat as soloist from the concert platform.[72] As Beethoven could no longer present concertos himself, he seized control as composer over the cadenzas, which in the Fifth Concerto are notated directly into the score. The cadenzas did not lose importance in this process but gained in significance. Thus the Fifth Concerto begins with a cadenza, an approach that Beethoven planned also for the unfinished Sixth Concerto from 1815.[73]

The wedding of such improvisatory or fantasy-like elements with structural control is perhaps most richly demonstrated in the C♯-Minor Quartet, op. 131, which moves far beyond the model of the C♯-Minor Sonata from twenty-five years earlier. For Gustav Nottebohm, no other quartet gave such a strong impression of spontaneous improvisation; for Kerman and others, it is the superb integration of the work that captures attention.[74] The innovations of op. 131 are not confined to the expanded narrative sequence of seven interconnected movements; they are embedded, as well, in the tonal language of the opening fugue, whose harmonic tensions destabilize the tonic while preparing what is to come. This is surely one of the pieces Felix Draeseke must have had in mind when he wrote in 1861, "Beethoven's third period seemed destined to shake the absolutist regime of the main tonality for the first time."[75] The directional unfolding of this fugue culminates in Beethoven's isolation and distillation of expressive dissonance, especially the drift of the music toward the Neapolitan D major—the key of the second movement. The octave gesture C♯–D that bridges these movements is part of an irreducible tensional network sustained across much of the composition (Example 11.12).

A quality of pointing beyond, of one movement foretelling the next, is characteristic of Beethoven, yet perhaps no other work carries the principle so far as the C♯-Minor Quartet. Every one of the movements yields up part of its autonomy in the interest of the work as a whole.[76] Yet this process goes beyond the transitions between

*Example 11.12.* Quartet in C♯ Minor, op. 131, end of fugue and beginning of second movement.

movements and the obvious thematic allusion in one of the finale's themes to the opening fugue. Most fascinating is the way the quality of pointing beyond—as an enlarged temporal presence—is manifested in the coda of the last movement.

How does a final movement foretell what is to come? Beethoven's strategy was to enact coexisting but incompatible sequences for closure or continuation. The first stage offers a narrowly aborted conclusion in the basic character of the movement—the tempestuous, agitated Allegro with its driving rhythms and extroverted rhetoric. One aspect of this progression—among many others—is the registral climax reaching C♯[4] in measures 6 and 10 of Example 11.13, where Beethoven has recalled the Neapolitan inflections of D major within a cadential progression in C♯ minor. Hammering away with emphatic cadential accents, Beethoven reached a specific viable point for closure at the downbeat of the third measure of the fourth system (m. 347)—whereupon the cadence *does not happen.*

*Example 11.13.* Quartet in C♯ Minor, op. 131, end of finale, mm. 327–88.

Ritmo di due battute.
350
363
370
f
p
pp

*Example 11.13, continued.*

After a measure of rests, Beethoven recalls at the "Ritmo di due battute" the theme whose four-note configuration binds it audibly to the opening fugue. Now, unlike the preceding appearances of the theme in the sonata form, there is a long downward extension spanning a tenth. An earlier passage leading into the coda had shown how this theme can be transformed to lead into the tempestuous musical idiom of the Allegro. Here, however, the melodically extended version of the referential theme is repeated in the first violin and viola, before it alights, in the passage beginning in m. 363, on the diminished-seventh chord supporting A as highest pitch. The emphasis given to this sonority, as well as the dwelling on A throughout the following passage, is remarkable. To make his point, Beethoven reiterated seven times a motive from his main theme that seems to assert the supremacy of A over G♯ (see mm. 369–82). G♯ is often left out altogether. This extreme reluctance to allow resolution is expressed furthermore through a slowing in tempo to Poco adagio and an increased espressivity, as reflected in Beethoven's performance directions. Consequently, Beethoven has ensured that it is virtually impossible for any quartet to convey a firmly decisive closure in C♯ major in the half-dozen measures that remain beginning at Tempo 1.

Why did Beethoven undercut both cadences, first the one in C♯ minor and then the one in C♯ major? Because he was after bigger game. The entire passage is steeped in the harmonic expressiveness, and indeed, the very notes and sonorities, of the opening fugue. Typically, Beethoven did not refer here merely to one passage in isolation, but to the first movement in a more encompassing sense. Thus the first violin dwells initially on the A above middle C, the crucial fourth note of the entire composition, whereas the second violin plays the notes B♯ and D♯ belonging to the diminished seventh heard at the end of the fugue. Having opened this window on the fugue, Beethoven could then afford to convey the same relationship—the semitone A–G♯—through the principal motive of the main theme of the last movement, while exploring the registers from the fugue in the many repeated entries of the four instruments. This may explain the point of his "Poco adagio" indication as the first violin plays this motive in the next-to-last system, since this A-to-G♯ motion in the same register had been heard at the very end of the fugue, just before the shift to D major for the second movement.

In a fundamental sense, the coda of this movement strives toward circularity, by conjuring up such a powerful presence of the fugue that the experience and process of memory is reenacted. The denial and weakening of closure allows for a paradoxical continuity, a kind of continued life in the imagination of the work as a whole. The quartet invites itself to be replayed in the mind's ear, as an experience that transcends merely linear concepts of time and termination.

Let us compare in this light the finales of the B♭-Major and C♯-Minor quartets. The comparison illustrates a principle once explicated by Donald Francis Tovey in his essay entitled "Normality and Freedom in Music," though in relation to op. 131, I will invert Tovey's titular description.[77] For op. 131—supposedly the more integrated work—radically undercuts its final cadential resolution, whereas the Great Fugue does not. Chua gets this wrong in his analysis, by bracketing off op. 131 from op. 130 on account of the greater coherence of the C♯-Minor Quartet, whereas he refuses to recognize or credit the powerful gestures of resolution and synthesis in the last section of the Great Fugue, including even a paired recall of snippets of the gapped fugue and Meno mosso that shows them to be but outwardly contrasting manifestations of identical material. As we have seen, the ending of the Great Fugue is more normal than the closing passages of op. 131, whose freedom is embodied in a provocative play with temporal relations and open circular form that represents one of the conspicuous innovations of Beethoven's ripest style. In this context, Beethoven found it impossible to use the theme in D♭ major that had been devised as a resolution of thematic material in C♯ minor from both of the outer movements of op. 131. The theme was set aside to become the starting point of the Lento assai of the final Quartet in F Major, op. 135.

The power of artistic effects like these, in addition to other innovations, such as the expanded cycles of interconnected movements in op. 132, op. 130, and op. 131, remind us how Beethoven's music continued to push toward fresh possibilities during 1825 and 1826. In op. 131, the preoccupation with fugue, carried over from the *Grosse Fuge,* was newly blended with fantasy. The last quartets—at least op. 132, op. 130 with the *Grosse Fuge* as finale, and op. 131—are bold, visionary works that seem to open a new creative period rather than close an old one. As he labored on these works, Beethoven pressed toward new metamorphoses that were not tied to any one of his earlier works, but that continued to reexamine basic principles and probe artistic meanings reaching deeper into the symbolic, mythic, and paradoxical.

## Coda

What had the artwork become in Beethoven's final productive years? More than ever before, it served as a tensional vessel for a "unity lying behind the diversity of the phenomena of human existence" and involved a search for "new paths" and new thresholds. The curious intermezzi along the journey of the A-Minor Quartet; the enigmatic contrasts of the B♭-Major Quartet; the unprecedented novelties of the inner movements in the C♯-Minor Quartet: all attest to the inclusiveness of this vision. For all its restless probing, this is not music born out of a spirit of negation and critique. Ultimately, it may be Beethoven's unceasing quest for a higher artistic perspective that allowed him to indulge so freely and even recklessly in embracing contrast and diversity, irony, and wit. No one stage in the artistic process was ever quite definitive, and principles of unification revealed themselves gradually anew through creative zeal and perseverance.

It is relevant here to recall the definition of *genius* offered by that most extravagantly colorful and unruly of early Romantic writers, the author and humorist Jean Paul. His literary works are invariably irregular in structure but show inexhaustible imagination and unusual sensitivity to the incongruity between ordinary life and ideal laws. As we have seen, Beethoven was described as a "musical Jean Paul" in the *Allgemeine musikalische Zeitung* in 1825. In the *Vorschule der Ästhetik,* Jean Paul wrote:

> If there are human beings, in whom the instinct for the divine speaks more loudly and clearly than in others; and if it guides in them the perspective on earthly things (rather than as in others the earthly taking precedence); [and] if it offers and controls a view of the whole: then the harmony and beauty of both worlds streams out and makes these into *one* entity, since before the divine there is only *one* and no contradiction of parts. And that is genius, and the reconciliation of both worlds is the so-called *ideal.*[78]

For Jean Paul, a higher, unchanging perspective regulates the untidy diversity of "earthly things." By implication, the overcoming of contradiction or avoidance of chaos in a work stems from an artist's conviction about a unified presence in reality.

What is the counterpart in music of such a unifying perspective? Consider in this regard Beethoven's preoccupation with nonlinear time as a manifestation of being. A more deterministic, forward-looking expectancy in the spirit of the Enlightenment is thereby complemented by a principle of static constancy. Dramatic action and unfolding based on the principle of change are juxtaposed with a sublime or even mystic presence founded on the unchanging. A deepening of Beethoven's engagement with nonlinear gestures occurred during his long labors on the *Missa solemnis,* and the results must have posed a critical dilemma for Adorno. The drastic contrasts of the Mass are often expressive of the gulf between humanity, on the one hand, and the deity or principle of eternity (such as the fugue on "Et vitam venturi"), on the other. In themselves, these wrenching discontinuities might tend to have been regarded by Adorno as marks of skepticism, but in the *Missa solemnis* they are bound up with something quite different: an awestruck vision of the sublime, an inspiring "Blick nach oben." Beethoven even devised an elaborate framework of high referential sonorities for this purpose: an impressive E♭-major sonority recurs a dozen times throughout the Credo and is transmuted and purified to become the lofty G-major tonic chord from which the solo violin descends in the Benedictus. A nonlinear dimension is evident at once in the very first chord of the Credo, which anticipates, quite independently of the text and musical context, the climax of the "Et vitam venturi" fugue, among other passages. Subsequently, Beethoven absorbed the same high sonority into his static, monolithic setting of the last line of the Schiller text in the finale of the Ninth Symphony: "Über Sternen muß er wohnen" ("Above the stars must he dwell").[79]

The last quartets are the final group of compositions Beethoven wrote after the Mass and Ninth Symphony. In these pieces, he went further than in earlier years in incorporating nonlinear gestures or temporal multiplicity into his instrumental music. In the "Heiliger Dankgesang" movement, for instance, the initial contrast between the lydian chorale and "Feeling new strength" is so profound that we may experience two separate, coexisting beginnings rather than a true sequence of ideas.[80] Equally bold explorations into enhanced temporality are contained in the quartets opp. 130/133 and op. 131, as we have seen. The rhythm of the Great Fugue signals its vitality, as Stravinsky said, but the incisiveness of the music is concentrated at once in its powerful reconstitution of notes drawn from the touching melodic climax of the gentle Cavatina. On the other hand, the expressive bending of the finale of the C♯-Minor Quartet toward "retrieval" of the opening fugue offers a thought-provoking perspective on some basic assumptions of the Classical style as embodied in a multimovement work. Foremost among these is Beethoven's protest against the cherished notion of closure. This music strives toward unending continuity through memory of its past and by recycling its own energies. The priority Beethoven granted to the imagination here comes to fulfillment in a manner that twists our expectations of the genre even more than earlier works while advancing his art toward new creative perspectives. In a hundred ways, these quartets confirm his stupendous understatement to Holz: "Thank God there is less lack of fantasy than ever before."

## Notes

1. Carl Dahlhaus, *Ludwig van Beethoven: Approaches to His Music,* trans. Mary Whittal (Oxford: Clarendon, 1991), 220.

2. See Kirkendale, "'The Great Fugue' Op. 133: Beethoven's 'Art of the Fugue,'" *Acta Musicologica* 35 (1963): 14–24; and his book *Fugue and Fugato in Rococo and Classical Chamber Music* (Durham, N.C.: Duke University Press, 1979), 255–69.

3. Igor Stravinsky, *The Observer,* June 17, 1962; cited in Kirkendale, *Fugue and Fugato,* 257.

4. See Stravinsky and Robert Craft, *Dialogues and a Diary* (New York: Doubleday, 1963), 62–65.

5. Daniel K. L. Chua, *The "Galitzin" Quartets of Beethoven* (Princeton, N.J.: Princeton University Press, 1995), 240.

6. Martin Cooper, *Beethoven: The Last Decade* (London: Oxford University Press, 1970), 416, 420.

7. For a discussion of the importance of Schiller's aesthetics—as articulated particularly in the *Aesthetic Letters* (1794–95)—to Beethoven, see the introduction to my monograph, *Beethoven* (Oxford: Clarendon, 1995), 1–14.

8. Notably unbalanced is the discussion of "The Beethoven Paradigm," in *The Imaginary Museum of Musical Works* (Oxford: Clarendon, 1992), by Lydia Goehr, who emphasizes the emergence of the "work-concept" around 1800. Her polar opposition of extemporization to formal composition stands at odds with Beethoven's aesthetics and compositional practice.

9. *Thayer's Life of Beethoven,* ed. Elliot Forbes (Princeton, N.J.: Princeton University Press, 1964), 741; *Beethoven Briefe,* L. 1318.

10. *Thayer's Life of Beethoven,* 982.

11. Franz Gerhard Wegeler and Ferdinand Ries, *Biographische Notizen über Ludwig van Beethoven* (Coblenz, 1838; reprinted Hildesheim: Georg Olms Verlag, 2000), 100.

12. Paul Bekker, *Beethoven* (Berlin: Schuster & Loeffler, 1911), 532; also Philip Radcliffe, *Beethoven's String Quartets* (New York: E. P. Dutton, 1968), 110.

13. Joseph Kerman, *The Beethoven Quartets* (New York: Norton, 1966), 295, 268.

14. Kramer even rewrites the continuation from this "gestural ending" as a normative classical bridge passage to point out the unusual context of this cadence. See his book *The Time of Music* (New York: Schirmer, 1988), esp. pp. 150–63; and his article "Multiple and Nonlinear Time in Beethoven's Opus 135," *Perspectives of New Music* 11 (1973): 122–45.

15. This argument is perhaps most clearly articulated in Theodor W. Adorno, "Verfremdetes Hauptwerk: Zur *Missa Solemnis,*" in his *Moments musicaux* (Frankfurt: Suhrkamp, 1964), 167–85; trans. Edmund Jephcott as "The Alienated *Magnum Opus:* On the *Missa Solemnis,*" in *Beethoven: The Philosophy of Music, Fragments and Texts,* ed. Rolf Tiedemann (Oxford: Polity Press, 1998), 141–53.

16. As Adorno himself admitted in 1964, his "projected philosophical work on Beethoven . . . has yet to be written, primarily because the author's exertions have foundered continually on the *Missa Solemnis*" (editor's preface of *Beethoven: The Philosophy of Music,* viii). Adorno tried to bridge the tension between his approach and the music by excluding several key works from the "late style," including the Mass, and he clearly had difficulty coming to terms with the idealistic or utopian dimension in these works.

17. It should not be assumed that Chua's approach is congruent with Adorno's. See in this regard my review of his book *The "Galitzin" Quartets of Beethoven* in *Intégral* 10 (1996): 167–75.

18. Sieghard Brandenburg, "Die Quellen zur Entstehungsgeschichte von Beethovens Streichquartett Es-Dur Op. 127," *Beethoven-Jahrbuch* 10 (1983): 221–76.

19. This is clear from Beethoven's letter to his nephew Karl from August 11, 1825, where he expressed concern about the possible loss of the autograph score of the "third to sixth" move-

ments, which Karl Holz had removed from Beethoven's lodging for purposes of copying. See *Beethoven Briefe* 6, L. 2029.

20. See in this connection Sieghard Brandenburg, "The Autograph of Beethoven's String Quartet in A Minor Opus 132," in *The String Quartets of Haydn, Mozart, and Beethoven: Studies of the Autograph Manuscripts,* ed. Christoph Wolff (Cambridge, Mass.: Harvard University Department of Music, 1980), 278–300.

21. See Robert Winter, *The Compositional Origins of Beethoven's Opus 131* (Ann Arbor, Mich.: UMI Research Press, 1982), 121–24, 167–74, 206–9; also Laura Bumpass, *Beethoven's Last Quartet,* p. i (Ph.D. dissertation, University of Illinois, Urbana-Champaign, 1982), 222–24

22. Cf. Sieghard Brandenburg, "Die Skizzen zur Neunten Symphonie," *Zu Beethoven: Aufsätze und Dokumente,* p. 2, ed. Harry Goldschmidt (Berlin: Verlag Neue Musik, 1984), esp. 128–29; and Gustav Nottebohm, *Zweite Beethoveniana: Nachgelassene Aufsätze* (Leipzig: Peters, 1887), 180–81.

23. Kerman, *The Beethoven Quartets,* 244. Kerman writes that "The violin *arpeggio* in bar 9—prolonging that F—is like a scream; the premature tonic chord in bar 10 is like a hand clapped over the mouth."

24. The larger context of this quotation, from Daniel Gottlob Türk's *Clavierschule* of 1789, is as follows: "Good taste has made it a rule that dissonances or dissonant chords must generally be struck with more force than consonant ones, for the reason that the passions should be generally aroused by dissonances" (trans. R. H. Haggh as *School of Piano Playing* (Lincoln: University of Nebraska Press, 1982), 340.

25. For a discussion of parenthetical structures in Beethoven's later music, see my essay "Thematic contrast and parenthetical enclosure in the piano sonatas, op. 109 and 111," *Zu Beethoven* 3, ed. Harry Goldschmidt (Berlin: Verlag Neue Musik, 1988), 43–59.

26. Susan McClary, *Conventional Wisdom: The Content of Musical Form* (Berkeley: University of California Press, 2000), 199–127.

27. Robert Hatten, *Interpreting Musical Gestures, Topics, and Tropes: Mozart, Beethoven, Schubert* (Bloomington: Indiana University Press, 2004), 270.

28. *Ludwig van Beethovens Konversationshefte* 7, ed. Karl-Heinz Köhler and Grita Herre (Leipzig: VEB Deutscher Verlag für Musik, 1978), 287; also see Brandenburg, "The Autograph of Beethoven's String Quartet in A Minor, Opus 132," 284.

29. This sketchbook has been published in facsimile and transcription, with a commentary, by Elena Vjaskova as *Ludwig van Beethoven. Moscow Sketchbook from 1825* (Moscow: The Gnesins Musical Academy of Russia, 1995).

30. See the comments by Marius Flothuis and Lewis Lockwood in relation to Brandenburg's study of op. 132 in *The String Quartets of Haydn, Mozart, and Beethoven,* 301.

31. Greg Vitercik, "Structure and Expression in Beethoven's Op. 132," *Journal of Musicological Research* 13 (1993): 249.

32. Kerman, *The Beethoven Quartets,* 260.

33. Donald Francis Tovey, *A Companion to Beethoven's Pianoforte Sonatas* (London: Oxford University Press, 1931), 169.

34. For my detailed discussion of op. 57, see my study *Beethoven* (Oxford: Clarendon, 1995), 99–102, and "Beethoven," *Nineteenth-Century Piano Music,* ed. R. Larry Todd (New York: Schirmer, 1990), 63–67.

35. See Kevin Korsyn, "J. W. N. Sullivan and the *Heiliger Dankgesang:* Questions of Meaning in Late Beethoven," *Beethoven Forum* 2 (1993): 173.

36. See Adorno, "Late Work without Late Style," in *Beethoven: The Philosophy of Music: Fragments and Texts,* ed. Rolf Tiedemann, trans. Edmund Jephcott (Oxford: Polity Press, 1998), 152.

37. Kerman, *The Beethoven Quartets,* 267.

38. Chua, *The "Galitzin" Quartets of Beethoven,* 159.

39. Ibid., 160, 161. It seems implausible that "exactly the same . . . patterns" are traced in these three movements.

40. See in this vein the aforementioned studies by Kerman, Korsyn, and Vitercik, the title of whose study, "Structure and Expression in Beethoven's Op. 132," itself affirms the aesthetic synthesis that Chua is prone to reject. There is good reason to believe that a synthesis of expression and structure remained fundamental to Beethoven's art throughout his life.

41. For discussion of the compositional genesis of op. 110, see my studies "Contrast and Continuity in Beethoven's Creative Process," in *Beethoven and His World,* ed. Scott Burnham and Michael P. Steinberg (Princeton: Princeton University Press, 2000), 215–18; and *Artaria 195: Beethoven's Sketchbook for the Missa solemnis and the Piano Sonata in E Major, Opus 109,* vol. 1 (commentary), 26–31 (Urbana and Chicago: University of Illinois Press, 2003). Earlier studies placed the beginning of Beethoven's work on the sonata in late 1821.

42. See in this regard my study "The Evolution of Beethoven's Late Style: Another 'New Path' after 1824?" *Beethoven Forum* 8 (2000): 83–84. Radcliffe draws a parallel between the finale of op. 110 and the "Heiliger Dankgesang" of op. 132 in *Beethoven's String Quartets,* 115.

43. The Largo e mesto of the Sonata in D Major, op. 10 no. 3, contains a dissolving coda foreshadowing the Funeral March of the *Eroica.* For discussion of these relationships, see my studies "The Piano Music: Concertos, Sonatas, Variations, Small Forms," in *The Cambridge Companion to Beethoven,* ed. Glenn Stanley (Cambridge: Cambridge University Press, 2000), 115–17; and *Beethoven,* 86–95.

44. Vitercik, "Structure and Expression in Beethoven's Op. 132," 246.

45. For a detailed account defending the role of the *Grosse Fuge* as a suitable finale, see Klaus Kropfinger, "Das gespaltene Werk-Beethovens Streichquartett Op. 130/133," in *Beiträge zu Beethovens Kammermusik: Symposion Bonn 1984,* ed. Sieghard Brandenburg and Helmut Loos (Munich: Henle, 1987), 296–335; see also Kropfinger's articles "Streichquartett B-Dur Op. 130," "Fuge B-Dur für Streichquartett 'Grosse Fuge' Op. 133," and "Bearbeitung der 'Grossen Fuge' Op. 133 für Klavier zu 4 Händen Op. 134," in *Beethoven: Interpretationen seiner Werke,* ed. Albrecht Riethmüller, Carl Dahlhaus, and Alexander Ringer (Laaber: Laaber, 1994), 299–316, 338–47. Also see in this regard Stefania M. de Kennessey, *The Quartet, the Finale and the Fugue: A Study of Beethoven's Op. 130/133* (Ann Arbor: UMI Research Press, 1984); and Richard Kramer, "Between Cavatina and Ouverture: Opus 130 and the Voices of Narrative," in *Beethoven Forum* 1 (1992):165–89. A discussion favoring the substitute finale is offered in Barry Cooper, *Beethoven and the Creative Process* (Oxford: Clarendon, 1990), 197–214.

46. See Barbara R. Barry, "Recycling the End of the 'Leibquartett': Models, Meaning and Propriety in Beethoven's Quartet in B-Flat Major, Opus 130," *Journal of Musicology* 13 (1995): 364–65.

47. See Kropfinger, "Streichquartett B-Dur op. 130," 301–4. Kropfinger rejects Barry Cooper's argument in his chapter "Planning the Later Movements: String Quartet in B flat, Op. 130," in *Beethoven and the Creative Process,* that Beethoven had no early intention of writing a fugal finale and that "the *Große Fuge* can be seen as something of an intrusion into the quartet, rather than the germ from which the work sprang" (214).

48. *Beethoven Briefe* 6, L. 2042, 2043.

49. Barry Cooper, *Beethoven and the Creative Process,* 197–214.

50. Rudolph Reti, *The Thematic Process in Music* (London: Faber & Faber, 1961), 228–29. Reti considers the D-flat tonic of the third movement to substitute for the D in the theme. The tonic of Beethoven's fourth movement is mistakenly given as G minor in Reti's book.

51. The "de Roda" sketchbook contains a draft for the movement without the intervening measures 5–14. See Cecilio de Roda, "Un Quaderno de autografi di Beethoven del 1825," *Rivista Musicale Italiana* 12 (1905): 596. Kropfinger comments on the role of the Adagio in this movement in "Zur thematischen Funktion der langsamen Einleitung bei Beethoven," in

Kropfinger, *Über Musik im Bilde* 1, ed. Bodo Bischoff et al (Cologne: Verlag Christoph Dohr, 1995), 213–29.

52. Elena Vjaskova, *Ludwig van Beethoven: Moscow Sketchbook from 1825*, 68.

53. Ludwig Misch, "Alla danza tedesca," in his collection of essays, *Beethoven Studies* (Norman: University of Oklahoma Press, 1953), 15–17.

54. *Ludwig van Beethovens Konversationshefte,* 8, ed. Karl-Heinz Köhler and Grita Herre (Leipzig: VEB Deutscher Verlag für Musik, 1981), 243, 245.

55. Ibid., 246.

56. This topic also may have been connected to Holz, because Beethoven could not resist making frequent puns on his friend's name, meaning "wood." When urging Holz to visit him, he would typically say, "Bring wood."

57. *Ludwig van Beethovens Konversationshefte,* 8, 250.

58. Ibid., 10, ed. Dagmar Beck (Leipzig: Deutscher Verlag für Musik, 1993), 185.

59. One exception is the Sixth Symphony, with its use of five movements.

60. Richard Kramer, "Between Cavatina and Ouverture," 180. Also see in this connection Ludwig Misch, "The Grand Fugue" and "Two B Flat Major Themes," in *Beethoven Studies* (Norman: University of Oklahoma Press, 1953), 3–13, 19–31.

61. "Between Cavatina and Ouverture," 184.

62. Ibid.

63. See in this regard especially Deryck Cooke, "The Unity of Beethoven's Late Quartets," *Music Review* 24 (1963): 30–49.

64. Cf. *Thayer's Life of Beethoven,* 975.

65. Robert Hatten, *Musical Meaning in Beethoven: Markedness, Correlation, and Interpretation* (Bloomington and Indianapolis: Indiana University Press, 1994), 202–23.

66. Another example is the B-minor episode in the finale of the "Hammerklavier" Sonata, where the fugue subject unfolds in reverse in the key that functions as a negative polarity in relation to the tonic B♭ major. Beethoven uses retrograde more briefly to effect a slowing of forward motion before the recapitulation of the Prestissimo of the Piano Sonata in E Major, op. 109. Near the end of the Alla danza tedesca of op. 130, on the other hand, several measures are presented in reverse order, delightfully subverting the expectations of the listener.

67. Chua, *The "Galitzin" Quartets of Beethoven,* 227, 240.

68. *Ludwig van Beethoven: Die Werke im Spiegel seiner Zeit,* ed. Stefan Kunze (Laaber: Laaber, 1987), 591. The passage in this review from the *Allgemeine musikalische Zeitung* is as follows: "What our musical Jean Paul has offered here is indeed great, marvelous, unusual, surprising and original, it must however not only be heard often, but really properly studied."

69. "Humoristische Totalität," in *Vorschule der Ästhetik, Jean Paul Werke* 9, ed. Norbert Miller (Munich and Vienna: Carl Hanser Verlag, 1975), 125–29.

70. This criticism of Wendt appeared in the *Allgemeine musikalische Zeitung* and is cited by Elaine Sisman in "After the Heroic Style: *Fantasia* and the 'Characteristic' Sonatas of 1809," *Beethoven Forum* 6 (1998): 96. Also see Robin Wallace, *Beethoven's Critics: Aesthetic Dilemmas and Resolutions during the Composer's Lifetime* (Cambridge: Cambridge University Press, 1986), 26–32.

71. *Thayer's Life of Beethoven,* 983, note 21.

72. Paul Mies, *Die Krise der Konzertkadenz bei Beethoven* (Bonn: Bouvier, 1970), esp. 52.

73. On the unfinished Sixth Concerto, see Lewis Lockwood, "Beethoven's Unfinished Piano Concerto of 1815: Sources and Problems," *Musical Quarterly* 56 (1970): 624–46. Also see Nicholas Cook, "Beethoven's Unfinished Piano Concerto: A Case of Double Vision?" in *Journal of the American Musicological Society* 42 (1989): 338–74; and the exchange between Lockwood and Cook in the *Journal of the American Musicological Society* 43 (1990): 376–82, 382–85.

74. Nottebohm, *Zweite Beethoveniana,* 54; Kerman, *The Beethoven Quartets,* 325–49.

75. Felix Draeseke, *Schriften, 1855–1861,* ed. Martella Gutiérrez-Denhoff and Helmut Loos

(Bad Honnef: Gudrun Schröder, 1987), 327. This essay was originally published in the *Neue Zeitschrift für Musik* 55 (1861).

76. For detailed discussion of the remarkable design of op. 131, see Kerman, *The Beethoven Quartets,* 295–302; 325–49; and his essay in this volume; and my study *Beethoven,* 308–23.

77. Tovey wrote an essay entitled "Normality and Freedom in Music" and another on "Some Aspects of Beethoven's Art Forms," in which he sets out to demonstrate the "fundamental normality of [Beethoven's] most unique work, the Quartet in C sharp minor." Both essays are contained in his *Essays and Lectures on Music* (London: Oxford University Press, 1949).

78. *Jean Paul Werke* 9, ed. Norbert Miller, 66.

79. These passages are discussed in detail in my studies "Beethoven's Symbol for the Deity in the *Missa solemnis* and the Ninth Symphony," *19th Century Music* 9 (1985): 102–18; and *Beethoven,* 238–50; 278–83.

80. See in this regard the discussion by Korsyn in "J. W. N. Sullivan and the *Heiliger Dankgesang,*" 149–61. Korsyn comments that "The two sections seem more like two independent movements than anything that Beethoven had dared within a single design" (p. 159).

# APPENDIX

## Chronology and Sources of the String Quartets

### Six Quartets in F Major, G Major, D Major, C Minor, A Major, and B♭ Major, op. 18

*Time of Composition*

*No. 1:* January to April 1799, first version preserved in a copy of parts sent to Karl Amenda dated 25 June 1799; revised during summer of 1800; *No. 2:* completed in May 1799; revised during summer of 1800; *No. 3:* autumn of 1798, completed in January 1799; possibly revised by 1800; copy of Nos. 1–3 made for Prince Lobkowitz in autumn 1799; *No. 4:* uncertain; possibly summer to autumn 1799; *No. 5:* June to August 1799; *No. 6:* April to summer 1800; copy of Nos. 4–6 made for Prince Lobkowitz in autumn 1800.

*Sketches*

The main sources for op. 18 are the first three bound sketchbooks used by Beethoven, manuscripts dating from 1798 to 1800 that are now held in Staatsbibliothek preussischer Kulturbesitz, Musikabteilung (hereafter SPK) in Berlin: Grasnick 1, Grasnick 2, and Autograph 19e, folios 12–31. Numerous other leaves that originally belonged to these sources have been identified; such source reconstruction is important with Grasnick 1 and especially Autograph 19e, parts of which were thoroughly dismembered. Editions of Grasnick 2 and Autograph 19e have been published in facsimile and transcription: *Beethoven: Ein Skizzenbuch zu Streichquartetten aus Op. 18,* ed. Wilhelm Virneisel (Bonn: Beethoven-Haus, 1972 [facsimile]; 1974 [transcription]); *Ludwig van Beethoven: A Sketchbook from the Summer of 1800,* ed. Richard Kramer (facsimile and transcription; Bonn: Beethoven-Haus, 1996); this publication is supplemented by *Ein neuentdecktes Skizzenblatt vom Sommer 1800 zu Beethovens Streichquartett op. 18 nr. 2,* ed. Richard Kramer (facsimile and transcription; Bonn: Beethoven-Haus, 1999). For a listing of leaves that originally belonged to Beethoven's sketchbooks of all periods, see Douglas Johnson, Alan Tyson, and Robert Winter, *The Beethoven Sketchbooks: History, Reconstruction, Inventory* (Berkeley: University of California Press, 1985). Some sketches are contained on leaves that did not belong to larger sketchbooks; one of these, now held in the Bibliothèque Nationale as MS 71, is published by Kramer in *A Sketchbook from the Summer of 1800,* transcription vol., p. 88. For a partial listing of other individual sketchleaves, consult Hans Schmidt, "Verzeichnis der Skizzen Beethovens," *Beethoven-Jahrbuch* 6 (1969): 7–128.

*No. 1:* Grasnick 1 sketchbook, SPK Berlin, fols. 37r–39v; Grasnick 2 sketchbook, SPK Berlin, fols. 1r–16v passim, 31v; Autograph 19e, fols. 18, 29–31; Artaria 166, p. 30 (rejected leaf from autograph), SPK Berlin; Landsberg 7, SPK Berlin, pp. 1, 100; 1 page in archive of Schott-Verlag, Mainz.

*No. 2:* Grasnick 2 sketchbook, SPK Berlin, fols.15v–18v, 20v–32r; Autograph 19e (in reconstructed form): fols. 20v–25r, and "Scala" leaf published in Kramer's *Ein neuentdecktes Skizzenblatt* (1999).

*No. 3:* Grasnick 1 sketchbook (in reconstructed form), SPK Berlin, fols. 1r–29v passim, augmented by sketchleaves from Paris and Bonn; Grasnick 2 Sketchbook, SPK Berlin, fol. 31v–32r; sketchleaf in Glinka Museum, Moscow.

*No. 4:* Grasnick 2 sketchbook, SPK Berlin; fol. 32v contains what may be early sketches for the first movement; British Library London Add. Ms 29997 fol. 8 relates to scherzo.

*No. 5:* Grasnick 2 sketchbook, SPK Berlin, fols. 26v, 28r, 32r–37v; British Library London Add. Ms. 29801, British Library "Kafka" sketchbook, fol. 152r.

*No. 6:* Autograph 19e, SPK Berlin, fols. 12–18 and 29–31 and leaves now in New York, Bonn, Berlin, St. Petersburg, and Berkeley that originally belonged in Autograph 19e.

*Autograph Scores and Early Copies*

No autograph scores are extant. The copy of op. 18 no. 1 in its first version that was prepared for Amenda is held at the Beethoven-Archiv, Bonn. The Lobkowitz copy of all six quartets is in the Music Department of the National Museum in Prague (Lobkowitz Collection Signatur X, He. 44). The version of nos. 1–3 in this copy is not identical to the version that Beethoven sent to Lobkowitz in October 1799, but corresponds to the later published version. The older version was presumably replaced by the newer one, probably in 1800.

*First Publication*

Nos. 1–3: Vienna, June 1801 (T. Mollo & Co.); Nos. 4–6: Vienna, October 1801 (T. Mollo & Co.).

*Complete Editions*

Old Complete Edition: Nos. 37–42 (Series 6 Nos. 1–6); New Complete Edition: Division VI, Vol. 3 (Munich: Henle).

## Quartet in F Major, Hess 34
## (Transcription of the Piano Sonata in E Major, op. 14 no. 1)

*Time of Composition*

Presumably 1802.

*Sketches*

None.

*Autograph and Early Copies*
None.

*First Publication*
Kunst- und Industriekomptoir, Vienna, May 1802.

*Complete Editions*
Not in Old Complete Edition; New Complete Edition, Division VI, Vol. 3.

## Three Quartets in F Major, E minor, and C major, op. 59
## "Rasumovsky" Quartets

*Time of Composition*
Late spring, summer, and autumn of 1806. By October 1806, the first quartet and first two movements of the second were in score, with other movements sketched; all three quartets were completed by November.

*Sketches*
*No. 1:* Mendelssohn 15 sketchbook, SPK Berlin, pp. 183–86 (these are interpolated leaves that did not belong to the original sketchbook).

*Nos. 1–3:* MS A 36, Gesellschaft der Musikfreunde, Vienna (25 of the 32 leaves relate to op. 59).

*No. 2:* Grasnick 20B, SPK Berlin, fol. 19r and v.; Landsberg 10, SPK Berlin, pp. 39–46.

*No. 3:* MS A 33, GdM Vienna; MSS BH 100 and Mh 72, Beethoven-Haus Bonn; MS 2175, Royal College of Music, London. For a discussion of these and other sources, see Alan Tyson, "The 'Razumovsky' Quartets: Some Aspects of the Sources," in *Beethoven Studies* 3, ed. Alan Tyson (Cambridge: Cambridge University Press, 1982), 107–40, esp. 113–14.

*Autograph Scores*
*No. 1:* Mendelssohn 10, SPK Berlin; published in facsimile, with an introduction by Alan Tyson (London: Scolar Press, 1980).

*No. 2:* Autograph 21, SPK Berlin; published in facsimile, with an introduction by Alan Tyson (London: Scolar Press, 1980).

*No. 3:* MS BH 62, Beethoven-Haus, Bonn.

*First Publication*
Bureau des Arts et d'Industrie, Vienna, 1808.

*Complete Editions*
Old Complete Edition: Nos. 43–45 (Series 6, Nos. 7–9); New Complete Edition: Division VI, Vol. 4.

## Quartet in E♭ Major, op. 74

*Time of Composition*

Summer to autumn 1809.

*Sketches*

Sketchbook Landsberg 5, SPK Berlin, pp. 70–97 passim. An edition of Landsberg 5 has been published as *Ludwig van Beethoven: Ein Skizzenbuch aus dem Jahre 1809 (Landsberg 5),* ed. Clemens Brenneis (facsimile and transcription Bonn: Beethoven-Haus, 1995). As Brenneis observes (commentary, p. 48), these sketches imply that in addition to the sketchbook, Beethoven also worked on op. 74 in a preliminary draft ("Arbeitspartitur") on separate papers, a document that has not been preserved.

*Autograph Score*

Biblioteka Jagiellońska, Kraków.

*First Publication*

Breitkopf & Härtel, Leipzig, 1810.

*Complete Editions*

Old Complete Edition: No. 46 (Series 6, No. 10); New Complete Edition: Division VI, Vol. 4.

## Quartet in F minor, op. 95

*Time of Composition*

Summer to autumn 1810; the quartet was presumably revised before its publication in 1816.

*First Performance*

In May 1814 by the Schuppanzigh Quartet in the context of a matinee performance in the Prater in Vienna. This report comes from Anton Schindler, who is often an unreliable witness. See Schindler, *Beethoven as I Knew Him,* ed. Donald MacArdle, trans. Constance Jolly (New York: Norton, 1972), 171.

*Sketches*

Landsberg 11 sketchbook, Biblioteka Jagiellońska, Kraków, Poland, pp. 31–35; 37–45; MS Grasnick 20A, SPK Berlin, fol. 8–9; Pierpont Morgan Library, New York (Schmidt Verzeichnis 390); MS owned by Dr. William Dreesmann; one leaf in Statens Musikbibliothek, Stockholm (Schmidt Verzeichnis 373).

*Autograph Score*

Österreichische Nationalbibliothek, Vienna, Music Department, Cod. 16.531.

*First Publication*

S. A. Steiner & Co., Vienna, 1816.

*Complete Editions*
Old Complete Edition: No. 47 (Series 6 No. 11); New Complete Edition: Division VI, Vol. 4.

## Quartet Movement in B Minor

*Time of Composition*
November 28, 1817. This brief quartet movement of twenty-three measures, marked "Allegretto," is a previously unknown piece composed by Beethoven for an English visitor, Richard Ford. It is a dance-like composition of somewhat contrapuntal character in 3/8 time, a kind of bagatelle for string quartet. The manuscript was auctioned at Sotheby's in December 1999 and sold into private hands. See *The Pencarrow Collection of Autographs Including the Newly-Discovered Beethoven Quartet Movement* (Sotheby's Auction Catalogue, London, 1999), 100–03.

## Quartet in E♭ Major, op. 127

*Time of Composition*
June 1824 until February 1825.

*First Performance*
March 6, 1825, by the Schuppanzigh Quartet in Vienna. After the initial performance, Joseph Böhm replaced Schuppanzigh as first violinist, and following a private performance on March 18, the work was played twice on the evening of March 23, 1825.

*Sketches*
Sketchbook Autograph 11/2, SPK Berlin, fols. 1–28 passim, and related leaves in other collections (see Johnson, Tyson, and Winter, *The Beethoven Sketchbooks,* 301–3); DeRoda sketchbook, Beethoven-Haus, Bonn, fol. 1r; Artaria 205/4 sketchbook, SPK Berlin, pp. 2–36 passim; Grasnick 4 sketchbook, Biblioteka Jagiellońska, Kraków, fols. 1–25 passim; MS BH 112, Beethoven-Haus, Bonn, pp. 3–4 (this MS belonged originally with MS A 50, Gesellschaft der Musikfreunde, Vienna). Score sketches are found in the Artaria 206 MS (Biblioteka Jagiellońska, Kraków), MSS A51 and A55 (Gesellschaft der Musikfreunde, Vienna), and related sources are listed in *The Beethoven Sketchbooks,* pp. 472–74, 477. A leaf containing score sketches for the first movement was sold at Sotheby's in December 2004. Several additional individual sketchleaves for op. 127 are listed by Brandenburg in "Die Quellen zur Entstehungsgeschichte von Beethovens Streichquartett Es-Dur Op. 127," *Beethoven-Jahrbuch* 10 (1983): 267–68.

*Autograph Score*
First and second movements: Biblioteka Jagiellońska, Kraków; third movement: Stiftelsen Musikkulturens Främjande, Stockholm (until sold into private hands at Sotheby's in December 2003); fourth movement: Beethoven-Haus, Bonn.

*First Publication*
Schott, Mainz, 1826.

*Complete Editions*
Old Complete Edition: No. 48 (Series 6, No. 12); New Complete Edition: Division VI, Vol. 5.

## Quartet in A Minor, op. 132

*Time of Composition*
February until July 1825. The second and fifth movements use some preexisting material.

*First Performances*
Private performances on September 9 and 11, and public performance on November 6, 1825, with the Schuppanzigh Quartet in Vienna.

*Sketches*
De Roda sketchbook, Beethoven-Haus, Bonn, fols. 5–18 passim; Moscow sketchbook, Glinka Museum, Moscow (and leaves that originally belonged to it), pp. 1–18 passim (see *Ludwig van Beethoven: Moscow Sketchbook from 1825*, ed. Elena Vjaskova (Moscow: Gnesins Musical Academy, 1995; and *The Beethoven Sketchbooks,* 423); Egerton 2795 Sketchbook, British Library, London, fols. 11r, 12r. Score sketches are found mainly in Artaria 213 MS, SPK Berlin, with related leaves in Koblenz, Stockholm, Berlin, Vienna, and London (see *The Beethoven Sketchbooks,* 475–77).

*Autograph Score, Parts, and Early Copies*
Autograph score (SPK Berlin) completed by July 1825, with some revisions made subsequently; parts with Beethoven's corrections in Beethoven-Haus Bonn (SBH 741), and in private collection in Paris; first copies date from July to October 1825.

*First Publication*
Score and parts: A. M. and M. Schlesinger, Berlin and Paris, 1827.

*Complete Edition*
Old Complete Edition: No. 51 (Series 6, No. 15).

## Quartet in B♭ Major, op. 130, and the "Great Fugue," op. 133

*Time of Composition*
First version with the *Grosse Fuge* as finale written between May 1825 and November–December 1825; the substitute finale of op. 130 dates from October to November 1826.

*First Performances*
First version (with the *Grosse Fuge* as finale): March 21, 1826, with the Schuppanzigh Quartet; second version (with the substitute finale): April 22, 1827; the second finale was already performed in December 1826.

*Sketches*
De Roda Sketchbook, Beethoven-Haus, Bonn, fols. 13–23; 28–39 passim; Kullak sketchbook (Autograph 24), SPK Berlin, fol. 1r–5r, 7r–10r, 12r, 52r, 59r–62r; Moscow Sketchbook, Glinka Museum, Moscow, pp. 25–26, 29–50 (and reconstructed individual leaves; see *The Beethoven Sketchbooks,* 423); Egerton 2795 Sketchbook, British Library, London, fols. 1–16 passim; Autograph 9/5, SPK, Berlin, fols. 1–8, 12–26 passim; Autograph 9/2, SPK Berlin; Autograph 9/1, SPK Berlin; Autograph 9/1a, fols. 1r–7v, 12r, 14r; MS 66/9, Bibliothèque Nationale, Paris; Autograph 19c, SPK Berlin, MS Artaria 216, SPK Berlin, p. 55. Score sketches in MS A 52, Gesellschaft der Musikfreunde, Vienna; Artaria 214, Biblioteka Jagiellońska, Kraków, with reconstructed individual leaves (see *The Beethoven Sketchbooks,* 478–81); and Artaria 209, SPK Berlin, with reconstructed leaves (this source is for the new finale of op. 130; see *The Beethoven Sketchbooks,* 503–8).

*Autograph Scores*
First movement: Biblioteka Jagiellońska, Kraków; second movement: Library of Congress, Washington; third movement: Bibliothèque Nationale, Paris; fourth movement: Moravian Museum, Institute of Music History, Brno; fifth and sixth movements: SPK Berlin. Autograph score of the *Grosse Fuge,* op. 133: Biblioteka Jagiellońska, Kraków.

*First Publication*
First version: printing in score prepared by middle of August 1826, but did not appear; second version (score and parts): M. Artaria, Vienna, 1827; second version (parts): M. Schlesinger, Paris, 1827.

*Complete Editions*
Old Complete Edition (second version): No. 49 (Series 6, No. 13); New Complete Edition: Division VI, Vol. 5.

## Quartet in C♯ minor, op. 131

*Time of Composition*
December 1825 until July 1826.

*First Performance*
In 1828 in Halberstadt, Müller Quartet.

*Sketches*
Kullak sketchbook (Autograph 24), SPK Berlin, fols. 9v–12v, 14r–v, 15v–47r; Autograph 9/1a, SPK Berlin, fols. 8v–20v passim; MSS Bonn BSK 22 and Mh 96 (Beethoven-Haus, Bonn), used exclusively for op. 131; Autograph 9/3, SPK Berlin, exclusively for op. 131; Autograph 9/4, SPK Berlin, exclusively for op. 131; Autograph 10/1, SPK Berlin, exclusively for op. 131; Artaria 205/3 MS, SPK Berlin, pp. 1–12, 15–16, 18–25, 28–30, 32, 35; MS Artaria 216, SPK Berlin, pp. 58, 99. Score sketches: Artaria 210 MS (165 leaves), SPK Berlin, with additional leaves in Berlin, Washington, D.C., London, Vienna, Paris, Coburg, Kraków (the twenty-four Kraków leaves are stored with the autograph score of movements 1–3 and 5–7, in MS Artaria 211), and Bonn (see *The Beethoven Sketchbooks,* 482–97). Other sketchleaves are housed in St. Petersburg, Baltimore, and Berlin. For a discussion of

manuscripts for op. 131, including numerous transcriptions, see Robert Winter, *Compositional Origins of Beethoven's Opus 131* (Ann Arbor: UMI Research Press, 1982).

*Autograph Score*
First to third, and fifth to seventh movements: Artaria 211, Biblioteka Jagiellońska, Kraków; fourth movement: Mendelssohn 19, SPK Berlin.

*First Edition*
Score and parts: Schott, Mainz, 1827.

*Complete Editions*
Old Complete Edition: No. 50 (Series 6, No. 14); New Complete Edition: Division VI, Vol. 5.

## Quartet in F Major, op. 135

*Time of Composition*
Summer of 1826.

*First Performance*
March 23, 1828, in the Musikvereinsaal, Vienna.

*Sketches*
Kullak sketchbook (Autograph 24), SPK Berlin, fols. 47v–58r passim; MS Artaria 205/3, pp. 16, 19, 22–25, 28–35; MSS Paris 62 and 66, Bibliothèque Nationale, Paris. Score sketches: MS Artaria 216, SPK Berlin; Paris MSS 66/1 and 66/13, Bibliothèque Nationale, Paris; leaves from MSS Artaria 210 and Artaria 209 (see *The Beethoven Sketchbooks,* 498–501).

*Autograph Score*
First movement: Beethoven-Haus, Bonn; second movement: last known in Ascher music shop, Vienna, in the 1860s; third movement: Musée de Mariemont, Brussels; fourth movement: Autograph 19b, SPK, Berlin.

*First Publication*
A. M. Schlesinger and M. Schlesinger, Vienna and Paris, 1827.

*Complete Editions*
Old Complete Edition: No. 52 (Series 6, No. 16); New Complete Edition: Division VI, Vol. 5.

# SELECTED BIBLIOGRAPHY


Abraham, Gerald. *Beethoven's Second-Period Quartets*. London: Oxford University Press, 1942.

Adelson, Robert. "Beethoven's String Quartet in E Flat Op. 127: A Study of the First Performances." *Music & Letters* 79 (1998): 219–43.

Adorno, Theodor W. *Beethoven: Philosophie der Musik; Fragmente und Texte*. Ed. Rolf Tiedemann. Frankfurt am Main: Suhrkamp, 1993. Trans. Edmund Jephcott as *Beethoven: The Philosophy of Music; Fragments and Texts*. Cambridge: Polity Press, 1998.

———. "Spätstil Beethoven." *Moments musicaux: Neu gedruckte Aufsätze 1928–62*. Frankfurt am Main: Suhrkamp, 1964.

Agawu, Kofi. "A Semiotic Interpretation of the First Movement of Beethoven's String Quartet in A Minor, Op. 132." In *Playing with Signs: A Semiotic Interpretation of Classic Music*. Princeton: Princeton University Press, 1991, 110–26.

Albrecht, Theodore. *Letters to Beethoven and Other Correspondence*. Lincoln: University of Nebraska Press, 1996.

Altmann, Wilhelm. *Beethoven String Quartet, Op. 59 No. 1*. Edition Eulenburg, No. 28. London: Ernst Eulenburg, Ltd, 1911.

———. "Ein Vergessenes Streichquartett Beethoven." *Die Musik* 5/1 (1905/6): 250–57.

Anderson, Emily, ed. and trans. *The Letters of Beethoven*. 3 vols. London: Macmillan, 1961, repr. 1985.

Baensch, Otto. *Aufbau und Sinn des Chorfinales in Beethovens Neunter Symphonie*. Berlin: Walter de Gruyter, 1930.

Barry, Barbara R. "Recycling the End of the 'Leibquartett': Models, Meaning, and Propriety in Beethoven's Quartet in B-Flat Major, Opus 130." *Journal of Musicology* 13/3 (1995): 355–76.

Bartlitz, Eveline. *Die Beethoven-Sammlung in der Musikabteilung der Deutschen Staatsbibliothek: Verzeichnis*. Berlin: Deutsche Staatsbibliothek, 1970.

Bashford, Christina M. "The Late Beethoven Quartets and the London Press, 1836–ca. 1850." *The Musical Quarterly* 84/1 (2000): 84–122.

Bekker, Paul. *Beethoven*. Berlin: Schuster & Loeffler, 1911.

Berlin, Isaiah. *The Roots of Romanticism*. Ed. Henry Hardy. Princeton, N.J.: Princeton University Press, 1999.

Biba, Otto. "Zu Beethovens Streichquartett Opus 95." *Münchener Beethoven-Studien*. Munich: Musikverlag Emil Katzbichler, 1992, 39–45.

Bishop, David M. "Chromatic and Diatonic Pitch-Class Motives and Their Influence on Closural Strategies: Analytical Studies of Three Middle-Period String Quartets of Ludwig van Beethoven." Ph.D. dissertation. University of Texas at Austin, 1999.

Blum, David. *The Art of Quartet Playing: The Guarneri Quartet in Conversation with David Blum*. New York: Alfred P. Knopf, 1986.

Borchard, Beatrix. "Quartettspiel und Kulturpolitik im Berlin der Kaiserzeit." In *Der "männliche" und der "weibliche" Beethoven*. Ed. Cornelia Bartsch, Beatrix Borchard, and Rainer Cadenbach. Bonn: Beethoven-Haus, 2003, 369–98.

Brandenburg, Sieghard. "The Autograph of Beethoven's Quartet in A Minor, Op. 132: The Structure of the Manuscript and Its Relevance for the Study of the Genesis of the Work." In *The String Quartets of Haydn, Mozart, and Beethoven*. Ed. Christoph Wolff. Cambridge, Mass.: Harvard University Press, 1980, 278–300.

———. "Die Beethovenhandschriften in der Musikaliensammlung des Erherzogs Rudolph." *Zu Beethoven 3*. Ed. Harry Goldschmidt. Berlin: Verlag Neue Musik, 1988.

———. "Beethovens Streichquartette Op. 18." In *Beethoven und Böhmen: Beiträge zu Biographie und Wirkungsgeschicht Beethovens*. Ed. Sieghard Brandenburg and Martella Gutiérrez-Denhoff. Bonn: Beethoven-Haus, 1998, 259–302.

———. "Bemerkungen zu Beethovens Op. 96." *Beethoven-Jahrbuch* 9 (1973/77): 11–25.

———. "The First Version of Beethoven's G Major Quartet, Op. 18 No. 2." *Music and Letters* 58 (1977): 127–52.

———, ed. *Haydn, Mozart, and Beethoven: Studies in the Music of the Classical Period: Essays in Honor of Alan Tyson*. Oxford: Oxford University Press, 1998.

———. "The Historical Background to the 'Heiliger Dankgesang' in Beethoven's A-minor Quartet Op. 132." In *Beethoven Studies 3*. Ed. Alan Tyson. Cambridge: Cambridge University Press, 1982, 161–91.

———, ed. *Ludwig van Beethoven: Briefwechsel Gesamtausgabe*. 8 vols. Munich: Henle, 1996.

———. "Die Quellen zur Entstehungsgeschichte von Beethovens Streichquartett Es-Dur Op. 127." *Beethoven-Jahrbuch* 10 (1978/81): 221–76.

———. "Die Skizzen zur Neunten Symphonie." In *Zu Beethoven* 2. Ed. Harry Goldschmidt. Berlin: Verlag Neue Musik, 1984.

Brenneis, Clemens. *Ludwig van Beethoven: Ein Skizzenbuch aus dem Jahre 1809*. 2 vols. Bonn: Beethoven-Haus, 1993.

Brinkmann, Reinhold. "Die Zeit der *Eroica*." In *Musik in der Zeit—Zeit in der Musik*. Ed. Richard Klein, Eckehard Kiem, and Wolfram Ette. Weilerswist: Velbrück Wissenschaft, 2000, 183–211. Trans. Irene Zedlacher as "In the Time of the *Eroica*." In *Beethoven and His World*. Ed. Scott Burnham and Michael P. Steinberg. Princeton, N.J.: Princeton University Press, 1–26.

Brodbeck, David L., and John Platoff. "Dissociation and Integration: The First Movement of Beethoven's Opus 130." *19th Century Music* 7 (1983): 149–62

Broyles, Michael. *Beethoven: The Emergence and Evolution of Beethoven's Heroic Style*. New York: Excelsior, 1987.

———. "Beethoven's Sonata Op. 14 No. 1—Originally for Strings?" *Journal of the American Musicological Society* 23 (1970): 405–19.

Buchholz, Helmut. *Perspektiven der Neuen Mythologie: Mythos, Religion und Poesie im Schnittpunkt von Idealismus und Romantik um 1800*. Frankfurt am Main: Peter Lang, 1990.

Bumpass, Laura Kathryn. "Beethoven's Last Quartet: A Study of Op. 135 Based on Autograph Materials." Ph.D. dissertation. University of Illinois at Urbana-Champaign, 1982.

Burnham, Scott. *Beethoven Hero.* Princeton, N.J.: Princeton University Press, 1995.

Campbell, Bruce. "Beethoven's Quartets Opus 59: An Investigation into Compositional Process." Ph.D. dissertation. Yale University, 1982.

Caplin, William. *Classical Form: A Theory of Formal Functions for the Instrumental Music of Haydn, Mozart, and Beethoven.* New York and Oxford: Oxford University Press, 1998.

———. "The 'Expanded Cadential Progression': A Category for the Analysis of Classical Form." *Journal of Musicological Research* 7 (1987): 215–57.

Carr-Richardson, Amy. "Rotational Symmetry as a Metaphor for the Scherzo of Beethoven's Opus 131." *Indiana Theory Review* 20/1 (1999): 1–23.

Cassirer, Ernst. *Sprache und Mythose: Ein Beitrag zum Problem der Götternamen.* Leipzig: B. G. Teubner, 1925.

Chua, Daniel. *Absolute Music and the Construction of Meaning.* Cambridge: Cambridge University Press, 1999.

———. *The "Galitzin" Quartets of Beethoven: Opp. 127, 132, 130.* Princeton, N.J.: Princeton University Press, 1995.

Cohn, Richard. "The Dramatization of Hypermetric Conflicts in the Scherzo of Beethoven's Ninth Symphony." *19th-Century Music* 15/3 (1992): 188–206.

Cone, Edward T. *Musical Form and Musical Performance.* New York: Norton, 1968.

Cook, Nicholas. "Beethoven's Unfinished Piano Concerto: A Case of Double Vision?" *Journal of the American Musicological Society* 42/2 (1989): 338–74.

Cooke, Deryck. "The Unity of Beethoven's Late Quartets." *Music Review* 24 (1963): 30–49.

Cooper, Barry. *Beethoven and the Creative Process.* Oxford: Clarendon, 1990.

———. "Newly Identified Sketches for Beethoven's Tenth Symphony." *Music & Letters* 66 (1985): 170–91.

———. "The Sketches for Beethoven's *Egmont* Overture: A Reassessment." In *Beethoven's Compositional Process.* Ed. William Kinderman. Lincoln: University of Nebraska Press, 1991, pp. 122–30.

Cooper, Martin. *Beethoven: The Last Decade, 1817–1827.* London: Oxford University Press, 1970.

Crotty, John Edward. "Design and Harmonic Organization in Beethoven's String Quartet, Opus 131." Ph.D. dissertation. University of Rochester, 1986.

Czerny, Carl. *Erinnerungen aus meinem Leben.* Ed. Walter Kolneder. Strasbourg: Heitz, 1968.

———. *On the Proper Performance of All Beethoven's Works for the Piano.* Ed. Paul Badura-Skoda. Vienna: Universal Edition, 1970.

Dahlhaus, Carl. *Beethoven und seine Zeit.* Laaber: Laaber, 1987. Eng. trans by Mary Whittall as *Ludwig van Beethoven: Approaches to His Music.* Oxford: Clarendon, 1991.

———. *Grundlagen der Musikgeschichte.* Cologne: Musikverlag Gerig, 1977.

———. "Zum Begriff des Thematischen bei Beethoven: Kommentare zu Opus 95 und Opus 102, 1." In *Beethoven '77.* Ed. Friedhelm Döhl. Zürich: Amadeus Verlag, 1979.

Danckwardt, Marianne. "Zu den Streichquartetten Op. 18 von Ludwig van Beethoven." *Neues musikwissenschaftliches Jahrbuch* 6 (1997): 121–61.

Danuser, Hermann. "Streichquartett f-Moll Quartetto serioso Op. 95." In *Beethoven: Interpretationen seiner Werke.* Ed. Albrecht Riethmüller, Carl Dahlhaus, and Alexander L. Ringer. Laaber: Laaber, 1994, vol. 2, 78–85.

Daverio, John. "Manner, Tone, and Tendency in Beethoven's Chamber Music for Strings." In *The Cambridge Companion to Beethoven.* Ed. Glenn Stanley. Cambridge: Cambridge University Press, 2000, 147–64.

Davies, Peter J. *Beethoven in Person: His Deafness, Illness, and Death.* Westport, Conn.: Greenwood, 2001.

———. *Character of a Genius: Beethoven in Perspective.* Westport, Conn.: Greenwood, 2002.

Del Mar, Jonathan. "A Problem Resolved? The Form of the Scherzo of Beethoven's String Quartet in F, Op. 59, No. 1." *Beethoven Forum* 8 (2000): 165–70.

Drabkin, William. "The Cello Part in Beethoven's Late Quartets." *Beethoven Forum* 7 (1999): 45–66.

Draeseke, Felix. *Schriften 1855–1861.* Ed. Martella Gutiérrez-Denhoff and Helmut Loos. Bad Honnef: Gudrun Schröder Verlag, 1987.

Elterlein, Ernst von. *Beethovens Clavier-Sonaten.* Leipzig: Heinrich Matthes, 1856.

Epstein, David. *Beyond Orpheus: Studies in Musical Structure.* Cambridge, Mass.: MIT Press, 1979.

Fecker, Adolf. *Die Entstehung von Beethovens Musik zu Goethes Trauerspiel Egmont: Eine Abhandlung über die Skizzen.* Hamburg: Verlag der Musiklienhandlung Karl Dieter Wagner, 1978.

Fink, Robert. "Going Flat: Post-Hierarchical Music Theory and the Musical Surface." In *Rethinking Musicology.* Ed. Nicholas Cook and Mark Everist. New York and Oxford: Oxford University Press, 1999.

Finscher, Ludwig. "Beethovens Streichquartett Op. 59, 3: Versuch einer Interpretation." In *Zur musikalischen Analyse.* Ed. Gerhard Schuhmacher. Darmstadt: Wissenschaftliche Buchgesellschaft, 1974, 122–60.

———. "'Das macht mir nicht so leicht ein anderer nach.' Beethovens Streichquartettbearbeitung der Klaviersonate op. 14 Nr. 1." In *Divertimento für Hermann J. Abs: Beethoven Studien.* Ed. Martin Staehelin. Bonn: Beethoven-Haus, 1981, 11–24.

———, ed. *Ludwig van Beethoven.* Wege der Forschung, vol. 428. Darmstadt: Wissenschaftliche Buchgesellschaft, 1983.

———. "Mythos und musikalische Struktur." In *Richard Wagner: Der Ring des Nibelungen; Ansichten des Mythos.* Ed. Udo Bermbach and Dieter Borchmeyer. Stuttgart: Metzler, 1995, 27–37.

———. *Studien zur Geschichte des Streichquartetts.* Kassel: Bärenreiter, 1974.

Fischer, Kurt von. "'Never to Be Performed in Public': Zu Beethovens Streichquartett Op. 95." *Beethoven-Jahrbuch* 9 (1973/77): 87–96.

Floros, Constantin. "Beethovens späte Streichquartette." *Musik/Revolution: Festschrift für Georg Knepler zum 90. Geburtstag.* Hamburg: Bockel, 1997, vol. II, 49–61.

Geck, Martin. "Das wilde Denken. Ein strukturalistischer Blick auf Beethovens op. 31, 2." *Archiv für Musikwissenschaft* 57 (2000): 64–77.

———. "Zur Philosophie von Beethovens Grosse Fuge." In *Festschrift Walter Wiora zum 90. Geburtstag.* Tutzing: Schneider, 1997, 123–31.

Gendolla, Peter. *Zeit: Zur Geschichte der Zeiterfahrung; Vom Mythos zur Punktzeit.* Cologne: DuMont 1992.

Gerstinger, Hans, ed. *Ludwig van Beethovens Stammbuch.* Facsimile. Bielefeld: Velhagen & Klasing, 1927.

Glauert, Amanda. "The Double Perspective in Beethoven's Opus 131." *19th Century Music* 4 (1980–81): 113–20.

Green, David B. *Temporal Processes in Beethoven's Music.* New York: Gordon and Breach, 1982.

Greenfield, Donald Tobias. "Sketch Studies for Three Movements of Beethoven's String Quartets, Opus 18, Nos. 1 and 2." Ph.D. dissertation. Princeton University, 1983.

Grew, Sidney. "The 'Grosse Fuge': An Analysis." *Music and Letters* 12 (1931): 253–61.

Griffiths, Paul. *The String Quartet.* London: Thames and Hudson, 1983.

Gülke, Peter. "Zur musikalischen Konzeption der Rasumowsky-Quartette Op. 59." "*. . . immer das Ganze vor Augen": Studien zu Beethoven.* Kassel: Metzler, 2000, 213–45.

Hatten, Robert. *Interpreting Musical Gestures, Topics, and Tropes: Mozart, Beethoven, Schubert.* Bloomington: Indiana University Press, 2004.

———. *Musical Meaning in Beethoven: Markedness, Correlation, and Interpretation.* Bloomington: Indiana University Press, 1994.

Hecker, Joachim von. "Untersuchungen an den Skizzen zum Streichquartett in cis-moll Op. 131 von Beethoven." Ph.D. dissertation. University of Freiburg, 1956.

Helm, Theodor. *Beethovens Streichquartette: Versuch einer technischen Analyse dieser Werke im Zusammenhange mit ihrem geistigen Gehalt.* Leipzig: Fritzsch, 1885.

Hirschbach, Hermann. "Über Beethovens letzte Streichquartette." *Neue Zeitschrift für Musik* 11/2–3 (1839): 5–6, 9–10, 13–14; 11/13 (1839): 49–51.

Hübsch, Lini. *Ludwig van Beethoven: Rasumowsky-Quartette.* Munich: Fink Verlag, 1983.

Imeson, Sylvia. *"The time gives it proofe": Paradox in the Late Music of Beethoven.* New York: Peter Lang, 1996.

Johnson, Douglas, Alan Tyson, and Robert Winter. *The Beethoven Sketchbooks: History, Reconstruction, Inventory.* Berkeley: University of California Press, 1985.

Jones, David Wyn. "Beethoven and the Viennese Legacy." In *The Cambridge Companion to the String Quartet.* Ed. Robin Stowell. Cambridge: Cambridge University Press, 2003 210–27.

Jones, Timothy. *The 'Moonlight' and Other Sonatas, Op. 27 and Op. 31.* Cambridge: Cambridge University Press, 1999.

Kamien, Roger. "Conflicting Metrical Patterns in Accompaniment and Melody in Works by Mozart and Beethoven: A Preliminary Study." *Journal of Music Theory* 37/2 (1993): 311–48.

Kaminsky, Peter. "Aspects of Harmony, Rhythm and Form in Schumann's *Papillons, Carnaval,* and *Davidsbündlertänze.*" Ph.D. dissertation. University of Rochester, 1989.

Kennessey, Stefania M. de. *The Quartet, the Finale, and the Fugue: A Study of Beethoven's Op. 130/133.* Ann Arbor, Mich.: UMI Research Press, 1984.

Kerman, Joseph. "Beethoven Quartet Audiences: Actual, Potential, Ideal." In *The Beethoven Quartet Companion.* Ed. Robert Winter and Robert Martin. Berkeley: University of California Press, 1994, 7–28.

———. *The Beethoven Quartets.* New York: Knopf, 1967.

———. "Close Readings of the Heard Kind." *19th-Century Music* 17/3 (1994): 209–19.

———. *Write All These Down.* Berkeley: University of California Press, 1994.

Kerman, Joseph, and Alan Tyson. "Beethoven, Ludwig van." In *The New Grove Dictionary of Music and Musicians.* Ed. Stanley Sadie. 20 vols. London: Macmillan, 1980, vol. 2, 354–414. Rev. Scott Burnham in 2nd ed. 29 vols. London: Macmillan, 2001, vol. 3, 73–140.

Kinderman, William. *Artaria 195: Beethoven's Sketchbook for the* Missa solemnis *and the Piano Sonata in E Major, Opus 109.* 3 vols. (Commentary, Facsimile, Transcription). Urbana and Chicago: University of Illinois Press, 2003.

———. *Beethoven.* Oxford: Oxford University Press, 1995.

———. "Beethoven." In *Nineteenth-Century Piano Music.* Ed. R. Larry Todd. New York: Schirmer, 1990, 55–96.

———, ed. *Beethoven's Compositional Process.* Lincoln: University of Nebraska Press, 1991.

———. *Beethoven's Diabelli Variations.* Oxford: Clarendon, 1987.

———. "Beethoven's High-Comic Style in Piano Sonatas of the 1790s, or Beethoven, Uncle Toby, and the 'Muckcart-driver.'" *Beethoven Forum* 5 (1996): 119–38.

———. "Beethoven's Symbol for the Deity in the *Missa solemnis* and the Ninth Symphony." *19th-Century Music* 9/2 (1985): 102–18.

———. "The Evolution of Beethoven's Late Style: Another 'New Path' after 1824?" *Beethoven Forum* 8 (2000): 71–99.

———. "Integration and Narrative Design in Beethoven's Piano Sonata in A♭ Major, Opus 110." *Beethoven Forum* 1 (1992): 111–45.

———. Review of *The "Galitzin" Quartets of Beethoven,* by Daniel K. L. Chua. *Intégral* 10 (1996): 167–75.

———. "Streichquartett Es-Dur Op. 127." In *Beethoven: Interpretationen seiner Werke.* Ed. Albrecht Riethmüller, Carl Dahlhaus, and Alexander L. Ringer. Laaber: Laaber, 1994, vol. 2, 278–91.

———. "Tonality and Form in the Variation Movements of Beethoven's Late Quartets." In *Beiträge zu Beethovens Kammermusik: Symposium Bonn 1984.* Ed. Sieghard Brandenburg and Helmut Loos. Munich: Henle, 1987, 135–51.

Kirkendale, Warren. *Fuge und Fugato in der Kammermusik des Rokoko und der Klassik.* Tutzing: H. Schneider, 1996. In English as *Fugue and Fugato in Rococo and Classical Chamber Music.* Rev. and exp. 2nd edition. Trans. Margaret Bent and Warren Kirkendale. Durham, N.C.: Duke University Press, 1979.

———. "The 'Great Fugue' Op. 133: Beethoven's Art of Fugue." *Acta Musicologica* 35 (1963): 14–24.

Klein, Hans-Günter, ed. *Ludwig van Beethoven: Autographe und Abschriften.* Berlin: Merseburger, 1975.

Knittel, K. M. "From Chaos to History: The Reception of Beethoven's Late Quartets." Ph.D. dissertation. Princeton University, 1992.

———. "Wagner, Deafness, and the Reception of Beethoven's Late Style." *Journal of the American Musicological Society* 51/1 (1998): 49–82.

Koch, Heinrich Christoph. *Musikalisches Lexikon.* Frankfurt am Main: August Hermann der Jüngere, 1802.

Köhler, Karl-Heinz, et al., ed. *Ludwig van Beethovens Konversationshefte.* 11 vols. Leipzig: VEB Deutscher Verlag für Musik, 1968– .

Kolisch, Rudolf. *Tempo und Charakter in Beethovens Musik.* Musik-Konzepte 76/77. Munich: text + kritik, 1992; in English as *Tempo and Character in Beethoven's Music. Musical Quarterly* 29/2–3 (1943): 169–87, 291–312; repr. in *Musical Quarterly* 77/1 (1993): 90–131.

Kopfermann, Michael. *Beiträge zur Musikalischen Analyse später Werke Ludwig van Beethovens.* Munich: Katzbichler, 1975.

Korsyn, Kevin. "J. W. N. Sullivan and the Heiliger Dankgesang: Questions of Meaning in Late Beethoven." *Beethoven Forum* 2 (1993): 133–74.

———. "Towards a New Poetics of Musical Influence." *Music Analysis* 10/1–2 (1991): 3–72.

Kramer, Jonathan. "Multiple and Nonlinear Time in Beethoven's Opus 135." *Perspectives of New Music* 11 (1973): 122–45.

———. *The Time of Music.* New York: Schirmer, 1988.

Kramer, Lawrence. *Music as Cultural Practice, 1800–1900.* Berkeley: University of California Press, 1990.

Kramer, Richard. "Ambiguities in *La Malinconia:* What the Sketches Say." *Beethoven Studies 3.* Ed. Alan Tyson. Cambridge: Cambridge University Press, 1982, 29–46.

———. "Between Cavatina and Ouverture: Opus 130 and the Voices of Narrative." *Beethoven Forum* 1 (1992): 165–89.

———. "'Das Organische der Fuge': On the Autograph of Beethoven's String Quartet in F major, Op. 59, No. 1." In *The String Quartets of Haydn, Mozart, and Beethoven.* Ed. Christoph Wolff. Cambridge, Mass.: Harvard University Press, 1980, 223–65.

———, ed. *Ein neuentdecktes Skizzenblatt von Sommer 1800 zu Beethovens Streichquartett Op. 18 Nr. 2.* Facsimile and transcription. Bonn: Beethoven-Haus, 1999.

———. "Gradus ad Parnassum: Beethoven, Schubert, and the Romance of Counterpoint." *19th-Century Music* 11/2 (1987): 107–20.

———. "Lisch aus, mein Licht: Song, fugue, and the symptoms of a late style." *Beethoven Forum* 7 (1999): 67–87.

———, ed. *Ludwig van Beethoven: A Sketchbook from the Summer of 1800.* Facsimile and transcription. Bonn: Beethoven-Haus, 1996.

———. "The Sketches for Beethoven's Violin Sonatas, Opus 30: History, Transcription, Analysis." Ph.D. dissertation. Princeton University, 1973.

Krebs, Harald. *Fantasy Pieces: Metrical Dissonance in the Music of Robert Schumann.* New York and Oxford: Oxford University Press, 1999.

———. "Rhythmische Konsonanz und Dissonanz." *Musiktheorie* 9/1 (1994): 27–37.

———. "Some Extensions of the Concepts of Metrical Consonance and Dissonance." *Journal of Music Theory* 31/1 (1987): 99–120.

Kreft, Ekkehard. *Die späten Quartette Beethovens.* Bonn: Bouvier, 1969.

Krones, Harmut. "Streichquartett Es-Dur 'Harfenquartett' Op. 74." In *Beethoven: Interpretationen seiner Werke.* Ed. Albrecht Riethmüller, Carl Dahlhaus, and Alexander L. Ringer. Laaber: Laaber, 1994, vol. 1, 585–92.

Kropfinger, Klaus. "Fuge B-Dur für Streichquartett 'Große Fuge' Op. 133." In *Beethoven: Interpretationen seiner Werke.* Ed. Albrecht Riethmüller, Carl Dahlhaus, and Alexander L. Ringer. Laaber: Laaber, 1994, vol. 2, 338–42.

———. "Das Gespaltene Werk—Beethovens Streichquartett Op. 130/133." In *Beiträge zu Beethovens Kammermusik.* Ed. Sieghard Brandenburg and Helmut Loos. Munich: Henle, 1987, 296–335.

———. "Streichquartett B-Dur Op. 130." In *Beethoven: Interpretationen seiner Werke.* Ed. Albrecht Riethmüller, Carl Dahlhaus, and Alexander L. Ringer. Laaber: Laaber, 1994, vol. 2, 299–316.

———. "Zur thematischen Funktion der langsamen Einleitung bei Beethoven." In *Colloquium amicorum Schmidt-Görg.* Ed. Siegfried Kross and Hans Schmidt. Bonn: Beethoven-Haus, 1967, 197–216.

Krummacher, Friedhelm. "Streichquartett f-Moll Op. 135." In *Beethoven: Interpretationen seiner Werke.* Ed. Albrecht Riethmüller, Carl Dahlhaus, and Alexander L. Ringer. Laaber: Laaber, 1994, vol. 2, 347–64.

Kunze, Stefan, ed. *Ludwig van Beethoven: Die Werke im Speigel seiner Zeit; Gesammelte Konzertberichte und Rezensionen bis 1830*. Laaber: Laaber, 1987.

Lam, Basil. *Beethoven String Quartets*. London: BBC, 1975.

Lenz, Wilhelm von. *Beethoven: Eine Kunststudie*. Repr. with notes by Alfred Kalischer. Berlin: Schuster and Loeffler, 1921.

———. *Beethoven et ses trois styles*. St. Petersburg: Bernard, 1852.

Lester, Joel. *The Rhythms of Tonal Music*. Carbondale: Southern Illinois University Press, 1986.

Lévi-Strauss, Claude. *Mythologiques*. Paris: Plon, 1964.

Levy, Janet M. *Beethoven's Compositional Choices: The Two Versions of the Opus 18, No. 1, First Movement*. Philadelphia: University of Pennsylvania Press, 1982.

Lindemann, Timothy H. "Strategies of Sonata Form in the First Movements of the Beethoven String Quartets." Ph.D. dissertation, Indiana University, 1987.

Lockwood, Lewis. "The Autograph of the First Movement of Beethoven's Sonata for Violoncello and Pianoforte, Opus 69." *Music Forum* 2 (1970): 1–109.

———. *Beethoven: The Music and the Life*. New York: Norton, 2003.

———. *Beethoven: Studies in the Creative Process*. Cambridge, Mass.: Harvard University Press, 1992.

———. "Beethoven as Colourist: Another Look at His String Quartet Arrangement of the Piano Sonata, Op. 14 No. 1." In *Haydn, Mozart, and Beethoven. Studies in the Music of the Classical Period. Essays in Honour of Alan Tyson*. Ed. Sieghard Brandenburg. Oxford: Clarendon, 1998, 175–80.

———. "Beethoven's Unfinished Piano Concerto of 1815: Sources and Problems." *Musical Quarterly* 56 (1970): 624–46.

———. "On Beethoven's Sketches and Autographs: Some Problems of Definition and Interpretation." *Acta Musicologica* 42 (1970): 32–47.

———. "On Schoenberg's View of the Beethoven Quartets." In *Music of My Future: The Schoenberg Quartets and Trio*. Ed. Reinhold Brinkmann and Christoph Wolff. Cambridge, Mass.: Harvard University Department of Music, 2000, 39–57.

———. "A Problem of Form: The 'Scherzo' of Beethoven's String Quartet in F Major, Op. 59, No. 1." *Beethoven Forum* 2 (1993): 83–95.

———. "Recent Writings on Beethoven's Late Quartets." *Beethoven Forum* 9 (2002): 84–99.

———. "The State of Sketch Research." *Beethoven's Compositional Process*. Ed. William Kinderman. Lincoln: University of Nebraska Press, 1991, 6–13.

Lodes, Birgit. "Beethovens individuelle Aneignung der langsamen Einleitung. Zum Kopfsatz des Streichquartetts op. 127." *Musica* 49 (1995): 311–20.

———. "Probing the Sacred Genres: Beethoven's Religious Songs, Oratorio, and Masses." In *The Cambridge Companion to Beethoven*. Ed. Glenn Stanley. Cambridge: Cambridge University Press, 2000, 218–36.

Lomnas, Bonnie, and Erling Lomnas. *Catalogue of Music Manuscripts*. Stockholm: Musikaliska akademiens bibliotek, 1995.

Lonchampt, Jacques. *Les quatuors à cordes de Beethoven*. Paris: Broché, 1987.

Macek, Jaroslav. "Die Musik bei den Lobkowicz." In *Ludwig van Beethoven im Herzen Europas*. Ed. Oldrich Pulkert and Hans-Werner Küthen. Prague: Ceské lupovké Závodny A. G., 2000, 171–216.

Mahaim, Ivan. *Naissance et renaissance des derniers quatuors de Beethoven.* 2 vols. Paris: Desclée de Brouwer, 1964.

Mahnkopf, Claus-Steffen. "Beethovens Grosse Fuge: Multiperspektivität im Spätwerk." *Musik & Ästhetik* 2/8 (1998): 12–38.

Marliave, Joseph de. *Beethoven's Quartets.* Ed. Jean Escarra. Trans. Hilda Andrews. London: Oxford University Press, 1928. Originally published as *Les quatuors de Beethoven.* Paris: F. Alcan, 1925.

Marston, Nicholas. "Analysing Variations: The Finale of Beethoven's String Quartet Op. 74." *Music Analysis* 8/3 (1989): 303–24.

———. "Landsberg 5 and Future Prospects for the *Skizzenausgabe.*" *Beethoven Forum* 6 (1998): 207–33.

Marx, Adolf Bernhard. *Ludwig van Beethoven: Leben und Schaffen.* Berlin: Otto Janke, 1859. Repr. Hildesheim and New York: Georg Olms, 1979.

Mason, Daniel Gregory. *The Quartets of Beethoven.* New York: Oxford University Press, 1947.

Meyer, Leonard B. *Explaining Music: Essays and Explorations.* Chicago: University of Chicago Press, 1973.

McCallum, Peter. "The Analytic Significance of Beethoven's Sketches for the String Quartet in F Major, Opus 135." Ph.D. dissertation. University of Sydney, 1996.

McClary, Susan. *Conventional Wisdom: The Content of Musical Form.* Berkeley: University of California Press, 2000.

Mies, Paul. *Die Krise der Konzertkadenz bei Beethoven.* Bonn: Bouvier, 1970.

Mikulicz, Karl Lothar, ed. *Ein Notierungsbuch von Beethoven aus dem Besitze der Preussischen Staatsbibliothek zu Berlin.* Leipzig: Breitkopf & Härtel, 1927. Repr. Hildesheim and New York: Georg Olms, 1972.

Mila, M. "Lettura della 'Grande fuga,' Op. 133." In *Scritti in onore di Luigi Ronga.* Milan: R. Ricciardi, 1973, 345–66.

Miller, Malcolm. "Beethoven's Early Piano Quartets WoO 36 and the Seeds of Genius." *Arietta* 4 (2004): 18–24.

———. "Beethoven's String Quartets: A Classic or Modernist Legacy?" *Beethoven Journal* 16/1 (2001): 26–29.

Misch, Ludwig. *Beethoven Studies.* Norman: University of Oklahoma Press, 1953.

Mitchell, W. J. "Beethoven's *La Malinconia* from the String Quartet, Opus 18, No. 6: Technique and Structure." *Music Forum* 3 (1973): 269–80.

Narmour, Eugene. *The Analysis and Cognition of Basic Melodic Structures: The Impact-Realization Model.* Chicago: Chicago University Press, 1977.

Nottebohm, Gustav. "Generalbass und Compositionslehre betreffende Handschriften Beethovens und J. R. v. Seyfrieds Buch 'Ludwig van Beethovens Studien im Generalbasse, Contrapuncte' u.s.w." In *Beethoveniana: Aufsätze und Mittheilungen.* Leipzig: Peters, 1872, 154–203.

———. *Zweite Beethoveniana: Nachgelassene Aufsätze.* Leipzig: Peters, 1887.

Obelkevich, Mary R. "The Growth of a Musical Idea—Beethoven's Op. 96." *Currrent Musicology* 11 (1971): 91–114.

Ong, Seow-Chin. "The Autograph of Beethoven's 'Archduke' Trio." *Beethoven Forum* 11/2 (2004): 181–208.

———. "Source Studies for Beethoven's Piano Trio in B-flat Major, Op. 97 ('Archduke')." Ph.D. dissertation. University of California at Berkeley, 1995.

Osthoff, Wolfgang. "Mozarts Cavatinen und Ihre Tradition." *Helmuth Osthoff zu seinem siebzigsten Geburtstag.* Ed. W. Stauder. Tutzing: H. Schneider, 1969, 139–77.

Platen, Emil. "Eine Frühfassung zum ersten Satz des Streichquartetts Op. 131 von Beethoven." *Beethoven-Jahrbuch* 10 (1978/81): 277–304.

Potter, Tully. "From Chamber to Concert Hall." In *The Cambridge Companion to the String Quartet.* Ed. Robin Stowell. Cambridge: Cambridge University Press, 2003, 41–59.

Pulkert, Oldřich. "Das Knabenquartett des Fürsten Lichnowsky." Trans. Václav Maidl. In *Ludwig van Beethoven im Herzen Europas: Leben und Nachleben in den Bömischen Ländern.* Ed. Oldřich Pulkert and Hans-Werner Küthen. Prague: Ceské lupkové závody A.G., 2000, 451–58.

Radcliffe, Philip. *Beethoven's String Quartets.* London: Hutchinson, 1965.

Ratner, Leonard. *Beethoven's String Quartets: Compositional Strategies and Rhetoric.* Stanford, Calif.: Stanford Bookstore, 1995.

———. *Classic Music: Expression, Form, and Style.* New York: Schirmer, 1980.

Ratz, Erwin. *Einführung in die musikalische Formenlehre. Über Formprinzipien in den Inventionen J. S. Bachs und ihre Bedeutung für die Kompositionstechnik Beethovens.* Vienna: Österreichischer Bundesverlag für Unterricht, Wissenschaft und Kunst, 1951.

Reynolds, Christopher. "From Berlioz's Fugitives to Godard's Terrorists: Artistic Responses to Beethoven's Late Quartets." *Beethoven Forum* 8 (2000): 147–63.

———. "The Representational Impulse in Late Beethoven, II: String Quartet in F Major, Op. 135." *Acta Musicologica* 60 (1988): 180–94.

Richards, Annette. *The Free Fantasia and the Musical Picturesque.* Cambridge: Cambridge University Press, 2001.

Riemann, Hugo. *Beethoven's Streichquartette.* Berlin: Schlesinger'sche Buch- und Musikhandlung, 1910.

Riezler, Walter. *Beethoven.* Trans. G. D. H. Pidcock. London: Forrester, 1938.

Roda, Cecilio de. "Un quaderno de autografi di Beethoven del 1825." *Rivista Musicale Italiana* 12 (1905): 63–108; 592–622; 734–67.

Rolland, Romain. "La Cathédrale Interrompue: Tome II. Le derniers Quatuors." In *Beethoven: les Grandes Époques Créatices.* Vol. 5. Paris: Éditions du Sablier, 1943.

Rothstein, William. "Beethoven with and without 'Kunstgepräng': Metrical Ambiguity Reconsidered." *Beethoven Forum* 4 (1995): 165–93.

Rumph, Stephen. *Beethoven after Napoleon: Political Romanticism in the Late Works.* Berkeley: University of California Press, 2004.

Salmen, Walter. "3 Streichquartette F-Dur, e-moll und C-dur 'Rasumowsky-Quartette' op. 59." In *Beethoven: Interpretationen seiner Werke.* Ed. Albrecht Riethmüller, Carl Dahlhaus, and Alexander L. Ringer. Laaber: Laaber, 1994, vol. 1, 430–38.

———. "Zur Gestaltung der 'Thèmes russe' in Beethovens op. 59." In *Festschrift für Walter Wiora.* Kassel: Barenreiter, 1967.

Schachter, Carl. "Mozart's Last and Beethoven's First: Echoes of K. 551 in the First Movement of Opus 21." In *Mozart Studies.* Ed. Cliff Eisen. Oxford: Clarendon, 1991, 227–51.

Schenker, Heinrich. "Beethoven zu seinem Opus 127." *Der Tonwille* 4 (1924): 39–41.

Schleuning, Peter. *The Fantasia II: 18th to 20th Centuries.* Trans. A. C. Howie. Cologne: Arno Volk Verlag, 1971.

Schmid, Manfred Hermann. "Streichquartett a-Moll op. 132." In *Beethoven: Interpretationen seiner Werke*. Ed. Albrecht Riethmüller, Carl Dahlhaus, and Alexander L. Ringer. Laaber: Laaber, 1994, vol. 2, 326–37.

———. "Streichquartett cis-Moll Op. 131." In *Beethoven: Interpretationen seiner Werke*. Ed. Albrecht Riethmüller, Carl Dahlhaus, and Alexander L. Ringer. Laaber: Laaber, 1994, vol. 2, 317–26.

Schmidt, Dörte. "'. . . in vierfach geschlungener Bruderumarmung aufschweben.' Beethoven und das Streichquartett als ästhetische, politische und soziale Idee in der Zeitgenössischen Publizistik." In *Der "männliche" und der "weibliche" Beethoven*. Ed. Cornelia Bartsch, Beatrix Borchard, and Rainer Cadenbach. Bonn: Beethoven-Haus, 2003, 351–68.

Schmidt, Hans. "Verzeichnis der Skizzen Beethovens." *Beethoven-Jahrbuch* 6 (1969): 7–128.

Schmidt-Görg, Joseph, and Hans Schmidt, eds. *Ludwig van Beethoven*. Translated from the German by the editorial department of the Deutsche Grammophon Gesellschaft. New York: Praeger, 1970.

Schneider, Herbert. "6 Streichquartette F-Dur, G-Dur, D-Dur, c-moll, A-Dur und B-Dur Op. 18." In *Beethoven: Interpretationen seiner Werke*. Ed. Albrecht Riethmüller, Carl Dahlhaus, Alexander L. Ringer. Laaber: Laaber, 1994, vol. 1, 133–50.

Schubring, Walther. "Beethovens indische Aufzeichnungen." *Die Musikforschung* 6 (1953): 207–14.

Schwab-Felisch, Oliver. "Die Logik der Koinzidenz: Modell und Modellverarbeitung in Ludwig van Beethovens Streichquartett Es-dur, Op. 127." In *Musikwissenschaft zwischen Kunst, Ästhetik und Experiment: Festschrift Helga de la Motte-Haber zum 60. Geburtstag*. Wurzburg: Königshausen & Neumann, 1998, 545–54.

Siegele, Ulrich. *Beethoven: Formale Strategien der späten Quartette*. Munich: text + kritik, 1990.

Simpson, Robert. "The Chamber Music for Strings." In *The Beethoven Companion*. Ed. Dennis Arnold and Nigel Fortune. London: Faber, 1967, 241–78. Rpr. as *The Beethoven Reader*, New York: Norton, 1971.

Sisman, Elaine R. "After the Heroic Style: Fantasia and the 'Characteristic' Sonatas of 1809." *Beethoven Forum* 6 (1998): 67–96.

———. *Haydn and the Classical Variation*. Cambridge, Mass.: Harvard University Press, 1993.

———. "Pathos and the Pathétique: Rhetorical Stance in Beethoven's C-minor Sonata, Op. 13." *Beethoven Forum* 3 (1994): 81–105.

Smyth, David H. "Beethoven's Revision of the Scherzo of the Quartet, Opus 18, No. 1." *Beethoven Forum* 1 (1992): 147–63.

Solomon, Maynard. *Beethoven*. New York: Schirmer, 1977.

———. *Beethoven Essays*. Cambridge, Mass.: Harvard University Press, 1988.

———. "Beethoven, Freemasonry, and the Tagebuch of 1812–1818." *Beethoven Forum* 8 (2000): 101–46.

———. *Beethovens Tagebuch*. Ed. Sieghard Brandenburg. Mainz: Hase & Koehler, 1990.

———. *Late Beethoven: Music, Thought, Imagination*. Berkeley: University of California Press, 2003.

Somfai, László. "Ludwig van Beethoven: String Quartets." CD notes in *Ludwig van Beethoven: String Quartets*. Bartók Quartet. Hungaroton, 2001.

Staehelin, Martin. "Another Approach to Beethoven's Last Quartet Oeuvre: The Unfinished String Quintet of 1826/27." In *The String Quartets of Haydn, Mozart, and Beethoven*. Ed. Christoph Wolff. Cambridge, Mass.: Harvard University Press, 1980, 302–23.

Stanley, Glenn, ed. *The Cambridge Companion to Beethoven.* Cambridge: Cambridge University Press, 2000.

Stephan, Rudolf. "Zu Beethovens letzten Quartetten." *Die Musikforschung* 23 (1970): 245–56.

Steinberg, Michael. "Notes on the Quartets." In *The Beethoven Quartet Companion.* Ed. Robert Winter and Robert Martin. Berkeley: University of California Press, 1994, 144–282.

Stravinsky, Igor, and Robert Craft. *Dialogues and a Diary.* London: Faber, 1968.

Sullivan, J. W. N. *Beethoven: His Spiritual Development.* New York: Knopf, 1927.

Thayer, Alexander Wheelock. *Ludwig van Beethovens Leben.* Ed. Hermann Deiters. 3 vols. Berlin, 1866–79; 2nd ed. by Hugo Riemann. Berlin: Brietkopf & Härtel, 1907–15; Eng. ed. by H. E. Krehbiel from Thayer's notes, 3 vols., New York: Beethoven Association, 1921; rev. ed. by Elliot Forbes as *Thayer's Life of Beethoven.* Princeton, N.J.: Princeton University Press, 1964.

Tovey, Donald Francis. *Beethoven.* Oxford: Oxford University Press, 1973.

———. *A Companion to Beethoven's Pianoforte Sonatas.* London: Oxford University Press, 1931.

———. *Essays and Lectures on Music.* Oxford: Oxford University Press, 1949.

Truscott, Harold. *Beethoven's Late String Quartets.* London: Dobson, 1968.

Tyson, Alan. *The Authentic English Editions of Beethoven.* London: Faber and Faber, 1963.

———. "The 'Razumovsky' Quartets: Some Aspects of the Sources." In *Beethoven Studies 3.* Ed. Alan Tyson. Cambridge: Cambridge University Press, 1982, 107–40.

———. "The Home-Made Sketchbook of 1807–08." *Beethoven-Jahrbuch* 10 (1978/81): 185–200.

Ulrich, Homer. *Chamber Music.* New York and London: Columbia University Press, 1948.

Unger, Max. *Eine Schweizer Beethovensammlung: Katalog.* Zurich: Verlag der Corona, 1939.

Viaskova, Elena, ed. *Ludwig van Beethoven: Moscow Sketchbook from 1825.* Facsimile. Moscow: Gnesins Musical Academy, 1995.

Virneisel, Wilhelm. *Beethoven: Ein Skizzenbuch zu Streichquartetten aus Op. 18.* Bonn: Beethoven-Haus, 1972 (facsimilie); 1974 (transcription).

Vitercik, Greg. "Structure and Expression in Beethoven's Op. 132." *The Journal of Musicological Research* 13/3–4 (1993): 233–53.

Waack, Carl. "Beethovens F-Dur Streichquartett Op. 18 No. 1 in seiner ursprünglichen Fassung." *Die Musik* 3/2 (1903/4): 418–20.

Wagner, Richard. *Prose Works.* 8 vols. Trans. William Ashton Ellis. London: K. Paul, Trench, Trübner, 1893–99. Vol. 5, containing Wagner's "Beethoven" essay, is repr. as *Actors and Singers.* Lincoln: University of Nebraska Press, 1995.

Wallace, Robin. "Background and Expression in the First Movement of Beethoven's Op. 132." *The Journal of Musicology* 7/1 (1989): 3–20.

———. *Beethoven's Critics: Aesthetic Dilemmas and Resolutions during the Composer's Lifetime.* Cambridge: Cambridge University Press, 1986.

Webster, James. "The Concept of Beethoven's 'Early' Period in the Context of Periodizations in General." *Beethoven Forum* 3 (1994): 1–27.

———. "Traditional Elements in Beethoven's Middle-Period String Quartets." In *Beethoven, Performers, and Critics: The International Beethoven Congress, Detroit, 1977.* Ed. Robert Winter and Bruce Carr. Detroit: Wayne State University Press, 1980, 94–133.

Wedig, Hans Josef. *Beethovens Streichquartett Op. 18 Nr. 1 und seine erste Fassung.* Bonn: Beethoven-Haus, 1922.

Wegeler, Franz Gerhard, and Ferdinand Ries. *Biographische Notizen über Ludwig van Beethoven.* Coblenz: K. Bädeker, 1838; repr. Hildesheim: George Olms Verlag, 2000.

Wendorff, Rudolf. *Zeit und Kultur: Geschichte des Zeitbewusstseins in Europa.* Opladen: Westdeutscher Verlag, 1985.

Wendt, Amadeus. "Thoughts about Recent Musical Art, and van Beethoven's Music, Specifically His *Fidelio.*" In *The Critical Reception of Beethoven's Compositions by His German Contemporaries.* Ed. Wayne M. Senner. Trans. Robin Wallace. 2 vols. Lincoln: University of Nebraska Press, 2001, vol. 2, 185–222.

Willson, Amos Leslie. *A Mythical Image: The Ideal of India in German Romanticism.* Durham, N.C.: Duke University Press, 1964.

Winter, Robert. *Compositional Origins of Beethoven's Opus 131.* Ann Arbor, Mich.: UMI Research Press, 1982.

———. "Performing the Beethoven Quartets in Their First Century." In *The Beethoven Quartet Companion.* Ed. Robert Winter and Robert Martin. Berkeley: University of California Press, 1994, 29–57.

———. "Plans for the Structure of the String Quartet in C Sharp Minor, Op. 131." *Beethoven Studies* 2. Ed. Alan Tyson. London: Oxford University Press, 1977, 106–37.

Winter, Robert and Robert Martin, eds. *The Beethoven Quartet Companion.* Berkeley: University of California Press, 1994 .

Witte, Reinhard. "Beethoven, Homer und die Antike." *Das Altertum* 48 (2003): 3–54.

Wjaskowa, Jelena. "Das Anfangsstadium des schöpferischen Prozesses bei Beethoven: Eine Untersuchung anhand der Skizzen zum ersten Satz des Quartetts Op. 130." In *Zu Beethoven 3.* Ed. Harry Goldschmidt. Berlin: Verlag Neue Musik, 1988, 60–82.

Yudkin, Jeremy. "Beethoven's 'Mozart' Quartet." *Journal of the American Musicological Society* 45 (1992), 30–74.

Zehentreiter, Ferdinand. "Bruch und Kontinuität in Beethovens späten Quartetten: Einige Überlegungen zur Werk- und Bedeutungsanalyse." *Musiktheorie* 11/3 (1996): 211–40.

# INDEX

Page numbers in boldface type refer to illustrations and music examples. References in endnotes have only been indexed if they contain distinctive information not found in the main text. For a list of manuscripts pertaining to the quartets, see "Appendix: Chronology and Sources of the String Quartets" (pp. 323–30).


Adorno, Theodor W., 10, 262–63, 266, 274, 276, 281–82, 291, 317, 318n16
Albrechtsberger, Johann, 90, 125, 279
*Allgemeine musikalische Zeitung,* 2, 109–11, 316, 321n68
Altmann, Wilhelm, 87n31
Amenda, Karl, 2, 13–14
Artaria, Matthias, 215
avoidance of sonata-form hierarchies, 181–84

Bach, Carl Philipp Emanuel, 90, 125
—Fantasia, Wq. 61, 125
Bach, Johann Sebastian, 39, 90, 125, 280, 295
Bach, Wilhelm Friedemann, 125
Baillot, Pierre, 101, 104
Beethoven, Karl van, 172
Beethoven, Ludwig van
Bagatelle, Op. 119, No. 1, 61
—Cantatas
Cello Sonatas, Op. 102, 163
Choral Fantasy, Op. 80, 90, 123
*Christus am Ölberge,* Op. 85, 197
*Der glorreiche Augenblick,* Op. 136, 197
*Die Ruinen von Athen* incidental music, Op. 113, 138
Duet for Viola and Cello "with two eyeglasses obbligato," WoO 32, 3
*Egmont* music, Op. 84, 31, 132–37, 293
Fantasy, Op. 77, 90, 123
*Fidelio,* Op. 72, 159, 197, 293, 295
*Kantate auf den Tod Kaiser Josephs II,* WoO 87, 197
*Kantate auf die Erhebung Leopolds II,* WoO 88, 197
*König Stephan* incidental music, Op. 117, 138
Mass, Op. 86, 185
*Missa solemnis,* Op. 123, 197–98, **199**, 200, 262, 317
—Overtures
*Coriolan* Overture, Op. 62, 31
*Egmont* Overture, Op. 84, 31, 132–37
*Namensfeier* Overture, Op. 115, 197
—Piano Concertos
Third, Op. 37, 278n12
Fifth, Op. 73, 90, 310
Piano piece "Lustig-traurig," WoO 54, 24
Sketch for a Piano Concerto in A Minor, **106**
—Piano Sonatas
Op. 2, No. 2, 216, **217**

Op. 7, 21
Op. 10, No. 3, 25, **26,** 121, 293
Op. 13 (*Sonate pathétique*), 3, 24–25
Op. 14, No. 1, 1, 121
Op. 22, 30n19
Op. 26, 121
Op. 27, No. 1, 120–22, 280
Op. 27, No. 2, 120–21, 275, 280, 309
Op. 28, 121
Op. 31, No. 2 ("Tempest"), 310
Op. 31, No. 3, 122
Op. 53 ("Waldstein"), 295
Op. 54, 216
Op. 57 ("Appassionata"), 289–91
Op. 78, 90, 123
Op. 79, 90, 123, 302
Op. 81a ("Lebewohl"), 90, 123, 124
Op. 90, 121
Op. 101, 163
Op. 106 ("Hammerklavier"), 159
Op. 109, 61, 121, 263
Op. 110, 28–29, 168, 277, 294
Op. 111, 121, 168, 197, 296
—Piano Trios
Op. 1, No. 2, **8**
Op. 70, No. 1 ("Ghost"), 121
Op. 70, No. 2, 122
Op. 97 ("Archduke"), 138, 166n46
*Prometheus* Ballet, Op. 43, 91
—Songs
*An die ferne Geliebte,* Op. 98, 58n6, 163
*An die Hoffnung,* Op. 32, 91
Gellert songs, Op. 48, 91, 197
*Sehnsucht,* WoO 146, 260
—String Quartets
Op. 14, No. 1 (as a string quartet in F major), 1
Op. 18, No. 1, 2–3, 13–14, **15–16,** 17, **18–19, 36,** 45, **46–49,** 50, **51–55,** 56, **57**
Op. 18, Nos. 1–6, 1–2, 13, 110
Op. 18, No. 2, 3, 13, 19, **20,** 21, **22–23**
Op. 18, No. 3, 3, 13, **33**
Op. 18, No. 4, 3–4, 13, 121, 263
Op. 18, No. 5, 3, 13, **33,** 119
Op. 18, No. 6, 13–14, 24–25, **26–27,** 28, **40–41,** 42–43, **44–45, 94**
Op. 59, No. 1, 4–5, **37, 64–72, 95**
Op. 59, Nos. 1–3, 1, 4, 60–61, 82, 85, 110
Op. 59, No. 2, 5, **36, 73–77,** 121, 275, 276
Op. 59, No. 3, 5–6, **8, 37, 78–81,** 82, **83–84**
Op. 74, 1, 6, **34,** 89–94, **96,** 97, **98–103,** 104, **105–6,** 107, 109–13, **115, 117–19,** 120–25, **127–28,** 129
Op. 95, 1, 6–7, **33,** 132–34, **135–37,** 138–45, **146–54,** 155–63
Op. 127, 1, 7, 10, 168–69, 171, **172–75,** 176, **177–79,** 180–82, **183–84,** 185–91, **192–93,** 194–203, 235, 276, 282, **283**
Op. 130, **frontispiece,** 1, 10, 214–17, **218–24,** 225–28, **229–30,** 230–31, 276, 279, 281, 294–95, **296,** 297, **298–300,** 301, **302,** 303, **304–7,** 308–9
Op. 131, 1, 7, 9–10, 121, **236,** 262–63, **264–65,** 266, **267,** 268–69, **270–72,** 273, **274,** 275–77, 281, 309–10, **311–14,** 315–17
Op. 132, 1, **34, 37–38, 236,** 262, 276, 282–84, **285–86,** 287, **288–90,** 291–94, 309
Op. 133 (*Grosse Fuge*), 1, 8, 234–35, **236–37,** 238, **239–40,** 241, **242–60,** 279, 283, 302
Op. 135, 1, **34, 36,** 277, 281, 283, 315
—String Trios
Op. 9, No. 2, 121
Op. 9, No. 3, 121, 278n12
—Symphonies
First, Op. 21, 119
Second, Op. 36, 205n26
Third ("Eroica"), Op. 55, 31, 189–96, 280
Fourth, Op. 60, 31
Fifth, Op. 67, 134, 276, 277
Seventh, Op. 92, 204n9
Eighth, Op. 93, 278n12
Ninth, Op. 125, 168, 185, 197, 198, 202, 224, 234, 245–46, 266, 277, 284, 303, 317
—Variations
Op. 34, 280
Op. 35 ("Prometheus"), 280
Op. 76, 90
Op. 120 ("Diabelli"), 197, 309
—Violin Sonatas
Op. 12, No. 2, 121
Op. 23, 121

Op. 30, No. 1, 295
Op. 47 ("Kreutzer"), 295
Op. 96, 155, 166n46
Bekker, Paul, 281
Berger, Karol, 202
Berlin, Isaiah, 5
Berlioz, Hector, 58n10
binary oppositions, 23–29, 187, 196, 201–2, 231, 285, 287, 289–93
Bloom, Harold, 125
Bonaparte, Jérôme, 89
Brandenburg, Sieghard, 139, 282
Breitkopf and Härtel, 89–90
Brenneis, Clemens, 90, 92, 100–101, 107n2
Brinkmann, Reinhold, 189–90, 196
Broyles, Michael, 31, 57n
Brunsvik, Count Franz, 155
Bülow, Hans von, 9
Burnham, Scott, 112, 262

Campbell, Bruce, 61, 73, 77, 80–82
Caplin, William E., 59n19
Chua, Daniel, 172, 174–76, 276, 277n5, 280, 282, 292, 308–9
Cohn, Richard, 31
Cone, Edward T., 31
Congress of Vienna, 196
Cooke, Deryck, 198
Cooper, Barry, 31, 214–15, 241, 254, 295
Cooper, Martin, 280
Czerny, Carl, 74, 119

Dahlhaus, Carl, 25, 31, 195, 279, 303
Dalley, John, 262, 277
deformations (of sonata forms), 278
directionality, 176, 184, 190–96, 310
Draeseke, Felix, 9, 310
Dreesmann, William, 138, 326

Elterlein, Ernst von, 9
Epstein, David, 31, 172–73
expressive doubling, 216–20, 223–24

fairy tales, 266
Fink, Robert, 62, 86n
Finscher, Ludwig, 10n1
Forster, Georg, 170, 200
Freud, Sigmund, 276–77
Fuchs, Aloys, 160
fugal techniques, 234–60
Fux, Johann Joseph, 90, 112

Galitzin, Prince Nikolas, 295
Geertz, Clifford, 169
Gellert, Christian Fürchtegott, 185, 197
Gendolla, Peter, 187
Gluck, Christoph Willibald, 266
—*Iphigenia in Tauris,* 266
Goethe, Johann Wolfgang von, 1, 28, 132, 137, 139; *Egmont,* 137
Griffiths, Paul, 111
Guarneri Quartet, 277n1

Hammer, Joseph von, 185
Handel, Georg Friedrich, 280
Haslinger, Tobias, 203
Hatten, Robert, 10, 287, 297, 304
Haydn, Franz Joseph, 1–3, 4–5, 13, 25, 39, 90, 93, 110–20, 123–29, 279
—String Quartets, Op. 20, 279
—String Quartet, Op. 20, No. 2, 4
—String Quartets, Op. 33 ("Russian"), 1, 13
—String Quartet, Op. 33, No. 5, 3
—String Quartets, Op. 76, 6
—String Quartet, Op. 76, No. 4 ("Sunrise"), 124, **126–27**
—String Quartet, Op. 76, No. 6, 58–59n16, 112–13, **114–18,** 119–20, 123, **126**
—String Quartets, Op. 77, 59n16
Hellmesberger Quartet, 7–8
Helm, Theodor, 3, 4, 9, 111
Hepokoski, James, 134, 276
Herder, Johann Gottfried, 169
Hippocrates, 281
Hirschbach, Hermann, 8–9
Hoffmann, E. T. A., 277, 280
Holz, Karl, 215, 280, 295, 302, 304, 317, 321n56
Homer, 170, 185–86; *Iliad,* 186; *Odyssey,* 186

Imeson, Sylvia, 58n7
improvisatory style, 6, 104, **106,** 107, 119–21, 123, 263, 281, 209–10

Jones, Sir William, 170, 188, 201

Kamien, Roger, 31
Kant, Immanuel, 200–201
Kerman, Joseph, 3, 9–10, 16–17, 19, 21–22, 26, 38, 60, 68, 73, 79–80, 85, 111–

12, 133, 163n, 180–81, 231, 281, 284, 289, 292–93, 310
Kinderman, William, 31, 63, 87n, 198, 202, 234, 263, 269, 275
Kinsky, Prince Ferdinand Johann Nepomuk, 89
Kirkendale, Warren, 198, 279
Kirnberger, Johann Philipp, 90
Kleuker, Johann Friedrich, 170, 200
Knittel, K. M., 7
Kolisch, Rudolf, 209n78
Korsyn, Kevin, 291, 293
Kraft, Nikolaus, 2
Kramer, Jonathan D., 210n92, 281, 318n14
Kramer, Lawrence, 216–17
Kramer, Richard, 19–21, 24, 29n, 30n, 43–45, 59n17, 125, 232n9, 303
Kreutzer, Rodolphe, 101
Krones, Hartmut, 6, 119
Kropfinger, Klaus, 215, 241, 254, 295, 320n45
Krumpholz, Wenzel, 2

Lafayette Quartet, 10
Lenz, Wilhelm von, 7, 110
Lester, Joel, 58n5
Lévi-Strauss, Claude, 169, 187, 197
Levy, Janet, 14–15, 59n24
Lichnowsky, Prince Karl, 2
Linke, Joseph, 2
Liszt, Franz, 9
Lobkowitz, Prince Franz Joseph, 2, 89, 91
Lockwood, Lewis, 6, 60–61, 86n, 155, 260
Lodes, Birgit, 10
Lombez, Ambrosius von, 200

Marliave, Joseph de, 3, 9
Marston, Nicholas, 6, 92, 176, 241
Martin, Robert, 111
Marx, Adolph Bernhard, 9, 110–11, 124
Mason, Daniel Gregory, 74
Masonic ideas, 107n5, 185, 202, 206n39, 212n117
McClary, Susan, 287
metrical dissonance, 31–59
Meyer, Leonard, 63–64, 85
Mies, Paul, 310
Misch, Ludwig, 302
Mongredien, Jean, 107n8
Moritz, Karl Philipp, 169
Mozart, Wolfgang Amadeus, 2–3, 4–5, 6, 13, 93, 110, 119, 129, 282, 292
—*Die Zauberflöte,* 292
—Fugue for two pianos, K. 426, 282
—"Haydn" Quartets, 1, 13
—"Jupiter" Symphony, K. 551, 119
—String Quartet, K. 464, 3, 119
—String Quartet, K. 465 ("Dissonant"), 5
Müller Quartet, 7
mythology, 168–203

nonlinear time, 184–86, 188–89, 196, 281–82, 297, 302, 308, 315–17
Nottebohm, Gustav, 97, 241, 310

Ong, Seow-Chin, 6
Oster, Ernst, 61, 64

parenthetical form, 263, 268
Paul, Jean. *See* Jean Paul Richter
Plantinga, Leon, 108n11
Platen, Emil, 206n32
plenitude, 224–32, 297
Pleyel, Ignaz, 6
—String Quartet, Op. 8, No. 2, 6
Plutarch, 186

Quintilian, 123

Radcliffe, Philip, 111, 125
Ratner, Leonard, 224, 274
Razumovsky, Count Andreas, 2, 5, 60
registral continuities, 60–85, 285
Reti, Rudolph, 265, 296, 320n50
Richards, Annette, 123
Richter, Jean Paul, 309, 316; *Vorschule der Ästhetik,* 316
Riemann, Hugo, 3, 26
Ries, Ferdinand, 281
Riezler, Walter, 111, 273
Rode, Cecilio de, 241
Rode, Pierre, 101
Rolland, Romain, 273
Rothstein, William, 31
Rudolph, Archduke, 89, 104, 119, 125, 280
Rumph, Stephen, 266

Schelling, Friedrich, 169, 203n
Schenker, Heinrich, 61–62, 64, 85

Schering, Arnold, 203
Schiller, Friedrich, 185, 280, 317
Schindler, Anton, 167n60
Schlegel, Friedrich, 169, 201; *Lucinde,* 201
Schlemmer, Wenzel, 160
Schleuning, Peter, 125
Schmid, Manfred Hermann, 277n2
Schoenberg, Arnold, 92, 107n4
Schubert, Franz, 28, 61
—*Gretchen am Spinnrade,* 28
—Piano Sonata, K. 960, 303
Schumann, Clara, 9
Schuppanzigh, Ignaz, 2, 8, 302
Schuppanzigh Quartet, 2, 8
Shakespeare, William, 25; *Hamlet,* 269; *Julius Caesar,* 131n50; *Romeo and Juliet,* 25–26
Siegele, Ulrich, 180, 204n10
Simpson, Robert, 3–4
Sina, Louis, 2
Sisman, Elaine, 112, 123, 131n
Solomon, Maynard, 85, 111, 170, 185–86, 202, 204n6, 206n39, 207n
Stadlen, Peter, 235, 260n3, 261n4
Steinberg, Michael, 189
Stravinsky, Igor, 279–80, 317
Sullivan, J. W. N., 263
temporality, 168–203, 281–82, 287, 303, 308–17
Thayer, Alexander Wheelock, 5
Tiedemann, Rolf, 262
Tovey, Donald Francis, 9, 145, 273, 276, 289, 315
transformational processes, 13–29
Türk, Daniel Gottlob, 90, 319n24
Tyson, Alan, 138–39, 161–63

Unger, Max, 108n11

Virneisel, Wilhelm, 51–55, 59n22
Vitercik, Greg, 289, 293–94
Vjaskova, Elena, 296

Waack, Carl, 14
Wagner, Richard, 7, 9, 276
Webster, James, 4, 112
Wedig, Hans Josef, 14
Weiß, Franz, 2
Wendt, August, 309
Winter, Robert, 10, 111, 121, 265, 319n21

Zmeskall, Baron Nikolaus von Domanovecz, 2, 6, 154–55

William E. Caplin is James McGill Professor of Music Theory at McGill University. He is the author of *Classical Form: A Theory of Formal Functions for the Instrumental Music of Haydn, Mozart, and Beethoven,* among other studies.

Robert Hatten is a professor of music theory at Indiana University. He is the author of *Musical Meaning in Beethoven: Markedness, Correlation, and Interpretation* (1994), as well as many other critical and semiotic studies, and has recently completed a book entitled *Interpreting Musical Gestures, Topics, and Tropes: Mozart, Beethoven, Schubert* (2004). He is also editor of the monograph series Musical Meaning and Interpretation, published by Indiana University Press.

Joseph Kerman is the author of many books, including *Opera as Drama, The Beethoven Quartets,* an edition of Beethoven's "Kafka" Sketchbook, *Contemplating Music, The New Grove Beethoven* (with Alan Tyson), and *Concerto Conversations* (1999). He is a professor emeritus of music at the University of California at Berkeley.

William Kinderman is a professor of music at the University of Illinois at Urbana-Champaign. His books include *Beethoven's Diabelli Variations, Beethoven,* and *Artaria 195: Beethoven's Sketchbook for the Missa solemnis and the Piano Sonata in E Major, Opus 109.* As pianist, he has recorded Beethoven's last sonatas and Diabelli Variations for Hyperion Records. He is editor of the Beethoven Sketchbook Series, published by the University of Illinois Press.

Harald Krebs is a professor of music theory at the University of Victoria and has written widely on harmonic, rhythmic, and metrical aspects of nineteenth-century music, as well as on Schoenberg and Nielsen. His book *Fantasy Pieces: Metrical Dissonance in the Music of Robert Schumann* (1999) won the Wallace Berry Award of the Society for Music Theory in 2002.

Lewis Lockwood is Fanny Peabody Research Professor of Music at Harvard University and author of *Beethoven: Studies in the Creative Process* (1992) and *Beethoven: The Music and the Life* (2002), among many other studies. He served as the editor of *Studies in Musical Genesis and Structure* and is currently working on an edition of Beethoven's sketches for the *Eroica* Symphony.

Birgit Lodes is a professor of historical musicology at the University of Vienna. She is the author of *Das Gloria in Beethovens Missa Solemnis,* as well as other studies devoted to Beethoven's vocal works, such as her essay "Probing the sacred genres: Beethoven's religious songs, oratorio, and masses," published in the recent *Cambridge Companion to Beethoven.* Lodes also has written on aspects of music in the Renaissance and on the music of Franz Schubert, Franz Lachner, and Richard Strauss.

Nicholas Marston is a reader in music theory and analysis at the University of Cambridge and a fellow of King's College. His publications include *Beethoven's Piano Sonata in E, Op. 109* (1995) and *Schumann: Fantasie, Op. 17* (1992). He is a coauthor of *The Beethoven Compendium* (1991) and has published work on Beethoven, Schumann, Schubert, and Heinrich Schenker in scholarly journals. His book *Heinrich Schenker and Beethoven's "Hammerklavier" Sonata* is scheduled for publication in 2007.

Malcolm Miller is a research associate and associate lecturer in music at the Open University, London. He is the editor of *Arietta,* the journal of the Beethoven Piano Society of Europe, and is a frequent contributor to scholarly journals and publications, including *Tempo* and *The New Grove Dictionary of Music and Musicians.* Miller received his Ph.D. at King's College London with a study of Wagner's Wesendonck Lieder.

Seow-Chin Ong is an associate professor of music history at the University of Louisville. His work on Beethoven has appeared in *Bonner Beethoven-Studien* and *Beethoven Forum.* He recently received a grant from the NEH to complete his project entitled *Landsberg 11: Beethoven's Sketchbook for the 'Egmont' Music, Quartet in F minor, and the 'Archduke' Trio.*

The University of Illinois Press
is a founding member of the
Association of American University Presses.

UNIVERSITY OF ILLINOIS PRESS
1325 South Oak Street Champaign, IL 61820-6903
www.press.uillinois.edu